OXFORD WORLD'S CLASSICS

THE KALEVALA

THE KALEVALA is an epic poem published in its final form in 1849, though much of its material goes back to the first millennium of our era. It is based on Finnish oral poetry, some of the richest and best-documented in the world. It begins with an account of the Creation from broken eggs, and ends with a strange interpretation of the Virgin Birth; in between, a northern people's negotiation with its environment and the conduct of its affairs is set forth in a text that is by turns epic, lyrical, ritual, and magical. The poem's overall structure is the work of Elias Lönnrot, the most famous of the Finnish scholars who saw in their oral tradition an expression of national identity.

ELIAS LÖNNROT (1802–84) was both a scholar and a district health officer covering a wide area of north-eastern Finland. In 1835 he published the first edition of the *Kalevala*, and in 1840–1 the *Kanteletar*, a companion volume of lyrics still almost unknown to the English-speaking world; in 1849 he published the second and final edition of the epic, nearly twice the length of its predecessor. In Finland, a province of Sweden from 1155 till 1809, when it became a Grand Duchy of Russia, he was hailed as a national figure, and the *Kalevala* as the national epic.

KEITH BOSLEY has published several collections of poems and a good deal of translations, mainly from French, Portuguese, German, and Finnish. Besides the *Kalevala*, his translations from Finnish include books of oral poetry, Eino Leino, Aleksis Kivi, a selection from the *Kanteletar*, and a historical anthology, *Skating on the Sea*. In 1991 he was made a Knight, First Class, of the Order of the White Rose of Finland.

ALBERT B. LORD worked with Milman Parry in the 1930s, revolutionizing Homeric scholarship in the light of their study of oral epic among the South Slavs. He was Arthur Kingsley Porter Professor of Slavic and Comparative Literature, Emeritus, in Harvard University.

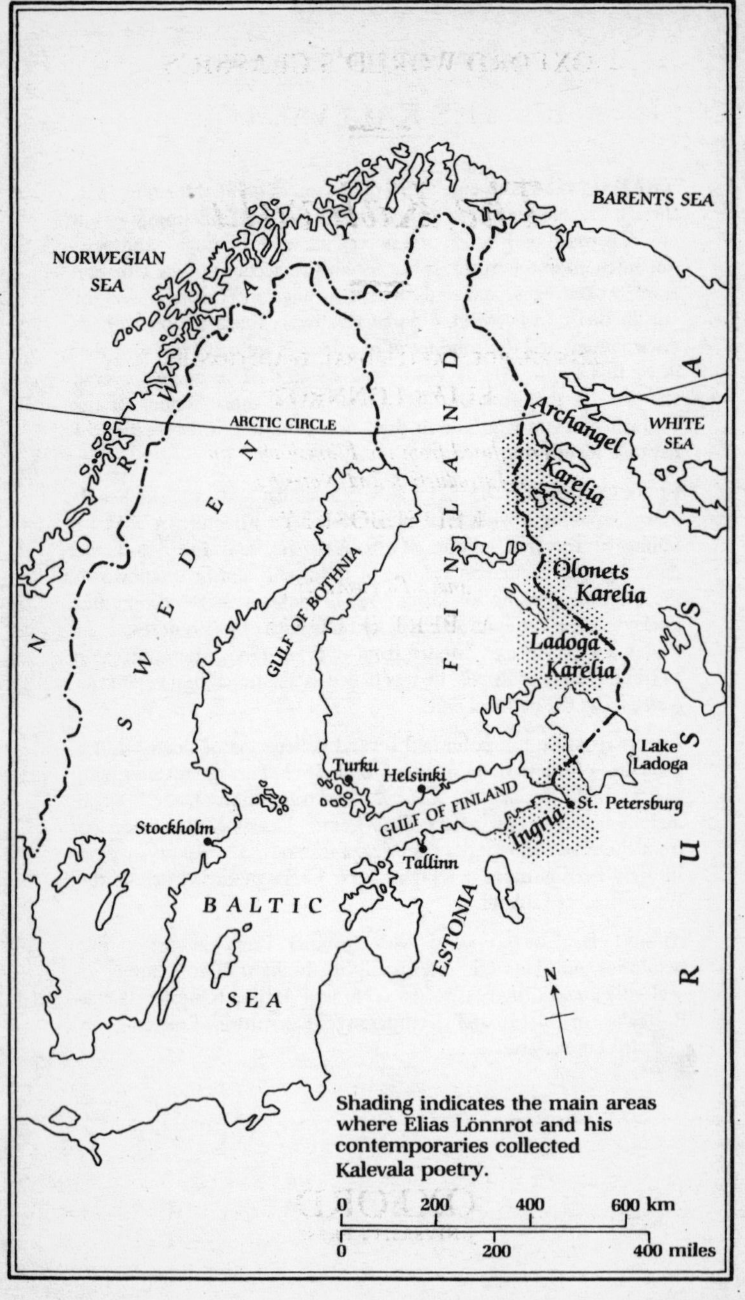

Shading indicates the main areas where Elias Lönnrot and his contemporaries collected Kalevala poetry.

OXFORD WORLD'S CLASSICS

The Kalevala

AN EPIC POEM AFTER ORAL TRADITION BY

ELIAS LÖNNROT

Translated from the Finnish with an Introduction and Notes by

KEITH BOSLEY

and a Foreword by

ALBERT B. LORD

OXFORD
UNIVERSITY PRESS

Great Clarendon Street, Oxford OX2 6DP

Oxford University Press is a department of the University of Oxford.
It furthers the University's objective of excellence in research, scholarship,
and education by publishing worldwide in

Oxford New York

Athens Auckland Bangkok Bogotá Buenos Aires Calcutta
Cape Town Chennai Dar es Salaam Delhi Florence Hong Kong Istanbul
Karachi Kuala Lumpur Madrid Melbourne Mexico City Mumbai
Nairobi Paris São Paulo Singapore Taipei Tokyo Toronto Warsaw

with associated companies in Berlin Ibadan

Oxford is a registered trade mark of Oxford University Press
in the UK and in certain other countries

Published in the United States
by Oxford University Press Inc., New York

First published as a World's Classics paperback 1989
Reissued as an Oxford World's Classics paperback 1999

British Library Cataloguing in Publication Data
Data available

Library of Congress Cataloging in Publication Data
Data available

ISBN 0–19–283570–X

5 7 9 10 8 6

Printed in Great Britain by
Cox & Wyman Ltd.
Reading, Berkshire

CONTENTS

FOREWORD

THE Finnish epic in English translation has been part of my consciousness of heroic poetry since my undergraduate and graduate days, and it has informed my teaching as well as my scholarly activities for some years. It draws one to revisit it frequently, because it has elements of subject and a general atmosphere that are not found in epic and romance as I know them in the European tradition from Homer through the eighteenth century. For the key to an understanding of the *Kalevala* is the power of the word, the power of incantation and of the story that brings power. Its heroes are word-masters and wonder-workers.

In the early 1950s I introduced the *Kalevala* into a course of Comparative Epic. The English translation of the *Kalevala* that I used for teaching at that time was W. F. Kirby's (1907). In the fifties there was little in English beyond Domenico Comparetti's *The Traditional Poetry of the Finns* (1892) to aid one in understanding how this strangely haunting epic from the North came into being. But that book, written by a classicist, was especially helpful for students of Homer, because it explained how Elias Lönnrot had not only collected but also assembled and shaped the great epic from its constituent shorter traditional songs.

In time in my course, Kirby's translation was superseded by that of Francis Peabody Magoun, Jr. (1963), who had been my teacher in Anglo-Saxon; it was during those years that he was working on his translation of the *Kalevala*. After Comparetti's book, Martti Haavio's *Väinämöinen, Eternal Sage* (1952), with its study in depth of several of the songs used for the composition of the *Kalevala*, was of very great help, for it also adduced comparative thematic material from all over the world and throughout time. With the appearance of *Finnish*

Folk Poetry: Epic (1977), and now with Keith Bosley's new and exciting translation, the student and scholar, as well as the more general reader, have acquired the means for a rich perspective on the *Kalevala*.

In Matti Kuusi's introduction to *Finnish Folk Poetry: Epic* and Michael Branch's to the 1985 edition of the Kirby translation of the *Kalevala*, one reads of the stages through which Finnish folk poetry has gone from that of myth to that which it had assumed when Lönnrot shaped the epic finally in 1849. It is remarkable how well-documented this epic is, thanks to the vast efforts of collecting that have brought together so many variants of so many songs. Variants are indispensable for the investigation of how singers in an oral tradition of sung narrative learn and compose their songs, and the *Kalevala*, with the large collections made since Lönnrot's day, makes ideal material available to comparatists for such research. We are also fortunate in having the earlier forms of Lönnrot's epic, the *Proto-Kalevala* (manuscript 1833–4, published 1929) and the *Old Kalevala* (the first edition, 1835).

Elias Lönnrot collected the songs that he used, among others, in composing the *Kalevala* by writing them down from the dictation of singers of the epic. That is the hard way. Those who have done extensive collecting in the field in these days of sophisticated, lightweight, portable sound equipment may find the concept of collecting with pen and paper, and nothing more, primitive in the extreme. It has its disadvantages, of course. When the pause at the end of a line is lengthened in the process of dictating beyond the customary interval, the rhythm of sequences of ideas is interrupted, and the singer finds himself in an awkward position in respect to the tempo of composition. Moreover, the musical element is often absent, and the context is not exactly that of regular performance. Yet dictation permits a closer and more 'uncluttered' communing with the singer than does electronic recording. There is no strange apparatus to take the attention of both singer and collector, the former wondering what is going on and the latter wondering if the electric box is operating properly, whether there is enough current of the right kind, and so forth. There is no crowd of wondering onlookers to make the singer feel uncomfortable.

Elias Lönnrot simply sat down with his singer and wrote; there were no complications. I have seen such collecting 'events' many times in the thirties in Yugoslavia, and with the years I have come to appreciate their directness. Texts collected in that way may, indeed, be better, truer to the singer's regular performance, than texts obtained with video cameras and sound equipment under artificially staged circumstances.

Lönnrot, as any other collector thoroughly versed in his tradition and not a mere novice, had heard many singers, and did not need to reproduce the 'normal' performance every time that he wanted to collect a song text. At any rate, ordinarily when a singer is asked to dictate a song he will have with him a few friends to listen to him and keep him company. They usually are the people who hear him whenever he sings, and he feels at ease with them. He is 'performing', therefore, to a small group that is not unlike his regular audience, so that the greatest lack that he may feel—and it is a real one, I admit—is the music and the rhythm afforded by the instrumental accompaniment and the singing. Our great collections from the past, from the Homeric poems to the medieval songs and epics, have very probably been set down in just this way. In the hands of a skilled scribe and/or collector such a performance has in the past produced great poetry. Prime examples are the *Iliad* and the *Odyssey* of Homer! Lönnrot knew his tradition, was constantly learning more and more about it as he wrote, and he knew the minds and the art of the Finnish singers. Keith Bosley has also penetrated into the singers' way of thinking and of expressing thought and feeling in the images, music, and rhythm of great poetry. All of that comes once more to life in his translation of the *Kalevala*.

Harvard University
December 1987

ALBERT B. LORD

DEDICATION

To Ben, Sebastian, Gabriel, my sons
big gentle brother to two little boys
your author dedicates another's lines
though this would not have taken by surprise
Lönnrot, our Finnish rhapsode who begins
and ends with those on whom a bard relies
to hold dear in a day beyond his knowing—
the youngsters rising and the people growing.

Do you remember Imatra, the town
built where the waters of a dozen lakes
slide off the granite table and tumble down
roaring to Russia till a man's hand takes
and turns them into power? Genius home-grown
blushed unseen till for all his people's sakes
one man took, turned it so that they would know
pressed between leaves, its colours still aglow

Kalevala. The people's heritage
is proved: again it comes before the world
as the last flower of a heroic age
when words meant more than iron, when they told
of holy origins, each word a gage
for what it named—the kind of truth unrolled
when Orpheus sang, till Homer came along
reporting blood and guts to prove him wrong.

Mallarmé, who said that, remains my guide:
poems are made of words, of phrases too
for bards who have no letters. I have tried
to show you how they sang, working anew
what they received—a mix to set beside
literature with its names and dates. And you?
Read, for your mix was made from two tongues' meeting
and any pudding's proof is in the eating.

FINNISH PRONUNCIATION

Spelling is almost entirely phonetic, so *kantele* has three syllables; a double vowel is long, a double consonant is lingered over—*Kyl-lik-ki*; accent is always on the first syllable; *a* and *ä* sound as the vowel in northern and southern English 'pat' respectively, so the first syllable of *Aino* rhymes with 'pie' and the first syllable of *Väinämöinen* with 'pay'; *h* is always sounded; *j* sounds as in 'hallelujah'; *ö* sounds as in German; *u* sounds as in 'put', so the first syllable of *sauna* rhymes with 'pow!'; *y* sounds as German *ü*.

INTRODUCTION

Romantic epic

Kalewala, taikka Wanhoja Karjalan Runoja Suomen kansan muinosista ajoista ('The Kalevala, or old Karelian poems about ancient times of the Finnish people'): so reads the title-page of the first edition of the epic, published in Helsinki in 1835. It was a work of literature based on the oral poetry of Karelia, the region that straddles the border of eastern Finland and north-western Russia; it was a compilation of heroic poetry edited to form a more or less continuous narrative by Elias Lönnrot (1802–84), a Finnish scholar and district health officer. Finland, a province of Sweden since the twelfth century, had been annexed in 1809 by Russia, which had made it an autonomous Grand Duchy; but it was beginning to think of itself as a nation in its own right. In his preface Lönnrot wrote of 'trying to set in some kind of order' poems about 'memorable ancestors', as the Greeks and the Icelanders had done. He was referring to Homer and the unknown thirteenth-century editor of the *Elder Edda*; but where the latter was little more than a compiler, as Lönnrot's Finnish predecessors had been, Homer had shaped some of his heritage into two monumental epics. Lönnrot's ambition was of this order, to present the Finnish nation and language as capable not only of poetry, but of epic. How far he succeeded in the eyes of his countrymen can be judged initially from the response of his colleagues, who placed material they had collected at his disposal: in 1840–1 he published the *Kanteletar*, a companion volume of lyrics and ballads, and in 1849 the second and final edition of the *Kalevala*, at 22,795 lines nearly twice the length of the first edition. The work became a rallying-flag for national aspirations, and is regarded as the 'national epic' by modern Finland, which celebrates Kalevala Day on 28 February, the date of Lönnrot's 1835 preface. How far he succeeded in the eyes of the world outside Finland can be judged from the fact that the epic has been translated into forty-seven languages; the present translation is one of five into English. Its status as one of the 'World's Classics' is enhanced by its informing presence in some of the greatest music of Sibelius, which is fully documented at the end of this book. The *Kanteletar*, though in many ways more representative of the tradition on which both works are based, has not had the same international success.

From a Western point of view the *Kalevala* is a double anachronism, an epic produced at a time when epic was regarded as a thing of the past, set in a world more archaic than that of *Beowulf*. To see the *Kalevala* as a work of European literature rather than an attractive curiosity, we need to adjust our sights. First, outside the mainstream of the Renaissance tradition, epic had a new lease of life thanks to Romanticism; second, in backwaters like Finland, oral tradition, long the Cinderella of Western culture, was still the major vehicle of talent. In other circumstances its unlettered bards and healers, with their prodigious memories, might have become leading figures in the arts and sciences.

Epic is about heroes making history, or what passes for history. The last heroes of Renaissance epic were Milton's Satan and Klopstock's Messiah: history had lost its nerve to pietism, and the large nations of Europe were settling down to the fruits of 'civilization'. But in this Age of Reason a new spirit was moving: Rousseau was singing the praises of the *bon sauvage* (after the 'noble savage' of seventeenth-century English fiction), and Herder, the future theorist of the *Sturm und Drang* ('Storm and Stress') movement in Germany whose rising star was the young Goethe, was developing ideas of a world of nations defined by vernacular and by folk culture. He urged his disciples to refresh the muse at the pure spring of folk song: in Germany, and later in England, poets wrote the rough-hewn, 'artless' lyrics and ballads beloved of *Lieder* composers—what Schiller was to call *naive* (as against *sentimentalische*) *Dichtung*.

Among the models Herder proposed was Ossian, allegedly a third-century Gaelic epic bard, translated into English prose by James Macpherson. Dr Johnson had dismissed Macpherson's texts, published in the 1760s, as 'impudent forgeries'; but Scotland, still smarting after Culloden, had welcomed Ossian, while the response on the Continent had amounted to a craze. Modern research has shown that the texts are based on genuine material, but that Macpherson lacked the scholarship to do it justice. Such scholarship was, meanwhile, evolving on the other side of Europe, where the Finnish historian Henrik Gabriel Porthan and his students saw in Macpherson at least a kindred spirit.

Ossian marks the beginning of what might be called Romantic epic, though it was not always epic in form. In the wake of the French Revolution poets proclaimed ideals of universal brotherhood in epic fragments like *L'Aveugle* by Chénier, in which a group of shepherds rescues a blind wandering bard—originally Ossian, but Chénier changed him to Homer. The epic fragment gathered momentum, culminating with Victor Hugo, who used what he dubbed the *petite épopée* for *La Légende des Siècles* (1859–83); the type was to live on for another hundred years with the *Canto general* (1950) of Pablo Neruda. Conversely, Goethe's *Hermann und Dorothea* (1797) is epic in form but hardly so in character. For the large-scale 'poem including history'—Pound's famous definition in *ABC of Reading* (1934)—one must turn to nations that felt a need to explore their history. For these, Romanticism offered the freedom not so much of personal expression as of national self-determination. *Zalán futása* ('The Flight of Zalán', 1825) by Vörösmarty the Hungarian and *Pan Tadeusz* ('Master Thaddaeus', 1834) by Mickiewicz the Pole are two of many 'national' epics to appear, mainly in Eastern Europe; to these might be added *Mirèio* ('Mireille', 1859) by the Provençal poet Mistral, though the dedication to Lamartine by an author styling himself a *païsan* is hardly compelling.

Herder's ideas about national identity had their greatest impact among nations with little by way of recorded history or literature, small nations that for centuries had been mostly unlettered peasants under masters speaking another language. In such nations a rising educated minority was inspired to return to its roots, and apply its learning to the hitherto despised vernacular and folk culture. This meant going out and finding them, and from the Baltic to the Balkans there followed a collecting and 'correcting' (as Alecsandri the Rumanian put it) of folk poetry, concerned less with fidelity to sources than with validation of a national culture. The antiquarian interest that had prompted Bishop Percy to collect and publish his *Reliques of Ancient English Poetry* (1765–94) had become a political imperative. Among the host of collectors who ventured into the wilds of the Russian, Austro-Hungarian, and Ottoman empires, it was Lönnrot who made the double leap: from oral poetry to publication, and from publication to literature.

By the end of the nineteenth century the *Kalevala* had been translated into eight languages, including English—though John Martin Crawford's version (1888, the first in English) was made from Schiefner's German (1852). The latter also produced a curious offshoot in English: after reading Schiefner, the indefatigable Longfellow was moved to pen *The Song of Hiawatha* (1855), adapting metre, theme, and character to his purpose. Although the West was already aware of poetic stirrings in the northern forests from reports and samples in travel books (one such book had prompted Goethe to write his *Finnisches Lied*, a translation of a folk lyric), the *Kalevala* came as a revelation. In Finland its effect was immeasurably greater. At first, during the years that followed annexation, the Russian authorities welcomed Finnish nationalism as a way of severing links with Sweden, and the destruction by fire in 1827 of Turku, the old capital on the south-west coast, with its university, led to the founding a year later of Alexander's University (named after the Tsar) in Helsinki, the capital since 1812. Here the Finnish Literature Society was founded in 1831, and four years later it published the first edition of the *Kalevala*. The reading public was still more at home in Swedish, but the Finnish of its servants and tradesmen was clearly the language of the future. The *Kanteletar* appeared soon after, and in 1847 a cartoon portrayed Lönnrot with walking-stick and scroll hurrying barefoot across open country over a caption based on Ennius: *Unus homo nobis cursando restituit rem* ('One man by running about is restoring to us our state'). The misquotation acquires further point from the knowledge that Ennius, and Virgil after him, have *cunctando* 'by delaying'. Two years later came the definitive *Kalevala*: Finland had its 'poem including history', and was preparing to make history.

In any serious approach to the *Kalevala*, literary studies cannot ignore the oral tradition behind it. The text of a folk poem is no more than the record of a performance; if the collector has been trained in what has come to be known as the Finnish Method, there will be the name of the bard, his or her age, the place of performance, and the date. The text itself is called a variant, which implies an original; but the original may exist only in the mind of the collector, who knows of other texts similar enough to be fellow variants. Bards would draw on a repertoire often learned from a relative (since talent tends to run in families) which they would handle in their own way, rearranging set-pieces or 'formulas' of a phrase, a line, or several lines, leaving some material out, adding new. There was no problem of personal style: the ancient poetry which is now called Kalevala poetry has a single style transcending not only individual talent but even region and century. One is tempted by this to wonder whether some ancient poetry from oral sources—such as Homer—has not led scholars to infer a single author from a single style.

The present approach to the *Kalevala* will look first at the oral tradition and its background, then at how the epic was assembled, and at the *Kalevala* as a text. Finally, the present translation will be discussed.

The Finnish tradition

'The Fenni are remarkably brutish and appallingly wretched: no weapons, no horses, no dwellings; their food vegetation, their clothing skins, their bed the ground; their only hope is in arrows which, lacking iron, they sharpen with bone.' Tacitus' laconic description of a Stone-Age people in the final chapter of his *Germania* is the earliest surviving written reference to people living in Finland, which is named after them in most languages; but the Fenni were probably Lapps, not Finns. In the first century AD, when the Roman historian wrote, the Lapps were being partly assimilated, partly displaced by a more advanced people, the Finns. It was during the first millennium AD that the foundations of Kalevala poetry were laid in a society with animistic beliefs, whose shamans negotiated with an otherworld through magic.

Who are the Finns, speaking a language so different from those of their Russian and Scandinavian neighbours? Neighbours they have long been, ethnically and culturally; but linguistically they are outside the Indo-European group, which ranges from Bengali to Gaelic. Their language group is Uralic, comprising Finno-Ugrian and Samoyed. Some five thousand years ago a group of tribes of non-Indo-European speech were living between the Volga and the Urals, whence the name. Most of the group migrated westward, and between three and two thousand years ago settled where their linguistic descendants now live. That is all that can be said with any certainty: the movement of language and culture is most often like wave motion, whereby a wave travels but the water merely goes up and down. Today, of roughly twenty million who speak a Uralic language, about two-thirds speak Hungarian; the rest speak up to twenty languages, of which the biggest are Mordvin (spoken south of Gorky, Russia) and Estonian with about a million speakers each, and Finnish, with not quite five million.

Some of the earliest references to Uralic-speakers are in Alfred the Great's ninth-century adaptation of a fifth-century Latin history of the world, whose lack of information about northern Europe he made good with travellers' tales. One such traveller was Ohthere, a Norwegian walrus-hunter, who sailed round the North Cape and the Kola Peninsula to the White Sea, then up the Northern Dvina where he met the prosperous 'Beormas'. The name is cognate with Old Norse *Bjarmar* 'Permians', a Uralic-speaking people skilled in metalwork, but Ohthere's hosts were more probably North Karelians, also smiths; he reported to Alfred that they seemed to speak 'almost the same language' as the Uralic-speaking Lapps. He also mentioned the 'Terfinns', Lapps of Turja or Tyrjä, that is eastern Kola (there is a warning against them in canto 12 of the *Kalevala*), and the 'Finns', that is Lapps, who did not get on with their Norwegian neighbours. Another of Alfred's travellers was Wulfstan, perhaps an Englishman, who reported on the alarming funeral customs of the Estonians.

The Finns themselves enter recorded history in 1155, when the Swedish King Eric the Good and the English-born Bishop Henry of Uppsala made Finland a province of Sweden. According to a folk poem Henry, the patron saint of Finland, came from Cabbageland—the English taste for the vegetable was already an international talking-point; and the modern Finnish writer Veijo Meri has observed that the first Finn known to history was a murderer, Lalli, the peasant responsible for Henry's martyrdom in 1156. In 1240 Alexander Nevsky turned the Swedes back from Russia, and much of Karelia has been Orthodox ever since, venerating Alexander as a saint. Here the clergy was more tolerant of the pagan oral tradition and it was here that Lönnrot found most of his material. During the sixteenth century, the rest of Finland became Lutheran, and written Finnish was advanced by Bishop Mikael Agricola, whose translation of the New Testament appeared in 1548. In 1809 Finland became a Grand Duchy under the Tsar, but during the nineteenth century its growing sense of national identity—fed in no small measure by the *Kalevala*—led to increasing oppression, till in 1917 it declared itself independent of a Russia preoccupied with other things. During the Second World War Finland ceded to the USSR some of Finnish Karelia, whose population moved west, where their lively temperament and sense of oral tradition still set them off from their countrymen.

'I used to be reckoned a good singer before these here *tunes* came in': the old Suffolk labourer's celebrated grumble about commercial popular music could have been uttered centuries earlier by a Finnish bard on hearing the kind of folk song that entered Finland from Western Europe after the Middle Ages. There are examples in Lönnrot's preface to the *Kanteletar* and in any book containing Finnish folk songs. The Finns have a ballad, *Velisurmaaja* ('The Brother-Slayer'), which has a parallel in Scotland ('Edward, Edward', the inspiration of the first of Brahms's *Ballads*, op. 10), and the plants intertwining from the graves of Lord Thomas and Fair Eleanor also appear in the Hungarian ballad *Kádár Kata* ('Kate Cooper'). But such songs, with their tuneful rhymed stanzas, have nothing to do with the starker music of the Kalevala tradition. This too shows international influence, albeit more ancient: Finnish bear-hunting ritual (recalled in canto 46 of the epic) shares a distant ancestor with the bear dances Bartók knew. As the Finnish scholar Kustaa Vilkuna remarked in 1974: 'No nation has its own culture, only its own barbarism.'

In Finnish folk poetry we hear the influence of Baltic song and Russian storytelling (the *bylina* tradition), of Viking and early Christian cultures. This brings in the historical dimension, as another Finnish scholar, Matti Kuusi, has written (1977) of the problems of dating a folk poem:

> A poem noted down in the eighteenth, nineteenth or twentieth century can be compared to the numerous strata of a burial mound in which many generations of men and their artefacts have been buried, although even this does not fully depict the magnitude of the scholar's task because the strata of a folk poem do not occur in a relatively clearly defined historical order—it is as if the burial mound had been disturbed by a bulldozer.

Of the various influences mentioned, the Baltic seems to have been the most radical, if—as is now thought—it reshaped the Finns' (and the Estonians') style of singing. The Indo-European-speaking Balts—Latvians, Lithuanians, and the now extinct Old Prussians—have a form called the *daina* which strongly resembles what is now known as Kalevala metre. Of all Uralic-speakers only those in the Baltic region used this metre.

Kalevala metre seems to be basically a trochaic tetrameter measured quantitatively—that is, four feet each consisting of a long and a short syllable: *Niin sanoopi Väinämöinen* ('Thus says Väinämöinen'). As in Classical prosody, accent—always on the first syllable in Finnish—does not feature, so there is often a tension between verse rhythm and speech rhythm entirely absent from Hiawatha metre, which replaces quantity with stress, the Germanic counterpart of accent; the *daina* is similarly quantitative. The foregoing description, it should be pointed out, is controversial; more will be said about metre when the translation is discussed.

Kalevala poetry was usually sung to tunes built on a pentachord (the first five notes of a scale) with an ambiguous third (between major and minor), corresponding to the five strings of the earliest kantele, a kind of zither which sometimes accompanied the singer. The rhythm varied, but narrative poetry was sung to tunes of five beats setting two or four lines:

That was the first appearance in print (1795) of such a tune. The text (in black-letter Finnish and roman Swedish) reads: 'There went a command from heaven' (twice) 'from all creation's Guardian' (twice)—the lines are not in the *Kalevala*, and the repetition is not typical. The grouping of lines into pairs suggests a caesura at the end of the first line of a pair. Perhaps the Homeric hexameter was originally such a pair of lines; whether it was or not, some editions of the *Kalevala* run pairs of lines together, though Lönnrot and his colleagues never did.

Kalevala poetry has neither rhyme nor stanza; its other formal features are alliteration and parallelism, often inverted into chiasmus. Alliteration is irregular and sometimes absent, but it often determines word choice, as in canto 46 of the epic when the bear's skull is set up to face east: east is *itä*, and the only part of the skull that alliterates with it is *ikenet*, the gums. Alliteration on a vowel requires the same vowel, unlike in Anglo-Saxon. Parallelism corresponds to the pairing of lines just mentioned, though this too varies: the sources often have odd lines, which suggests that they were spoken rather than sung. Lönnrot, however, always (with the solitary exception of 5:131–3, which is why the epic has an odd number of lines) thought in pairs of lines, even when they were not parallel. Such pairing recalls the description of performance in Porthan's seminal work *De Poësi Fennica* (1766–78): he describes two men, a lead singer and an assistant, singing antiphonally as they 'sit either side by side or facing each other, close enough to lock hands and knees . . . their bodies gently swaying . . . their expressions thoughtful and serious'—we have a glimpse of this in the opening lines of the epic. When women sang, the lead singer would be accompanied by a group. Antiphonal singing was already in decline before Lönnrot's day, but solo singing survived long after in a few areas: the granddaughter of a man who sang for Lönnrot was still singing in 1942. In the *Kalevala*, Lönnrot sought to reconstruct the original setting.

As in other places where it has been possible to study a singing tradition, narrative poems were what the South Slavs called 'men's songs', the rest were 'women's songs'; this is the basis of Väinämöinen's taunt in the singing-match in canto 3, that the upstart Joukahainen sings only 'child's wisdom, woman's recall' which 'is for no bearded fellow'. But in Finland, as the tradition declined during the nineteenth century, women took over the songs which men no longer sang, giving rise to what Finnish scholars call 'lyrical epic' because the women would lace the stories with fragments of their own songs, adding a new warmth, or would tell stories of their own in epic style, giving ballad material an unforeseen gravity. The best example of 'lyrical epic' in the *Kalevala* is canto 4, whose source was a woman; we shall be looking at it and meeting her later. But why did the Finnish tradition decline and eventually die out?

All oral tradition thrives on want—of material progress, of education. The Marxist notion of culture produced only from an economic surplus (Brecht's 'grub first, then ethics') is soon dispelled by the knowledge that most Finnish bards lived in abject poverty; references in the *Kalevala* to gold and silver, to ownership of land and of serfs, are usually epic hyperbole. In Finland for centuries there was little opportunity for self-advancement: the tolerance mentioned earlier of Orthodox clergy amounted in the long term to indifference. Gifted individuals had nowhere to go, so they stayed at home, and developed their gifts as best they could. Gray's 'mute inglorious *Milton*' buried in Upton churchyard was a victim of English privilege, like Clare; but the Finnish bard lived at the back of beyond, and did not even speak the language of his rulers. Yet, in his own small world at least, he was respected: Arhippa Perttunen (1769–1840), an important source of the *Kalevala*, told Lönnrot that at singing-matches 'his village used to put him forward, and he did not remember ever being beaten'. An idea of the richness of the tradition can be had from the same bard's boyhood recollections of fishing-trips with the village men: 'They often sang all night hand in hand by the fire, and the same song was never sung twice' (1835 preface).

Finnish folk poetry was first written down in the 1670s: ironically perhaps, the palm belongs to a variant about the murder of Bishop Henry, one of the most modern themes. The following century saw a trickle of collectors at work, which in the nineteenth became a flood. The main interest was in the older, Kalevala tradition, with its vast range of material all in the same metre. It included epic narratives, lyrics, rites, magic incantations, and lullabies and children's songs, some of which are still in use today. One poem might have up to two hundred variants scattered across the country. The richest areas were the Orthodox borderlands of Finland and Russia—Archangel Karelia towards the Arctic Circle, Olonets Karelia, Ladoga Karelia, and Ingria, stretching from the St Petersburg area westward along the south coast of the Gulf of Finland towards Estonia. A village in Archangel Karelia, some 375 miles north of St Petersburg, was the home of Arhippa, who sang 4,000 lines to Lönnrot, and of his son Blind Miihkali (1815–99) who was to continue the family tradition. Of a later generation still was the Ingrian bard Larin Paraske (1834–1904), who had an astonishing repertoire of more than 11,000 lines. She was a national celebrity when, in 1891, the young Sibelius heard her and was deeply affected: his first *Kalevala* setting, the *Kullervo* symphonic poem, was performed the following year. Of the material collected, about a million and a quarter lines were eventually published in *Suomen Kansan Vanhat Runot* ('Old Poems of the Finnish People', 33 volumes, Helsinki, 1908–48), from which a selection with an English translation has been published as *Finnish Folk Poetry: Epic* (hereinafter FFPE); a selection of lyrics is projected. There is half as much again unpublished material in the archives of the Finnish Literature Society, and large collections in Russian Karelia and Estonia.

Lönnrot's 'old poems' led, as we have seen, to a co-operative effort among collectors. Though some of these complained that he had tampered with his source material, most educated Finns were so enthusiastic that, around the turn of the century, the identification of Karelia with the emerging Finnishness prompted a vogue for pilgrimages into the eastern wilds, where, with luck, one might meet a poetic backwoodsman and persuade him to sing. Karelianism, as the vogue was called, attracted a number of creative spirits including the protean 'national artist' Axel Gallén, who later finnicized his name to Akseli Gallen-Kallela, and his friend Jean Sibelius.

It will be clear by now that folklore has an importance

in Finland it cannot claim in the West. A review of an English Baroque violinist in a Finnish newspaper a few years ago likened her playing to that of a folk fiddler: this was intended as high praise. The American scholar Robert Redfield speaks of 'great' and 'little' traditions, meaning educated and folk traditions respectively. In most Western nations 'great' tradition has long been dominant, influencing 'little' tradition from above—a process known as seepage. In countries like Finland the situation is reversed: for centuries it had only 'little' tradition, which eventually influenced an emerging 'great' tradition from below—a process described by the English scholar Michael Branch as 'rising damp'. Before we see the beginning of this process in Finland with the *Kalevala*, we need to look at how the poetry of 'little' tradition was composed—and still is in some parts of the world.

A village might claim a 'singing family': though the Western world may still dream of noble savages composing in committee, oral epic was the preserve of a talented few. A bard's repertoire can be compared with what one uses to build a garden wall—bricks, mortar, and a length of string to guide the builder. The bricks are the 'formulas' mentioned earlier: they may be whole or half bricks, chunks of stone, pebbles, flints, shards. The mortar is the bard's powers of invention: here, where the bricks are regular, only a thin layer is needed; there more is needed, in which to set the awkward pieces. To guide the performance there is the 'thread' of the story to be told, the mood to be communicated, the rite to be celebrated, the spell to be recited. Underlying all this is the ability to do the job—a command of the *métier*, of the metre: anyone, even a politician, can improvise in prose, but only a bard can keep a poem alive.

The American scholar Milman Parry (1902–35) revolutionized Homeric studies by demonstrating the 'composition in performance' technique behind the *Iliad* and the *Odyssey* in the light of his research among the bards of Yugoslavia. His 'formulaic system', which accounts for 'swift-footed Achilles', 'rosy-fingered dawn', 'wine-dark sea', and much else in Homer, also accounts for 'steady old Väinämöinen', 'the sky all into windows', 'on the blue high seas', and much else in the *Kalevala*. Here are two passages describing a journey:

He lashed the courser	. . . struck the courser with the lash
whacked it with the beaded belt:	whacked it with the beaded belt:
courser ran and journey sped	courser ran and journey sped
the sledge rolled, the road shortened	the sledge rolled, the road shortened.
the birchwood runner thudded	
the rowan collar-bow slammed.	
He rumbles along	He rumbles along
by swamps and by lands	paces his journey
by wide open glades.	
He went one day, he went two	
till on the third day	
he came to the long quay's end	
upon Kalevala's heath	upon those heaths of the North
at the edge of Osmo's field.	the broad borders of Lapland . . .
(10:7–20)	(35:125–32)

Both passages are built entirely of formulas, as are similar journey passages in cantos 6, 8, 12 (twice), 24, 26, and 35 (again). Birchwood runners appear in other contexts, as do swamps and lands, and the counting of days. Earlier in canto 35 a line corresponding with the fourth quoted above reads 'the road rolled, the sledge clattered' (104)—memorably set by Sibelius in *Kullervo*. There are hundreds of such formulas in the *Kalevala*; they enabled the bard to pace the narrative, here taking the strain, there free-wheeling. The lack of an anticipated repetition could be used for dramatic effect, as when in canto 4 Aino tells in turn her father, her brother, and her sister why she is weeping: she has lost her trinkets in the forest. Then she tells her mother the real reason: an old man accosted her, and she tore them off to appear less attractive. We shall soon look in more detail at this episode, to see how Lönnrot turned folk poetry into literature.

'For the primitive, art is a means; for the decadent, it becomes an end', writes Pierre Reverdy (*Le Livre de mon Bord*, 1948). What was the function of this poetry by the time Lönnrot and his colleagues came to write it down? There were no more shamans to demonstrate their power over the otherworld, though some poems were still sung for good luck, and charms were still valued. Scholars believe that lyrics and ballads continued to be composed, but that the ancient epic narratives had long since established their main features and become feats of memory rather than acts of 'composition in performance'; the evidence for this is the similarity of variants many miles or generations apart. So when a bard performed, his listeners knew the story already: the interest lay in how he would do it this time—a sophisticated (or 'decadent') approach not unlike comparing interpretations of a piece of music. But this might be in a remote community of Archangel Karelia.

The shaping of the Kalevala

'Then it takes the usual course of the iron spell. . . . Then the wedding poems are to be sung, which you'll get from the women.' Such prose asides by a bard in mid-performance proved a breakthrough for Lönnrot, on his fourth field trip in September 1833. For the first time he saw how separate poems could be combined into an epic narrative. The following April he returned to the bard's parish of Vuokkiniemi in Archangel Karelia, whose biggest village, Uhtua, has since been renamed Kalevala by the Soviet authorities. Of eleven field trips Lönnrot made between 1828 and 1845, the fifth was the most momentous for the shaping of the *Kalevala*. In a fortnight he collected over 13,000 lines: literary epic was within his reach. He was not the first collector to visit

Vuokkiniemi, but it owes its fame to him. What he called 'the best and richest home of poems' (1849 preface) is a good place to watch him at work: we shall see how three poems from there (FFPE 10, 104, 56) became cantos 3, 4, and most of canto 5 of the 1849 *Kalevala*.

The first poem was sung by Ontrei Malinen (1780–1855), one of the great bards, to A. J. Sjögren, an older contemporary of Lönnrot, in 1825. It tells of a quarrel between two men on a narrow road about who should make way for the other; the settling of the score by a contest of magic suggests that they were shamans. The younger, Joukavainen or Joukahainen, who throws down the challenge, sings commonplaces about birds, fish, trees, land, and sea, whereupon the older, Väinämöinen, scornfully declares that he assisted at the creation of the world,

> bearing the arch of heaven
> and fixing the sky's pillar
> filling the heaven with stars
> and stretching out the Great Bear.
>
> (35–8; translation revised)

To teach him a lesson, he magics his young rival into a swamp—and for a moment, interestingly, feels ashamed of abusing his powers. To save his skin, his victim offers gold, silver, his horse—in vain; but when he offers his sister the spell is reversed, and he goes 'weeping home / wailing to the farm', expecting his parents to be furious; but the poem ends with his mother delighted at the prospect of such a gifted son-in-law.

The second poem was sung to Lönnrot on that remarkable fifth field trip in 1834, by a homeless widow known only as Matro, who scraped a meagre living by knitting socks. Her poem tells of Anni, a 'matchless (*aini*) girl' who is accosted in the forest by a man. She goes weeping home (like the young shaman above—this is a formula), and fobs off her father, brothers, and sisters with a story about losing trinkets, but—as we have seen—tells her mother the real reason for her tears. Her mother bids her fatten herself up and dress splendidly, but Anni, in 'the shed on the hill' where the family trousseau is kept,

> strangled herself with the belts
> choked herself with the girdles
> she staggered, she slumped
> hanged herself with her own thread . . .
> (78–81)

Her mother finds her, and the poem ends with a moving passage describing how her tears swell to rivers, on whose banks birches rise with cuckoos on their boughs lamenting Anni. An Estonian variant tells of a girl accosted by a man, whom she stabs dead 'through his splendid wooing-shirt', then goes weeping home to be congratulated by her mother on getting rid of the landlord's son who was a common nuisance: as so often in folk poetry, similar elements produce a different compound.

The third, much shorter poem was again sung by Ontrei, this time to Lönnrot on his third field trip in 1833. It concerns Väinämöinen again, out fishing. He catches a strange fish, and prepares to cut it up, but it slips from his grasp back into the water. It is in fact no fish, but a mermaid, who calls him a 'wretched old man', and says that was no way to treat a potential wife. The poem is of Christian origin, designed to discredit belief in Väinämöinen as a water-god.

The three poems have little enough in common; yet Lönnrot joined them together to form one of the most powerful episodes of the *Kalevala*. After the Creation cantos in which we meet Väinämöinen as a culture-hero, Lönnrot introduces the young upstart Joukahainen who, when his 'child's wisdom, woman's recall' fails to impress, starts boasting (3:215–34); Väinämöinen's reply (235–54) has some of the splendour of Job's God (cf. Job 38). He no longer feels compunction for singing his rival into a swamp, because he has been challenged to a sword-fight. In canto 4 the promised sister becomes Matro's Anni, whom Lönnrot renames Aino, his own invention after the adjective *aini* (of Germanic origin, cognate with English 'one' in the sense of unique—the name has been in use ever since) and Väinämöinen becomes the suitor. Aino's distress is dwelt on by the addition of two lyrics ('How do the lucky ones feel' and 'Better it would be for me', 197–230); then, arriving at the shed, she puts on her wedding dress and wanders off. She comes to a lake, undresses, swims, and drowns. Suicide? The text is evasive, dreamlike. Why Lönnrot drowns her instead of hanging her we shall see in a moment. As she dies, Aino identifies herself with the lake—the waters are her blood, the fish her flesh (363–70)—a turning back to inanimate nature often found in Finnish folk poems about death. Instead of her mother discovering her, various animals are detailed to bear the news of her death: only the hare does so, and her mother weeps as in Matro's poem, with a beautiful last word from Lönnrot about the cuckoo changing its role from harbinger of summer to recaller of grief. Canto 5 opens with Väinämöinen, but now he is mourning: he learns where there are mermaids, and goes fishing there. He catches a wondrous fish, and all follows as in Ontrei's poem until the fish says it used to be Joukahainen's sister (126): the 'wretched old man' taunt (129) acquires a new emotional charge.

Lönnrot did his work so well that some people thought he had restored a lost epic from its scattered fragments: that is at least a tribute to his literary sense. For the *Kalevala* is not Finnish oral poetry in epitome. In the first place there is more lyric than epic poetry, and the *Kanteletar* is the fatter book; in the second, Lönnrot fitted his material to his purpose, which was not that of a modern folklorist. If this son of a poor tailor from Sammatti (a village not far from Helsinki, now on the tourist trail) was not a Homer in the accepted sense—his own poetic achievement in the literary sphere is modest—then he was a great rhapsode, performing in print as Homer's interpreters had performed at festivals in the fifth century BC: as it happens, a rhapsode was literally a 'stitcher together' of (presumably) separate poems into a performance, a rhapsody. Lönnrot's first epic 'performance' was the 1835 *Kalevala*; that of 1849 shows him warming to his theme, filling out his portrait of the 'heroic age' of the Finns with lyrics and incantations. It was a massive labour of assembly that involved not only stitching poems together, but patching some with scraps of others. Lönnrot, like Homer, unified dialects into a kind of national demotic: 'The language in these poems is ordinary Karelian Finnish, not much different from the speech of other Finnish provinces, so a Finn from anywhere will with a little adjustment easily understand them' (1849 preface)—though, it should be added, with the help of such glosses as accompany the work of later 'unifiers' like Kazantzakis and MacDiarmid. Some of Lönnrot's characters are likewise 'unified'. The opening lines of canto 11 refer to Ahti the Islander, Lemminkäinen (alias *lieto Lemmin poika* 'wanton Loverboy'), and Farmind (*Kaukomieli*, a footloose Viking figure) as one man, whereas in the source material there are three. In one variant (FFPE 34) Lemminkäinen even fights Ahti, and cuts off his head 'like cropping a turnip', a fate Lönnrot transfers to the Master of Northland (27:382); but this is nothing beside the bard Arhippa (FFPE 37), who has Farmind cropping Herod. Lönnrot virtually invented the Kullervo of cantos 31–36 by combining poems about an orphan child of Herculean strength (for example FFPE 41–43), about a departing warrior (137), about incest (44, 45), and about reacting to news of death (137–141); the main characters of these poems have various names, including Kullervo, while the incestuous brother is sometimes Lemminkäinen.

The society depicted is highly improbable—a water-god turned shaman and a sky-god turned smith sailing off together on a Viking-style raid (canto 39). But this is not Lönnrot's invention: his source is Arhippa himself (FFPE 12, one of the tradition's masterpieces). Folklorists call such a poem an example of syncretism, mixing the incompatible: for an English example,

> There is an old tale goes that Herne the hunter,
> Sometime a keeper here in Windsor Forest,
> Doth all the winter-time, at still midnight,
> Walk round about an oak, with great ragg'd horns . . .
>
> (*The Merry Wives of Windsor*, IV. iv)

The 'old tale' tells of his being wounded by a stag, killing it, going mad, tying its antlers on his head, running naked through the forest, and hanging himself: the sheer improbability of it all suggests a mix of, say, a known Tudor poacher called Horne and the Celtic horned god Cernunnos, whose image in turn recalls a shaman in full regalia. Oral tradition projects a timeless present full of such contradictions, faithfully echoed by Lönnrot except in one particular, the Christian element. His historical scheme shows Christianity suddenly arriving to take over in the last act, like Fortinbras in *Hamlet* (canto 50). In fact, as we have seen, it coexisted with pagan beliefs for centuries, especially in Karelia: Väinämöinen's journey to the otherworld for a tool to mend his sledge (25: 673–738) arises, according to the source material, from a mishap on his way to church (FFPE 30).

Christianity apart, Lönnrot followed the example of his best sources, shaping existing material into new wholes; but with the advantage of literacy he took the process further.

The *Kalevala*, then, is not for folklorists, who are amply provided for in the archives of the Finnish Literature Society. The Finns have their national epic, but what of the rest of us? What are we to make of myth, 'sacred narrative', turned long since into legend, then served up as history? It is time to turn away from folklore towards the *Kalevala* as literature: whatever went into its making, the proof of the pudding is in the eating.

The Kalevala *as literature*

In a young nation state concerned about its place in the Western world, the national epic has had a mixed reception over the last decade or so: current interest is centred more on the oral tradition behind it. The shift, reflected in the school textbook *Kansanruno-Kalevala* ('The Folk Poem *Kalevala*' ed. Matti Kuusi, Helsinki, 1976) and the bulky anthology *Runojen kirja: neljä vuosisataa suomalaista runoutta* ('The Book of Poems: four centuries of Finnish poetry' ed. Veikko Polameri, Helsinki, 1977), is readily understood: Finland has folklore archives that are virtually unrivalled, and related disciplines more exportable than what some Finns regard as a literary monument to local aspirations. The fact remains, however, that the *Kalevala* is the work of Finnish literature best known abroad, where it must stand or fall as a text in its own right. Having seen it in its historical and cultural setting, we might now try to see it in the setting it creates for itself, the 'heroic' world of the Dark Ages when the Kalevala tradition was being formed.

'It is the nature of epic poetry to be at ease in regard to its subject matter', writes W. P. Ker in his still indispensable study of medieval narrative, *Epic and Romance* (London, 1908). The *Kalevala* tells its story unselfconsciously, without straining for effect, almost without abstraction or moralizing; it has the dramatic sense for which Aristotle praises Homer of revealing character mainly through speech; like a good film, it cuts from one close-up to another, adding the occasional long shot for contrast. Ker identifies two styles in early Teutonic epic, the broadly sweeping western style (for example, *Beowulf*) with its enjambements, its sentences beginning and ending in mid-line, like the blank verse of centuries later, and the terser, end-stopped northern (for example, the *Elder Edda*), which led to the ballad and the lyric poetry of the skalds, so that epic narrative had to switch to prose, whence the sagas. Then, around the twelfth century, came romance, replacing local heroic values with those of cosmopolitan chivalry. Ker's range of reference, breathtaking though it still is, did not extend to Finnish epic: had it done so, he might have decided that this lies somewhere between *Beowulf* and the *Edda*. It has some of the former's breadth, but without enjambement, and some of the latter's terseness, but without a tendency to short forms. All three epic styles share a taste for alliteration, but beyond that prosodies diverge. The leap and thump of Teutonic, not only in poetry but in ordinary speech (as Hopkins knew when he tried to bring the rhythms of English poetry back to those of speech), gives way to a dance of light consonants and harmonizing vowels. All three epic styles, too, are oral in origin, and the Finnish experience suggests that some of the difference observed by Ker may be due to different methods of recording oral material. While the Anglo-Saxon and Icelandic bards were performing, and while they were being written down, Finnish epic was flourishing in communities on the eastern edge of the Viking homelands; but Europe became aware of their poetic achievement only in the nineteenth century, after a time-lag of up to a millennium. When Western scholars include the *Kalevala* and its sources in their studies of early European epic, they may feel the kind of excitement that palaeontologists felt on discovering a live coelacanth.

The *Kalevala* moves with ease between epic proper, lyric, rite, and magic, four modes derived from the four principal types of poem in the tradition. There is the epic splendour of the eagle formed from a sheet of flame refusing to return to its master after catching the great pike in the river of Death:

Well, the iron-foot eagle
at that flared up into flight—
up into the sky it soared
on to a long bank of cloud:
the clouds squirmed, the heavens mewed
the lids of the sky tilted
  the Old Man's bow snapped
so did the moon's horny points.

(19:305–12)

A notable feature of Finnish epic is its humour—nothing subtle or dignified, but the kind of comic relief one meets in Shakespearean tragedy. Our heroes have stolen the Sampo while Northland sleeps, and as they sail away with their booty Lemminkäinen, against advice, bursts into song 'with his surly voice / with his rasping throat' (42:283–4). He disturbs a crane 'counting its toe bones' (295), which 'let out a weird croak' (299) and wakes Northland, leading to the climactic battle scene of the next canto. No wonder Lönnrot's colleagues complained of his tampering with his material, for according to the source—Arhippa singing for Lönnrot himself—the crane is disturbed because 'an ant, a ballocking boy (*mulkupoika*) / pissed' on its leg (FFPE 12:269–70).

Then there is the lyric delicacy of the Maid of the North about to leave her childhood home with her bridegroom:

This is how the lucky feel
  how the blessed think—
  like daybreak in spring
the sun on a spring morning.
  But how do I feel
  in my gloomy depths?—
like the flat brink of a cloud
like a dark night in autumn
  a black winter day;
  no, darker than that—
gloomier than an autumn night.

(22:173–84)

Rite and magic are less common in literature. The longest ritual passages accompany the wedding (cantos 21–5) and the bear hunt and feast (canto 46). The wedding sequence is remarkable for its comprehensiveness: one is reminded of *Les Noces* by Stravinsky, who uses Russian material, though childhood memories of his birthplace Kaarasti (Russian Oranienbaum) in Finnish-speaking Ingria could have contributed. There is sensible advice to the bride about living in an extended family where food may be in short supply:

> Should you see a child upon the floor
> even if 'tis sister-in-law's child
> lift the child on to a bench
> wash its eyes and smooth its hair
> put some bread into its hand
> spread some butter on the bread;
> if there's no bread in the house
> put a wood-chip in its hand.
>
> (23:185–92)

The bridegroom too receives advice, such as to avoid his wife's face when beating her, for 'a lump / would come up on the eyebrow / a blueberry on the eye' (24:253–4), which would lead to gossip. Nevertheless, he is urged to defend her against his family when necessary: he must 'stand as a wall before her / stay as a doorpost' (24:199–200).

This is a formula, which features more often in charms to stop blood, as in one of the longest incantations, which forms most of canto 9. Väinämöinen has gashed his knee with his axe. To heal the wound, two things are required—magic and medicine. A spell (27–266) recites the origin or 'birth' (*synty*) of the offending substance, to demonstrate one's power over it: this is sound psychotherapy, as we have since discovered. As a shaman, Väinämöinen is a kind of consultant: he makes a diagnosis, then refers the patient—here himself—for treatment to a practitioner—here an unnamed old man whose son acts as a nurse. The diagnosis ('thorough knowledge') consists of showing that the shaman knows all about iron, of which the axe is made. An odd tale of milk from heavenly nipples producing iron ore leads to the lowlier magic of rebuke and threat, recited by the old man (271–342), who goes on to the final exorcism (343–416). The blood is commanded to stop flowing:

Blood, stand like a wall
stay, gore, like a fence
like an iris in a lake
stand, like sedge among moss, like
a boulder at a field-edge
a rock in a steep rapid!
(347–52)

Should it refuse to stop flowing, a higher power—the Demon—is invoked to boil the blood dry. Should that not work either, God himself is called upon to 'press your fat thumb' (408) on the wound. Then a salve is prepared, tested (spectacularly), and applied, and all is well. This is the basic technique; there are many variations. Origin spells are not always such flights of fancy: the beer spell in canto 20 is a coded recipe—barley, hops, water, and saliva from fighting bears to stimulate fermentation; while the snake spell in canto 26 is a loathsomely vivid metaphor—a blob of mucus spat on water, stretched lengthwise and 'blessed' with eyes. Charms—spells in miniature—often use metaphor too, but in a more compressed way, as in the labour charm which commands a nature spirit:

Take up a golden
club in your right hand:
with it shatter bars
and break the doorposts
dislodge the Creator's locks
and snap off the inner bolts

for the great to go, the small
to go, the puny to pass!

(45:139–46)

The incantations of the epic are like coloratura arias, with both medium and performer showing what they are capable of.

Following the example of Aristotle, who in the *Poetics* summarizes the *Odyssey* in three sentences ('This is essential; the rest is episode'), one might offer a still briefer account of the *Kalevala* thus: 'The Sampo is forged, a rogue screws; there's a wedding, a murder, the blues; a serf bites the dust, the Sampo gets bust, and Finland receives the Good News.' For a fuller description, the *Kalevala* can be divided into eight cycles, each with a leading character.

1. The first Väinämöinen cycle (cantos 1–10). Väinämöinen (the name is probably derived from archaic *väinä* 'slow-flowing river', whence he is also called 'Calm Waters man') is the dominant figure of the epic and culture-hero of the tradition, in which he sometimes appears as a water-god creating the world; in the epic he is a shaman. The first man on earth, he founds the land of Kalevala, twice fails to find a wife, and nominates Ilmarinen to forge the mysterious Sampo for Northland.
2. The first Lemminkäinen cycle (cantos 11–15). Lemminkäinen (probably from *lempi*, cf. Greek *erōs*) is a many-named (see earlier) adventurer in every sense, who leaves his wife to woo the Maid of the North, is killed, but is then restored to life by his mother.
3. The second Väinämöinen cycle (cantos 16–25). Väinämöinen and Ilmarinen compete for the Maid of the North; Ilmarinen wins, and Väinämöinen sings at the wedding.
4. The second Lemminkäinen cycle (cantos 26–30). Angry at not being invited to the wedding, Lemminkäinen kills the Master of Northland, has more

amorous adventures, and is finally thwarted by the Frost.

5. The Kullervo cycle (cantos 31–6). Sold as a serf to Ilmarinen after a family feud, Kullervo causes the death of Ilmarinen's wife. He unwittingly seduces his sister, revives the feud, is defeated, and kills himself.
6. The Ilmarinen cycle (cantos 37–8). In the tradition Ilmarinen (perhaps from *ilma* 'sky, air') is sometimes a sky-god; in the epic he is a smith, and friend and comrade to Väinämöinen. Here he is briefly dominant as a widower who tries to make a new wife out of gold.
7. The third Väinämöinen cycle (cantos 39–49). The climax of the epic: the men of Kalevala sail to Northland, steal the Sampo, but lose it overboard in battle. Kalevala prospers nevertheless, and despite the plagues sent by Louhi, Mistress of Northland.
8. The Marjatta cycle (canto 50). The virgin Marjatta (a form of Mary or Margaret) is impregnated by a berry (*marja*) and produces a son to whom the heavens defer. Väinämöinen ungraciously hands Finland over to him, and sails away, leaving his songs behind.

Beyond these characters, the cast-list remains elegantly short. We have already met Joukahainen and his sister Aino. Louhi is the leading Northland character; her unnamed husband appears only in canto 27, to be killed by Lemminkäinen. She is first a friend, then a foe; her daughter, known only as the Maid of the North, is wooed in turn by Väinämöinen, Lemminkäinen, and Ilmarinen, who must each perform tasks to win her. Kyllikki, Lemminkäinen's wife, is surprisingly modern in her insistence on equal rights (canto 11). Lesser characters requiring comment are dealt with in the Notes.

The human world of the epic is, as it were, a commonwealth of heroes: the protagonists Väinämöinen and Louhi have their followers, Ilmarinen has serfs to work his bellows, Marjatta has a servant, but there is no precedence, no sense of lord and retainer. This is due not to any early experiment in democracy, as in the Icelandic sagas, but to the primitiveness of the society depicted. The otherworld, in contrast, is strictly hierarchical. As we saw in the blood-stopping charm earlier, there are three classes of spirits, forming a pyramid. At the base the animistic world-view generates any number of resident spirits, sometimes personifications ('Blood, stand like a wall'), sometimes named after what they inhabit—nature-daughters, Sampsa 'the field's son', Sinew-daughter, and many others. Above them are spirits with 'proper' names like Tapio, lord of the forests, and Tuoni, lord of the dead. Neither good nor evil in themselves, they must be treated with respect, or the hunter will not catch his prey, and the shaman who visits the dead will not come back. Some such spirits, if not evil, are at least mischievous—the Demon (*Hiisi*), alias the Devil (*Lempo*), who causes Väinämöinen's wound in canto 8, whose followers are demons (*hiiet*, *pirut*) or judases (*juuttahat*). At the apex of the pyramid is the Old Man (*Ukko*, cf. modern Finnish *ukkonen* 'thunder'), who is identified with God (*Jumala*, the name adopted by Christianity).

The central narrative of the epic concerns the changing relations between Kalevala and Northland (*Pohjola*), which hinge on the Sampo—its manufacture (canto 10), its theft (42), and loss in battle (43). Much scholarly ink has flowed into speculation on two questions: Where was Northland? What was the Sampo? What little remains to be said must be prefaced by two caveats: the bards themselves could not answer either question, and Lönnrot's guesses were based on historical theories long since discredited. But the reader coming to the epic for the first time deserves at least something to quiet Eliot's house-dog of the mind.

The epic identifies Kalevala with Finland, Northland with Lapland. But even if the names refer to two peoples who were once neighbours in southern Finland—the Finns and Tacitus' Fenni, who were probably Lapps—there is no evidence of the former helping the latter until these overtook their benefactors and had to be brought back into line. As Lönnrot himself wondered: 'When would any other people have been subject to taxation by the Lapps?' (1849 preface). His answer to his own question was that Northland belonged to Alfred's 'Beormas', North Karelians: 'Here indeed is the central bond or unity of the Kalevala poems, that they tell how Kalevala gradually caught up with Northland and finally overtook it' (ibid.). This, as Michael Branch has pointed out (1985), needs to be seen in the context of an emerging nineteenth-century nation state, itself busy with catching up, and hoping to overtake. We are left with the text and the tale it tells.

The Sampo offers the house-dog richer meat. According to canto 10, it is a mill with a decorated lid, made by a smith and hence of metal, that grinds corn, salt, and money; but its subsequent history is hardly consonant with a mill, be it never so versatile. The very notion of a mill may be a Scandinavian importation: scholars have cited the poem in the *Elder Edda* about a magic mill (*Gróttasöngr*, 'The Song of the Grinders' in Auden and Taylor trans., *Norse Poems*, London, 1981). Guesses have included an idol (Lönnrot), a chest containing treasure or a document, a world pillar or tree, a model of the cosmos . . . The modern Finnish poet Paavo Haavikko has even proposed at some length a mint stolen by Vikings from Byzantium, since forged Byzantine coins have been found in Finland. But it is difficult to square any of these with the ingredients in the epic for its manufacture specified by Louhi, who asks Ilmarinen to make the Sampo

from a swan's quill tip
a barren cow's milk
a small barley grain
a summer ewe's down . . .
(10:263–6)

Suddenly, it seems, the 'Beormas' need something of metal, about which they have no idea; indeed, Ilmarinen can find no facilities for making it—'no forge, no anvil / no hammer, no handle even!' (287–8). Or are they driving a hard bargain, though they are in no position to do so? When the smith eventually sets to work, he produces first a crossbow, then a boat, a heifer, and a plough—a neat summary, perhaps, of hunting, fishing, stock-breeding, and agriculture—and only then the Sampo itself. Exeunt Beormas; enter Fenni, bearing arrows sharpened with bone. For a more palatable interpretation we need to turn to the tradition. Michael Branch sees the Sampo as a 'parody of courtship', with Väinämöinen as matchmaker. The Sampo ingredients are part of the suitor's 'impossible tasks' like those facing Väinämöinen (canto 8), Lemminkäinen (13–14) and Ilmarinen again (19). The rest, as Aristotle says, is episode. Readers of the epic must be content with the Sampo for what it is, and was meant to be—a mysterious object.

The most interesting relationship in the epic is that between Ilmarinen and Väinämöinen. Traces of their sometime divine status can be discerned in Väinämöinen's association with water and water-spirits, and in Ilmarinen's unanswerable self-qualification for making the Sampo as the smith who made the sky (canto 10). As mortals they are portrayed as friends and comrades ('brothers'). Though they occasionally appear together in the source material (for example, FFPE 12, the great Sampo raid poem), their comradeship in the epic is mostly Lönnrot's invention, a Finnish Roland and Oliver. But it is a very unequal comradeship: apart from the smith's success in their rivalry to win the Maid of the North (canto 18), the shaman has the upper hand, as when he tricks the smith into first going to Northland (10), mocks him for making a woman of gold (37), proves him wrong over what to do with fishbones (40), and mocks him again for making a replacement moon and sun (49). The Maid prefers youth, however grimy, to age, however rich; but when it comes to intelligence the shaman repeatedly outwits the smith. What is Lönnrot doing here? Is he arguing the superiority of magic to metalworking, as if to say that the Finns in their 'heroic age' were peaceful, resolving their conflicts with spells rather than cold steel? The epic generally bears this out, so that when violence does take place it is shocking: in canto 27 the duel between Lemminkäinen and the Master of Northland becomes bloody only when a contest of magic proves inconclusive, and in canto 49 even Väinämöinen does not scruple to lay about him when all else fails. Most of the time, however, magic rules, often at the smith's expense. Even in his solo performance in canto 37 he is finally upstaged by the shaman, who, on being offered the Golden Bride the smith has made but failed to warm up, dismisses her as 'this golden bugbear' (216), and suggests she be melted down to make something useful, or sold to greedy foreigners. This episode can be seen from another angle when it is compared with a later (1858) Ingrian variant in the tradition: FFPE 22 tells of a smith tired of making tools that are taken for granted, so he makes an idol of a kind often found in the far North (St Stephen of Perm reported 'a golden woman' in the fourteenth century), which frightens everyone but pleases him. Something of this surfaces in canto 37 when the serfs working the bellows are 'badly scared' (143) as the woman emerges. But Väinämöinen's rejection has more than a touch of Stephen about it when he warns the young against 'bowing to gold / scraping to silver' (237–8), and it is the shaman who gives way to the virgin Marjatta's son in canto 50, the old magic giving way to the new.

Magic remains the biggest problem for the modern reader. We can accept it when the context supplies clues—there is blood to be stopped (canto 9), game to be caught (14), even a corpse to be resurrected (15); but what of the magic that is dumped without preliminaries in the lap of the unsuspecting foreigner or city-dweller who no longer grasps the language of myth?

To go to Northland, Väinämöinen 'took a stallion of straw / a horse of pea stalks' (6: 5–6). Learned opinion has tended to regard this as a description of the beast's colour, but Felix Oinas (1985) argues that a shaman would mount a stick of straw and proclaim it a horse; in English folklore one is reminded of a witch's broomstick. Here the epic supplies its own critique: in the wedding ritual, Kaleva-daughter says she would praise even 'a stallion of straw' if it were bringing the bridegroom to the feast (23:63–6), implying *a fortiori* how much more welcome a real horse would be. The boat 'born uncarved / the ship with no shaving pared' (17:627–8), the animals invoked in the duel (27:205–56), the smith's fire that leaves the serfs unscorched (canto 37) exist only in the poem: they are products of the creative Word as uttered by culture-heroes like Orpheus, whose rule ended with what Mallarmé, with characteristic panache, called *la grande déviation homérique* of poetry as reportage.

The *Kalevala*, then, has some extraordinarily archaic features, but these very features can bring it to life in a world that has inherited the preoccupations of Modernism: if we enjoy a Picasso influenced by African masks, or a Stravinsky who has learned from pagan rites of passage, then the *Kalevala* is for us. What once mystified as magic can challenge us as poetic truth: across the centuries, across the great divide between oral tradition and literature, the epic invites our attention as that most universal of spells, a poem.

The translation

As we have seen, the shaping of the *Kalevala* involved a certain dislocation—from oral tradition to literature, from scattered fragments to monumental epic, from 'little' tradition to 'great'. Such dislocation is eased when a nation knows that 'one man . . . is restoring to us our state', but it is compounded when we move outside the national context by way of translation. How is a translator to keep alive a work whose cultural setting has so little in common with that of his readers? From the English-speaker's point of view, the *Kalevala* is the Finns' Chaucer, Shakespeare, Milton, Pope, and Wordsworth rolled into one; but the genius of its sources could neither read nor write. It is as though English literature had begun with Percy's *Reliques*, and everything before had been written in French. That is the size of the translator's problem.

One translator can ignore the problem, and give an account, as accurate as he can make it, in plain prose, like Magoun (1963): the result will please students of the exotic. Another translator can assume a cultural equivalent, and thus complete the dislocation, like Kirby (1907): the result will please nearly everybody (many of us owe our first contact with the epic to Kirby), who will wonder why such charming fairy-tales are considered so important. Somewhere between Magoun's Scylla and Kirby's Charybdis a third translator may steer a way, combining accuracy without dullness and readability without falsification. The Fromms (1967) have achieved it in German, despite their commitment to reproducing the original metre, or rather the German adaptation of it. The present translation departs from the practice of many translators of the epic into many tongues by replacing the original metre with another. This, after all, has been the usual method in English since Gavin Douglas's *Aeneid* (1513), though one need not follow the example of the unknown Augustan translating a Lappish folk poem (one of two published by Johannes Scheffer in 1673) in *The Spectator*:

Haste, my rein-deer! and let us nimbly go
Our am'rous journey through this dreary waste;
Haste, my rein-deer! still thou art too slow,
Impetuous love demands the lightning's haste . . .

The verse translator must first be a good listener. Finnish is pure *bel canto*: where 'standard' English has some twelve vowels and twenty-four consonants, Lönnrot's 'ordinary Karelian Finnish' has only eight vowels and twelve consonants, which seldom cluster more than two together. So alliteration, far from being the maker's hammer-mark, is sometimes hard to avoid, and translators have found that any consistent attempt to reproduce it would not only take them too far from an original full of concrete particulars, but would weigh down a version in a 'heavier' language like English or German; besides which English alliterative verse was already 'uncouth' to Dunbar's ear five hundred years ago.

Unlike Germanic with its stress accent, Finnish has a tonic (or pitch) accent. Languages with a tonic accent tend not to use it as a metrical feature: if quantity is functional, they use that, like ancient Greek and Latin; if it is not, they count syllables, like modern Greek, and the Romance and Celtic languages. In the present foreigner's view, the basis of Kalevala poetry is quantitative, which is why it sounds 'irregular' to Germanic and even to modern Finnish ears, so strong has Germanic cultural influence been. While Finnish scholars observe that a long syllable cannot occur in an 'unstressed' position, they admit that roughly half of all known Kalevala poetry consists of 'broken lines', meaning lines that do not scan accentually, like the opening lines of the epic:

Mieleni minun tekevi,
aivoni ajattelevi . . .

('I have a good mind / take into my head . . .'). Kirby 'corrects' the metre thus: 'I am driven by my longing, /

And my understanding urges . . .'. The Fromms, likewise, running two lines into one: '*Mich verlangt in meinem Sinne, mich bewegen die Gedanken* . . .'. But no scientist would tolerate a law that is broken half the time. Could Kalevala metre be syllabic? If it were, there would not be the variation one finds in the sources. Could the parallelism point to a syntactical basis, as in biblical poetry? But even in the epic (which is smoother than the sources) parallelism presents wide variations, including what sounds like parallelism but in fact is not:

vyöltä vanhan Väinämöisen,
alta ahjon Ilmarisen . . .

(literally 'from-the-belt of-old Väinämöinen, / from-beneath the-forge of-Ilmarinen', 1:31–2). In modern Finnish this would be *vanhan Väinämöisen vyöltä, Ilmarisen ahjon alta*: beyond what Finns call the 'winnowing principle', whereby longer words gravitate towards the end of the line, another law is operating here, pitting sound against sense. In the opening lines quoted above, it is surely a quantitative law one hears when one knows that the Karelian verb-ending *-evi* is often recorded as *-eepi* (cf. modern Finnish *-ee*); though the law's application throughout Kalevala poetry is more relaxed Greek than rigid Roman.

The apparent confusion of accent and quantity could go back to eighteenth-century German adaptations of Classical metres and forms, and to their Swedish derivatives. English poets have rarely gone further than adapting a few metrical feet (iambus, anapaest, and so on), but some of the greatest German poetry is in 'Classical' hexameters, alcaics and others. The adaptation consisted of exchanging long syllables for stressed, short for unstressed. It was still flourishing in Finland in 1917, when Koskenniemi published his *Elegioja* ('Elegies'):

Yksin oot sinä, ihminen, kaiken keskellä yksin,
yksin syntynyt oot, yksin sa lähtevä oot . . .

('You are alone, man, alone amid everything, / alone you were born, alone you will depart . . .'). Whether or not Finns listen to their own folk poetry with Germanic ears—and there are many examples elsewhere of such alienation in similar circumstances—it has certainly been heard that way by translators. The model seems to have been Goethe, in whose *Finnisches Lied* (1810) the 'broken lines' are all mended. The poem is worth quoting in full beside the original, first printed in a Swedish travel book in French (1801), which partly accounts for the strange Finnish. 'Broken lines'—fewer than average—are marked below with asterisks; Goethe's metre has become the *anakreontisch* of Gleim:

*Jos mun tuttuni tulissi	Käm der liebe Wohlbekannte,
*Ennen näh tyni näkyissi,	Völlig so wie er geschieden,
Sillen suuta suika jaissin	Kuß erkläng an seinen Lippen,
*Olis sun suden weressä,	Hätt auch Wolfsblut sie gerötet;
Sillen kättä käppä jaissin	Ihm den Handschlag gäb ich, wären
Jospa kärmä kämmen päässä!	Seine Fingerspitzen Schlangen.
Olisko tuuli mielelissä!	Wind! o hättest du Verständnis,
Aha wainen kielelissä,	. . .
Sanan toisi, sanan weisi,	Wort um Worte trügst du wechselnd,
Sanan liian liikuttäissi	Sollt auch einiges verhallen,
*Kahden rahkaan wälillä.	Zwischen zwei entfernten Liebchen.
Ennembä heitän herkurruat,	Gern entbehrt ich gute Bissen,
*Paisit papillan unohdan	Priesters Tafelfleisch vergäß ich
Ennen kun hei tän hertaiseni	Eher, als dem Freund entsagen,
Kesan kestytel dyäni	Den ich, Sommers rasch bezwungen,
Talwen taiwulel duäni.	Winters langer Weis bezähmte.

('If the one I know came now / the one I've seen were in sight / I'd snatch a kiss from his mouth / though his mouth bled from a wolf / I would grasp him by the hand / though a snake were in his palm! / Had the wind a mind / and the gale a tongue / it would bring word, take a word / set an extra word astir / between two lovers. / I will sooner leave fine foods / and forget rectory roasts / before I leave my sweetheart / the one I tamed all summer

/ and persuaded all winter.') Seventy variants of this lyric have been recorded. The first Finnish folk poem to reach the outside world, it was accompanied by a *traduction verbale* and first appeared in English in 1802. Goethe's translation, the first in verse, demonstrates the principle still in use by a later generation of Weimar translators, who signed their work with *fertaitsht un ferbessert* 'translated into Yiddish and improved'. Then came Schiefner, Longfellow, Crawford, Kirby, the Fromms . . . It is a pity that the common sense translators have applied to the question of alliteration in Kalevala poetry has not also been applied to that of metre, especially when the metre of their translations is a travesty of the original. As any reader of *Hiawatha* knows, the metre is not only monotonous, it restricts language to the point of triviality—in English, at least. This matters little in a romance of Indians without cowboys, but it matters a great deal in an epic of world stature, most of whose readers approach it in translation.

The only way I could devise of reflecting the vitality of Kalevala metre was to invent my own, based on syllables rather than feet. While translating over 17,000 lines of Finnish folk poetry before I started on the epic, I found that a line settled usually into seven syllables of English, often less, occasionally more. I eventually arrived at seven, five, and nine syllables respectively, using the *impair* (odd number) as a formal device and letting the stresses fall where they would. Syllable-based metres are not new to English verse: Wyatt adapts the Italian *endecasillabo*, and like any metre evolved through the demands of translation—such as blank verse itself, invented by Surrey for translating Virgil—they can explore unfamiliar rhythms.

The present translation attempts to provide a counterpart for as much as possible of Lönnrot's text. Not an equivalent—there can be none; not a substitute—there is not the shared background. A counterpart, then, for its many rhythms, its formulaic construction, its foundation in popular speech. The subtitle and canto titles are mine; the latter replace Lönnrot's detailed Renaissance-style 'arguments' in rather quaint Finnish (*Runo alotteleikse* 'The poem causes itself to be beginning'—an old Karelian reflexive). My only textual interference has been to run together many of the original's shorter paragraphs; changes of punctuation have been dictated largely by the often considerable difference of idiom. For the rest, I hope I have produced a version that is both readable and accurate: several Finns with good English claim to have 'heard' the *Kalevala* when I have read from the present translation. Much of the power of Kalevala Finnish lies in its verbs, whose frequently wayward tenses I have faithfully rendered ('He says with this word / he spoke with this speech'): 'to roll' has nine derivatives in the epic, for many of which English has quite separate words. There is nothing like translation for improving knowledge of one's mother tongue. Among nouns, diminutives proliferate: I have thrown in the odd 'little' or 'dear' or the like where it seemed necessary.

The essential structural feature of formula repetition has been kept with the help of a concordance. Of course one does not always translate a word in the same way, but a formula needs to be recognizable. Problems of tone arise when a formula occurs in widely varying contexts: the line *Jo vainen valehtelitki!* occurs twice in canto 15 when Lemminkäinen's mother asks desperately about her missing son, and twice in canto 43 when Väinämöinen inquires about a cloud. In isolation these might be rendered respectively 'You're fobbing me off!' and 'You're having me on!' The translator of both can only be more literal in the hope of encompassing both with 'Surely you have lied!' The original listeners would have responded to the same words fitting both contexts: like Mallarmé they knew that poems are made not of ideas but of words.

The *Kalevala* is founded on popular speech because

for the bards there was no other, except for what they heard in church. It has much in common with English rural speech, which changes little from one generation to the next: one still hears ''tis' and ''twas', wenches (servant girls) are still luckless, fellows are still wroth enough to rise betimes (early) and smite their foes. Occasionally a Scottish word or usage has been preferable or necessary—'calloo' rather than 'long-tailed duck' (*Clangula hyemalis*), associated in Finnish tradition with sorrow; the literal rendering 'hen' rather than 'chick' or 'duck' as a term of endearment; 'tine' to render a dialect word for 'spark' (tiny?) already in use. Gavin Douglas's 'rurall vulgar gros' applies here to the original as well as to the translation. But this is not an exercise in pastoral nostalgia. All these words were needed to match the original's rich vocabulary of synonyms and near-synonyms, due in part to a wealth of dialect words: 'grass' and 'turf' being already spoken for, 'sward' is more appropriate than the educated 'verdure'. A few nonsense words generated by play have been rendered, in our less tolerant tongue, with rare words—'braes', 'swashed', 'gillaroo'. Names have been translated where they have an obvious meaning. Popular usage has guided syntax too. When the innocent Marjatta's mother demands to know how she came to be pregnant, she asks: *Kenen oot makaelema* (literally 'Of-whom are-you the-having-been-laid', 50:164). Previous English translators have spoken of resting and bedfellows, but resting, even sleeping with, are euphemisms not in the original, and no bed need come into it; she could even have been raped. The Finnish verb has the same overtones as the English: 'By whom have you been laid' is better, but 'Who were you laid by' is better still.

Early versions by me of extracts from the *Kalevala* appeared in my first book *Tales from the Long Lakes* (Gollancz, 1966), in my collection for children *And I Dance* (Angus & Robertson, 1972), in *Young Winter's Tales 3*, ed. M. R. Hodgkin (Macmillan, 1972), and a version of canto 4 was published as *The Song of Aino* by Mr Robert Richardson's Moonbird Publications (1973). The following year I became involved in a continuing project to prepare a series of anthologies presenting Finnish folk poetry and that of all Finno-Ugrian-speaking peoples in the original languages and in English translation; it was through this work that Mr Urpo Vento of the Finnish Literature Society in Helsinki invited me to make a new English translation of the *Kalevala*, and a grant was awarded through the Finnish Ministry of Education. A version of cantos 11–15 was published as *Wanton Loverboy* by the Finnish Literature Society in 1985, when Finland celebrated the sesquicentenary of the epic's first edition; a *Kalevala* issue of *Books from Finland* published a few extracts, and BBC radio broadcast a few more. Other extracts appeared in the *Poetry Review*, in programmes for BBC Henry Wood Promenade Concerts, for concerts promoted by Van Walsum Management and the Brighton Festival, in the score of *Lemminkäinen*, op. 103, by Mr Erik Bergman (Edition Pan, Helsinki), in Timo Martin and Douglas Sivén, *Akseli Gallen-Kallela: National Artist of Finland* (Watti-Kustannus, Helsinki), on two postcards from the Menard Press of Mr Anthony Rudolf, conversation with whom is always fruitful, and in the catalogue of an exhibition, *The Language of Wood*, mounted by the Museum of Applied Arts, Helsinki. The genial godfather of all my Finnish excursions has been Professor Michael Branch, Director of the School of Slavonic and East European Studies in the University of London; Academician Matti Kuusi of the University of Helsinki has inspired and guided all of us who seek poetic excellence in oral tradition. Ms Senni Timonen of the Finnish Literature Society has monitored the translation throughout; her energy was inexhaustible, her contribution is inestimable. The BBC has been a good-natured employer, and Bush House colleagues have been helpful. Most 'thanksworthy', as Finns would say, is my wife

Satu Salo, who has shared me with the *Kalevala* for most of our married life, kept me in touch with modern Finnish usage, and saved me from silly mistakes. Such shortcomings as remain can only be my responsibility. Let this translation of the *Kalevala* go on its way with a closing formula from an unknown Ingrian bard performing in 1858 (FFPE 26:141–5):

> Of what use are we singers
> what good we cuckoo-callers
> if no fire spurts from our mouths
> no brand from beneath our tongues
> and no smoke after our words!

Upton-cum-Chalvey K.B.

SELECT BIBLIOGRAPHY

In English

Francis Peabody Magoun, Jr. (trans.), *The Kalevala, or Poems of the Kaleva District, compiled by Elias Lönnrot. A Prose Translation with Foreword and Appendices* (Cambridge, Mass., 1963, 1985). The appendices contain articles by Finnish scholars, Lönnrot's 1835 and 1849 prefaces, an extract from Porthan's *De Poësi Fennica*, and lists of names and charms.

W. F. Kirby (trans.), *Kalevala, the Land of (the) Heroes* (London and Dover, NH, 1985). A reissue of the 1907 Everyman's Library verse translation, the first in English from the original, introduced and annotated by Michael Branch.

Matti Kuusi, Keith Bosley, Michael Branch (ed. and trans.), *Finnish Folk Poetry: Epic. An Anthology in Finnish and English* (Helsinki, London, Montreal, 1977). Texts of such sources as formed the basis of the *Kalevala*, but covering a wider range, with extensive introduction and commentary.

Lauri Honko, Senni Timonen, Keith Bosley, Michael Branch (ed. and trans.), *The Great Bear. A Thematic Anthology of Oral Poetry in the Finno-Ugrian Languages* (Helsinki, 1993). Texts in fifteen languages, with translation, introduction, and commentary.

Felix J. Oinas, *Studies in Finnic Folklore: Homage to the Kalevala* (Helsinki, 1985). Essays by an Estonian-American scholar, some of which explore links with Slav folklore.

Books from Finland 1 (1985). *Kalevala* issue of the journal of the Finnish Literature Information Centre, Helsinki.

Pentti Leino, *Language and Metre: metrics and the metrical system of Finnish* (Helsinki, 1986).

In German

Lore and Hans Fromm (trans.), *Kalevala. Das finnische Epos des Elias Lönnrot* (Munich, 1967; Stuttgart, 1984). Hans Fromm's introduction and commentary are the fullest outside Finnish.

In Finnish

Kalevala (Helsinki, always in print). The school edition of the Finnish Literature Society (Suomalaisen Kirjallisuuden Seura, SKS) gives the plain text with Lönnrot's 1849 preface. There are many other editions, some illustrated.

Väinö Kaukonen (ed.), *Elias Lönnrotin Kalevalan Toinen Painos* ['The Second Edition of Elias Lönnrot's *Kalevala*'] (Helsinki, 1956, still in print). With an introduction, a history of the text, a commentary that includes background on Lönnrot's predecessors and contemporaries, and Ahlqvist's concordance.

Aimo Turunen, *Kalevalan Sanat ja niiden taustat* ['The Words of the *Kalevala* and their background'] (Lappeenranta, 1979). The standard work on the epic's vocabulary.

Toivo Vuorela, *Kansanperinteen Sanakirja* ['Dictionary of the Folk Tradition'] (Helsinki, 1979).

Matti Kuusi and Pertti Anttonen, *Kalevala-Lipas* ['The *Kalevala* Box'] (Helsinki, 1985). A popular survey, full of useful and curious information.

1. *In the Beginning*

I have a good mind
take into my head
to start off singing
begin reciting
reeling off a tale of kin
and singing a tale of kind.
The words unfreeze in my mouth
and the phrases are tumbling
upon my tongue they scramble
along my teeth they scatter.
Brother dear, little brother
fair one who grew up with me
start off now singing with me
begin reciting with me
since we have got together
since we have come from two ways!
We seldom get together
and meet each other
on these poor borders
the luckless lands of the North.
Let's strike hand to hand*
fingers into finger-gaps
that we may sing some good things
set some of the best things forth
for those darling ones to hear
for those with a mind to know
among the youngsters rising
among the people growing—
those words we have got
tales we have kindled
from old Väinämöinen's belt
up from Ilmarinen's forge
from the tip of Farmind's brand

from the path of Joukahainen's bow
from the North's furthest fields, from
the heaths of Kalevala.*

My father used to sing them
as he cut an axe handle;
    my mother taught them
    turning her distaff
and I a child on the floor
fidgeting before her knee
    a milk-bearded scamp
    a curd-mouthed toddler.
The Sampo did not lack words
    nor did Louhi spells:
the Sampo grew old with words
and Louhi was lost with spells
and with tales Vipunen died
and Lemminkäinen with games.
There are yet other words too
    and mysteries learned—
    snatched from the roadside
    plucked from the heather
    torn from the brushwood
    tugged from the saplings
    rubbed from a grass-head
    ripped from a footpath
    as I went herding
as a child in the pastures
on the honey-sweet hummocks
    on the golden knolls
following black Buttercup
beside Bouncy the brindled.
The cold told a tale to me
the rain suggested poems:*
another tale the winds brought
    the sea's* billows drove;
    the birds added words
    the treetops phrases.

I wound them into a ball
and arranged them in a coil
slipped the ball into my sled
and the coil into my sledge;
I took it home in the sled
in the sledge towards the kiln*
put it up in the shed loft*
in a little copper box.

Long my tale's been in the cold
for ages has lain hidden:
shall I take the tales out of the cold
scoop the songs out of the frost
bring my little box indoors
the casket to the seat end
under the famous roof beam
    under the fair roof
shall I open the word-chest
and unlock the box of tales
unwind the top of the ball
untie the knot of the coil?
I will sing quite a good tale
quite a fair one I'll beat out
    after some rye bread
    and some barley beer.
    If beer is not brought
    and ale not offered
I'll sing from a leaner mouth
after water I will lilt
to cheer this evening of ours
to honour the famous day
or to amuse the morrow
and to start the new morning.

* * *

I heard it recited thus
I knew how the tale was made:
with us the nights come alone

the days dawn alone, so was
Väinämöinen born alone
the eternal bard appeared
from the woman who bore him
from Air-daughter his mother.

There was a lass, an air-girl
a nice nature-daughter:* she
    long remained holy
    for ever girlish
    in the air's long yards
    on its level grounds.
    Her times grew weary
    and her life felt strange
from being always alone
    living as a lass
    in the air's long yards
    in the empty wastes.
So now she steps further down
launched herself upon the waves
    on the clear high seas
upon the open expanse.
There came a great gust of wind
from the east nasty weather
    lashed the sea to foam
    whipped it into waves.
    The wind lulled the maid
and the billow drove the lass
    about the blue main
    and the froth-capped waves;
and the wind blew her womb full
    the sea makes her fat.

    She bore a hard womb
a difficult bellyful
    seven hundred years
    nine ages of man;
    but no birth was born

no creature was created.
The lass rolled as the water-mother:
    she swims east, swims west
    swims north-west and south
    swims all the skylines
    in fiery birth-pangs
    in hard belly-woes;
    but no birth was born
no creature was created.
    She weeps and whimpers;
she uttered a word, spoke thus:
'Woe, luckless me, for my days
poor child, for my way of life:
now I have come to something—
for ever under the sky
    by the wind to be
    lulled, by billows driven
    on these wide waters
    upon these vast waves!
    Better 'twould have been
to live as lass of the air
than just now to toss about
as water-mother: it is
chilly for me to be here
woeful for me to shiver
in billows for me to dwell
in the water to wallow.
    O Old Man, chief god
upholder of all the sky
come here when you are needed
come this way when you are called:
free a wench from a tight spot
a woman from belly-throes;
come quickly, arrive promptly
most promptly where the need is!'

    A little time passed
    a moment sped by.

Came a scaup, straightforward bird
    and it flaps about
in search of a nesting-place
working out somewhere to live.
    It flew east, flew west
    flew north-west and south
    but it finds no room
not even the worst spot where
    it might build its nest
    take up residence.
    It glides, it hovers
    it thinks, considers:
'Shall I build my cabin on the wind
my dwelling on the billows?
The wind will fell the cabin
the billow will bear off my dwelling.'

So then the water-mother
the water-mother, air-lass
raised her knee out of the sea
her shoulderblade from the wave
for the scaup a nesting-place
    sweet land to live on.
    That scaup, pretty bird
    glides and hovers; it
spied the water-mother's knee
    on the bluish main;
thought it was a grass hummock
    a clump of fresh sward.
    It flutters, it glides
and it lands on the kneecap.
    There it builds its nest
    laid its golden eggs:
    six eggs were of gold
an iron egg the seventh.

It began to hatch the eggs
    to warm the kneecap:

it hatched one day, it hatched two
soon it hatched a third as well.
At that the water-mother
the water-mother, air-lass
feels that she is catching fire
that her skin is smouldering;
she thought her knee was ablaze
all her sinews were melting.
    And she jerked her knee
    and she shook her limbs:
the eggs rolled in the water
sink into the sea's billow;
    the eggs smashed to bits
    broke into pieces.
The eggs don't fall in the mud
the fragments in the water.
The bits changed into good things
the pieces into fair things:
    an egg's lower half
became mother earth below
    an egg's upper half
    became heaven above;
the upper half that was yolk
became the sun for shining
the upper half that was white
became the moon for gleaming;
what in an egg was mottled
became the stars in the sky
what in an egg was blackish
became the clouds of the air.

    The ages go on
    the years beyond that
    as the new sun shines
    as the new moon gleams.
Still the water-mother swims

the water-mother, air-lass
    on those mild waters
    on the misty waves
before her the slack water
and behind her the clear sky.

    Now in the ninth year
    in the tenth summer
she raised her head from the sea
    she lifts up her poll:
she began her creation
    forming her creatures
    on the clear high seas
upon the open expanse.
Where she turned her hand around
there she arranged the headlands;
where her foot touched the bottom
there she dug out the fish troughs;
    where else she bubbled
there she hollowed out the depths.
She turned her side to the land:
there she brought forth the smooth shores;
she turned her feet to the land:
there she formed the salmon haunts;
with her head she reached the land:
    there she shaped the bays.
Then she swam further from land
    paused upon the main;
formed the crags in the water
    grew the hidden reefs
to be places for shipwreck
the dispatch of sailors' heads.

Now the islands were arranged
and the crags formed in the sea
the sky's pillars set upright
the lands and mainlands called up
patterns* cut upon the rocks

lines drawn on the cliffs; but still
Väinämöinen was not born
nor fledged the eternal bard.
Steady old Väinämöinen
went round in his mother's womb
    for thirty summers
and as many winters too
    on those mild waters
    on the misty waves.
    He thinks, considers
how to be, which way to live
    in his dark hideout
in his narrow dwelling where
he has never seen the moon
    nor beheld the sun.
    He says with this word
    he spoke with this speech:
'Moon, unloose, and sun, set free
    and Great Bear,* still guide
a man out from the strange doors
    from the foreign gates
    from these little nests
    and narrow dwellings!
Bring the traveller to land
man's child into the open
to look at the moon in heaven
    to admire the sun
    observe the Great Bear
    and study the stars!'

When the moon did not loose him
nor did the sun set him free
    all his times felt strange
    his life felt irksome:
he shifted the stronghold* gate
    with his ring finger
    slid the lock of bone
    with his left toe, came

with his nails from the threshold
with his knees from the doorway.
Then he tripped head first seaward
hands first he tumbled waveward;
the man stays in the sea's care
the fellow in the billows.
    He lolled there five years
    both five years and six
    seven years and eight.
He stood on the main at last
on a headland with no name
on a mainland with no trees.
With his knees he tensed upward
with his arms pulled himself round:
he rose to look at the moon
    to admire the sun
    observe the Great Bear
    and study the stars.

That was Väinämöinen's birth
how the bold bard came to be
from the woman who bore him
from Air-daughter his mother.

2. *Felling and Sowing*

At that Väinämöinen rose
planted both feet on the heath
on the island on the main
on the mainland with no trees.
He lingered there many years
    continued living
on the island with no words
on the mainland with no trees.
    He thinks, considers
    and long he ponders:
    who is to sow lands
    and make crops fruitful?
Pellervoinen, the field's son
    Sampsa,* tiny boy—
    he is to sow lands
    and make crops fruitful!
He got down to sowing lands
    he sowed lands, sowed swamps
    he sowed sandy glades
    he has boulders set.
    Hills he sowed for pines
    sowed mounds for spruces
    and heaths for heather
and hollows for young saplings.
On lowlands he sowed birches
    alders in light soils
sowed bird cherries in new soils
and goat willows in fresh soils
and rowans on holy ground
and willows on rising ground
junipers on barren lands
and oaks on the banks of streams.

The trees started to come up
and the young saplings to rise:
spruces grew with flowery tops
    shock-headed pines spread;
birch trees rose on the marshes
and alders in the light soils
bird cherries in the new soils
junipers on the bare lands
on the juniper a fair berry
on the bird cherry good fruit.

Steady old Väinämöinen
    went to look at where
    Sampsa had seeded
and Pellervoinen had sown:
he saw the trees had come up
the young saplings had risen;
only the oak is shootless
and rootless the tree of God.
He left the damned thing alone
    to sort itself out
and he waited three more nights
and the same number of days.
    Then he went to look
after a week at the most:
    the oak had not grown
nor rooted the tree of God.

    So, he sees four maids
yes, five brides of the water:
    they were mowing turf
    cutting down dew-straw
on the misty island's tip
at the foggy island's end;
    what they mowed they raked
dragged it all into a stack.
Out of the sea came the Beast
the fellow rose out of the billows:

he thrust the hay into fire
and the power of naked flame
    burnt it all to ash
    reduced it to dust.
A heap of cinders arose
and a pile of dry ashes.
And there was a lovely leaf
a lovely leaf, an acorn
from which grew a fair seedling
a green shoot came up; it rose
from earth like a strawberry
    it grew with twin stalks.
    It reached out its boughs
it spread out its foliage;
its top filled out heavenward
its foliage spread skyward:
it stopped the clouds from scudding
and the vapours from drizzling
it blocked the sun from shining
    the moon from gleaming.

Then the old Väinämöinen
    thinks and considers:
might there be an oak-breaker
a cutter of the fine tree?
It is dull for man to live
    grim for fish to swim
    without the sunshine
    without the moon's gleam.
    But there's no fellow
nor yet a brave man
    who could fell the oak
or lay low the hundred-leaved.
At that old Väinämöinen
    put this into words:
'Woman, mother who bore me
nature-daughter who raised me:
    make the water-folk

(in the water are many)
    break this oak tree down
and destroy this evil tree
from before the shining sun
away from the gleaming moon!'

Out of the sea a man rose
a fellow came up from the billow:
he was not big as big goes
nor all that small as small goes
but as tall as a man's thumb
as high as a woman's span.
Copper was the hat on his shoulders
copper the boots on his feet
copper mittens on his hands
copper the patterns on the mittens
copper the belt round his waist
copper the axe at his belt
its handle tall as a thumb
blade high as a fingernail.

Steady old Väinämöinen
    thinks and considers:
it is a man by his looks
a fellow by appearance
as tall as an upright thumb
as high as an ox's hoof!
Then he put this into words
    he uttered, declared:
'What sort of a man are you
wretch, which sort of fellow?
Little better than a corpse
or fairer than a dead man!'

The small man from the sea said
the billow-fellow answered:
'I am quite a man, a small
fellow of the water-folk.

I have come to break the oak
to shatter the brittle tree.'

Steady old Väinämöinen
    put this into words:
'I do not think you were made
neither made nor appointed
to be the great oak's breaker
to be the grim tree's feller.'

He just managed to say that;
    he glances once more:
    he saw the man changed
    the fellow renewed!
His foot stamps upon the ground
    his head holds the clouds;
his beard goes over his knee
and his hair beyond his heels;
a fathom between his eyes
fathom-wide his trouser-leg
one and a half from his knee
two from his breeches' border.
    He fingers his axe
he sharpened the even blade
    upon six whetstones
on the tip of seven hones
    and he swings along
    whistles on his way
    in his wide trousers
    in his broad breeches:
    he stepped once nimbly
    upon the fine sand
    twice rambled along
upon the liver-hued ground
    a third time ambled
up to the fiery oak's root.
He struck the tree with his axe

bashed it with his even blade;
    he struck once, struck twice
    soon a third time tried:
    fire flashed from the axe
and a blaze flew from the oak
and the oak wanted to tilt
the world-sallow to topple.
    So at the third time
    he could fell the oak
and shatter the world-sallow
and bring down the hundred-leaved.
The base he thrust to the east
the top he lowered north-west
the foliage to the great
south, the boughs half way northward.

    Who then took a bough
took eternal happiness
and who then broke off the top
broke off eternal magic;
who cut off a leafy twig
he cut off eternal love.
    What slivers flew up
    what chips of wood leapt
    on the clear high seas
    upon the vast waves
    'twas those the sea lulled
    and the sea spray rocked
as boats on open water
and as ships upon the waves.

The wind bore them to Northland:
a tiny wench of the North
is washing out her kerchiefs
    and rinsing out clothes
on a wet rock on the shore
upon a long headland's tip.
She saw a sliver floating
gathered it into her bag

in the bag carried it home
in the long-strapped to the yard
to make her witch's arrows
her weapons of enchantment.

When the oak had been broken
    and felled the mean tree
    suns were free to shine
    moons were free to gleam
    clouds to scud along
and heaven's arches to curve
on the misty headland's tip
at the foggy island's end.
Then the backwoods began to flourish
the forests to sprout gladly
leaf on tree and grass on ground
and birds on a tree to sing
    thrushes to rejoice
the cuckoo on top to call.
On the ground berry stalks grew
golden flowers upon the lea;
grasses grew of every kind
    of many forms sprang.
Only barley did not rise
the precious crop did not grow.

At that old Väinämöinen
    paces, considers
on the shore of the blue main
    the great water's banks
    and he found six grains
    seven seeds he found
    upon the seashore
    upon the fine sand
hid them in a marten-skin
in a summer squirrel's shank.
He went to sow them in earth
    to broadcast the seed

by the well of Kaleva
on the bank of Osmo's field.
A tomtit chirped from a tree:
'Osmo's barley will not rise
Kaleva's oats will not grow
unless the earth is pressed down
unless a clearing is felled
    and is burned with fire.'*

Steady old Väinämöinen
    had a sharp axe made;
then he felled a great clearing
and pressed down the powerless earth.
He cut down all the fine trees
    but he left one birch
to be the birds' resting-place
and the cuckoo's calling-tree.

An eagle flew across heaven
a bird over the sky; it
    came to look at this:
    'Why has this been left—
    the birch tree not felled
    the fine tree not cut?'

The old Väinämöinen said:
'This is why it has been left—
    for birds to rest on
the sky's eagle to sit on.'

The eagle, the sky's bird said:
    'And you have done well:
you have left the birch growing
    the fine tree standing
    for birds to rest on
    myself to sit on.'

The sky's bird struck fire
    made a flame flare up.
The north wind burnt the clearing
the north-east quite consumed it:
it burnt all the trees to ash
    reduced them to dust.
At that old Väinämöinen
    took up the six grains
    the seven seeds took
out of the one marten-skin
from the summer squirrel's shank
out of the summer stoat's paw.
He went to sow them in earth
    to broadcast the seed
and he put this into words:
    'I get down to sow
between the Lord's fingers, by
way of the Almighty's hand
on this earth that is growing
this glade that is coming up.
Old woman of underground
    soil-dame, earth-mistress
now set the sward pushing up
    the strong earth heaving!
The earth will not want for strength
    ever in this world
while there's love from the givers
and leave from nature's daughters.
    Rise, earth, from your bed
    the Lord's turf from sleep!
    Set the stems teeming
    the stalks sticking up!
    Raise shoots in thousands
scatter branches in hundreds
from my ploughing, my sowing
all the pains I have taken!
    O Old Man, chief god—
that is, heavenly father

keeper of the cloudy realm
governor of the vapours:
    in the clouds hold court
in the bright heights clear council!
Rear a cloud out of the east
raise a bank from the north-west
send others out of the west
out of the south hurry them!
Sprinkle water from the sky
and from the clouds drip honey
    on the rising shoots
    on the rustling crops!'

    That Old Man, chief god
father and ruler of heaven
    in the clouds held court
in the bright heights clear council;
he reared a cloud from the east
raised a bank from the north-west
sent another from the west
out of the south hurried them;
pushed them together edge-on
knocked them against each other;
sprinkled water from the sky
and from the clouds dripped honey
    on the growing shoots
    on the rustling crops.
    A spiky shoot rose
    one stump-hued came up
    from the field's soft earth
where Väinämöinen had toiled.

And there on the second day
at the end of two, three nights
after a week at the most
steady old Väinämöinen
    went to look at where

he had ploughed, had sown
taken all the pains:
barley grew as he wanted
ears pointing six ways
and stems with three joints.
There the old Väinämöinen
looks and turns round.
A spring cuckoo came
Saw the birch growing:
'Why has that been left—
the birch tree unfelled?'

The old Väinämöinen said:
'This is why it has been left
the birch tree growing—
for you, for a calling-tree.
There call now, cuckoo
and carol, fine-breast
warble, silver-breast
tin-breast,* tinkle forth!
Call evenings and call mornings
once at midday too
that my weather may be fair
my forests pleasant
my shores prosperous
my sides full of corn!'

3. *The Singing Match*

Steady old Väinämöinen
  is living his times
in those glades of Väinö-land
on the Kalevala heaths
  is singing his tales
singing, practising his craft.
  He sang day by day
night by night he recited
  ancient memories
  those deep Origins
which not all the children sing
only fellows understand
  in this evil age
  with time running out.
Far and wide the news is heard
outward the tidings travel
of Väinämöinen's singing
  the fellow's cunning;
the tidings travelled southward
  the news reached Northland.

Now, the young Joukahainen
  a lean Lappish lad
  once went visiting
and he heard of wondrous words
of songs being put about
better ones being set forth
in those glades of Väinö-land
on the Kalevala heaths
than the ones he knew himself
he had learned from his father.
He took that very badly

spent all his time envying
Väinämöinen, said to be
a better singer than him.
Now he came to his mother
    his honoured parent
and announced that he would go
    said he hoped to come
to those Väinö-land cabins
    to take on Väinö.

The father forbade his son
father forbade, mother banned
his going to Väinö-land
    to take on Väinö:
    'There you will be sung*
you'll be sung and chanted, face
into snow, head into drifts
    fists into hard air
until your hands cannot turn
until your feet cannot move.'

The young Joukahainen said:
'My father's wisdom is good
my mother's even better
but my own is the highest.
If I want to draw level
    measure up to men
I'll sing at who sings at me
and recite at who recites at me
I'll sing at the best singer
till he is the worst singer—
on his feet sing shoes of stone
trousers of wood on his loins
a stone anchor on his breast
a stone slab on his shoulders
mittens of stone on his hands
on his head a rock helmet.'

At that he left, did not heed.
He took off his own gelding
    whose muzzle struck fire
    and whose shanks struck sparks
harnessed the fiery gelding
in front of the golden sleigh.
    He sits in the sledge
    settles in his sleigh
struck the courser with the lash
hit it with the beaded whip
and off the courser galloped
    the horse dashed away.
    He swishes along
he drove one day, he drove two
soon he drove a third as well.
Now upon the third day he
reached the glades of Väinö-land
the heaths of Kalevala.

Steady old Väinämöinen
the everlasting wise man*
was driving along his roads
    pacing out his ways
in those glades of Väinö-land
on the Kalevala heaths.
The young Joukahainen came
drove down the road to face him:
    shaft seized on shaft-end
traces tangled with traces
    hames were jammed with hames
and collar-bow tip with tip.
Then and there was a full stop
a full stop, a pause for thought . . .
sweat poured from the collar-bow
    from the shafts steam rose.

The old Väinämöinen asked:
    'Of what kin are you

coming foolishly forward
    this way recklessly
smashing the hames of bent wood
the collar-bows of young wood
    my sleigh to splinters
into bits the toboggan?'

Then the young Joukahainen
uttered a word and spoke thus:
'I am young Joukahainen.
But say what your own kin is:
    of what kin are you
    of what rabble, wretch?'

Steady old Väinämöinen
thereupon said who he was
    and then he declared:
'Since you're young Joukahainen
    draw aside a bit!
    You're younger than me.'

Then the young Joukahainen
uttered a word and spoke thus:
'Not a bit does a man's youth
his youth or his age matter!
Who is better in wisdom
mightier in recalling—
let him stand fast on the road
the other shift off the road.
If you're old Väinämöinen
the everlasting singer
    let us start singing
    begin reciting
    with man testing man
one defeating the other!'

Steady old Väinämöinen
uttered a word and spoke thus:
    'Well now, what of me

as singer, as cunning man?
I've lived all my time only
in these glades, at these edges
of the home-field, listening
    to the home-cuckoo.
    Be that as it may
tell me that my ears may hear:
what do you know most about
understand above others?'

The young Joukahainen said:
'Well, I know a thing or two!
    This I know plainly
    and grasp thoroughly:
the smoke-hole is in the roof
    the flame in the hearth.
The seal enjoys a good life
the water-dog rolls about:
it eats salmon close by it
    whitefish at its side.
The whitefish's fields are smooth
the salmon's roof is level.
The pike spawns during the frost
slobber-chops in hard weather.
    The perch, shy, crook-necked
in autumn swims in the deep
in summer spawns on dry land
thrashes about on the shores.

'Should not enough come of that
I know other wisdom too
I am aware of one thing:
the north ploughed with the reindeer
    the south with the mare
far Lapland with the wild ox.
I know trees on Pisa Hill
the firs on the Demon's Cliff:
tall the trees on Pisa Hill

and the firs on Demon's Cliff.
    Three there are of steep
    rapids, three great lakes
    and three high mountains
    under this sky's vault:
in Häme* are Hällä Falls
Kaatra in Karelia;
but none has conquered Vuoksi*
nor gone over Imatra.'*

The old Väinämöinen said:
'Child's wisdom, woman's recall
is for no bearded fellow
nor for a man with a wife!
Tell me of deep Origins
    of eternal things!'

    Young Joukahainen
uttered a word and spoke thus:
'I know of the tomtit's Origin
that the tomtit is a bird
the green viper is a snake
    the ruff is a fish.
Iron I know is brittle
    black soil is bitter
    and hot water hurts
    and a burn is bad.
Water is the oldest of ointments
rapid-foam of remedies
and the Lord of soothsayers
    and God of healers.
A mountain is water's Origin
and fire's Origin is heaven
the source of iron is rust
and copper's root is a cliff.
A wet hummock is the oldest land
a willow the first of trees

a fir root first of dwellings
and a stone the first crude pot.'

Steady old Väinämöinen
    put this into words:
'Do you recall any more
or has your babble ended?'

The young Joukahainen said:
'I recall a bit more too!
Now, I recall such a time
as I was ploughing the sea
    grubbing the sea's gulfs
    digging the fish-troughs
    deepening the depths
laying out the pool-waters
    stirring up the hills
    piling up the crags.
What's more, I was the sixth man
    the seventh fellow
    when this earth was made
    when the sky was built
when the sky's pillar was fixed
when heaven's arch was borne up
    when the moon was moved
    when the sun was helped
when the Great Bear was stretched out
when heaven was filled with stars.'

The old Väinämöinen said:
    'Truly you have lied!
    You were never seen
    when the sea was ploughed
    the sea's gulfs were grubbed
    the fish-troughs were dug
    the depths were deepened
the pool-waters were laid out
    the hills were stirred up

and the crags piled up
nor yet were you seen
neither seen nor heard
when this earth was made
when the sky was built
when the sky's pillar was fixed
when heaven's arch was borne up
when the moon was moved
when the sun was helped
when the Great Bear was stretched out
when heaven was filled with stars.'

Young Joukahainen
at that put this into words:
'Since I do not have the wits
I shall ask wits of my sword.
Old Väinämöinen
singer with the gaping mouth
let the sword decide
go with the brand's view!'

The old Väinämöinen said:
'I shall not much fear
those swords of yours, wits of yours
those ice-picks, those tricks of yours.
Be that as it may
I'll not let the sword decide
with you, you mean boy
with yourself, poor wretch.'

At that young Joukahainen
twisted his mouth, turned his head
and twisted his black whiskers
and he put this into words:
'Who'll not let the sword decide
and not go with the brand's view
I will sing into a pig
put into a low-snouted

and I will treat such fellows
that one thus and this one so—
will tread into a dunghill
dump in a cowshed corner.'

Väinämöinen grew angry
at that, angry and ashamed.
He himself started singing
himself began reciting:
the songs are not children's songs
children's songs, women's cackle
but for a bearded fellow
which not all the children sing
    nor do half the boys
nor a third of the suitors
    in this evil age
    with time running out.
The old Väinämöinen sang:
the lakes rippled, the earth shook
the copper mountains trembled
the sturdy boulders rumbled
    the cliffs flew in two
the rocks cracked upon the shores.
He sang young Joukahainen—
saplings on his collar-bow
a willow shrub on his hames
goat willows on his trace-tip
    sang his gold-trimmed sleigh
sang it to treetrunks in pools
sang his whip knotted with beads
    to reeds on a shore
    sang his blaze-browed horse
to rocks on a rapid's bank;
he sang his gold-hilted sword
    to lightnings in heaven
then his bright-butted crossbow
to rainbows upon waters

and then his feathered arrows
    to swift-flying hawks
and then his dog of hooked jaw
    to rocks on the ground;
he sang the cap off his head
to a piled-up bank of cloud
sang the mittens off his hands
to lilies on a still pool
    then his blue cloth coat
    to vapours in heaven
from his waist the fine-wove belt
    to stars across heaven;
he sang him, Joukahainen
in a swamp up to his waist
in a meadow to his groin
in the heath to his armpits.

By now young Joukahainen
    knew and realized—
knew that he had come this way
undertaken the journey
    to take on, to sing
with the old Väinämöinen.
    He worked his foot free
    but could not lift it;
so he tried the other too
but it wore a shoe of stone.
Then for young Joukahainen
    things become painful
things turn out more troublesome.
He uttered a word, spoke thus:
    'Shrewd Väinämöinen
O everlasting wise man
whirl your holy words around
    take back your phrases:
get me out of this tight spot
from this matter set me free!

I will lay down the best price
pay the heaviest ransom.'

The old Väinämöinen said:
'All right, what will you give me
if I whirl my holy words
around, take back my phrases
get you out of that tight spot
from that matter set you free?'

The young Joukahainen said:
    'Well, I have two bows
    two handsome crossbows:
    one is quick to strike
    one has a straight aim.
    Take either of them!'

The old Väinämöinen said:
'I don't care for your crossbows
wild one, for your bows, mean one!
    I have some myself
stacked up against every wall
    stored on every peg:
without men they go hunting
without fellows work outdoors.'
He sang young Joukahainen
    sang him still deeper.

The young Joukahainen said:
    'Well, I have two craft
    two beautiful boats:
    one is light to race
    one carries a lot.
    Take either of them!'

The old Väinämöinen said:
'I do not care for your craft

for your boats I don't complain!
  I have some myself
hauled up on every roller
and laid up in every cove:
one is steady in the wind
one makes way in bad weather.'
He sang young Joukahainen
  sang him still deeper.

The young Joukahainen said:
  'I have two stallions
  two handsome horses:
  one runs more nimbly
  one frisks in traces.
  Take either of them!'

The old Väinämöinen said:
'I don't care for your horses
grieve for your white-fetlocked ones!
  I have some myself
tied up in every manger
led into every barnyard
with clear water on their backs
with pools of fat on their rumps.'*
He sang young Joukahainen
  sang him still deeper.

The young Joukahainen said:
  'Old Väinämöinen
whirl your holy words around
take back your phrases! I'll give
a helmetful of gold coins
a felt hatful of silver—
  my father's war-spoils
  brought home from battle.'

The old Väinämöinen said:
'I don't care for your silver

nor ask, wretch, for your gold coins!
    I have some myself
    crammed in every shed
    stored in every box—
gold eternal as the moon
silver ancient as the sun.'
He sang young Joukahainen
    sang him still deeper.

The young Joukahainen said:
    'Old Väinämöinen
get me out of this tight spot
from this matter set me free!
I will give my ricks at home
surrender my sandy fields
    to save my own skin
    to redeem myself.'

The old Väinämöinen said:
'I do not yearn for your ricks
rascal, for your sandy fields!
    I have some myself—
fields in every direction
    ricks in every glade
and my own are better fields
    my own ricks sweeter.'
He sang young Joukahainen
sang him even further down.

Then the young Joukahainen
    was at his wits' end
up to his chin in the slime
to his beard in the bad place
to his mouth in swamp mosses
his teeth stuck in a treetrunk.
And young Joukahainen said:
    'Shrewd Väinämöinen

O everlasting wise man
	sing your song backwards
	spare yet a weak life
and get me away from here!
Now the stream tugs at my foot
the sand is grinding my eyes.
If you whirl your holy words
around and call off your spell
I'll give Aino my sister
I will yield my mother's child
	to clean out your hut
	and to sweep your floor
	rinse your wooden plates
	to wash out your cloaks
	weave your golden cloak
	bake your honey-bread.'

Then the old Väinämöinen
was utterly delighted
to have Joukahainen's maid
care for him in his old age.
He sits on the rock of joy*
on the song-boulder settles:
he sang one moment, sang two
sang a third moment as well
whirled his holy words away
	took back his phrases.
Young Joukahainen was free
with his chin out of the slime
his beard out of the bad place
the horse from the rapid-rock
the sledge from the shore treetrunk
and the whip from the shore reed.
He clambered into his sleigh
flung himself into his sledge
went away in bad spirits
	with a gloomy heart
	to his dear mother
towards his honoured parent.

He rumbles along
    he drove home oddly
smashed his sledge against the kiln
the shafts to bits on the steps.
His mother began to guess
and his father says a word:
'Needlessly you've smashed your sledge
on purpose broken the shaft!
So why do you ride oddly
    come home stupidly?'

At that young Joukahainen
    weeps a flood of tears
his head down, in bad spirits
    helmet all askew
    his lips grimly set
his nose drooped over his mouth.
His mother hastened to ask
the pains-taker to question:
'Why do you weep, my offspring
fruit of my youth, why lament?
Why are your lips grimly set
your nose drooped over your mouth?'

The young Joukahainen said:
'O mother who carried me!
    Cause has arisen
and magic has taken place—
cause enough for me to weep
magic for me to lament!
For this I'll weep all my days
    grieve my lifetime through:
I have given my sister
Aino, pledged my mother's child
to care for Väinämöinen
to be mate to the singer
refuge for the dodderer
shelter for the nook-haunter.'

The mother rubbed her
    two palms together;
she uttered a word, spoke thus:
    'Don't weep, my offspring!
There is nothing to weep for
    to grieve greatly for:
this I've hoped for all my days
    longed my lifetime through—
    a great man for my
kin, a bold man for my stock;
Väinämöinen for my son-in-law
the singer for my brother-in-law.'*

Young Joukahainen's sister
for her part fell to weeping.
She wept one day, she wept two
    sideways on the steps:
    she wept from great grief
    and from low spirits.
Her mother began to say:
'Why do you weep, my Aino
when you will come to a great
bridegroom's, a lofty man's home
    to sit at windows
    prattle on benches?'

The daughter put this in words:
'O mother who carried me!
I have something to weep for—
the beauty of my tresses
the thickness of my young locks
and the fineness of my hair
if they're hidden while I'm small
covered while I am growing.
For this I'll weep all my days—
for the sweetness of the sun
for the splendid moonlight's grace
for all the sky's loveliness

if while young I must leave them
as a child leave them behind
to my brother's carving-grounds
to my father's window seats.'

The mother says to the girl
the eldest spoke to her child:
'Begone, madcap, with your cares
good-for-nothing, with your tears!
There is no cause to be glum
no reason to be downcast.
    God's sun also shines
    elsewhere in the world—
not at your father's windows
    your brother's gateway.
There are berries on a hill
and in glades strawberries too
for you, luckless one, to pick
further afield, not always
in your father's glades, upon
your brother's burnt-over heaths.'

4. *The Drowned Maid*

Now, that Aino, the young maid
young Joukahainen's sister
went for a broom from the grove
and for bath-whisks* from the scrub;
broke off one for her father
another for her mother
    gathered a third too
for her full-blooded brother.
She was just stepping homeward
    tripping through alders
when old Väinämöinen came.
He saw the maid in the grove
the fine-hemmed in the grasses
and uttered a word, spoke thus:
'Don't for anyone, young maid
    except me, young maid
wear the beads around your neck
set the cross upon your breast
put your head into a braid
    bind your hair with silk!'

The maid put this into words:
'Not for you nor anyone
do I wear crosses upon
my breast, tie my hair with silk.
I don't care for cogware,* for
wheat slices I don't complain:
    I live in tight clothes
    I grow on breadcrusts
    by my good father
    with my dear mother.'

She wrenched the cross from her breast
and the rings from her finger

the beads she shook from her neck
and the red threads off her head
left them on the ground for the ground's sake
in the grove for the grove's sake
    and went weeping home
    wailing to the farm.*

Her father at the window
sat adorning an axe haft:
'Why are you weeping, poor girl
    poor girl, young maiden?'

    'I have cause to weep
    woes to complain of!
For this I weep, my papa
for this I weep and complain:
the cross came loose from my breast
the bauble shook from my belt
from my breast the silver cross
the copper threads off my belt.'

Her brother at the gateway
is carving collar-bow wood:
'Why do you weep, poor sister
    poor sister, young maid?'

    'I have cause to weep
    woes to complain of!
For this I weep, poor brother
for this I weep and complain:
the ring slipped off my finger
and the beads fell from my neck
the gold ring from my finger
from my neck the silver beads.'

Her sister at the floor seam
is weaving a belt of gold:

'Why do you weep, poor sister
    poor sister, young maid?'

    'The weeper has cause
    she who whines has woes!
For this I weep, poor sister
for this I weep and complain:
the gold came loose from my brows
and the silver from my hair
and the blue silks from my eyes
the red ribbons off my head.'

Her mother on the shed step
is skimming cream off the milk:
'Why are you weeping, poor girl
    poor girl, young maiden?'

'O mamma who carried me
O mother who suckled me!
    There are dark causes
    very low spirits!
For this I weep, poor mother
for this, mamma, complain: I
went for a broom from the grove
for bath-whisk tips from the scrub
broke off one for my father
another for my mother
    gathered a third too
for my full-blooded brother.
I began to step homeward
was just stepping through the glade
when from the dell, from the land
burnt over, the Great One* said:
"Don't for anyone, poor maid
    except me, poor maid
wear the beads around your neck
set the cross upon your breast

put your head into a braid
    bind your hair with silk!"
I wrenched the cross from my breast
the beads I shook from my neck
and the blue threads from my eyes
and the red threads off my head
cast them on the ground for the ground's sake
in the grove for the grove's sake
and I put this into words:
"Not for you nor anyone
do I wear the cross upon
my breast, tie my head with silk.
I don't care for cogware, for
wheat slices I don't complain:
    I live in tight clothes
    I grow on breadcrusts
    by my good father
    with my dear mother."'

The mother put this in words
the eldest spoke to her child:
    'Don't weep, my daughter
fruit of my youth, don't lament!
One year eat melted butter:
you'll grow plumper than others;
    the next year eat pork:
you'll grow sleeker than others;
a third year eat cream pancakes:
you'll grow fairer than others.
Step to the shed on the hill
    open the best shed:
there is chest on top of chest
    and box beside box.
    Open the best chest
    slam the bright lid back:
inside are six golden belts
    and seven blue skirts

all woven by Moon-daughter
finished off by Sun-daughter.

'Long since, when I was a maid
and lived as a lass, I went
for berries in the forest
raspberries under the slope.
I heard Moon-daughter weaving
    Sun-daughter spinning
    beside blue backwoods
at the edge of a sweet grove.
    I went up to them
    I came close, approached;
I began to beg of them
    I uttered and said:
"Give, Moon-daughter, of your gold
Sun-daughter, of your silver
to this girl who has nothing
    to this child who begs!"
Moon-daughter gave of her gold
Sun-daughter of her silver:
I put the gold on my brows
on my head the good silver
    and came home a flower
to my father's yards a joy.
I wore them for one day, two
    till on the third day
I stripped the gold from my brows
from my head the good silver
took them to the hilltop shed
put them under the chest lid:
there they have been ever since
all this time unlooked upon.

'Bind now the silks to your eyes
and to your brows lift the gold
around your neck the bright beads
the gold crosses on your breasts!

Put on a shirt of linen
one of hempen lawn on top;
pull on a skirt of broadcloth
on top of it a silk belt
    fine stockings of silk
    handsome leather shoes!
Twine your hair into a braid
tie it with ribbons of silk
on your fingers put gold rings
and on your hands gold bracelets!
Like that you will come back home
you will step in from the shed
to be your kinsfolk's sweetness
the softness of all your clan:
you will walk the lanes a flower
you will roam a raspberry
more graceful than you once were
better than you were before.'

The mother put that in words
that's what she said to her child
but the daughter did not heed
did not hear the mother's words:
she went weeping to the yard
pining into the farmyard.
    She says with this word
    she spoke with this speech:
'How do the lucky ones feel
and how do the blessed think?
This is how the lucky feel
    how the blessed think—
    like water stirring
or a ripple on a trough.
But how do the luckless feel
and how do the calloos think?
This is how the luckless feel
    how the calloos think—
like hard snow under a ridge

like water in a deep well.
    Often in my gloom
now, often, a gloomy child
my mood is to tread dead grass
and through undergrowth to crawl
    on turf to loiter
in a bush to roll about—
my mood no better than tar
my heart no whiter than coal.
Better it would be for me
and better it would have been
had I not been born, not grown
    not sprung to full size
    in these evil days
    in this joyless world.
Had I died a six-night-old
and been lost an eight-night-old
I would not have needed much—
    a span of linen
    a tiny field edge
a few tears from my mother
still fewer from my father
not even a few from my brother.'

She wept one day, she wept two.
Her mother began to ask:
'Why are you weeping, poor lass
why, woebegone, complaining?'

'This is why I, poor lass, weep
    all my time complain:
you have given luckless me
and your own child you have pledged
made me care for an old man
gladden an aged man, be
refuge for a dodderer
shelter for a nook-haunter.
Sooner had you bidden me

go below the deep billows
to be sister to whitefish
and brother to the fishes!
Better to be in the sea
to dwell below the billows
to be sister to whitefish
and brother to the fishes
than to care for an old man
be a dodderer's refuge
one who trips on his stockings
who falls over a dry twig.'

Then she stepped to the shed-hill
    stepped inside the shed
    opened the best chest
    slammed the bright lid back
and she found six golden belts
    and seven blue skirts
    and she put them on
    she decks her body.
She set the gold on her brows
the silver upon her hair
the blue silks upon her eyes
the red threads upon her head.
    Then she stepped away
across one glade, along two;
    she roamed swamps, roamed lands
    roamed gloomy backwoods.
    She sang as she went
    uttered as she roamed:
'In my heart there is a hurt
in my head there is an ache
but the hurt would not hurt more
and the ache would not more ache
if I, hapless, were to die
    were cut off, mean one
    from these great sorrows
    from these low spirits.

Now would be the time for me
    to part from this world—
the time to go to Death, the
age to come to Tuonela:
father would not weep for me
mother would not take it ill
sister's face would not be wet
brother's eyes would not shed tears
though I rolled in the water
fell into the fishy sea
down below the deep billows
    upon the black mud.'

She stepped one day, she stepped two
    till on the third day
    she came upon sea
    faced a reedy shore:
there the night overtakes her
    the dark detains her.
There the lass wept all evening
    whimpered all night long
on a wet rock on the shore
    at the broad bay-end.

Early in the morning she
looked out at a headland's tip:
three maids at the headland's tip
there were, bathing in the sea!
The maid Aino would be fourth
and the slip of a girl fifth!
She cast her shirt on willow
her skirt upon an aspen
her stockings on the bare ground
her shoes upon the wet rock
her beads on the sandy shore
her rings upon the shingle.
A rock was bright on the main
a boulder glittering gold:

she strove to swim to the rock
she would flee to the boulder.
    Then, when she got there
    she sits herself down
    upon the bright rock
on the glittering boulder:
the rock plopped in the water
    the boulder sank down
    the maid with the rock
Aino beside the boulder.

That is where the hen was lost
    there the poor lass died.
She said while she was dying
spoke as she was still rolling:
'I went to bathe in the sea
arrived to swim in the main
and there I, a hen, was lost
I, a bird, untimely died:*
    let not my father
    ever in this world
    draw any fishes
    from this mighty main!
I went to wash at the shore
I went to bathe in the sea
and there I, a hen, was lost
I, a bird, untimely died:
    let not my mother
    ever in this world
    put water in dough
    from the broad home-bay!
I went to wash at the shore
I went to bathe in the sea
and there I, a hen, was lost
I, a bird, untimely died:
    let not my brother
    ever in this world

water his war-horse
upon the seashore!
I went to wash at the shore
I went to bathe in the sea
and there I, a hen, was lost
I, a bird, untimely died:
let not my sister
ever in this world
wash her eyes here, at
the home-bay landing!
Waters of the sea
so much blood of mine;
fishes of the sea
so much flesh of mine;
brushwood on the shore
is a poor one's ribs;
grasses of the shore
are her tousled hair.'
Such the death of the young maid
end of the fair little hen.

Who now will carry the news
will tell it by word of mouth
to the maid's famous
home, to the fair farm?
A bear will carry the news
will tell it by word of mouth!
But the bear does not: it was
lost among a herd of cows.
Who now will carry the news
will tell it by word of mouth
to the maid's famous
home, to the fair farm?
A wolf will carry the news
will tell it by word of mouth!
But the wolf does not: it was
lost among a flock of sheep.
Who now will carry the news

will tell it by word of mouth
  to the maid's famous
  home, to the fair farm?
A fox will carry the news
will tell it by word of mouth!
But the fox does not: it was
lost among a flock of geese.
Who now will carry the news
Will tell it by word of mouth
  to the maid's famous
  home, to the fair farm?
A hare will carry the news
will tell it by word of mouth!
The hare said for sure: 'The news
will not be lost on this man!'
  And the hare ran off
  the long-ear lolloped
  the wry-leg rushed off
  the cross-mouth careered
  to the maid's famous
  home, to the fair farm.

To the sauna threshold it
ran, on the threshold it squats.
The sauna is full of maids;
whisks in hand they greet: 'Sly one
have you come here to be cooked
pop-eye, to be roasted for
  the master's supper
  the mistress's meal
  for the daughter's snacks
  or for the son's lunch?'

The hare manages to say
and the round-eye to speak out:
'Perhaps the Devil has come
  to stew in the pans!
I have come carrying news

to tell it by word of mouth:
    the fair has fallen
the tin-breast has pined away
sunken the silver-buckle
the copper-belt slipped away—
gone into the wanton sea
    down to the vast deeps
to be sister to whitefish
and brother to the fishes.'

The mother started weeping
and a stream of tears rolling
and then she began to say
the woebegone to complain:
    'Don't, luckless mothers
    ever in this world
    don't lull your daughters
    or rock your children
to marry against their will
as I, a luckless mother
    have lulled my daughters
    reared my little hens.'

The mother wept, a tear rolled:
her plentiful waters rolled
    out of her blue eyes
    to her luckless cheeks.
One tear rolled, another rolled
her plentiful waters rolled
    from her luckless cheeks
    to her ample breasts.
One tear rolled, another rolled
her plentiful waters rolled
    from her ample breasts
    upon her fine hems.
One tear rolled, another rolled
her plentiful waters rolled
    down from her fine hems

upon her red-topped stockings.
One tear rolled, another rolled
her plentiful waters rolled
down from her red-topped stockings
to her gilded shoe-uppers.
One tear rolled, another rolled
her plentiful waters rolled
from her gilded shoe-uppers
to the ground beneath her feet;
they rolled to the ground for the ground's sake
to the water for the water's sake.
The waters reaching the ground
began to form a river
    and three rivers grew
    from the tears she wept
    that came from her head
that went from beneath her brow.
    In each river grew
    three fiery rapids;
    on each rapid's foam
    three crags sprouted up
    and on each crag's edge
    a golden knoll rose
    and on each knoll's peak
    there grew three birches;
    in each birch's top
there were three golden cuckoos.

The cuckoos started calling:
    the first called *love, love!*
the second *bridegroom, bridegroom!*
    and the third *joy, joy!*
    That which called *love, love!*
    called out for three months
    to the loveless girl
    lying in the sea;
that which called *bridegroom, bridegroom!*
    called out for six months

to the comfortless bridegroom
    sitting and longing;
    that which called *joy, joy!*
called out for all her lifetime
to the mother without joy
    weeping all her days.

The mother put this in words
listening to the cuckoo:
'Let a luckless mother not
listen long to the cuckoo!
When the cuckoo is calling
    my heart is throbbing
    tears come to my eyes
    waters down my cheeks
    flow thicker than peas
    and fatter than beans:
by an ell my life passes
by a span my frame grows old
my whole body is blighted
when I hear the spring cuckoo.'

5. *The Mermaid*

Now the news had been carried
and the tidings borne abroad
    of the young maid's sleep
    of the fair one's loss.
Steady old Väinämöinen
    he took it badly:
he wept evenings, wept mornings
and nights most of all he wept
that the fair one had fallen
the maid had fallen asleep
gone into the wanton sea
down below the deep billows.
He stepped, full of care and sighs
    with a gloomy heart
to the shore of the blue sea;
he uttered a word, spoke thus:
'Tell now, O Dreamer, your dream
O stretched in earth, your vision:
    where is Ahto-land
where do his Wave-wife's maids stretch?'

Well, the Dreamer told his dream
the stretched in earth his vision:
    'Here is Ahto-land
and here his Wave-wife's maids stretch—
on the misty headland's tip
at the foggy island's end
down below the deep billows
    upon the black mud.
    There is Ahto-land
and there his Wave-wife's maids stretch—
    in a tiny room

a narrow chamber
beside a bright rock
lodged beneath a thick boulder.'

At that old Väinämöinen
dragged himself to the boatyards;
glances at his fishing-lines
and looks over his fish-hooks;
put a hook in his pocket
an iron barb in his bag.
He paddles along
he reaches the island's end
and the misty headland's tip
and the foggy island's end.
There he stayed with the fish-hook
remained with the fishing-line
turned the hand-net to and fro.
He cast the gorge on the sea
he angled, dangled:
the rod of copper trembled
the silver line whirred
and the cord of gold jingled.

On a day among others
one morrow among many
a fish took his hook
a sewin his barb:
he pulled it into his boat
landed it upon his bilge.
He looks, he turns it over
and uttered a word, spoke thus:
'Now, that is a fishy fish
I never saw the like of!—
rather smooth for a whitefish
rather light-hued for a trout
rather grizzled for a pike
too finless for a spawner;
but weird for a person too—

too bareheaded for a maid
beltless for a water-girl
too earless for a home-bird
too mild for a sea salmon
a perch of the deep billow.'

At his belt Väinämöinen
has a silver-tipped sheath-knife:
he drew the knife from his side
from its sheath the silver-tipped
    to divide the fish
    cut up the salmon
    for meals at morning
    for breakfast titbits
    for salmon lunches
    and for big suppers.
He made to cut the salmon
with the knife to slash the fish:
into the sea the salmon
    flashed, the bright fish flared
from the bilge of the red craft
out of Väinämöinen's boat.
Only then it raised its head
    and its right shoulder
    upon the fifth squall
    on the sixth high wave;
    held up its right hand
    revealed its left foot
    on the seventh main
on top of the ninth billow.
From there it put this in words
    it declared, chattered:
'O you old Väinämöinen!
    I was not to be
a salmon for you to cut
a fish for you to divide
    for meals at morning
    for breakfast titbits

for salmon lunches
and for big suppers.'

The old Väinämöinen said:
'What were you to be?'
'Well, I was to be
a hen tucked under your arm
one who would sit for ever
a lifelong mate on your knee*
to lay out your bed
to place your pillow
to clean your small hut
one to sweep your floor
to bring fire indoors
to kindle your light
to make your thick bread
bake your honey-bread
carry your beer mug
and set out your meal.
I was not a sea salmon
a perch of the deep billow:
I was a girl, a young maid
young Joukahainen's sister
who you hunted all your days
throughout your lifetime longed for.
You wretched old man
you foolish Väinämöinen
for you knew no way to keep
the Wave-wife's watery maid
Ahto's peerless child!'

The old Väinämöinen said
his head down, in bad spirits:
'O Joukahainen's sister!
Come but once again!'

But she did not come again
not ever again:

now she drew back, flopped back, was
lost from the water's surface
    within the bright rock
the cleft of the liver-hued.
Steady old Väinämöinen
    at that considers
how to be, which way to live.
Now he wove a silken seine
    criss-crossed the water
along one strait, across two;
    he dragged calm waters
    between salmon-crags
those waters of Väinö-land
Kalevala's land-bridges
    dragged the gloomy depths
    and the main's great poles
the rivers of Jouko-land
and the bay-shores of Lapland.
He caught enough other fish
    all kinds of fishes
but he did not catch the fish
    he'd set his heart on—
the Wave-wife's watery maid
    Ahto's peerless child.

Then the old Väinämöinen
his head down, in bad spirits
    helmet all askew
    put this into words:
'O madman, for my madness
    fool, for my manhood!
    Once I had a mind
    and thought was given
    a great heart crammed full—
    that was long ago.
    But now, nowadays
    in this evil age
    this life running short

all my mind is anyhow
    my thoughts are priceless*
all my sense is somewhere else.
She I waited for always
    and half my lifetime
the Wave-wife's watery maid
the water's latest daughter
to be a friend for ever
    and a lifetime's mate
    came on to my hook
    flopped into my boat:
    I could not keep her
    carry her off home
but lost again to the waves
down below the deep billows.'

And he went a little way
he stepped, full of care and sighs;
    he trudges homeward.
He uttered a word, spoke thus:
'Time was when my cuckoos called
former cuckoos of my joy
used to call evenings, mornings
    once at midday too:
what has stifled their great voice
    lost their voice so fair?
Grief has stifled their great voice
care brought down their voice so sweet
because no calling is heard
and at sundown no singing
    to cheer my evenings
    to ease my morrows.
Nor do I know now at all
how to be, which way to live
    in this world to dwell
    in these lands to roam.
If my mother were alive
    my parent awake

she would be able to say
how to stand upright
unbroken by griefs
unstricken by cares
in these evil days
in these low spirits!'

From the grave his mother heard
from below the wave answered:
'Your mother is still alive
your parent awake
she who is able to say
how to be all right
unbroken by griefs
unstricken by cares
in these evil days
in these low spirits:
go among the North's daughters!
There daughters are comelier
maids are twice fairer
five times, six times livelier—
none of Jouko's frumps
gawky children of Lapland.
Get a wife from there, my boy
the best of the North's daughters
who is pretty-eyed
fair to look upon
ever fleet of foot
and brisk of movement!'

6. *A Brother's Revenge*

Steady old Väinämöinen
    intended to go
yonder to the cold village
    off to dark Northland.
He took a stallion of straw
    a horse of pea stalks
bridled the golden one, put
the silver one's headstall on;
    he sat on its back
    leapt on, straddled it
    and he trots along
    paces his journey
astride the stallion of straw
astride the horse of pea stalks.
He rode the Väinö-land glades
the heaths of Kalevala:
the horse ran, the journey sped
his home stays, the road shortened.
Now he rode upon the main
upon the open expanse
without a hoof getting wet
without a fetlock sinking.

As for young Joukahainen
    the lean Lappish lad
    he bore long hatred
    a lasting envy
towards old Väinämöinen
for the eternal singer.
He makes a fiery crossbow
a handsome bow he adorns:
the bow he built of iron

in copper he casts the back;
    with gold he trimmed them
    in silver worked them.
Where to get a cord for it
    where to find a string?—
from the sinews of the Demon's elk
from the Devil's hempen threads!
And he finished off his bow
made his crossbow quite ready.
The bow was fair to look on
the crossbow somewhat costly:
a horse stood upon its back
a foal ran along the butt
a girl lay upon the bow
and a hare where the rack was.*
And he cut a stack of darts
a pile of three-feathered ones
and the shafts he shapes in oak
the tips he makes of tar-wood.
    What he makes ready
    he puts feathers on—
small feathers of a swallow
tail feathers of a sparrow;
and he hardened his arrows
    he tempered his darts
    in black worm poison
in a snake's venomous blood;
and he made the bolts ready
the crossbow fit to be drawn.
Then he waited for Väinämöinen
to catch him of Calm Waters;
waited evening and morning
    waited once at noon;
long he waited for Väinämöinen
long he waited unweary
    sitting at windows
watching at the ends of huts
listening behind the lane

on his guard in the acre
the quiverful on his back
the good bow under his arm;
he waited further out too
on the far side of next door
on a fiery headland's tip
under a fiery cape's arm
on a fiery rapid's brink
upon a holy stream's bank.

So one day among others
one morrow among many
he cast his eyes north-west, turned
his head to below the sun
spied a black speck on the sea
something bluish on the waves:
'In the east is that a cloud
the sunrise in the north-east?'

In the east it was no cloud
no sunrise in the north-east:
it was old Väinämöinen
the everlasting singer
    heading for Northland
    making for Darkland
astride the stallion of straw
astride the horse of pea stalks.
Now, that young Joukahainen
    the lean Lappish lad
prepared the fiery crossbow
    grabbed the fairest bow
meant for Väinämöinen's head
to slay him of Calm Waters.

His mother hastened to ask
and his parent to inquire:
'Who is the crossbow primed for
the iron bow ready for?'

Now, that young Joukahainen
uttered a word and spoke thus:
'The crossbow is primed for him
the iron bow is ready—
meant for Väinämöinen's head
to slay him of Calm Waters.
I'll shoot old Väinämöinen
down the eternal singer
through the heart, by the liver
and cleaving the shoulder flesh.'

Mother forbade him to shoot
his mother forbade and banned:
'Do not shoot Väinämöinen
or fell Kalevala's man!
Väinö is of great kin, my
brother-in-law's sister's son.
Should you shoot Väinämöinen
and fell Kalevala's man
joy would be lost from the world
and song would fall from the earth.
Joy is better in the world
song more fitting on the earth
    than in the Dead Lands
those cabins of Tuonela.'

With that young Joukahainen
now considers a little
    and ponders a bit:
    his hand bade him shoot
one hand bade and one forbade
his sinewy fingers ached.
At last he put this in words
    he declared, spoke thus:
'Though it were twice over, let
all our worldly joys be lost
    let all the songs fall!
No, I'll shoot, I'll not beware.'

He tensed the fiery crossbow
    drew the copper wheel
    against his left knee
from underneath his right foot
from the quiver drew a bolt
a feather from the three-shank
he took the swiftest arrow
chose the one with the best shaft
    placed this in the groove
joined it to the hemp bowstring
aligned the fiery crossbow
    on his right shoulder
and places himself to shoot—
to shoot at Väinämöinen
and he put this into words:
    'Strike now, birch-tipped one
    pine-backed one, now smite
    hemp bowstring, hit hard:
    where my hand may dip
    let the arrow lift;
    where my hand may lift
    let the arrow dip!'

    He touched the trigger
    shot the first arrow:
    it went very high
    overhead to heaven
    to the hurtling clouds
    the whirling vapours.
Still he shot, did not heed, shot
another of his arrows:
    it went very low
into mother earth below;
the earth wished to go to Death
the shady ridge to be cleft.
Soon he shot a third as well:
it travelled straight the third time
into the blue elk's shoulder

beneath old Väinämöinen;
he shot the stallion of straw
    the horse of pea stalks
    through its bladebone flesh
    by its left foreleg.

At that old Väinämöinen
dives fingers first in the wet
turned hands first into the wave
fists first plunged into the foam
from the back of the blue elk
    the horse of pea stalks.
    Then a great wind rose
a rough billow on the sea;
it bore old Väinämöinen
and washed him further from land
out on to those wide waters
to the open expanses.
With that young Joukahainen
    boasted with his tongue:
'Never, old Väinämöinen
never more with eyes alive
    never in this world
not in a month of Sundays*
will you tread Väinö-land's glades
the heaths of Kalevala!
    Bob there now six years
    ride seven summers
    and drift for eight years
    on those wide waters
    upon the vast waves—
    six years as spruce wood
    seven as pine wood
    as a stump-log eight!'

    Then he slipped indoors.
His mother began to ask:

'Have you shot Väinämöinen
lost the son of Kaleva?'

Well, that young Joukahainen
    says words in answer:
'Yes, I've shot Väinämöinen
felled the Kalevala man
    made him broom the sea
    made him sweep the wave.
    In that wanton sea
in the midst of the billows
the old man on his fingers
has sunk, has turned on his palms;
there he has slumped on his side
on his back has stopped, to be
driven by the sea's billows
to be steered by the sea surf.'

The mother put this in words:
'You did wrong, you luckless one
when you shot Väinämöinen
lost the Kalevala man
the great man of Calm Waters
fairest of Kalevala!'

7. *The Castaway*

Steady old Väinämöinen
    swims the vasty deeps
moved as a rotting spruce trunk
    a rotting pine stump
    for six summer days
    six nights in a row
before him the slack water
and behind him a clear sky.
    He swims two nights more
and two of the longest days
    till on the ninth night
    at the eighth day's end
    he feels a great pain
    pressing till it hurts
for there's no nail on his toes
and on his fingers no joint.
At that old Väinämöinen
    put this into words:
'Woe is me, a luckless boy
woe, a boy down on his luck
that I went from my own lands
the lands where I used to live
    to be for ever
in the open, night and day
    to be lulled by wind
to be driven by billows
    on these wide waters
these open expanses! 'Tis
chilly for me to be here
woeful for me to shiver
always on billows to dwell
    on the main to float.
    Neither do I know

how to be, which way to live
    in this evil age
    with time running out:
shall I build my cabin on the wind
on the water shall I carve my hut?
If I build my cabin on the wind
on the wind is no support;
if I carve my hut on the water
the water will bear it off.'

A bird flew out of Lapland
an eagle from the north-east—
not a great big eagle, nor
a little tiny eagle:
one wing ruffled the water
and the other swept the sky
    its tail skimmed the sea
and its beak clattered on crags.
    It flutters, it glides
    it looks, it turns round;
it saw old Väinämöinen
    on the blue high seas:
'Why, man, are you in the sea
fellow, among the billows?'

Steady old Väinämöinen
uttered a word and spoke thus:
'This is why I'm a man in the sea
a fellow amid billows:
I'm off for a Northland maid
    for a Darkland lass.
    I was galloping
along the unfrozen sea
till one day among others
one morrow among many
    I reached Cragland Bay
Jouko-land's river waters:
from under me my horse was

shot, someone was after me.
Then I flopped in the water
sank fingers first in the wave
    to be lulled by wind
to be driven by billows.
A wind came from the north-west
out of the east a big squall;
it had me borne far away
and washed me further from land.
Many days I have struggled
and many nights swum about
    on these wide waters
on these open expanses;
    neither can I know
    guess nor understand
    which death is to come
    which will arrive first—
    yielding to hunger
or sinking in the water.'

The eagle, bird of the air
said: 'Don't you worry at all!
    Get up on my back
rise upon my wingbone tips!
I'll carry you from the sea
where you have a mind to go.
I still remember that day
and think of the better time
when you cleared Kaleva's trees
and slashed Osmo-land's backwoods:
you left a birch tree growing
    a fine tree standing
    for birds to rest on
    for me to sit on.'

    Old Väinämöinen
    then lifts up his poll;
the man rises from the sea

the fellow from the billow comes up
on its wings places himself
on the eagle's wingbone tips.
That eagle, bird of the air
carried old Väinämöinen
bears him along the wind's road
    along the gale's path
    to the furthest North
to dreary Sariola.
There it left Väinämöinen
and soared off into the sky;
and there Väinämöinen wept
    there he wept and groaned
    upon a seashore
    whose name was unknown
a hundred wounds in his side
by a thousand winds battered
his beard too the worse for wear
and his hair in a tangle.
    He wept two, three nights
the same number of days too;
did not know the way to go
nor, a stranger, know the route
    for returning home
to go to familiar lands
to those places of his birth
the lands where he used to live.

A tiny wench of the North
    a fair-skinned woman
made a bargain with the sun
with the sun and with the moon
    that at the same time
as they rose, she would awake;
but she made it before them
before the moon, the sunlight—
without even the cockcrow

or the song of the hen's child.
    Five fleeces she sheared
six sheepfuls she teased, she made
the fleeces into homespun;
she worked all up into clothes
    before the sun rose
before the sunlight came up.
Then she washed the long tables
    the wide floors she swept
    with a brush of twigs
    with a broom of leaves;
    she scooped her rubbish
into a small copper box
which she took out through the door
to the field beside the yard
out to the furthest field's end
out to the lowest fence gap.
She stood on the rubbish heap
she listened, she turned around:
she hears weeping from the sea
crying across the river.
    Running she returns
    quickly goes indoors
and she said when she got there
    explained when she came:
'I heard weeping from the sea
crying across the river.'

Louhi, mistress of Northland
the gap-toothed hag of the North
quickly slipped into the yard
    bowled to the gateway;
there with her ears she listens.
She uttered a word, spoke thus:
'That is not a child weeping
and not women complaining;
that is a bearded fellow weeping
a hairy-chinned one crying.'

And she launched a boat
one with three planks on the waves
and started rowing.
She both rowed and sped:
she rowed to Väinämöinen
towards the weeping fellow.
And there Väinämöinen wept
the swain of Calm Waters groaned
by an evil willow brook
a thick clump of bird cherries:
his mouth moved and his beard shook
but his chin did not quiver.
The mistress of Northland said
she talked, she chattered:
'You wretched old man!
Now you are in a strange land.'

Steady old Väinämöinen
makes to lift his head.
He uttered a word, spoke thus:
'Now I know it too:
yes, I am in a strange land
utterly unknown.
In my land I was better
at home loftier.'

Louhi, mistress of Northland
uttered a word and spoke thus:
'Might I say something
would I be allowed to ask
what kind of man you may be
what sort of fellow?'

Steady old Väinämöinen
uttered a word and spoke thus:
'Well, I have been talked about
and valued from time to time
as a merrymaker at evening

as a singer everywhere
in those glades of Väinö-land
on the Kalevala heaths;
but how mean I may be now
I myself can hardly tell.'

Louhi, mistress of Northland
uttered a word and spoke thus:
'Rise now out of your marsh, man,
fellow, on to a new track
  to speak your sorrows
  to tell some stories!'

She took the man from weeping
and the fellow from groaning;
brought him from there to her craft
and sat him in the boat's stern.
She settled down at the oars
and straightened herself to row;
she rowed across to Northland
takes him to a strange cabin.
And she fed the hungry one
and the wet one she dried out;
then a long time she rubs him
  rubs him and warms him:
  she made the man well
  the fellow better.
  She inquired, she talked
  she uttered, spoke thus:
'Why were you weeping, Väinämöinen,
whining, man of Calm Waters
  in that evil place
on the shore beside the sea?'

Steady old Väinämöinen
uttered a word and spoke thus:
  'I have cause to weep
  woes to complain of!

For long I have swum the seas
    and shovelled the waves
    on those wide waters
on the open expanses.
For this I weep all my days
and throughout my lifetime grieve
that I swam from my own lands
and came from familiar lands
    towards these strange doors
    to these foreign gates.
    All the trees here bite
    all the fir sprigs beat
    every birch tree knocks
    every alder cuts:
only the wind do I know
and the sun have seen before
    in these foreign lands
    utterly strange doors.'

Louhi, mistress of Northland
    then came out with this:
'Do not weep, Väinämöinen
don't whine, man of Calm Waters!
'Tis good for you to be here
sweet for you to tarry here
to eat salmon off the plate
    and pork beside it.'

Then the old Väinämöinen
    put this into words:
'Strange food goes down the wrong way
even in a good lodging;
in his land a man's better
    at home loftier.
If only sweet God would grant
the kind Creator allow
me to come to my own lands
the lands where I used to live!

Better in your own country
even water off your sole
than in a foreign country
honey from a golden bowl.'

Louhi, mistress of Northland
uttered a word and spoke thus:
'So, what will you give me if
I bring you to your own lands
    back to your own field
all the way to your sauna?'

The old Väinämöinen said:
'What do you ask of me if
you bring me to my own lands
    back to my own field
to where my own cuckoo calls
where my own bird sings? Will you
take a capful of gold coins
a felt hatful of silver?'

Louhi, mistress of Northland
uttered a word and spoke thus:
    'Shrewd Väinämöinen
O everlasting wise man
I don't ask for your gold coins
nor do I want your silver:
gold coins are children's playthings
silver coins are horse-trinkets.
If you can forge the Sampo
    beat out the bright-lid
    from a swan's quill tip
    a barren cow's milk
    from one barley grain
    the wool of one ewe
    I'll give you a girl
pay you a maid for wages

I'll bring you to your own lands
    where your own bird sings
where your own cockerel is heard
    back to your own field.'

Steady old Väinämöinen
uttered a word and spoke thus:
'I cannot forge the Sampo
    brighten the bright-lid.
But bring me to my own lands:
I will send Ilmarinen
the smith—he'll forge your Sampo
    beat out the bright-lid
    suit your maid and make
    your daughter happy.
    He is quite a smith
the highly skilful craftsman
    who has forged the sky
beaten out the lid of heaven
but there is no hammer mark
nor trace of where tongs have gripped.'

Louhi, mistress of Northland
uttered a word and spoke thus:
'I will bestow my daughter
on him, pledge my child to him
who forges the dear Sampo
    brightens the bright-lid
    from a swan's quill tip
    a barren cow's milk
    from one barley grain
    the down of one ewe.'

She put a foal in harness
a bay in front of a sledge
saw old Väinämöinen off
sat him in the stallion's sledge

and then she uttered a word
  she declared, spoke thus:
  'Do not raise your head
  nor lift up your poll
while the stallion does not tire
  nor evening arrive;
but if you do raise your head
  or lift up your poll
then indeed ruin will come
an evil day will befall.'

At that old Väinämöinen
beat the stallion to a run
the hemp-mane into movement
  and he rumbles off
  out of dark Northland
from dreary Sariola.

8. *The Wound*

'Twas the fair maid of the North
the land's famous, water's choice
sat on the sky's collar-bow
upon heaven's arch
shimmered in clean clothes
and in white garments;
cloth of gold she is weaving
of silver she is working
from a gold shuttle
with a silver reed.
The shuttle whizzed in her grasp
in her hand the spool swivelled
the heddles of copper creaked
the silver reed slammed
as the maid wove cloth
worked cloth of silver.

Steady old Väinämöinen
is rumbling along
out of dark Northland
from dreary Sariola.
He drove a bit of a way
a tiny way he traced, when
he heard a shuttle buzzing
up above his head.
He lifted his head
glances heavenward:
the arch is fair in the sky
the maid at the arch's edge;
cloth of gold she is weaving
of silver she is tinkling.
Steady old Väinämöinen
stopped his horse at once

and he put this into words
    he declared, spoke thus:
    'Come, maid, into my
sleigh, step down into my sledge!'

The maid put this into words
    she declared and asks:
'Why get a maid into your
sleigh, a girl into your sledge?'

Steady old Väinämöinen
    well, he answered that:
'Why get a maid into my
sleigh, a girl into my sledge?—
that she may bake honey-bread
    know how to brew beer
    sing on every bench
rejoice at every window
on those farms of Väinö-land
in those Kalevala yards.'

The maid put this into words
she declared, chattered: 'As I
walked on the maddery ground
skipped upon the yellow heath
yesterday at evening late
as the sun was going down
a bird carolled in a grove
    a fieldfare twittered—
carolled how daughters feel, sang
how a daughter-in-law feels.
    I made to say this
    and to ask the bird:
    "Little fieldfare, sing
    that my ears may hear:
    whose lot is better
and whose more highly thought of—
a daughter's in father's house, or a

daughter-in-law's in a husband's house?"
Well, the tomtit informed me
    the fieldfare twittered:
    "Bright a summer day
but a maid's state is brighter;
chilly is iron in frost
chillier a daughter-in-law's state.
A maid in father's house is
like a berry on good land;
daughter-in-law in a husband's house
is like a dog on a chain.
Seldom is a serf cherished;
a daughter-in-law never."'

Steady old Väinämöinen
    put this into words:
'Idle are a tomtit's tales
and a fieldfare's twitterings!
A daughter at home's a child;
she's only a maid when wed.*
    Come, maid, into my
sleigh, step down into my sledge!
I am not a man of no account
a fellow sleepier than others.'

The maid skilfully answered
uttered a word and spoke thus:
    'I'd call you a man
I'd reckon you a fellow
if you could split a horsehair
    with a pointless knife
pull an egg into a knot
so that the knot did not show.'

Steady old Väinämöinen
    splits a horsehair through
    with a pointless knife
    quite without a tip;

pulls an egg into a knot
so that the knot does not show.
He bade the maid into his
sleigh, the girl into his sledge.

The maid skilfully answered:
'Well, perhaps I'll marry you
  when you peel a stone
  cut fence poles of ice
without a piece breaking off
  or a chip flying.'

Steady old Väinämöinen
does not greatly fret at that:
  he just peeled a stone
  cut fence poles of ice
without a scrap breaking off
  or a chip flying.
He called the maid into his
sleigh, the girl into his sledge.

The maid skilfully answers
  and says with this word:
  'Well, I'd marry one
  who could carve a boat
out of bits of my spindle
from pieces of my drawknife
  who could launch the boat
and the new ship on the waves
  his knee not nudging
  his fist not touching
  his arm not turning
his shoulder not reaching out.'

At that old Väinämöinen
  put this into words:
'Not on earth, not in the world
not under all the sky's vault

is there such a boatbuilder
a carver the likes of me.'

He took bits of the distaff
    whorls of the spindle
set about carving a boat
building a hundred-planked one
    on a steel mountain
    on an iron cliff.
Rashly he carved at the boat
the wooden craft recklessly;
he carved one day, he carved two
soon he carved a third as well:
the axe does not touch the rock
nor the blade tip strike the cliff.

    So on the third day
the Demon swung the handle
round, the Devil wrenched the blade
the Evil One jogged the haft:
into the rock the axe went
and the blade tip struck the cliff
and the axe bounced off the rock
and the blade slid into flesh
into the worthy boy's knee
into Väinämöinen's toe;
the Devil slipped it upon his flesh
the Demon tried it on his sinews
    and the blood spilled out
    the gore rippled forth.
Steady old Väinämöinen
the everlasting wise man
at that put this into words
he declared and chattered thus:
    'O you hook-beaked axe
you hatchet of even blade
did you think you had a tree

to bite, a fir to attack
    a pine to put down
    a birch to meet with
when you slipped into my flesh
slithered upon my sinews?'

He started then singing charms
    began reciting:
he told Origins in depth
    and spells in order
but he cannot remember
some of the great iron words
    which would prove a bar
    serve as a firm lock
against those rents of iron
those slashes of the blue-mouth.
The blood as a river ran
the gore as a rapid roared:
on the ground it covered berry stalks
heather plants upon the heath.
    There was no hummock
    that was not flooded
by that overflow of blood
    of gore that frothed forth
    from the true boy's knee
out of Väinämöinen's toe.
Steady old Väinämöinen
snatched some fibres from a rock
from a swamp took some mosses
from the ground a clump he ripped
    to block the harsh hole
to stop up the evil gate;
but it will not yield at all
nor a tiny bit hold off.
Well, now things become painful
things turn out more troublesome.
Steady old Väinämöinen
    he burst into tears:
he put his foal in harness

the bay in front of the sledge
then flings himself in the sledge
    settled in his sleigh.
    He lashed the courser
whacked it with the beaded belt:
courser ran and journey sped
the sledge rolled, the road shortened.
    Now soon a village
    comes up: three roads meet.

Steady old Väinämöinen
drives along the lowest road
    to the lowest house.
Over the threshold he asks:
'Might there be one in this house
    who treats iron's toil
knows about a fellow's pain
    explains injuries?'

There was a child on the floor
a small boy on the stove seat.
    This one answers that:
'There is no one in this house
    who treats iron's toil
knows about a fellow's pain
    takes hold of an ache
    explains injuries.
    He's in the next house:
    drive to the next house!'

Steady old Väinämöinen
    he lashed the courser
    drives off with a swish.
He drove a bit of a way
along the middlemost road
up to the middlemost house.
He asked back from the threshold
begged from below the window:

'Might there be one in this house
    who treats iron's toil
    who bars a blood-rain
    who checks vein-rapids?'

There was an old hag under a cloak
a gossip on the stove seat
and the hag indeed answered
    the three-toothed one clacked:
'There is no one in this house
    who treats iron's toil
knows the Origin of blood
    takes hold of an ache.
    He's in the next house:
    drive to the next house!'

Steady old Väinämöinen
    he lashed the courser
    drives off with a swish.
He drove a bit of a way
along the uppermost road
up to the uppermost house.
Over the threshold he asks
spoke from beyond the rooftree:
'Might there be one in this house
    who treats iron's toil
    who will block this flood
    shut the dreary blood?'

An old man dwelt on the stove*
a greybeard under the ridge.
The old man growled from the stove
    the greybeard boomed out:
'Bigger things yet have been shut
greater things yet overcome
with the Creator's three words
the deep Origin's decree—

rivers at mouths, lakes at heads
and furious streams at the neck
bays at the tips of headlands
land-bridges where they taper.'

9. *Iron and Blood*

At that old Väinämöinen
got out of the sleigh himself
rose from the sledge, was not raised
got up, but was not helped up;
from there comes into the hut
under the roofs makes his way.
A silver flagon is brought
a golden jug is carried:
it will not take a little
not even a drop will hold
of old Väinämöinen's blood
of the mighty fellow's gore.
The old man growled from the stove
    the greybeard boomed out:
'What kind of man may you be
    what sort of fellow?
Of blood there's seven boatfuls
    of bucketfuls eight
    luckless, from your knee
    fallen to the floor!
Other words I would recall
but cannot work out iron's
Origin, where it was born
or where the hapless dross grew.'

Then the old Väinämöinen
uttered a word and spoke thus:
'I know iron's birth myself
can work out steel's Origin:
air is the first of mothers
water eldest of brothers
iron youngest of brothers
and fire was once the midmost.

That Old Man, high creator
    the god of the skies
from the sky parted water
from the water laid out land.
Iron, poor thing, was unborn
    unborn and ungrown.
The Old Man, god of the sky
rubbed his two palms together
    pressed both together
    on his left kneecap
and from that were born three maids
all three daughters of nature
to be mothers of rust-hued iron
conceivers of the blue-mouth.
    The maids bounced along
the lasses trod a cloud's rim
    with their dugs bursting
    their nipples aching:
they squeezed their milk on the earth
    they let their dugs burst;
they squeezed on lands, squeezed on swamps
    squeezed on calm waters.
    One squeezed black milk: she
was the eldest of the maids;
the second spilled white: she was
the middlemost of the maids;
    the third showered red: she
was the youngest of the maids.
    She who squeezed black milk
from her was born soft iron;
    she who squeezed white milk
from her were made things of steel;
    she who showered red milk
from her was got pig iron.

    'A little time passed.
Iron was eager to meet

its eldest brother
to get to know fire.
Fire started being naughty
it grew to be quite dreadful:
it was burning the luckless
the poor iron, its brother.
But iron managed to hide—
to hide, to keep safe
from that harsh fire's hands
from the mouth of furious flame.
At that and then iron hid
both hid and kept safe
in a moving mire
in a spilling spring
on the largest open swamp
on a harsh fell-top
where the swans lay eggs
and the goose hatches her young.
Iron sprawls out in the swamp
and in the slack place stretches;
it hid one year, it hid two
soon it hid a third as well
between two treestumps
under three roots of a birch.
But no, it did not escape
the harsh hands of fire:
it must come a second time
and go to fire's cabins, while
it was made into a blade
and was forged into a sword.
A wolf ran along the swamp
a bear rambled on the heath;
the swamp moved at the wolf's tread
and the heath at the bear's paws:
there iron rust rose
and a steel rod grew
where the wolf's feet had been, where
the bear's heel had dug.

'Smith Ilmarinen was born
    both was born and grew
was born on a hill of coal
grew on a heath of charcoal
holding a copper hammer
    gripping tiny tongs.
By night born, Ilmarinen
by day built a workshop: he
sought a spot for the workshop
    space for the smithy.
He saw a small strip of swamp
    a little damp ground;
he went off to look at it
to inspect it from close by:
there he pressed down his bellows
    there set up his forge.
He followed in the wolf's tracks
and where the bear's heel had been;
he saw iron-coloured shoots
and steel-coloured balls of snow
    in the wolf's great tracks
    the bear's paw-places.
    He says with this word:
"Alas for you, poor iron
being in a wretched spot
    a lowly dwelling
on the swamp in the wolf's prints
always in the bear's footsteps!"
    He thinks, considers:
    "What would come of it
if I thrust it in the fire
    in the forge set it?"
    Poor iron started—
    started and took fright
when it heard fire spoken of
    fire harshly mentioned.
    The smith Ilmarinen said:

"Don't worry at all!
Fire will not burn one it knows
nor abuse its clan.
When you come to fire's cabins
and to flame's fortress
there you will grow to be fair
come up to be most graceful
to be men's good swords
women's ribbon clasps."

'Well, at that day's end
iron was drained from the swamp
from the slack place was stirred up
and brought to the smith's workshop:
the smith thrust it in the fire
down into his forge pushed it.
He puffed once, puffed twice
puffed a third time too:
iron as gruel
lolls, as dross it foams;
it stretched as wheat paste
as dough of rye flour
in the smith's great fires
in the power of naked flame.
At that poor iron cried out:
"Smith Ilmarinen!
Ah, take me away from here
out of the pain of red fire!"
The smith Ilmarinen said:
"If I take you from the fire
perhaps you will grow dreadful
and fly quite into a rage
and even carve your brother
chop your mother's child."
Thereupon poor iron swore—
swore a solemn oath
on the forge, on the anvil

on the hammers, the mallets;
    it says with this word
    it spoke with this speech:
"There is wood for me to bite
a rock's heart for me to eat
so I'll not carve my brother
    chop my mother's child.
'Tis better for me to be
pleasanter for me to live
as a rover's companion
    a walking man's tool
than to eat my own kinsman
    to abuse my clan."
Then the smith Ilmarinen
the everlasting craftsman
snatched iron out of the fire
set it upon the anvil;
he works it till it is soft
makes it into things with blades
into spears, into axes
into all manner of things.
But still a bit was missing
and poor iron was in need
for iron's tongue will not boil
nor will a steel-mouth be formed
iron will not harden if
it is not steeped in water.
At that smith Ilmarinen
    gives some thought to this:
he prepared a bit of ash
    and some lye he mixed
into steel-making poison
iron-tempering waters.
The smith tested with his tongue
tasted it to his liking
and he put this into words:
"No, these are no good to me

for steel-making waters, for
 working iron things."

'A bee rose up from the ground
a blue-wing from a hummock;
 it flutters, it glides
 round the smith's workshop.
The smith put this into words:
 "O bee, lightweight man
 bring mead on your wing
carry honey on your tongue
 from six flowery tips
 from seven grass tops
for steel things to be made, for
 iron to be wrought!"
But a wasp, the Demon's bird
is looking, is listening
 looked from the roof edge
from beneath the birch bark gazed
at the iron to be wrought
at the steel things to be made.
 It buzzes about;
it tossed the Demon's terrors
 carried snake venom
 a worm's black poison
 an ant's itchy juice
 a frog's secret hates
in the steel-making poison
iron-tempering water.
As for smith Ilmarinen
the perpetual craftsman, he
 believes, considers
 that the bee has come
 and has brought honey
 and has carried mead.
He uttered a word, spoke thus:
"Now then, these are good for me
for the steel-making waters

and for working iron things!"
Thereupon he snatched the steel
thereupon steeped poor iron
as it was brought from the fire
and taken out of the forge.
At that the steel grew evil
iron flew into a rage
and the wretch forsook its oath
ate its honour like a dog:
the poor one carved its brother
held its kinsman in its mouth
    freed the blood to spill
    the gore to gush forth.'

The old man growled from the stove
the beard sang and the head quaked:
'Now I know the Origin
of iron, I grasp steel's ways.
Alas for you, poor iron
poor iron and hapless dross
and steel, victim of witchcraft!
Is that how you came to be
how you grew to be dreadful
sprang up to be very big?
    You were not big then
    neither big nor small
not very handsome at all
    nor extremely cross
    when as milk you lay
    as fresh milk languished
    in the young maid's teats
grew under the lass's arm
on the edge of the long cloud
    beneath level heaven;
    nor were you big then
you were neither big nor small
when as ooze you were resting
were standing as clear water

on the largest open swamp
    on a harsh fell-top
when you changed there into mud
and turned into rusty soil;
    nor were you big then
you were neither big nor small
when elk rubbed you on the swamp
reindeer ground you on the heath
the wolf mashed you with its feet
the bear with its little paws;
    nor were you big then
you were neither big nor small
when you were tilled from the swamp
shaped up out of the earth's mud
taken to the smith's workshop
down to Ilmarinen's forge;
    nor were you big then
you were neither big nor small
when as dross you were roaring
and rippling as warm water
    in harsh fireplaces
and you swore your solemn oath
on the forge, on the anvil
on the hammers, the mallets
on the smith's standing-places
    on his forging-grounds.
Have you sprung now to full size
    have you turned surly
wretch, have you broken your oath
doglike eaten your honour
now that you have harmed your tribe
held your kinsman in your mouth?
Who told you to work evil
who compelled you to be mean—
your father or your mother
the eldest of your brothers
the youngest of your sisters
or other of your great kin?

Not your father, your mother
the eldest of your brothers
the youngest of your sisters
nor other of your great kin:
you did the foul deed yourself
split the death-coloured open.
Come now, realize your deed
    mend your evil ways
before I tell your mother
and to your parent complain!
    Mother has more work
great trouble the parent has
    when her son does wrong
her child gets up to mischief.

    'Hold, blood, your spilling
    and gore, your rippling
    upon me spraying
    spurting on my breast!
    Blood, stand like a wall
    stay, gore, like a fence
like an iris in a lake
stand, like sedge among moss, like
a boulder at a field edge
a rock in a steep rapid!
But if you should have a mind
    to move more swiftly
    then move in the flesh
    and in the bones glide!
Inside is better for you
beneath the skin is fairer—
    coursing through the veins
    gliding through the bones
than spilling upon the ground
    trickling on the dirt.
Yours, milk, is not to fall down
upon the turf, blameless blood
sweetheart of men, on the grass,

on a mound, fellows' darling:
within the heart is your place
beneath the lung your cellar;
    slip in between there
    run quickly in there!
You are no river to run
    nor a pool to flow
nor a swamp-mire to gurgle
no shipwreck to spill over.
Have done now, dear, with dripping
    red one, with dropping!
If you have not done, then clot!
Lapland's rapid once had done
Tuonela's river clotted
the sea dried up, heaven dried
in that great year of clear skies
of fires no one could deal with.

'Should you not heed even that
other things will be thought of
and new means found out: I'll shout
for a pot from the Demon
in which the blood will be boiled
and the gore will be heated
without a trickle dripping
    a red one dropping
no blood spilling on the earth
    no gore gushing forth.

'Should I not be man enough
nor fellow enough the Old Man's son
    to block off this flood
    check this vein-rapid
there's the heavenly father
    god above the clouds
    who counts among men
and holds good among fellows
for shutting the mouth of blood
    blocking what comes forth.

O Old Man, high creator
    heaven-dwelling god
come here when you are needed
walk this way when you are called:
    thrust your chubby hand
    and press your fat thumb
    to block the harsh hole
to stop up the evil gate;
draw a sweet leaf over it
a golden water lily
slap on, to bar the blood's road
    to block what comes forth
that it may not splash my beard
    run on to my rags!'

Thus he shut the mouth of blood
barred the road of gore. He sent
his son into the workshop
    to make some ointments
    from those husks of hay
those tips of the thousand-leaved
that spill honey on the earth
    drip trickles of mead.
The lad went to the workshop
set about making ointment.
He came up to an oak tree
and inquired of his oak tree:
'Is there honey on your boughs
    mead beneath your bark?'

The oak skilfully answers:
    'Only yesterday
    mead dripped on my boughs
    honey daubed my top
    from drizzling clouds, from
    scattering vapours.'

He took some slivers of oak
fragments of the brittle tree;
    he took some good hay
    many kinds of grass
which are not seen on these lands
    growing everywhere.
He puts a pot on the fire
he brought the stew to the boil
    full of oak tree bark
    of good-looking hay.
    The pot boiled, rumbled
    for three nights in all
    for three days of spring;
then he looked to see whether
the ointments were steadfast, the
remedies reliable.

The ointments were not steadfast
the remedies not reliable.
He put in some extra hay
    many kinds of grass
which had been brought from elsewhere
brought back from a hundred trips
    from nine soothsayers
    from eight who treat ills.
    He cooked three nights more
    for nine nights on end;
he lifts the pot from the fire
    looks to see whether
the ointments are steadfast, the
remedies reliable.

    A branchy aspen
    grew at a field edge.
The murderer shattered it
quite into two he split it;
he anointed it with those ointments
he treated it with those remedies
and he put this into words:
'If something in these ointments

can be put upon a hurt
can be poured on injuries
aspen, heal together, be
more graceful than you once were!'

The aspen healed together
more graceful than it once was—
  grew fair at the top
  quite healthy below.
Then he tested the ointments
he looks at the remedies
tried them on cracks in a rock
  on clefts in boulders:
already rocks stuck to rocks
boulders to a boulder joined.
The lad came from the workshop
  from making ointments
  from preparing salves
thrust them in the old man's hand:
'These ointments are steadfast, these
remedies reliable
though you should anoint mountains
and make all cliffs into one.'

The old man tested them with his tongue
tasted them with his sweet mouth
and he knew the remedies
were good, the ointments steadfast.
Then he anointed Väinämöinen
the ill-befallen he healed—
anointed below, above
  slapped the middle once.
  He says with this word
  he spoke with this speech:
'I move not with my own flesh
but with my Creator's flesh
I act not by my own power
but by the Almighty's power

I talk not with my own mouth
I talk with the mouth of God.
Now, if I have a sweet mouth
sweeter is the mouth of God
and if my hand is fair, the
Creator's hand is fairer.'

When the ointment was put on
and those steadfast remedies
they sent him into half-swoons
Väinämöinen into faints:
he thrashes here, thrashes there
    but he found no rest.
So the old man drove the aches
thrust from there the points of pain
to the middle of Ache Hill
    the peak of Mount Ache
    to make a rock ache
    to break a boulder.
He seized a handful of silk
    smoothed it into sheets
    tore it into strips
into bandages shaped it;
    he bound with those silks
    swathed with those fair ones
the knee of the worthy boy
the toes of Väinämöinen.
    He says with this word
    he spoke with this speech:
'Be a bandage the Lord's silk
the Lord's cape be a cover
    upon this good knee
    on these steadfast toes!
    Look now, O fair God
keep him, steadfast Creator
lest he be taken hurtward
towards injury be hauled!'

At that old Väinämöinen
now felt it really helping.
    Soon he became well
    and his flesh grew fair
    quite healthy below
with the middle not aching
    the side not hurting
    and on top no scar—
more graceful than it once was
better than it was before.
Already now he could walk
his knee was able to tread;
he does not suffer at all
does not groan even a bit.
At that old Väinämöinen
    lifted up his eyes
    glances handsomely
    overhead to heaven;
    he says with this word
    he spoke with this speech:
'From there mercies ever flow
    friendly refuge comes
out of heaven above, from
the almighty Creator.
    Be now praised, O God,
extolled, Creator, alone
    for giving me help
bringing me friendly refuge
    amid these harsh pains
    this sharp iron's toil!'

At that old Väinämöinen
put this also into words:
    'Do not, folk to come
    folk still to grow up
    rashly make a boat
recklessly a bow either!
God appoints how far to go

the Lord fixes the limit;
'tis not in a fellow's skill
even in a strong one's power.'

10. *Forging the Sampo*

Steady old Väinämöinen
    took his bay stallion
put his foal into harness
the bay in front of the sledge
flings himself into the sledge
    settles in his sleigh.
    He lashed the courser
whacked it with the beaded belt:
courser ran and journey sped
the sledge rolled, the road shortened
the birchwood runner thudded
the rowan collar-bow slammed.
    He rumbles along
    by swamps and by lands
    by wide open glades.
He went one day, he went two
    till on the third day
he came to the long quay's end
upon Kalevala's heath
at the edge of Osmo's field.
There he put this into words
    he declared, chattered:
    'Wolf, devour the seer
    disease, kill the Lapp!
She said I would not reach home
any more with eyes alive
    ever in this world
not in a month of Sundays
reach these glades of Väinö-land
the heaths of Kalevala.'

At that old Väinämöinen
sings and practises his craft:

he sang a spruce topped with flowers
topped with flowers and leaved with gold;
the top he pushed heavenward
through the clouds he lifted it
spread the foliage skyward
across heaven scattered it.
He sings, practises his craft—
    sang the moon to gleam
on the gold-topped spruce, he sang
the Great Bear on to its boughs.
    He rumbles along
    towards his dear home
his head down, in bad spirits
    helmet all askew
for he had promised the smith
the everlasting craftsman
Ilmarinen to redeem
    to save his own skin—
promised him to dark Northland
to dreary Sariola.
The stallion stopped at the end
    of Osmo's new field
and there old Väinämöinen
lifted his head from the sleigh:
from the workshop noise is heard
clanging from the charcoal-hut.
Steady old Väinämöinen
he slipped into the workshop:
there is smith Ilmarinen
    hammering away.
The smith Ilmarinen said:
    'Old Väinämöinen!
Where have you lingered so long
    spending all your time?'

Steady old Väinämöinen
    put this into words:

'There I have lingered so long
    living all my time—
    there in dark Northland
in dreary Sariola
gliding along Lappish trails
in the haunts of men who know.'

Then the smith Ilmarinen
uttered a word and spoke thus:
    'Old Väinämöinen
you everlasting wise man
what's to tell from your travels
    now you have come home?'

Old Väinämöinen uttered:
    'I have much to tell:
there is a maid in Northland
a lass in the cold village
who will not accept bridegrooms
    take to good husbands.
Half the North was praising her
for being very handsome:
the moon shone from her brow-bones
and from her breasts the sun beamed
the Great Bear from her shoulders
the Seven Stars from her back.
    Smith Ilmarinen
you everlasting craftsman
    go and fetch the maid
    look for the braid-head!
If you can forge the Sampo
    brighten the bright-lid
you'll get the maid for your pay
for your work the lovely girl.'

The smith Ilmarinen said:
'O-oh, old Väinämöinen!
    Have you promised me—

promised me to dark Northland
  to save your own skin
  to redeem yourself?
Never in this world shall I
not in a month of Sundays
set out for Northland's cabins
for Sariola's buildings
  for the man-eating
the fellow-drowning places!'

At that old Väinämöinen
  put this into words:
'There's another wonder yet—
  a spruce topped with flowers
topped with flowers and leaved with gold
at the edge of Osmo's field
and the moon gleamed in its top
on its boughs the Great Bear stood.'

The smith Ilmarinen said:
  'I'll not believe that
unless I go there to look
and see with these eyes of mine.'
The old Väinämöinen said:
'All right, if you don't believe
let us go and see whether
it is the truth or a lie!'

  They went off to look
upon that spruce topped with flowers:
first went old Väinämöinen
next the smith Ilmarinen.
  Then, when they got there
to the edge of Osmo's field
  the smith stops by it
wonders at the new spruce, for
on its boughs was the Great Bear
the moon in the spruce's top.

There the old Väinämöinen
    put this into words:
'Now, you smith, my dear brother
    climb to fetch the moon
    to take the Great Bear
out of the spruce topped with gold!'

Then the smith Ilmarinen
    climbed high in the tree
    up, up heavenward
    climbed to fetch the moon
    to take the Great Bear
out of the spruce topped with gold.
The spruce topped with flowers uttered
the shock-headed pine declared:
'Alas for a mindless man
an utterly strange fellow!
You climbed, strange man, on my boughs
child-witted, into my top
    to fetch a mock moon
for the sake of a false star!'

Then the old Väinämöinen
    sings under his breath—
sang the wind into a whirl
worked the air into a rage;
    he says with this word
    he spoke with this speech:
'Take him, wind, into your craft,
    gale, into your boat
    to whisk him away
    into dark Northland!'

The wind rose into a whirl
the air worked into a rage
took the smith Ilmarinen
    to sweep him away
    into dark Northland

to dreary Sariola.
There the smith Ilmarinen
    he both went and sped:
he went along the wind's road
    along the gale's path
over moon and under sun
across the Great Bear's shoulders;
    he reached Northland's yard
Sariola's sauna-road
but the dogs did not hear him
nor did the barkers notice.

Louhi, mistress of Northland
the gap-toothed hag of the North
    comes into the yard
    and hastened to say:
'What kind of man may you be
    what sort of fellow?
You came here by the wind's road
    by the gale's sledge path
and the dogs don't bark at you
nor do the fluffy-tails speak!'

The smith Ilmarinen said:
'I've certainly not come here
to amuse the village dogs
to enrage the fluffy-tails
    before these strange doors
    at these foreign gates!'

Then the mistress of Northland
inquired of the newcomer:
    'Have you come to see
    hear and know about
that Ilmarinen the smith
the most skilful of craftsmen?
He has long been waited for

and ages been longed for, here
in furthest Northland
to make up the new Sampo.'

Smith Ilmarinen
uttered a word and spoke thus:
'Perhaps I have come to see
that Ilmarinen the smith
for I am Ilmarinen
the skilful craftsman myself.'

Louhi, mistress of Northland
the gap-toothed hag of the North
quickly slipped indoors
and says with this word:
'My younger maiden
my child, my smallest baby!
Put on your best now
on your body the whitest
the softest upon your hems
the most splendid on your breasts
around your neck the fairest
the most blooming on your brows
put red on your cheeks
and show off your face
for the smith Ilmarinen
the everlasting craftsman
has come to make the Sampo
brighten the bright-lid!'

'Twas the fair girl of the North
the land's famous, water's choice
took out her choice clothes
her cleanest garments
decks herself, dresses herself
fits herself out in headbands
puts herself in copper hoops
looks a wonder in gold belts

and she came in from the shed
tripping in from the farmyard
    with her eyes aglow
    with her ears gorgeous
    fair about the face
    with her cheeks blushing;
    gold hung at her breast
on her head silver glittered.

She, the mistress of Northland
showed the smith Ilmarinen
round those cabins of Northland
round Sariola's buildings;
    there she fed him full
she let the man drink his fill
entertained him very well.
Then she got round to saying:
    'Smith Ilmarinen
O everlasting craftsman
if you can forge the Sampo
    brighten the bright-lid
    from a swan's quill tip
    a barren cow's milk
    a small barley grain
    a summer ewe's down
you'll get the maid for your pay
for your work the lovely girl.'

Then the smith Ilmarinen
put this into words: 'I'll be
able to forge the Sampo
    beat out the bright-lid
    from a swan's quill tip
    a barren cow's milk
    a small barley grain
    a summer ewe's down
because I have forged the sky
beaten out the lid of heaven

with nothing to start off from
with not a shred ready made.'

He went to make the Sampo
    brighten the bright-lid:
he asked for a workshop site
    longed for forging-tools
but there was no workshop site
no workshop and no bellows
    no forge, no anvil
no hammer, no handle even!
Then the smith Ilmarinen
uttered a word and spoke thus:
    'Well, let the hags doubt
    the flighty break off—
but even a worse man won't
nor a sleepier fellow!'

He sought a base for a forge
    space for a smithy
upon those lands, those mainlands
upon the North's furthest fields;
he sought one day, he sought two
    till on the third day
he came upon a bright rock
a massive boulder in front.
    There the smith stopped, there
the craftsman put up his fire;
spent one day making bellows
the next setting up a forge.

Then the smith Ilmarinen
the everlasting craftsman
pushed the raw stuffs in the fire
his materials down in the forge;
    he took serfs to puff
    and striplings to press.
    The serfs puffed and flapped

the striplings pressed hard
for three summer days
and three summer nights;
rocks grew at their heels
and boulders where their toes were.

So on the first day
he, the smith Ilmarinen
leaned over to look
at his forge's underside
and see what might be coming
from the fire, out of the flame:
a crossbow pushed from the fire
a bow of gold from the heat
the bow gold, the top silver
the shaft copper-bright.
The crossbow is good-looking
only it is ill-mannered:
every day it claims a head
and on a good day two heads.
He, the smith Ilmarinen
was not greatly pleased with that
and he snapped the bow in two
then pushes it in the fire;
he made the serfs puff
and the striplings press.

Now the day after
he, the smith Ilmarinen
leaned over to look
at his forge's underside:
a boat pushed out of the fire
a red craft out of the heat
its prow bright with gold
its rowlocks cast in copper.
It is a good-looking boat
but it is not well-mannered:

vainly it would go to war
    needlessly to fight.
    Smith Ilmarinen
was not pleased with that either:
he shattered the boat to bits
pushes it in the fireplace;
    he made the serfs puff
    and the striplings press.

    Now on the third day
he, the smith Ilmarinen
    leaned over to look
at his forge's underside:
a heifer pushed from the fire
a gold-horned one from the heat
on its brow a Great Bear star
and on its head the sun's disc.
The heifer is good-looking
but it is not well-mannered:
it lies down in the forest
spills its milk upon the ground.
    Smith Ilmarinen
was not pleased with that either:
he cut the cow in pieces
then pushes it in the fire;
    he made the serfs puff
    and the striplings press.

    Now on the fourth day
he, the smith Ilmarinen
    leaned over to look
at his forge's underside:
a plough pushed out of the fire
a gold-shared one from the heat
the share gold, the stilt copper
silver on the handle top.
It is a good-looking plough
but it is not well-mannered:
    it ploughs others' fields

and tills their acres.
Smith Ilmarinen
was not pleased with that either
and he snapped the plough in two
and shoved it down in his forge.
He made the winds puff
and the strong gusts press.
The winds puffed and flapped:
the east puffed and puffed the west
and the south puffed more
and the north blasted.
They puffed one day, they puffed two
soon they puffed a third as well:
the fire flashed from the window
the sparks flew out of the door
the dirt rose skyward
the smoke thickened to the clouds.

Smith Ilmarinen
at the third day's end
leaned over to look
at his forge's underside—
saw the Sampo being born
the bright-lid growing.
Then the smith Ilmarinen
the everlasting craftsman
he hammers away
he tap-taps away.
He forged the Sampo with skill:
on one side there's a corn mill
on the second a salt mill
a money mill on the third.
And then the new Sampo ground
and the bright-lid rocked;
ground a binful at twilight—
one binful to eat
another it ground to sell
and a third to store at home.

The hag of the North was pleased;
then she took the great Sampo
into Northland's rocky hill
inside the slope of copper
    and behind nine locks.
    There she rooted roots
to a depth of nine fathoms;
sank one root in mother earth
and one in a riverbank
and a third in the home-hill.

Then the smith Ilmarinen
    went to beg the girl.
He uttered a word, spoke thus:
'Will you marry me, maid, now
that the Sampo is finished
    and the bright-lid fair?'

But that fair girl of the North
    put this into words:
    'And who here next year
    who the third summer
would set the cuckoo calling
    set the birds singing
if I went elsewhere and came,
a berry, to other lands!
If this hen were to be lost
if this goose were to wander
mother's offspring were to stray
the cowberry went away
all the cuckoos would be lost
the joy-birds would move away
    from the peaks of this
knoll, the shoulders of this ridge.
Nor am I free otherwise
cannot leave my maiden days
    these jobs to be done
    in the summer rush—

berries on the land unpicked
    the bay shores unsung
untrodden by me the glades
the groves unplayed in by me.'

Then the smith Ilmarinen
the everlasting craftsman
his head down, in bad spirits
    helmet all askew
    now considers there
    and long he ponders
    how to go homeward
    come to lands he knows
    out of dark Northland
from dreary Sariola.
The mistress of Northland said:
'Oh dear, smith Ilmarinen!
Why are you in bad spirits
    helmet all askew?
Would you have a mind to go
to the lands where once you lived?'

The smith Ilmarinen said:
'There I'd have a mind to go—
    to my home to die
to my land to pine away.'

Then the mistress of Northland
fed the man, gave him to drink
sat him astern in a craft
with a paddle of copper;
    told the wind to blow
and the north wind to bluster.
Then the smith Ilmarinen
the everlasting craftsman
    made for his own lands
    over the blue sea.

He sailed one day, he sailed two
    till on the third day
    now the smith came home
to those places of his birth.

    Old Väinämöinen
asked the smith Ilmarinen:
'Brother, smith Ilmarinen
O everlasting craftsman
have you made the new Sampo
    brightened the bright-lid?'

The smith Ilmarinen said
the maker himself chattered:
'The new Sampo's been grinding
    the bright-lid rocking;
ground a binful at twilight—
    one binful to eat
another it ground to sell
and a third to store away.'

11. *A Bond Made*

'Tis time to tell of Ahti
and to lilt about a rogue.
Ahti the Islander boy
he, the wanton Loverboy
grew up in a lofty home
    with his dear mother
at the broadest bay's far end
underneath Far Headland's arm.
On fish there Farmind grew up
and on perch Ahti came up
became a man of the best
a red-blooded one burst forth
    who has a good head
    and can hold his own;
but he went a little wrong
and rascally in his ways:
he kept going with women
    staying out all night
making merry with lasses
capering with braided heads.

Kylli was an Island maid
an Island maid, Island flower
who grew in a lofty home
came up in one most graceful
sitting in her father's rooms
    where the back bench sagged.
Long she grew up, far was famed:
    from far suitors came
    to the maid's famous
    home, to her fair farm.
The sun wooed her for his son

but she'd not go to Sunland
    to shine with the sun
    in the summer rush.
The moon wooed her for his son
but she'd not go to Moonland
    to gleam with the moon
    to go the sky's rounds.
A star wooed her for his son
but she'd not go to Starland
    to twinkle night-long
    in the winter skies.
From Estonia bridegrooms came
others from Ingria yonder
but she'd not go there either
    and she answered back:
'In vain is your gold used up
    your silver worn thin!
I'll not go to Estonia
I'll not go, nor pledge myself
to row Estonian water
    punt between islands
    eat Estonian fish
    gulp Estonian broth.
Nor will I go to Ingria
    to its banks and braes:
there is lack, lack of all things—
lack of trees and lack of splints*
lack of water, lack of wheat
    and lack of rye bread.'

Well, wanton Lemminkäinen
    he, the fair Farmind
    promised he would go
off to woo the Island flower
    that especial bride
the beautiful braided head.
His mother tried to forbid
    the old woman warned:

'Do not go, my boy
    among your betters!
You will not be accepted
among the Island's great kin.'

Wanton Lemminkäinen said
    fair Farmind uttered:
'Though my home is not handsome
    and my kin not great
I will choose with my body
take with my other good looks.'

And still his mother forbids
Lemminkäinen to go off
among the Island's great kin
and its mighty families:
'There the wenches will taunt you
the women will laugh at you.'

What did Lemminkäinen care!
He put this in words: 'Be sure
I'll ward off women's laughter
and the giggles of daughters:
I'll kick a boy at the breast
    and a babe-in-arms;
that will stop even good taunts
    better insults too.'

His mother put this in words:
'Woe, luckless me, for my days!
If you disgraced the Island
women, used the pure wenches
a quarrel would come of it
and a great war would befall!
All of the Island's bridegrooms
a hundred men with their swords
would fall on you, luckless one
would surround you on your own.'

What did Lemminkäinen care
about his mother's warning!
He takes the good stallion, he
    harnessed the choice foal
    and he rumbles off
to the Island's famed village
off to woo the Island flower
the Island's especial bride.

The women laughed at Lemminkäinen
the wenches poked fun, for he
drove oddly along the lane
grimly into the farmyard:
he drove his sleigh till it tipped
at the gate rolled it over.
There wanton Lemminkäinen
twisted his mouth, turned his head
and twisted his black whiskers
and he put this into words:
'I have not seen that before
    I've not seen nor heard
a woman laughing at me
nor suffered a wench's taunts.'

What did Lemminkäinen care!
He uttered a word, spoke thus:
'Is there space on the Island
land on the Island's mainland
    for me to play games
ground for me to dance, to make
merry with Island lasses
and caper with braided heads?'

And the Island lassies say
and the headland maids answer:
'Yes, there's space on the Island

land on the Island's mainland
    for you to play games
    ground for you to dance—
clearings fit for a cowherd
burnt land fit for a herd-boy:
the Island children are lean
    but the foals are fat.'

What did Lemminkäinen care!
He got hired as a herdsman
spent the days herding, the nights
making merry with lasses
    sporting with those maids
capering with braided heads.
Thus wanton Lemminkäinen
    he, the fair Farmind
warded off woman's laughter
and held off a wench's taunts:
    there was no daughter
not even the purest wench
    he did not touch up
    did not lie down with.

One lass there was of them all
among the Island's great kin
who would not accept bridegrooms
    take to good husbands:
that was Kyllikki the proud
the Island's beautiful flower.
Well, wanton Lemminkäinen
    he, the fair Farmind
wore away a hundred boots
rowed a hundred oars in half
    going for that maid
    hunting Kyllikki.
    Kyllikki, proud maid
    put this into words:

'Why, wretch, do you rush about,
    plover, drive about
asking after the girls here
inquiring about tin-belts?
I cannot be spared from here
before I've ground the quern down
beaten the stamper away
pounded the mortar to bits.
Nor do I care for birdbrains—
for birdbrains, for scatterbrains:
I want a shapely body
for my own shapely body
I want one finer looking
    for my own fine looks
    and a fairer face
    for my own fair face.'

    A little time passed
barely half a month went by
till one day among others
one evening among many
    the maids are sporting
the beauties are capering
on the backwoods' mainland side
    upon the fair heath—
Kyllikki above the rest
the Island's most famous flower;
and the full-blooded rogue came
wanton Lemminkäinen drove
    with his own stallion
    with his chosen foal
into the midst of their sport
of the beauties' capers, snatched
Kyllikki into his sledge
grabbed the maid into his sleigh
    dumped her on his hide
    put her on his planks
    and he whipped the horse

thrashed it with the thong
then he glided off
saying as he goes:
'Lasses, don't ever
give the game away
that I have been here
have taken a maid from here!
If you do not heed
it will be the worse for you:
I'll sing your bridegrooms to war
your young men beneath the sword
so they'll be heard nevermore
nor seen ever in this world
walking in the lanes
driving in the glades.'

Truly Kyllikki complained
the Island's flower moaned:
'Let me go now, give
a child her freedom
to go home, back to
her weeping mother!
If you will not give
me leave to go home
my five brothers yet
my uncle's seven children
will track the hare down
will demand the maid's head back.'

When she could find no way out
she burst into tears
and uttered a word, spoke thus:
'In vain was I, luckless, born
in vain born, in vain I grew
in vain lived my time;
now I'm left with an idler
with a man of no account

sheltered by a warmonger
a harsh one always fighting!'

Wanton Lemminkäinen said
    fair Farmind uttered:
'Kyllikki, my heart's delight
my luscious little berry
    don't worry at all!
    I shan't ill-treat you—
you in my arms as I eat
you in my hands as I walk
you at my side as I stand
you beside me as I lie—
    so why do you grieve
why do you sigh full of care?
    Is this why you grieve
and why you sigh full of care—
that you'll have no cows, no bread,
everything in short supply?
    Don't worry at all!
    I have many cows
    many milk-givers—
one, Buttercup on the swamp
two, Strawberry on the hill
three, Cowberry* on burnt land.
They are fine without eating
fair without looking after;
there's no evening tethering
and no morning letting out
no tossing of a hay-bale
no worry for salt or feed.
Or else is this why you grieve
and why you sigh full of care—
that my kinsfolk are not great
my home not very lofty?
Though I am not great of kin
    nor lofty of home

I have a fiery sword, a
    sparkling iron brand.
    This is great kin, this
is a mighty family—
one refined among demons
    polished among gods;
and thus I make my kin great
    all my kind mighty—
with a sword of fiery blade
    with a sparkling brand.'

    The hapless maid sighs
and she put this into words:
    'Ahti, Loverboy
if you want a maid like me
for an everlasting mate
for a hen under your arm
you, swear an oath for ever
that you will not go to war—
not even for need of gold
even for greed of silver.

There wanton Lemminkäinen
    put this into words:
'I swear an oath for ever
that I shall not go to war—
not even for need for gold
even for greed of silver.
    Now you, swear your oath
that you'll not go visiting—
not for greed of a good hop
even, for need of a dance!'

Thereupon they swore their oaths
made their pledges for ever
before the God known to all*
beneath the Almighty's face:
Ahti would not go to war

nor Kyllikki visiting.
Then wanton Lemminkäinen
    lashed the courser on
beat the stallion with the rein
and he put this into words:
    'Farewell, Island turfs
    spruce roots, tarry stumps
where I have walked in summer
    tramped all the winters
lurking upon cloudy nights
and fleeing in bad weather
as I was hunting this grouse
    chasing this calloo!'

    He canters away;
    soon his home appears.
The maid put this into words
    she declared, spoke thus:
'A cabin is looming there
a lean hovel's appearing.
    Whose is that cabin
whose is that ne'er-do-well's home?'

The wanton Lemminkäinen
uttered a word and spoke thus:
'Don't you grieve about cabins
    don't sigh about huts!
Other cabins will be built
better ones will be put up
from massive standing timber
    the best timberland.'

Then wanton Lemminkäinen
    quickly arrives home
    to his dear mother
beside his honoured parent.
His mother put this in words
    she declared, spoke thus:

'You have lingered long, my boy
    long in foreign lands.'

Wanton Lemminkäinen said
uttered a word and spoke thus:
'I had to disgrace the wives
and pay the pure wenches back
because they kept taunting me
    kept laughing at me.
I got the best in my sleigh
    dumped her on my hide
    put her on my planks
and under the rug rolled her.
Thus I paid the wives' laughter
and the wenches' mockery.
O my mother who bore me
my mamma who brought me up
what I set out for I got
and what I hunted I found:
lay now your best mattresses
    your softest pillows
for me in my own land to
    lie with my young maid!'

His mother put this in words
    she declared, chattered:
    'Be now praised, O God,
extolled, Creator, alone
for giving me a daughter-in-law
bringing a good fire-blower
an excellent cloth-weaver
a most capable spinner
a superb washerwoman
    and bleacher of clothes!
    And you, praise your luck:
good you got and good you found
good your Creator promised
good the merciful one gave.

Pure is the bunting on snow—
purer is the one you have;
white on the sea is the froth—
whiter is the one you hold;
fair on the sea is the duck—
fairer is the one you keep;
bright is the star in the sky—
brighter is the one you wed.
Prepare now floors that are wide
fetch windows that are bigger
raise walls that are new, and build
a whole cabin that's better
thresholds before the cabin
and new doors at the threshold
since you have got a young maid
and have looked out a fair one
  better than yourself
  greater than your kin!'

12. *A Bond Broken*

Then Ahti Lemminkäinen
he, the fair faraway man
    carried on living
    with the young maiden
and he did not go to war
nor Kyllikki visiting.
So, one day among others
one morrow among many
he, Ahti Lemminkäinen
goes off to catch fish spawning;
did not come home at evening
for the first night could not. Now
Kyllikki went visiting
    to sport with those maids.

Who is it carries the news
who is a tell-tale? Ahti
has a sister, Annikki;
she it is carries the news
    she is the tell-tale:
'Darling Ahti my brother!
Kyllikki's been visiting
    within foreign gates
sporting with the village maids
capering with braided heads.'

Ahti boy, the matchless boy
he, wanton Lemminkäinen
at that was angry, was wroth
    and was long furious;
and he put this into words:
'O my mother, old woman!

If you were to wash my shirt
    in black snake poison
and were quickly to dry it
    I could go to war
to the fires of the North's sons
the grounds of Lapland's children:
Kyllikki's been visiting
    within foreign gates
    sporting with those maids
capering with braided heads.'

And truly Kyllikki says
his wife hastens first to say:
    'My darling Ahti
    don't go off to war!
    I dreamed as I lay
    as I soundly slept:
fire as a forge was driving
    flame was flickering
right underneath the window
by the bank at the back wall;
    from there it swirled in
    as a rapid roared
    from floorboards to roof
    window to window.'

There wanton Lemminkäinen
    put this into words:
'I don't believe women's dreams
    nor the oaths of wives.
O my mother who bore me
    bring here my war-gear
carry here my battledress!
    I have a good mind
to go drink the beer of war
to taste the honey of war.'

His mother put this in words:
    'O Ahti my boy
    don't go off to war!
    We have beer at home
    in an alder keg
    behind an oak bung;
I will bring you some to drink
though you were to drink all day.'

Wanton Lemminkäinen said:
'I don't care for home beer! I'd
sooner drink river water
off a tarry paddle's blade:
that's sweeter for me to drink
    than all the home brews.
    Bring here my war-gear
carry here my battledress!
I'm off to Northland's cabins
the grounds of Lapland's children
    to lay claim to gold
    to demand silver.'

Lemminkäinen's mother said:
    'Oh, Ahti my boy!
    There is gold at home
    silver in our shed.
    Only yesterday
quite early in the morning
a serf ploughed a viper-field
turned over one full of snakes;
the plough lifted a chest lid
its back end raised a penny:
inside hundreds had been stacked
    thousands had been crammed.
I lugged the chest to the shed
put it up in the shed loft.'

Wanton Lemminkäinen said:
'I don't care about home wealth!

If I get one mark from war
I'll regard it as better
    than all the home gold
silver lifted by a plough.
    Bring here my war-gear
carry here my battledress!
I'm off to a Northland war
a fight with Lapland's children.
    I have a good mind
    take into my head
    to hear with my ears
and see with these eyes of mine
if there's a maid in Northland
    a wench in Darkland
who will not accept bridegrooms
    take to good husbands.'

Lemminkäinen's mother said:
    'Oh, Ahti my boy!
You have Kyllikki at home
a home-wife who's loftier.
It is grim to have two wives
    in one husband's bed.'

Wanton Lemminkäinen said:
'Kyllikki's a gadabout:
let her run in every sport
lie in every room, making
merry with village lasses
capering with braided heads!'

His mother tried to forbid
    the old woman warned:
    'Just don't, my offspring
don't go to Northland's cabins
unless you are wise in words
unless you can work wisdom
to the fires of the North's sons

the grounds of Lapland's children!
There a Lapp will sing,* a man
of Turja will shove your face
into coal, head into clay
and into dust your forearms
your fists into hot ashes
    and burning boulders.'

Lemminkäinen says: 'Witches
have already bewitched me
witches bewitched, vipers cursed:
three Lapps had a go at me
    in one summer night
naked upon an outcrop
    without belt or clothes
    without a stitch on;
    but they gained from me
and the mean ones got as good
as an axe gets from a rock
and an auger from a cliff
and a pick from an ice-sheet
Death from an empty cabin.
    Things looked grim one way
but they turned out differently.
They wanted to put me, they
    threatened to sink me
for a causeway upon swamps
boards upon dirty places
to put my chin into slime
my beard into a bad spot.
    But I, such a man
did not greatly fret at that;
I became a soothsayer
I turned reciter: I sang
the witches with their arrows
the shooters with their weapons
the wizards with their iron
knives, the wise men with their steels

into Tuoni's steep rapid
into the frightful eddy
down the highest waterfall
down into the worst whirlpool.
There let the witches sleep, there
    let the envious lie
    until the grass grows
through the head, through the helmet
through a witch's shoulderblades
cleaving the shoulder flesh off
    a witch where he lies
an envious man where he sleeps!'

    Still his mother banned
Lemminkäinen from going;
the mother forbade her son
and the woman banned her man:
    'Just don't go at all
yonder to the cold village
    into dark Northland!
Ruin at least will come, ruin
to the worthy boy, downfall
to wanton Lemminkäinen.
Say it with a hundred mouths
but I'll still not believe you:
there is no singer in you
to match the sons of the North
nor do you know Turja's tongue*
and you cannot speak Lappish.'

Then wanton Lemminkäinen
    he, the fair Farmind
    was combing his head
    and brushing his hair.
He flung the comb at the wall
the brush he hurled at the post
he uttered a word, spoke thus
    he declared, chattered:

'That will be Lemminkäinen's
downfall, the worthy boy's ruin
when the comb is pouring blood
and the brush is babbling gore.'

Wanton Lemminkäinen went
    off to dark Northland
although his mother forbade
    and his parent warned.
    He bolts up, belts up
    puts on iron shirts
    buckles on steel belts
and he put this into words:
'In armour a man's tougher
in an iron shirt better
in a steel belt more powerful
among those witches, so he
does not care about worse ones
fret about good ones even.'

    He took his own sword
    snatched his fiery blade
refined among the demons
    ground among the gods;
    to his side binds it
thrust it into the scabbard.
Where does the man guard himself
the harsh fellow shield himself?
Now he guards himself a bit
there the harsh one shields himself—
at the door beneath the beam
by the doorpost of the hut
in the yard where the lane ends
and within the furthest gates.
There the man guarded himself
    against womenfolk;
but that guard was not strong, nor
was the refuge trustworthy

so he further guards himself
    against the menfolk
    where two ways parted
on the back of a blue rock
    upon moving mires
    upon spilling springs
a rapid's steep waterfall
a swirl of mighty water.
There wanton Lemminkäinen
    declared, recited:
'Up out of the earth, swordsmen
fellows as old as the soil
out of the wells, brand-bearers
out of the rivers, bowmen!
Rise up, forest, with your men
    all wilds with your folk
old mountain-men with your power
water-demon with your ghouls
with your force, water-mistress
water's eldest with your host
maidens out of every marsh
fine-hemmed ones out of the mires
to help the man without match
to be with the famous boy
so witch-arrows do not work
    nor a wise man's steels
nor a wizard's iron knives
    no shooter's weapons!

'Should not enough come of that
I recall another way:
    higher I will sigh
to that Old Man of the sky
    him who keeps the clouds
    governs the vapours.
    O Old Man, chief god
    old father in heaven

who speak through the clouds
declare down the air:
bring for me a fiery sword
in a fiery sheath
with which I will shatter bars
snatch away jinxes
overturn the earth-envious
defeat the water-wizards
out in front of me
to the rear of me
above my head, to my side
on both my flanks; I will stick
witches upon their arrows
wizards on their iron knives
wise men on their steels
evil men upon their swords!'

Then wanton Lemminkäinen
he, the fair Farmind, whistled
his foal out of the thicket
from withered grass his gold-mane
slipped the foal into harness
between shafts the fiery-red
and he sat down in the sledge
rushed into his sleigh
and lashed the courser
goaded with the pebble-tipped.
Courser ran and journey sped
the sledge rolled, the road shortened
the silver sand rang
the golden heath boomed.
He went one day, he went two
soon he went a third as well
till on the third day
he comes upon a village.
Then wanton Lemminkäinen
rumbles on his way

along the outermost road
up to the outermost house.
Over the threshold he asks
spoke from beyond the rooftree:
'Might there be one in this house
who will take off my breast-straps
    will let down my shafts
unfasten the collar-bow?'

A child declared from the floor
a boy from the staircase end:
'There is no one in this house
who will take off your breast-straps
    will let down your shafts
unfasten the collar-bow.'

What did Lemminkäinen care!
    He lashed the courser
whacked it with the beaded belt;
    he rumbles away
along the middlemost road
up to the middlemost house.
Over the threshold he asks
speaks out from beyond the roof:
'Might there be one in this house
    who will take the reins
    tear off the breast-straps
    pull off the traces?'

A hag ranted from the hearth
a gossip from the stove seat:
'Yes, you'll get some in this house
    who will take your reins
    take off your breast-straps
    and let down your shafts;
    yes, there are dozens
you'll get (if you want) hundreds
    who'll give you a lift:

they will supply a draft horse
to go, scoundrel, to your home
to flee, villain, to your land
    where your master sits
    where your mistress steps
    your brother's gateway
    your sister's floor end
    before the day's out
    and the sun goes down!'

What did Lemminkäinen care!
He uttered a word, spoke thus:
    'The hag should be shot
    the hook-chin clobbered.'
He gave the courser its head;
    he swishes away
along the uppermost road
up to the uppermost house.
There wanton Lemminkäinen
as he approaches the house
    he says with this word
    he spoke with this speech:
'Demon, block the barker's mouth
and Devil, the dog's jawbone;
set a block before its mouth
and a gag between its teeth
so it makes no sound before
    the man has gone by!'

    So, reaching the yard
he smites the earth with his whip:
a mist rose from the whip's path
a little man in the mist;
'twas he took off the breast-straps
'twas he who let down the shafts.
Then wanton Lemminkäinen
    listens with his ears
with nobody spotting him

with no one noticing him:
from outside he heard poems
    through the moss heard words
    through the wall players
and through the shutter singers.
    He glanced in from there
    he peeped furtively:
the cabin was full of clever men
the benches full of singers
the side walls full of players
the doorway of cunning men
the back bench full of wise men
the inglenook of crooners;
they sang poems of Lapland
and a Demon-tale they squealed.

Then wanton Lemminkäinen
dared to become someone else
he made bold to change his shape;
from the corner he went in
got inside from the wall joint
and he put this into words:
'A song is good when it ends
when 'tis short a tale is fair;
it makes better sense to stay
than break off in the middle.'

She, the mistress of Northland
shifted at the floor seam, paced
in the middle of the floor
and uttered a word, spoke thus:
'There used to be a dog here
    a cur iron-hued
that ate the flesh, gnawed the bones
lapped the blood of someone new.
What kind of man may you be
what sort of fellow are you—
coming into this cabin

getting inside the building
without the dog hearing you
or the barker noticing?'

Wanton Lemminkäinen said:
'I've certainly not come here
without my skill, my wisdom
without my might, my knowledge
without my father's magic
and my parent's protection
to be eaten by your dogs
    chopped up by barkers.
    My mother washed me
washed me as a little sprout
three times in a summer night
nine times in an autumn night
to be wise on every road
and knowing in every land
to be a singer at home
and a cunning man abroad.'

Then wanton Lemminkäinen
    he, the fair Farmind
now became a soothsayer
and turned into a singer:
    his coat hems struck fire
    and his eyes poured flame
as Lemminkäinen sang, as
    he sang and chanted.
He sang the best of singers
into the worst of singers;
rammed rocks sideways in the mouths
piled boulders sidelong in those
    of the best singers
    the most skilful bards.
    So he sang such men
    one this way, one that—
    into barren glades

    upon unploughed lands
    into fishless pools
    ones quite without perch
into Rutja's* steep rapid
into the smoking whirlpool
to be froth-crests in the stream
and rocks amid the rapid
    to smoulder as fire
    and to shoot as sparks.
Wanton Lemminkäinen sang
the men thither with their swords
the fellows with their weapons;
he sang the young, sang the old
    sang the middle-aged;
    one he left unsung—
    a paltry herdsman
an old man, old and sightless.
    Dripcap* the herdsman
    put this into words:
'O you wanton Loverboy
you've sung the young, sung the old
    sung the middle-aged—
so why will you not sing me?'

Wanton Lemminkäinen said:
'This is why I'll not touch you:
you are mean to look upon
wretched without my touching.
    Still a younger man
    a paltry herdsman
you spoilt her your mother bore
    you raped your sister;
all the horses you abused
and the mare's foals you wore out
on open swamps, amid lands
upon shifting water-scum.'

    Dripcap the herdsman
at that was angry, furious

and he went out through the door
to the field across the yard
ran to Tuonela's river
to the holy stream's whirlpool.
There he looked out for Farmind
he waits for Lemminkäinen
on his return from Northland
    on his journey home.

13. *The Demon's Elk*

Then wanton Lemminkäinen
said to the hag of Northland:
'Hag, now give of your wenches
bring one of your girls this way
the best of the flock for me
the tallest of your wench-brood!'

Well, that mistress of Northland
uttered a word and spoke thus:
'I'll not give of my wenches
bestow any of my girls—
not the best, not the worst, not
the tallest, not the shortest
for you have a wedded wife
    a married mistress.'

Wanton Lemminkäinen said:
'I'll tie Kyllikki outside
to the village threshold steps
to foreign gates, and from here
I will get a better wife.
Now bring your daughter this way
loveliest of the lass-flock
fairest of the braided heads!'

The mistress of Northland said:
'No, I'll not give my girl to
    men of no account
    to idle fellows.
    Only beg for girls
ask after flower-heads when you
have skied for the Demon's elk
from the Demon's furthest fields!'

Then wanton Lemminkäinen
    put tips on his spears
    strung up his crossbows
    and stocked up his bolts
and he put this into words:
    'The spear may be tipped
    all the bolts ready
    the crossbow strung up
but I've no left ski* to push
no right for the heel to smite.'

There wanton Lemminkäinen
    thinks and considers
where he might get snowshoes from
    anything like skis.
He went to Kauppi's farm, he
stopped at Lyylikki's workshop:
    'O shrewd northerner
    fair Kauppi the Lapp:
    make me useful skis
groove handsome ones, right and left
to ski for the Demon's elk
from the Demon's furthest fields!'

And Lyylikki says a word
    Kauppi finds his tongue:
'Vainly, Lemminkäinen, you
go hunting the Demon's elk:
'tis a scrap of rotten wood
you'll get, and that with great grief.'

What did Lemminkäinen care!
And he put this into words:
'Make me a left ski to push
    a right ski to scoot!
I'm off to ski for the elk
from the Demon's furthest fields.'

Lyylikki, smith of left skis
Kauppi, maker of right skis
all autumn shaped a left ski
all winter grooved a right ski
all day he cut a pole shaft
all next put on a snow-disc.
The left ski was fit to push
the right for the heel to smite
and the pole shafts were ready
and the snow-discs were put on;
the pole shaft cost an otter
and the snow-disc a brown fox.
With butter he smeared his skis
greased them with reindeer tallow
    and at that he thinks
    he says with this word:
'Might there among these youngsters
among the folk growing be
someone to push this left ski
of mine, to heel-kick the right?'

Wanton Lemminkäinen said
the full-blooded rogue uttered:
'Indeed among these youngsters
among the folk growing there's
someone to push this left ski
of yours, to heel-kick the right.'

The quiver upon his back
he tied, shouldered the new bow
grasped the pole shaft in his hand;
he went to push the left ski
    to heel-kick the right
and he put this into words:
    'Surely in God's world
beneath the lid of this sky
there's nothing in the forest
    running on four feet

that is not overtaken
handsomely carried off, with
these skis of Kaleva's son
with Lemminkäinen's sliders.'

The demons happened to hear
the judases to take note
and the demons built an elk
the judases a reindeer:
they make a head from a block
antlers from goat willow forks
    feet from driftwood, legs
    from stakes in a swamp
    a back from fence poles
sinews from withered grasses
eyes out of pond lily buds
ears out of pond lily flowers
    skin out of spruce bark
other flesh from rotten wood.
The Demon advised his elk
to his reindeer spoke by mouth:
'Now run, you elk of demons
    foot it, noble deer
to where the reindeer breeds, to
the grounds of Lapland's children!
Make a man ski till he sweats—
Lemminkäinen most of all!'

At that the demons' elk ran
the wild reindeer trotted off
below the North's sheds and through
the grounds of Lapland's children:
it kicked over a cook-house
tub, knocked the pans off the fire
spoilt the meat in the cinders
spilt broth over the fireplace.
    Quite a din rose on

the grounds of Lapland's children—
    Lapland's dogs barking
and Lapland's children crying
and Lapland's women laughing
and other people grumbling!

He, wanton Lemminkäinen
kept skiing after the elk:
he skied on swamps, skied on lands
he skied upon open glades;
    fire swished from the skis
smoke from the tips of the poles
but he did not see his elk
neither saw it nor heard it.
He slid through one town, through twain
slid through lands beyond the sea
skied through all the Demon's woods
all the heaths of the grave too
skied before the mouth of Death
behind the farm of the grave:
    Death opens its mouth
    the grave tilts its head
    to take the fellow
to swallow Lemminkäinen;
but it did not score a hit
was not nearly quick enough.
A strip was yet unslid through
a nook of the wilds untouched
    in the furthest North
    in open Lapland:
he went sliding through that too
touching that nook of the wilds.
    Now, when he arrived
    he heard quite a din
    from the furthest North
the grounds of Lapland's children:
    he heard dogs barking
and Lapland's children crying

and Lapland's women laughing
and the other Lapps grumbling.
Then wanton Lemminkäinen
    went skiing straight off
to where the dogs were barking
the grounds of Lapland's children
and he said when he got there
    inquired when he came:
'Why did the women here laugh
women laugh and children cry
    the old people groan
what did the grey dogs bark at?'

'For this the women here laughed
women laughed and children cried
    the old people groaned
and for this the grey dogs barked:
the demons' elk ran this way
    the smooth-hoof galloped;
it kicked over a cook-house
tub, knocked the pans off the fire
it tipped the stew upside down
spilt gruel in the fireplace.'

At that the full-blooded rogue
that wanton Lemminkäinen
pushed his left ski on the snow
like a viper in the grass
made the swamp-pine one slither
    like a snake alive;
he uttered as he careered
    said with pole in hand:
'What men there be in Lapland
all shall carry off the elk
and what women in Lapland
    all shall wash a pan
and what children in Lapland
    all shall gather wood

and what pans a Lapp may have
    all shall cook the elk!'

He made fast, he braced himself
he kicked off, he tensed himself.
    The first time, he kicked
to where no eye could spot him;
    the next time, he thrust
to where no ear could hear him;
    the third, he jumps on
the rump of the demons' elk.
He took a maple tether
he snatched a birch withe, with which
he tied up the demons' elk
    inside an oak pen:
    'Stay there, demons' elk
    wild reindeer, trot there!'
    And he strokes its back
    and he pats its hide:
'This is just the place for me
just the right place to lie down
    beside a young maid
    with a growing hen!'

Then the Demon's elk, the wild
reindeer kicked out in alarm
and it uttered, this it says:
'May the Devil help you to
    lie down with young maids
    dally with daughters!'
It braced itself, tensed itself:
    the birch withe it tore
it snapped the maple tether
    the oak pen it smashed;
    then it scuttled off
    the elk skipped away
towards swamps and towards lands
    to a scrubby hill

to where no eye could spot it
to where no ear could hear it.

At that the full-blooded rogue
    was angry and wroth
sorely angry and furious:
he skied off after the elk
but with one kick the left ski
    buckled at the toe
the ski gave at the foot plate
the right ski snapped by the heel
    the spear at the tip
the pole at the snow-disc joint—
and the Demon's elk ran off
till its head could not be seen.
There wanton Lemminkäinen
his head down, in bad spirits
    gazes at his things
and he put this into words:
    'Never, nevermore
may another of our men
    go hunting rashly
skiing for the Demon's elk
    as I, luckless, went!
I have destroyed good snowshoes
and a fair pole I have lost
and the sharpest of my spears!'

14. *Elk, Horse, Swan*

Then wanton Lemminkäinen
    thought and considered
which path he should press upon
which trail he should go along:
should he leave the Demon's elks
    and make his way home
or should he keep on trying
    skiing at his ease
to please the forest mistress
gladden the backwoods lasses?
    He says with this word
    he spoke with this speech:
    'O Old Man, chief god—
that is, heavenly father:
    make me now straight skis
    light ones, left and right
on which I may ski along
across swamps and across lands
ski towards the Demon's lands
across the heaths of the North
to where the Demon's elk roams
the wild reindeer's stamping-grounds!

'I go from men forestward
from fellows to outdoor work
along Tapiola's roads
and through Tapio's houses.
    Hail, mountains, hail, slopes
    hail, soughing spruces
    hail, grizzled aspens
    hail one who hails you!
Be kind, forest, soften, wilds
and bend, precious Tapio;

bring a man to the islet
    lead him to that mound
where a catch is to be made
and a prey-task carried out!
Nyyrikki, Tapio's son
clear-skinned man, red-helmeted:
carve notches along the lands
blaze a trail upon the slopes
that this fool may feel the way
this utter stranger may know
    the road as I seek
    prey and beg for game!
Mielikki, forest mistress
clear-skinned crone, fair to look on:
    set gold in motion
    silver wandering
in front of the man seeking
in the steps of one who begs;
    take golden keys from
    the ring at your thigh
and open Tapio's shed
and shift the forest stronghold
on the days of my hunting
at the times of my prey-search!
Should you not care to yourself
    then force your wenches
    put in your hirelings
order those who take orders!
Surely you are no mistress
if you do not keep a wench
not keep a hundred wenches
a thousand order-takers
guardians of all your stock
cherishers of all your wealth.
    Tiny forest wench
mead-mouthed maid of Tapio:
play a honey-sweet whistle
on a mead-sweet whistle pipe

in the ear of the kindly
the pleasant forest mistress
    that she may hear soon
    and rise from her bed
for she does not hear at all
    hardly ever wakes
    though I keep begging
with golden tongue beseeching!'

Then wanton Lemminkäinen
    all the time gameless
skied on swamps and skied on lands
    skied through the hard wilds
    on God's hills of coal
the Demon's heaths of charcoal.
He skied one day, he skied two
    till on the third day
    he climbed a great hill
    rose on a great rock
    cast his eyes north-west
    across swamps northward:
Tapio's houses appeared
    and the doors gleamed gold
from across a swamp northward
from under a slope, from scrub.
That wanton Lemminkäinen
    straight away went up
    came near and approached
below Tapio's window.
    He crouched down to look
    through the sixth window:
    there the givers dwelt
    and the wealth-dames lolled
    in plain working-clothes
    in dirty tatters.
Wanton Lemminkäinen said:
'Why, forest mistess, do you
    dwell in working-clothes

in kiln-rags wallow
quite black to look on
of appearance grim
wicked of aspect
your frame ugly to behold?
When I walked through the forest
there were three strongholds—
one of wood and one of bone
and the third a stone stronghold;
six golden windows
were at each stronghold's corner.
I peered in through them
as I stood below the wall:
the master and the mistress
of Tapio's house
Tellervo, Tapio's maid
and Tapio's other folk
with them were swarming in gold
sauntering all in silver.
The forest mistress herself
the kindly forest mistress
had her hands in gold bracelets
fingers in gold rings
head adorned with gold
her hair coiled with gold
ears dangling with gold
her neck with good beads.
Sweet forest mistress
Forestland's honey-sweet crone:
cast off your hay shoes
shed your birchbark burning-shoes
take off your kiln-rags
drop your working-shirt;
dress in lucky clothes
put on shirts for game
on the days of my stalking
at the times of my prey-search!
I fill with boredom

fill up with boredom
in this idleness
at all this time without game
for at no time do you give
hardly ever look after.
Boring the joyless evening
long the day without a catch.

'Old forest greybeard
sprig-hatted, lichen-coated:
dress the forests in linens
clothe the backwoods in broadcloth
the aspens all in cloth coats
the alders in their best clothes;
in silver deck out the firs
set up the spruces in gold
the old firs in copper belts
and the pines in silver belts
the birches in golden flowers
the stumps in golden trinkets!
Dress them as of old
in your better days:
as the moon the spruce boughs shone
and as the sun the pine tops
the forest smelt of honey
and of mead the blue backwoods
the glade edges of wort, swamp
edges of melted butter.

'Forest girl, sweet maid
Tuulikki, daughter of Tapio:
drive the wealth towards the slopes
towards the most open glades!
If it be stiff in running
or lazy in galloping
take a lash from a thicket
a birch out of a wild dell
to tickle its loin

and prod its armpits!
Let it run swiftly
quickly dash along
in front of the man seeking
in the steps of one who plods!
When the wealth reaches the track
goad it up the track;
form with your two palms
a rail on two sides
lest the wealth swerve past
sheer away from the roadside!
But if the wealth does swerve past
sheer away from the roadside
guide it roadward by the ears
bring it by the horns trackward!
A trunk lies across the road:
well, push it aside;
trees on the ground in the way—
well, snap them in two.
It will come upon a fence:
knock the fence askew
leaving a gap five withes high
and seven stakes wide!
A river will lie in front
a brook flow across the road:
seize silk for a plank
red broadcloth for stepping-stones!
Bring it from across the straits
drag it across the waters
from across Northland's river
from over the rapid-foam!

'Master of Tapio's house
mistress of Tapio's house
old forest greybeard
golden forest king;
Mimerkki, forest mistress,

dear, game-giving forest crone
    blue-cloaked thicket dame
    red-socked swamp mistress:
    come now to change gold
    to trade with silver!
My gold is old as the moon
and the sun's age my silver
gained with defiance from war
    with threats from a fight;
but coins wear out in a purse
tarnish in a money-bag
when there's no one to change gold
    to trade with silver.'

So wanton Lemminkäinen
    long skied on his way
sang tales at a thicket top
sang three in a wild hollow:
he pleased the forest mistress
even the forest master
delighted all the lasses
and got round Tapio's maids.
    They chased, they hounded
the Demon's elk from its lair
behind Tapio's slope, the
bounds of the Demon's stronghold
in front of the man seeking
for the reciter to catch.
He, wanton Lemminkäinen
    let fly his lasso
at the Demon's elk's shoulders
the camel-colt's* neck, so that
it did not kick wickedly
    as he stroked its back;
then wanton Lemminkäinen
    put this into words:
'Lord of the woods, land master
fair one living on the heath;

Mielikki, forest mistress
dear, generous forest crone:
    come now, take the gold
    pick out the silver;
put your linen on the ground
your best hempen stuff spread out
underneath the gleaming gold
and the glittering silver
    without dropping it
    getting it dirty!'

Then he set out for Northland
and he said when he got there:
'I've skied for the Demon's elk
from the Demon's furthest fields:
    hag, give me your girl
    give me the young bride!'

Louhi, mistress of Northland
    this one answered that:
'I'll only give my daughter
    and the young bride, when
you've bridled the great gelding
    the Demon's bay horse
the Demon's foal whose jaw froths
from the Demon's furthest turfs.'

Then wanton Lemminkäinen
    took his golden reins
    a silver halter
sets off in search of the horse
to listen for the grass-mane
on the Demon's furthest turfs
    and he trips along
    whistles on his way
    to a green acre
    a holy field's edge:
    there he seeks the horse

listens for the grass-hued, the
yearling's bridle at his belt
shouldering the foal's harness.
He sought one day, he sought two
    till on the third day
    he climbed a great hill
clambered upon a rock's back;
he cast his eyes eastward, turned
his head to below the sun:
on the sand he saw the horse
the grass-mane among spruces
    and its hair flashed fire
    its mane billows smoke.
    Lemminkäinen says:
    'O Old Man, chief god
Old Man, keeper of the clouds
governor of the vapours:
    open heaven up
the sky all into windows;
    rain iron hailstones
    drop icy coolers
on the mane of the good horse
on the Demon's blaze-brow's flanks!'

That Old Man, high creator
    god above the clouds
rent the sky into a rage
    heaven's lid in half;
    he rained slush, rained ice
    he rained iron hail
smaller than a horse's head
but bigger than a man's head
on the mane of the good horse
on the Demon's blaze-brow's flanks.
Then wanton Lemminkäinen
went over to look at it
to inspect it from close by

and he put this into words:
'O good horse of Demonland
mountain foal of frothing jaw:
put now your golden muzzle
    slip your silver head
    into golden rings
    among silver bells!
I shall not treat you badly
    drive you all that hard:
I'll drive you a tiny bit
    but a little way
yonder to Northland's cabins
to a stern mother-in-law
and when I slap with a thong
    or smack with a lash
    I shall slap with silk
    smack with a cloth hem.'

    The Demon's bay horse
the Demon's foal whose jaw frothed
thrust then its golden muzzle
    slipped its silver head
    into golden rings
    among silver bells.
So wanton Lemminkäinen
now bridled the great gelding
bridled the golden one, put
the silver one's headstall on;
he leapt on the good one's back
on the Demon's blaze-brow's flanks.
    He lashed the courser
thrashed it with a willow switch
and he drove a little way
    cantered up a fell
up the north side of a hill
the top of a snowy slope
and came to Northland's cabins.

He went indoors from the yard
    said when he got there
    when he reached Northland:
'I've bridled the great gelding
the Demon's foal I've harnessed
    from a green acre
    a holy field's edge
and skied for the Demon's elk
from the Demon's furthest fields
so now, hag, give me your girl
    give me the young bride!'

Louhi, mistress of Northland
well, she put this into words:
'I'll only give my daughter
and the young bride when you have
shot the swan from the river
from the stream the splendid fowl
out of Tuoni's black river
from the holy stream's whirlpool
    at a single try
raising a single arrow.'

Then wanton Lemminkäinen
    he, the fair Farmind
went to the swan's whooping,* to
    look for the long-neck
out of Tuoni's black river
from the dale of the Dead Land
    and he swings along
    warbles on his way
towards Tuonela's river
to the holy stream's whirlpool
shouldering his great crossbow
a quiverful on his back.

    Dripcap the herdsman
the old blind man of Northland

is at Tuonela's river
at the holy stream's whirlpool
    looking, turning round
for Lemminkäinen's coming.
One day among others he
saw wanton Lemminkäinen
arriving and coming close
there at Tuonela's river
beside the furious rapid
at the holy stream's whirlpool
and he raised a water snake
a cowbane out of the waves
and hurled it through the man's heart
through Lemminkäinen's liver
    through his left armpit
into his right shoulderblade.

Now wanton Lemminkäinen
    felt a grievous pain.
He uttered a word, spoke thus:
'That was the worst thing I did
not remembering to ask
my mother, her who bore me
for two words by all accounts
(three would have been quite a lot)
how to be, which way to live
in these evil days: I don't
know the hurts of water snakes
    the stings of cowbane.
O my mother who bore me
pains-taker who cared for me!
If you knew, if you guessed where
    your luckless son is
of course you would come dashing
you would hasten to help me;
you would free your luckless son
from this road away from death

from falling asleep while young
rolling over full-blooded.'

Then the blind one of Northland
    Dripcap the herdsman
hurled wanton Lemminkäinen
lost the son of Kaleva
down in Tuoni's black river
    in the worst whirlpool:
wanton Lemminkäinen went—
went down the rapid roaring
with the current in a flash
towards Tuonela's cabins.
That bloody son of Tuoni
struck at the man with his sword
    bashed him with his brand
    with one flashing stroke
smote the man into five bits
into eight pieces, tossed him
into Tuonela's river
into the Dead Land's eddies:
    'Loll there for ever
with your crossbow, your arrows!
Shoot the swans on the river
the waterfowl on the banks!'

That was Lemminkäinen's end
the untiring suitor's death
down in Tuoni's black river
in the dale of the Dead Land.

15. *Resurrection*

The wanton Lemminkäinen's
mother at home keeps thinking:
'Where's Lemminkäinen got to
where has my Farmind vanished
that he is not heard coming
from his travels in the world?'
The luckless mother does not
nor the mean one who bore him
know where her flesh is moving
where her own blood is rolling
whether on a piny hill
    heathery heathland
or was he on the high seas
    on the froth-capped waves
    or in a great war
    a dreadful revolt
in which blood reaches the shin
    redness is knee-deep.

Kyllikki the handsome wife
looks about and turns about
in wanton Lemminkäinen's
home, on Farmind's farm. She looked
in the evening at his comb
on the morrow at his brush
and one day among others
one morrow among many
blood was leaking from the comb
gore was oozing from the brush.
Kyllikki the handsome wife
uttered a word and spoke thus:
'Now my man has gone from me
my fair Farmind has vanished

on travels without shelter
    and on unknown roads:
blood is leaking from the comb
gore is oozing from the brush!'

Then Lemminkäinen's mother
herself looks upon the comb
and she gave way to weeping:
'Woe, luckless me, for my days
afflicted one, for my times!
Now the son of luckless me
now, hapless me, my offspring
has come upon evil days!
Ruin to the worthy boy
downfall to wanton Lemminkäinen:
now the comb is pouring blood
and the brush is oozing gore!'

With her fists she grasped her hems
    with her arms her clothes
and soon she ran a long way
    she both ran and sped:
the hills thudded as she went
the marshes rose, the slopes sank
    the highlands came down
    the lowlands went up.
She came to Northland's cabins
    asked about her son—
    she asked and she spoke:
'You mistress of Northland, where
have you led Lemminkäinen
where have you dispatched my son?'

Louhi, mistress of Northland
    this one answered that:
'I know nothing of your son
where he has gone and vanished.
I sat him in a stallion's

sledge, a most fiery one's sleigh;
could he have drowned in slush, gone
    solid on sea ice
or got into the wolf's mouth
the jaws of the dreadful bear?'

Lemminkäinen's mother said:
    'Surely you have lied!
    No wolf eats my kin
no bear fells Lemminkäinen:
with his fingers he strangles
wolves, with his hands he fells bears.
Look, if you will not say where
you have led Lemminkäinen
I will smash the new kiln's door
and break the Sampo's hinges.'

The mistress of Northland said:
    'I fed the man full
    let him drink his fill
entertained him till he drooped;
I sat him in a boat's stern
sent him over the rapids.
But I cannot imagine
where the mean wretch has got to—
whether in foaming rapids
    or in swirling streams.'

Lemminkäinen's mother said:
    'Surely you have lied!
    Tell the truth with care
    and have done with lies
where you led Lemminkäinen
lost the Kalevala man
or else it will be your doom
    you will meet your death!'

The mistress of Northland said:
'Suppose now I tell the truth:
I set him to ski for elk
    flay the king of beasts*
    bridle great geldings
    and to harness foals;
I made him search for the swan
    hunt the holy fowl.
Now I cannot imagine
what has come by way of ruin
by way of hindrance turned up
that he is not heard coming
    to ask for a bride
    to beg for a girl.'

The mother sought the one gone
astray, for the lost she longs:
she ran great swamps as a wolf
trod the wilds as a bruin
waters as an otter roamed
lands she walked as a pismire
as a wasp headland edges
    as a hare lakeshores;
    rocks she shoved aside
    and stumps she tilted
moved dead boughs to the roadside
kicked dead trunks to form causeways.
Long she sought the one astray
long she sought, but does not find.
She asked trees about her son
    longed for her lost one;
a tree talked, a fir tree sighed
an oak skilfully answered:
'I have worries of my own
without worrying about your son
for I was formed for hardship
was put here for evil days—
to be chopped up for stacking

to be hewn down for faggots
to pine away for kiln-wood
to be felled for slash-and-burn.'

Long she sought the one astray
long she sought and does not find.
She comes upon a small road;
    to the road she bows:
'O small road, God's creature, have
    you not seen my son
    my apple of gold
    my staff of silver?'

The road skilfully answered
it both declared and chattered:
'I have worries of my own
without worrying about your son
for I was formed for hardship
was put here for evil days—
for every dog to run on
every horseman to ride on
every hard shoe to walk on
    every heel to scrape.'

Long she sought the one astray
long she sought, but does not find.
And she comes upon the moon;
    to the moon she bows:
'Darling moon, God's creature, have
    you not seen my son
    my apple of gold
    my staff of silver?'

    That moon, God's creature
skilfully enough answered:
'I have worries of my own
without worrying about your son
for I was formed for hardship

was put here for evil days—
to travel the nights alone
    to shine in the frost
to keep watch over winters
to vanish for the summer.'

Long she sought the one astray
long she sought and does not find.
And she comes upon the sun;
    to the sun she bows:
'O sun, creature of God, have
    you not seen my son
    my apple of gold
    my staff of silver?'

Well now, the sun knew something
    the daylight reckoned:
    'Your son, luckless you
    has been lost, been killed
down in Tuoni's black river
the Dead Land's ageless water—
gone through the rapids roaring
with the currents in a flash
towards furthest Tuonela
to the dales of the Dead Land.'

Then Lemminkäinen's mother
    she burst into tears.
She went to the smiths' workshop:
    'Smith Ilmarinen
you forged once, forged yesterday
    so forge today too:
    helve a copper rake
prong it with prongs of iron;
forge prongs a hundred fathoms
long, prepare a helve of five!'

Smith Ilmarinen
the everlasting craftsman
helved a copper rake
pronged it with prongs of iron;
forged prongs a hundred fathoms
long, prepared a helve of five.
She, Lemminkäinen's mother
gets the iron rake
flew to Tuonela's river.
She prays to the sun:
'O sun, God's creature, creature
of the Creator, our light:
shine for one moment sultry
for the next dimly swelter
for a third with all your might;
put the weary folk to sleep
tire the force of the Dead Land
wear down the host of Tuoni!'

That sun, God's creature, creature
of the Creator, daylight
flew on to a birch tree's crook
to an alder's warp it flapped:
it shone one moment sultry
for the next dimly sweltered
for a third with all its might
put the weary folk to sleep
tired the force of the Dead Land—
the young men upon their swords
and the old against their sticks
the middle-aged on their spears.
Then it slunk away
to the top of level heaven
to where it had been before
its former abode.

Then Lemminkäinen's mother
took the iron rake;
she rakes for her son

amid the roaring rapid
    in the flashing stream:
she rakes and she does not find.
Then she shifted further down—
went all the way to the sea
in slush to her stocking-top
in water up to her waist.
    She rakes for her son
along Tuonela's river
she dredges against the stream.
She dragged once, and for that twice:
all she gets of her son is
a shirt, much to her distress;
    she dragged once again:
got his stockings, hat she found—
the stockings to her great grief
hat to her dismay. From there
she stepped even further down
to the dale of the Dead Land
dragged once along the water
next time across the water
a third athwart the water;
and it was the third time that
a mass of entrails came forth
    on the iron rake.

Mass of entrails it was not
but wanton Lemminkäinen
    he, the fair Farmind
    stuck on the rake's prongs
    by his ring finger
    and by his left toe.
Wanton Lemminkäinen rose
and Kaleva's son came up
    on the copper rake
on top of the clear waters;
but there was a bit missing—

one hand, half his head
a lot of other
scraps, and breath as well.
There his mother thinks
and weeping she says:
'Could a man still come from this
a new fellow recover?'

A raven happened to hear
and this answers that:
'There is no man in one gone
in one come to grief: by now
whitefish have eaten his eyes
a pike has split his shoulders.
Let the man go in the sea
push him into Tuonela's river!
Perhaps he'll become a cod
do well as a whale.'

That Lemminkäinen's mother
will not push her son.
She dredges once more
with the copper rake
along Tuonela's river
both along it and across:
she gets some hand, gets some head
she gets half of a back bone
the other half of a rib
and many other scraps, built
from them some of a son, worked
on wanton Lemminkäinen
joining flesh to flesh
bones to bones fitting
and limbs to their limbs
sinews to sinew fractures.
She bound up sinews
knitted up ends of sinews
the yarn of sinew she tells

over, saying with this word:
'Sweet woman of the sinews
Sinew-daughter, sweet woman
comely spinner of sinews
    with the sweet spindle
    the copper distaff
    and the iron wheel:
come here when you are needed
walk this way when you are called
a bundle of sinews in your arms
a ball of membranes under your arm
    to bind up sinews
    knit up sinew-ends
in the wounds that are cloven
in the gashes that are torn!

'Should not enough come of that
there's a lass upon the air
    in a copper boat
    in a red-sterned craft:
    come, lass, off the air
    maid, from heaven's pole
row the boat down the sinews
    shake it down the limbs
    row through gaps in bone
    and through cracks in limbs!
Put the sinews in their place
and set them in their setting—
face to face the big sinews
the arteries eye to eye
overlapping set the veins
the small sinews end to end!
Then take up a fine needle
threaded with a silken thread:
    sew with fine needles
    with tin needles stitch
    knit up sinew-ends
with silken ribbons bind them!

'Should not enough come of that
you yourself, god of the sky
    harness up your foals
    make ready your steeds!
    Drive with your bright sleigh
    through bone and through limb
    through muscles and through
    slippery sinews!
    Join bone up to flesh
sinew up to sinew-end
    silver the bone-gap
and gild the sinew fracture!
Where a membrane is broken
    make the membrane grow
where a sinew is fractured
    knit up the sinew
where the blood has spilt over
    make the blood roll on
    where bone has gone soft
    fit some bone in there
    where some flesh is loose
    join flesh together
and bless it into its place
and set it in its setting—
bone to bone and flesh to flesh
    and limbs to their limbs!'

Thus Lemminkäinen's mother
made the man, formed the fellow
with the life he had before
with the looks he used to have;
she had the sinews all told
    the sinew-ends bound
but had not the man talking
    not the child speaking.
Then she put this into words
    she declared, spoke thus:
'Where now may ointment be got

a drop of mead brought
to anoint the weary one
to tend the ill-befallen
that the man may find his words
return to his tales?
O bee, bird of ours
king of forest flowers:
go now to fetch some honey
and to find some mead
out of pleasant Forestland
from careful Tapiola
from many flower petals, from
the husks of many grasses
to be ointments for the sick
and to heal the ill!'

The bee, a brisk bird
forthwith wafted off
into pleasant Forestland
to careful Tapiola:
it pecked flowers upon a lea
cooked honey upon its tongue
from six flower tips, from
a hundred grass-husks.
So it comes panting
travels doubled up
all its wings drenched in mead, its
feathers in melted honey.
She, Lemminkäinen's mother
took up those ointments, with them
anointed the weary one
tended the ill-befallen;
but no help came from them, no
words came to the man.
Then she put this into words:
'Bee, my little bird
fly that other way
right over nine seas

to an island on the main
  a honeyed mainland
  to Thor's new cabin*
the Worshipful's boundless one!
There is pleasant honey there
  and good ointment there
  which will suit sinews
  and be good for limbs
so bring some of those ointments
bear some of those remedies
for me to put on the hurt
to pour on the injuries!'

  The bee, a slight man
  again flitted off
  right over nine seas
  half a tenth sea too:
it flew one day, it flew two
soon it flew a third as well
without sitting on a reed
without perching on a leaf
to the island on the main
  the honeyed mainland
to a fiery rapid's brink
to a holy stream's whirlpool.
There honey was being cooked
salves were being made ready
  in tiny cauldrons
  in beautiful pans
  that would hold a thumb
  fit a fingertip.
  The bee, slight man, got
  some of those ointments.
  A short time passes
  a moment speeds by:
  now it comes buzzing
  hither and thither
  six cups in its arms

seven at its back—
they're full of ointments
and full of good salves.

She, Lemminkäinen's mother
anointed with those ointments
with the nine ointments
the eight remedies:
still she got no help—
no, found none from it.
She said with this word
she spoke with this speech:
'Bee, bird of the air
fly there a third time
high up into heaven
above nine heavens!
There is mead in plenty there
honey to the heart's content
with which once the Creator
sang charms and the pure God talked
the Lord anointed his brood
injured by an evil power.
Dip your wings in mead, and your
feathers in melted honey
bring mead on your wing
and bear honey on your cape
to be ointment for the sick
to pour on the injuries!'

The bee, kindly bird
managed to put this in words:
'But how am I to get there—
I, a puny man?'
'You will get there easily
trip there handsomely—
over the moon, underneath
the sun, between heaven's stars.
For one day you will flutter
to the moon's brow-bones

for another you will whizz
to the Great Bear's shoulderblades
for a third you will soar up
on to the Seven Stars' back;
then 'tis a mite of a way
    a tiny circuit
to where God the holy lives
to the blessed one's dwellings.'

And the bee rose from the earth
the mead-wing from the hummock;
    now it fluttered off
    whizzed on little wings.
It flew beside the moon's ring
the sun's border it skirted
past the Great Bear's shoulderblades
the back of the Seven Stars;
it flew to the Lord's cellar
to the Almighty's chamber.
There ointment is being made
and salves are being prepared
    in pots of silver
    and in pans of gold:
honey boiled in the middles
at the brims melted butter
    mead at the south tip
    at the north end salves.
The bee, the bird of the air
    then got enough mead
honey to its heart's content.
    A little time passed:
    now it comes panting
    arrives doubled up
with a hundred hornfuls in its arms
a thousand other bulges—
this one honey, that water
the other the best ointment.

Then Lemminkäinen's mother
took them into her own mouth
she tested them with her tongue
tasted them to her liking:
'These are some of those ointments
the Almighty's remedies
with which God has anointed
the Lord poured on injuries.'
Then she anointed the weary one
tended the ill-befallen—
anointed through gaps in bone
    and through cracks in limbs
anointed below, above
    slapped the middle once.
Then she put this into words
    she declared, chattered:
    'Rise up out of sleep
    get up out of dream
from these evil places, from
    the bed of hard luck!'

And the man rose out of sleep
    he woke out of dream.
Now he manages to say
    to tell with his tongue:
'Long I, wretched, have slumbered
ages I, hapless, have slept!
    I've slept a sweet sleep
    a sound snooze I've had.'

Lemminkäinen's mother said
    she declared, chattered:
'You would have slept more ages
still longer you would have stretched
but for your poor old mother
for the mean one who bore you.
Say now, luckless son of mine
tell so that my ears may hear:

what led you to Death, pushed you
into Tuonela's river?'

Wanton Lemminkäinen said
    answered his mother:
    'Dripcap the herdsman
    Dreamland's sightless one—
he led me to Death, pushed me
into Tuonela's river.
He raised a snake out of the water
a dragon out of the waves
    against woeful me
and I knew nothing of it
did not know the hate of water snakes
    the stings of cowbane.'

Lemminkäinen's mother said:
'Alas for a mindless man!
You boasted of bewitching
witches, of singing at Lapps
but don't know the hate of water snakes
    the stings of cowbane!
From water the water snake was born
and the cowbane from the waves
from the calloo's good brains, from
inside the sea-swallow's head.
On the waters the Ogress
spat, dropped a blob on the waves;
the water stretched it out long
the sun shone till it was soft.
    Then the wind lulled it
and the water's breath rocked it;
the billows washed it ashore
and the surf steered it to land.'

Then Lemminkäinen's mother
    lulled the one she knew
to the shape he had before
to the looks he used to have

till he was a bit better
even, fitter than before.
Then she asked her son whether
he was short of anything.
Wanton Lemminkäinen said:
'There's a lot I'm still short of:
    there my heart's desire
    there my longing lies—
among those maids of the North
    those fair braided heads.
The mould-eared dame of the North
    will not give her girl
    unless I shoot the
    calloo, hit the swan
on that Tuonela river
on the holy stream's whirlpool.'

Lemminkäinen's mother said
    she declared, chattered:
    'Leave your blasted swans
    let the calloos be
upon Tuoni's black river
    the smoking whirlpools!
    You just come home now
    with your mean mother
    and still thank your luck
    your God known to all
for giving you real help
and bringing you back to life
from Tuoni's undoubted road
the abode of the Dead Land!
    I could do nothing
    nothing by myself
without the mercy of God
the guidance of the true Lord.'

Then wanton Lemminkäinen
    went home straight away

with his dear mother
beside his honoured parent.

There now I lose my Farmind
leave wanton Lemminkäinen
out of my tale for some time
and I turn my tale meanwhile
I'll let the song go elsewhere
I'll push on to a new track.

16. *To Build a Boat*

Steady old Väinämöinen
the everlasting wise man
was about to carve a boat
    work on a new craft
on the misty headland's tip
at the foggy island's end
but the craft-smith needed trees
    the boatbuilder planks:
    now, who will seek wood
    go after oak for
    Väinämöinen's boat
    for the singer's keel?
Pellervoinen, the field's son
    tiny boy Sampsa—
he it is who will seek wood
    go after oak for
    Väinämöinen's boat
    for the singer's keel.
    He treads the road, steps
    to north-eastern worlds:
he walked one hill, he walks two
soon he went a third as well
shouldering a golden axe
a copper haft on the axe.
He came up to an aspen
    of three fathoms' height.
He wished to touch the aspen
to thrash the tree with the axe.
    The aspen speaks up
    and it finds its tongue:
'What, man, do you wish of me—
what anyway do you want?'

Boy Sampsa Pellervoinen
    put this into words:
'This is what I wish of you
this is what I seek and want—
a boat for Väinämöinen
some craft-wood for the singer.'

The aspen spoke more oddly
and the hundred-bough managed:
'Full of leaks a boat from me
and a craft likely to sink!
I am hollow at the base:
    three times this summer
the maggot has eaten my
heart, the worm has laid my roots.'

Boy Sampsa Pellervoinen
    at that fares further;
    he thinks he will step
    towards northern worlds
and he came upon a fir
    of six fathoms' height.
He struck the tree with the axe
    whacked it with his adze
    he asked and he talked:
    'Fir, could you become
a boat for Väinämöinen
and ship-wood for the singer?'

The fir blurted an answer
    gave a great bellow:
'Not from me will a craft come
    one that bears six ribs!
    I am a gnarled fir:
    three times this summer
the raven croaked at my top
the crow has cawed on my boughs.'

Boy Sampsa Pellervoinen
    fares even further;
    he thinks he will step
    towards southern worlds
and he came upon an oak
    of nine fathoms' girth.
    He asked and he talked:
    'Oak, would you become
the hull of a hunting-boat
    or a war-craft's keel?'

The oak skilfully answered
and the acorn-tree managed:
'Indeed there is wood in me
    for one small boat's hull
for I am no gnarled bean-pole
nor am I hollow inside:
    three times this summer
this great summertime, the sun
has gone round my middle wood
the moon has gleamed at my top
cuckoos have called on my boughs
birds have rested in my leaves.'

Boy Sampsa Pellervoinen
took the axe from his shoulder
he struck the tree with the axe
the oak with the even blade;
soon he was able to fell
the oak, lay the fine tree low.
First he took the top away
and the base he cleaves right through:
    from it he carved keels
    planks without number
for building the singer's ship
    Väinämöinen's boat.

At that old Väinämöinen
the everlasting wise man

started building the boat with wisdom
making the craft with singing
    from one oak's fragments
    the brittle tree's bits.
He sang one tale, fixed the keel
he sang two, joined on a side
soon he sang a third as well
    while he hewed rowlocks
    and finished rib-tops
    and joined overlaps.
When the little boat was ribbed
    and the side joints joined
    he needed three words
for putting on the handrails
    for raising the prow
    rounding off the stern.
Steady old Väinämöinen
the everlasting wise man
uttered a word and spoke thus:
'Woe, luckless me, for my days!
The boat did not reach waters
    the new ship the waves!'

    He thinks, considers
    where to get words from
    fetch the right spells from—
    the scalps of swallows
the heads of a flight of swans
from a skein of geese' shoulders?
He set off to get some words:
he ruined a flock of swans
a gaggle of geese destroyed
    no end of swallows;
but he got no word at all—
    no word, not a half.
    He thinks, considers:
'There would be a hundred words
under a summer reindeer's

tongue, in a white squirrel's mouth.'
He set off to get some words
take some mysteries: he cut
a field of reindeer open
a big beamful of squirrels;
from there he got many words—
    all of them useless.
    He thinks, considers:
'There I'll get a hundred words—
from Tuonela's dwelling, from
the Dead Land's ageless abode.'

He went to Tuonela for
words, to the Dead Land for powers
    and he trips along:
for one week he trod through brush
for two weeks through bird cherry
for a third through juniper;
now the Dead Land's isle appeared
    Tuoni's hillock gleams.
Steady old Väinämöinen
    now shouted out loud
at that Tuonela river
in the dale of the Dead Land:
'Bring a boat, girl of Tuoni
a raft, child of the Dead Land
to get me over the strait
reach me across the river!'

A stunted girl of Tuoni
a squat maid of the Dead Land
    was at her washing
    pounding her laundry
in Tuoni's black river, in
    the Dead Land's eddy.
She uttered a word, spoke thus
    she declared, chattered:
'A boat will be brought from here

if the reason is stated—
    what led you to Death
killed by no disease, taken
by no natural causes
shattered by no other doom.'

Steady old Väinämöinen
uttered a word and spoke thus:
    'Tuoni brought me here
and Death dragged me from my lands.'

The stunted girl of Tuoni
the squat maid of the Dead Land
    put this into words:
'Now I have spotted a fraud!
For if Tuoni brought you here
Death dislodged you from your lands
Tuoni would have brought you when
he came, Death when he travelled
with Tuoni's hood over your
head, Death's mittens on your hands.
Say truly, Väinämöinen:
    what led you to Death?'

Steady old Väinämöinen
    there put into words:
'Iron has led me to Death
steel snatched me to Tuonela.'

The stunted girl of Tuoni
the squat maid of the Dead Land
uttered a word and spoke thus:
'There I recognize a fraud!
If iron got you to Death
steel brought you to Tuonela
your clothes would be pouring blood
    would be gushing gore.

Say truly, Väinämöinen
say truly the second time!'

Steady old Väinämöinen
    uttered and spoke thus:
'Water has got me to Death
the billow to Tuonela.'

The stunted girl of Tuoni
the squat maid of the Dead Land
uttered a word and spoke thus:
    'I can see a liar!
If water got you to Death
the billow to Tuonela
your clothes would pour water, your
    hems would be dripping.
    Tell the truth with care:
    what led you to Death?'

There the old Väinämöinen
    is once more a fraud:
'Fire brought me to Tuonela
    flame led me to Death.'

The stunted girl of Tuoni
the squat maid of the Dead Land
    put this into words:
    'I can guess a liar!
If fire had brought you to Death
    flame to Tuonela
    your curls would be scorched
your beard badly burnt as well.
    Old Väinämöinen
if you want a boat from here
    tell the truth with care
    and have done with lies
about how you came to Death
killed by no disease, taken

by no natural causes
broken by no other doom.'

The old Väinämöinen said:
'If I did lie a little
was a fraud the second time
now I'll tell the truth. I was
building a boat with wisdom
making a craft with singing;
I sang one day, I sang two
    till on the third day
    the poem-sledge smashed
the phrase-runner snapped: I've come
to Tuonela for a spike
to the Dead Land for a drill
    to build my sledge with
    to make my song-sleigh.
Now bring a little boat here
make ready your raft for me
to get me over the strait
reach me across the river!'

Truly Tuoni-daughter scolds
    and Death's maid quarrels:
    'Fool, for your folly
man, for your madness! You come
without cause to Tuonela
undiseased to Death's abodes!
Better it would be for you
to return to your own lands:
    plenty have come here
but not many have returned.'

The old Väinämöinen said:
'Let a hag turn off the road
but even a worse man won't
nor a sleepier fellow!

Bring a boat, girl of Tuoni
a raft, child of the Dead Land!'

And Tuoni's girl took a boat;
on it old Väinämöinen
she gets over the strait, she
reaches across the river
and she put this into words:
'Woe to you, Väinämöinen:
you have come unslain to Death
still alive to Tuonela!'

Tuoni-daughter, good mistress
Dead Land Daughter, old woman
brought beer in a flagon, fetched
some in a two-handled one
and she put this into words:
'Drink up, old Väinämöinen!'

Steady old Väinämöinen
looked down into his flagon:
there were frogs spawning within
worms on the sides clustering.
Then he put this into words:
'I did not come here to drink
the bowls of the Dead Land, to
lap the flagons of Tuoni:
    beer drinkers get drunk
guzzlers of the jug fall down.'

And Tuonela's mistress said:
    'Old Väinämöinen
what did you come to Death for
why to Tuonela's cabins
before Tuoni wished, before
you were summoned from Death's lands?'

The old Väinämöinen said:
'As I was carving a boat
was working on a new craft
    I needed three words
    to round off the stern
    and to raise the prow;
when I could get them nowhere
not find them on lands, in skies
I must come to Tuonela
    go to Death's abodes
    where I'd get those words
    learn those mysteries.'

That mistress of Tuonela
uttered a word and spoke thus:
    'Tuoni gives no words
    Death does not share power!
You won't get away from here
    ever in this world
    to go to your home
    to crawl to your lands.'
And she wore the man to sleep
made the traveller lie down
upon Tuoni's bed of rugs
and there the man is lying
the fellow taking a sleep:
the man lay, the bedclothes watched.

In Tuonela was a hag
an old hag of pointed chin
a spinner of iron yarn
a caster of copper threads:
she spun a hundred-mesh seine
and a thousand-mesh she wound
    in one summer night
    upon one wet rock.
In Tuonela was a man
an old man with three fingers

a weaver of iron nets
a maker of copper seines:
he wove the hundred-mesh seine
the thousand-mesh he knitted
    that same summer night
    on the same wet rock.
Tuoni's son of hooked finger
of hooked finger iron-tipped
he drew the hundred-mesh seine
across Tuonela's river
both across it and along
and athwart it too, to stop
Väinämöinen getting out
the man of Calm Waters free
    ever in this world
not in a month of Sundays
from Tuonela's dwellings, from
the Dead Land's ageless abodes.

Steady old Väinämöinen
uttered a word and spoke thus:
'Could my ruin have come, my
day of trouble have arrived
in these Tuonela cabins
these abodes of the Dead Land?'
    Soon he changed his shape
promptly became something else—
went as something black to sea
as an otter to the sedge;
he crawled as an iron worm
moved as a viperish snake
across Tuonela's river
    through Tuoni's netting.
Tuoni's son of hooked finger
of hooked finger iron-tipped
walked early in the morning
    to look at his nets:
he has a hundred sewin

and a thousand fry, but he
has not caught Väinämöinen
the old man of Calm Waters.

At that old Väinämöinen
when he came from Tuonela
    he says with this word
    he spoke with this speech:
    'May the good God not
may he not bring this about—
he who himself went to Death
penetrated Tuonela!
    Plenty have got there
    few have come from there
from Tuonela's dwellings, from
the Dead Land's ageless abodes.'
He put this too into words
    he declared, thus told
    the youngsters rising
    the folk coming up:
    'Don't, children of man
    ever in this world
lay the guilt on the guiltless
or the blame on the blameless!
    Wages are ill paid
there in Tuonela's dwellings:
the guilty have a place there
    those to blame have beds
the bedsteads are of hot rocks
    of burning boulders
the quilts of vipers, of snakes
woven from Tuoni's maggots.'

17. *Inside the Giant*

Steady old Väinämöinen
when he got no words
from Tuonela's dwellings, from
the Dead Land's ageless abodes
keeps considering
and long he ponders
where to get words from
fetch the right spells from.
He meets a herdsman
who put this in words:
'You will get a hundred words
and a thousand tale-charms from
Antero Vipunen's* mouth
from the word-hoarder's belly.
But he has to be gone to
and the track picked out—
it is not a good journey
but not quite the worst either:
at first you must run
upon women's needle points
then next you must walk
on a man's sword tips*
and third must amble
on a fellow's hatchet blades.'

Steady old Väinämöinen
certainly meant to go. He
ducks into the smith's workshop
and says with this word:
'Smith Ilmarinen
forge iron footwear
forge iron gauntlets
make an iron shirt!

Prepare an iron cowlstaff
    obtain one of steel:
    put steel at its core
and on top draw soft iron!
I am off to get some words
    take some mysteries
from the word-hoarder's belly
Antero Vipunen's mouth.'

    Smith Ilmarinen
uttered a word and spoke thus:
'Vipunen has long been dead
Antero for ages has
vanished, left the trap he'd set
    the path he'd baited;
from there you will get no word—
no, not even half a word.'

Steady old Väinämöinen
    still went, did not heed:
for one day he stepped clinking
upon women's needle points
for two he rambled along
    upon men's sword tips
for a third too he ambled
on a fellow's hatchet blades.

Vipunen, he full of tales
    old man word-hoarder
    he lolls with his tales
    with his spells he sprawls;
an aspen grew upon his shoulders
on his eyebrows a birch rose
an alder upon his chin
a willow shrub on his beard
on his brow a squirrel-spruce
a cony fir on his teeth.
Now Väinämöinen comes: he

drew his sword, snatched the iron
out of the holder of hide
out of the belt of leather;
he felled the aspen from the shoulders
from the eyebrows toppled the birches
from the jaws the broad alders
the willow shrubs from the beard
from the brow felled the squirrel-spruces
the cony firs from the teeth.
He plunged the iron cowlstaff
into Antero Vipunen's mouth
    in his grinning gums
    in his squelching jaws
and uttered a word, spoke thus:
    'Rise up, serf of man
from where you lie underground
from the long sleep you're taking!'

That Vipunen full of tales
    was startled from sleep.
He felt the one touching hard
and with pain the one teasing:
he bit the iron cowlstaff
he bit off the soft iron
but he could not bite the steel
could not eat the iron core.
At that old Väinämöinen's
(as he stood beside the mouth)
    other foot stumbles
his left foot slithers into
Antero Vipunen's mouth
    on his jawbone slid
and Vipunen full of tales
at once opened his mouth more
    flung his jaw-posts wide—
swallowed the man with his sword
    into his throat gulped
    old Väinämöinen.

There Vipunen full of tales
    put this into words:
'I've eaten a thing or two:
I've eaten ewe, eaten goat
    eaten barren cow
    eaten boar, but I
    have not yet eaten
a morsel that tastes like this!'

    Old Väinämöinen
    put this into words:
'My ruin could be coming
my day of trouble looming
in this lair of a demon
this inglenook of the grave.'

    He thinks, considers
how to be, which way to live.
At his belt he has a knife
with a curly-birch handle;
out of it he built a boat
he built a boat with wisdom.
    He rows, he glides from
    gut end to gut end
    he rowed every nook
every cranny he went round.
Old Vipunen full of tales
was not going to heed that.
Then the old Väinämöinen
made himself into a smith
became a blacksmith; he changed
his shirt into a workshop
his shirtsleeves into bellows
his coat into a blower
his trousers he turned to pipes
stockings to pipe-mouthpieces
his knee into an anvil

to a hammer his elbow.
    He hammers away
    he tap-taps away;
hammered all night without rest
all day without a breather
in the word-hoarder's belly
the eloquent one's bosom.

Then Vipunen full of tales
    put this into words:
'What kind of man may you be
what sort of fellow? I have
eaten a hundred fellows
destroyed a thousand men, but
I don't think I've eaten such:
coal is coming into my
mouth, firebrands on to my tongue
iron dross into my throat!
Go now, wonder, on your way
earth's evil, get a move on
before I seek your mother
and fetch your honoured parent!
If I tell your mother, speak,
report you to your parent
    mother has more work
great trouble a parent has
    when her son does wrong
    her child misbehaves.
I have no idea at all
cannot guess your Origin
demon, where you latched on from
pest, where you have come here from
    to bite, to nibble
to eat and to gnaw: are you
disease the Lord created
    death decreed by God
    or are you man-made

brought and wrought by someone else
    put here for payment
    set up for money?
If disease, the Lord's creature
    death decreed by God
I will trust my Creator
cast myself upon my God:
he'll not cast away the good
he'll not let the fair be lost.
But if you are man-made, a
problem caused by someone else
be sure I shall learn your kin
I'll find out where you were born!

'From there problems used to spring
    from there plights arose—
from the haunts of men who know
the pastures of singing men
    the homes of scoundrels
    the grounds of wizards;
from there—the heaths of the grave
    from inside the earth
from the home of a dead man
from the farm of one vanished
    from crumbling soils, from
    earth being disturbed
    from whirling gravels
    from sands that jingle
    from marshy hollows
    from swamps without moss
    from overflowing
    mires, from spilling springs
from a forest demon's lair
a gorge between five mountains
from a copper slope's summit
    a coppery peak
from spruces that whisper, from
    firs that sough and sigh

from a rotten pine tree's top
from the decayed heads of pines
    from where the fox screams
from heaths where elk is hunted
from the bruin's rocky den
    the bear's craggy cell
    from the furthest North
    from Lapland's vastness
    from the barren glades
    from the unsown lands
    from great battlefields
    from men's killing-grounds
    from rustling grasses
    from the steaming gore
    from the great high seas
from the open expanses
    from the sea's black mud
from a thousand fathoms down
    from the rushing streams
    the smoking whirlpools
from Rutja's steep rapid, from
the swirl of mighty water
from the further heavens, from
the furthest fair-weather clouds
the thoroughfares of the gale
the nurseries of the wind.
Is that where you too sprang from
and where, plight, you arose from
to enter my guiltless heart
    my blameless belly
    to eat and to gnaw
    to bite, to devour?

'Ease now, Demon's hound
    soften, Dead Land's cur
    leave my lap, scoundrel
grim of the earth, my liver

from eating my inmost heart
    scrabbling at my spleen
    fulling my belly
    twisting up my lungs
    chewing my navel
    grasping at my bowels
    crunching my back bones
    slashing at my sides!
Should I not be man enough
I will put in my betters
    to solve this problem
    lose this dreadful thing.
I raise from earth the soil-dames
from the field the first masters
from the earth all the swordsmen
from the sand all the horsemen
to be my strength and my power
my support and my refuge
    in this hard labour
    in this grievous pain.

'Should it not heed even that
and not yield even a bit
rise, O forest, with your men
junipers with your people
    pines with your household
O still pool with your children
a hundred men armed with swords
a thousand iron fellows
    to chafe this demon
    crumple this judas!

'Should it not heed even that
and not yield even a bit
rise from the water, water
mistress, blue-capped from the waves
    fine-hemmed from the mire
clear of face out of the mud

to be a small fellow's strength
and a little man's manhood
lest I'm eaten without cause
    killed without disease!

'Should it not heed even that
and not yield even a bit
    O dame, nature's girl
O handsome woman of gold
who are the eldest of wives
    the first of matrons
come now to feel out the pains
to oust the days of trouble
    to deal with this deal
    ward off this attack!

    'But should it not heed
not give way even a bit
Old Man at the pole of heaven
at the thundercloud's edges
come here when you are needed
make your way when you are asked
to undo the wretched deeds
    take away the woes
with a sword of fiery blade
    with a sparkling brand!

'Go now, wonder, on your way
earth's evil, get a move on!
There is no room here for you
even if you needed room:
    move your house elsewhere
your dwelling-place further off
to where your master sits down
to where your mistress steps out!
    When you have got there
    reached your journey's end
at the haunts of your maker

the pastures of your builder
show that you are there, give a
secret sign that you've arrived—
    a boom like thunder
    a flash like lightning!
Kick the gate of the yard, throw
open the window shutter
and from there sidle within
fly as a whirlwind indoors
    and grab by the hock
    by their skinniest heel
your masters crouched at the rear
mistresses crouched by the door
and gouge out the master's eye
and smash the mistress's head
bend their fingers the wrong way
and twist their heads round and round!

'If little should come of that
fly as a cock to the lane
as a hen's chick to the farm
abreast of the rubbish heap:
crush the horse at the manger
and the horned beast in the byre
    stick its horns in filth
drop its tail upon the floor
    turn their eyes askew
and give their necks a quick jerk!

'If you're a wind-borne disease
    wind-borne, water-driven
    shared out by the gale
    carried by chill air
    go by the wind's way
    by the gale's sledge track
without sitting in a tree
or resting in an alder

to a copper slope's summit
    a coppery peak
there to be lulled by the wind
    cared for by the gale!
If you've come from heaven, from
the furthest fair-weather clouds
    rise again to heaven
go up there into the sky
    to the drizzling clouds
    to the trembling stars
    to smoulder as fire
    to sparkle as sparks
    where the sun drives, where
    the moon-ring revolves!
Should you, weakling, have been drawn
by water, by billows driven
weakling, enter the water
and drive below the billows
to the mud-stronghold's edges
the water-ridge's shoulders
there to be driven by the billows
tossed by the gloomy water!
Should you be from the grave's heath
the abodes of ever-gone
    try hard to get home
to those farmyards of the grave
    to the crumbling soils
    earth being disturbed
in which people have fallen
    strong folk have toppled!

'If, evil one, you have come
from a forest demon's lair
    from hideouts of pine
    from lodges of fir
that is where I banish you—
to the forest demon's lair
    the lodges of fir

the hideouts of pine
that you may stay there
until the floors rot
and the wall beams grow mushrooms
and the roof comes tumbling down.
There I banish you
there, wretch, I compel you—to
gaffer bruin's home
to gammer bear's farm
to marshy hollows
upon unthawed swamps
into moving mires
into spilling springs
into pools that are
fishless, quite perchless.

'Should you not get a place there
yonder I will banish you—
to the furthest North
to Lapland's vastness
to the barren glades
to the unsown lands
where there is no moon, no sun
nor daylight for evermore.
You will enjoy being there
you will love it flitting there:
elk have been hung up on trees
the kings of beasts overcome
for a hungry man to eat
for one who wants it to bite.
There I banish you
there tell and compel you—to
Rutja's steep rapid
the smoking whirlpool
into which trees fall headlong
pines roll root and branch
the great firs base first plunging

the shock-headed pines top first:
    swim there, bad heathen
in the rapid's steep foaming
in the wide waters swirl round
in the narrow waters dwell!

'Should you not get a place there
yonder I will banish you—
to Tuoni's black river, to
the Dead Land's eternal brook
from where you'll never get out
never in this world be free
unless I get to letting you out
get round to unloosing you
    with nine wethers, born
    of a single ewe
    with nine oxen, calves
    of a single cow
    with nine stallions, foals
    of a single mare.
If you should ask for a lift
beg for draught horses—oh, yes
I'll arrange a lift for you
and I'll give you a draught horse:
the Demon has a good horse
one with red hair on a fell
    whose muzzle flashed fire
    its snout flame indeed
all its hoofs are of iron
    its haulers of steel;
    they can go uphill
raise a hollow to a bank
with a good man at the reins
    with a strict driver.

'Should not enough come of that
get the Demon's skiing-things
the Devil's alder snowshoes

the evil one's thick ski-stick
to ski on the Demon's lands
and to roam the Devil's groves
hopping on the Demon's lands
skipping on the evil one's!
A rock lies across the road:
    let it smash to bits;
a log lies along the road:
    let this snap in two;
a fellow stands in the road:
    send him to one side!

'Go now, idler, on your feet
evil man, get a move on
    before the day breaks
    and the dawn god dawns
    and the sun comes up
    and the cockcrow sounds!
Now's the idler's on-foot time
the evil one's move-on time
with moonlight for your going
brightness for your wandering.
    Should you not quickly
yield, depart, motherless cur
I'll get claws from an eagle
talons from a blood-drinker
grippers of flesh from a bird
    graspers from a hawk
with which I will seize scoundrels
set the wicked for ever
so that their heads will not twitch
so that their breath will not pant.
A created devil stopped
and a mother's son too strayed
    when God's trance-hour* came
and the Lord's help unfolded:
will you not, motherless, stray
    stop, unlucky brat

disappear, keeperless dog
and depart, motherless cur
with the ending of this hour
with the passing of this moon?'

Steady old Väinämöinen
    then put this in words:
''Tis good for me to be here
sweet for me to tarry here:
the liver will serve for bread
the marrow to eat with it
the lungs will be right for stew
    the fats for good food.
I will set up my anvil
deeper upon the heart-flesh
slam my sledgehammer harder
    on still worse places
so that you'll never get out
never in this world be free
unless I come to hear words
    and fetch the right spells
    and hear enough words
    and a thousand charms.
    Words shall not be hid
    nor spells be buried;*
might shall not sink underground
    though the mighty go.'

Then Vipunen full of tales
    the old word-hoarder
with great wisdom in his mouth
boundless might in his bosom
    opened his word-chest
and flung wide his box of tales
    to sing some good things
set some of the best things forth—
    those deep Origins
spells about the Beginning

which not all the children sing
only fellows understand
    in this evil age
    with time running out:
he sang Origins in depth
    and spells in order
how by their Creator's leave
at the Almighty's command
of itself the sky was born
from the sky water parted
from the water land stretched forth
on the land all growing things;
he sang of the moon's shaping
the sun's placing, the fixing
    of the sky's pillars
heaven being filled with stars.
There Vipunen full of tales
indeed sang, showed what he knew!
    Never in this world
    was heard or was seen
    a better singer
a more careful cunning man:
    that mouth hurled forth words
    the tongue flung phrases
    as a colt its legs
    a steed sturdy feet.
    He sang day by day
night by night he recited
and the sun stopped to listen
the golden moon to take note;
billows stood still on the main
    waves at the bay-end;
    streams left off rolling
and Rutja's rapid foaming
and Vuoksi's rapid flowing—
and Jordan's river halted.

At that old Väinämöinen
    when he had heard words

had got enough words
and fetched the right spells
sets about quitting
Antero Vipunen's mouth
and the word-hoarder's belly
the eloquent one's bosom.
And old Väinämöinen said:
'O Antero Vipunen
open your mouth more
fling your jaw-posts wide, so that
I may get out of your gut
on to the ground and go home!'

There Vipunen full of tales
put this into words: 'Many
have I eaten, many drunk
destroyed thousands all told; but
I've not yet eaten any
such as old Väinämöinen!
You did well to come:
you'll do better to return.'

Then Antero Vipunen
grinned and showed his gums
opened his mouth more
flung his jaw-posts wide:
old Väinämöinen
quitted the great wise one's mouth
and the word-hoarder's belly
the eloquent one's bosom;
slips out of his mouth
trips upon the heath
like a golden squirrel, or
a gold-breasted pine marten.
He stepped from there on his way
and came to his smith's workshop.
The smith Ilmarinen said:

'Did you get to hear some words
    to fetch the right spells
    for fixing the side
    joining on the stern
    and raising the bows?'

Steady old Väinämöinen
    put this into words:
'Now I've got a hundred words
and thousands of charms, I have
brought the words out of hiding
    unburied the spells.'
    He went to his boat
on the knowledgeable stocks:
the little boat was finished
    the side joint was joined
    the stern-end ended
    and the bows were raised
and the boat was born uncarved
the ship with no shaving pared.

18. *The Rivals*

Steady old Väinämöinen
    thought and considered
going to woo the maiden
to look up the braided head
    out in dark Northland
in dreary Sariola
the famous girl of the North
the special bride of the North.
He rigged the vessel in blue
in red the side of the craft
the bows he adorned with gold
and overlaid with silver.
One morrow among others
quite early in the morning
    he pushed the boat out
the hundred-planked on the waves
from the rollers stripped of bark
    from the stocks of pine.
    He raised up his mast
on the mast he hoisted sails:
he hoisted a sail of red
and another sail of blue;
into the ship he goes down
into the vessel he steps
and he sailed off on the sea
    sped off on the blue.
There he put this into words
    he declared, chattered:
'Come now into the craft, God,
in the vessel, merciful
to be a small fellow's strength
and a little man's manhood
    on those wide waters

upon those vast waves!
Lull, O wind, the craft,
billow, drive the ship
with my fingers not rowing
the water's sheen unbroken
on the wide high seas
upon the open expanse!'

Annikki, she of good name
girl of night, maiden of dusk
keeper of a long twilight
and morning's early riser
chanced to be at her washing
and soaking her clothes
at the end of a red stair
on a broad landing
on the misty headland's tip
at the foggy island's end.
She looks, turns her gaze
round the lovely air
towards the sky overhead
shoreward by the seas:
above, the sun shone
below, the billows glittered.
She cast her eyes seaward, turned
her head to below the sun
past Finlandia's* river-mouth
past Väinö-land's waters' end
spied a black speck on the sea
a bluish one on the waves.

She uttered a word, spoke thus
she declared, chattered:
'What are you, black on the sea
who, bluish upon the waves?
If you're a gaggle of geese
or a flock of dear calloos
then waft into flight
up into the sky!

If you're a shoal of salmon
or some other school of fish
    splash into a swim
take off into the water!
Should you be a shoal of rock
or a log in the water
the billow would cover you
the water wash over you.'

    The boat rolls nearer
    and the new craft sails
past the misty headland's tip
past the foggy island's end.
Annikki, she of good name
now saw 'twas a boat coming
a hundred-planked one tacking.
She uttered a word, spoke thus:
'If you are my brother's boat
or perhaps my father's craft
    wend your way homeward
and turn towards your own lands
with your prow to these moorings
your stern to other moorings!
If you are a stranger's craft
    float further away
and make for other moorings
with your stern to these moorings!'

But it was not a home-boat
    nor a stranger's craft:
it was Väinämöinen's craft
the eternal singer's ship.
    He was approaching
pressing onward for a chat
to take one word, to bring two
to speak a third forcefully.
Annikki, she of good name
girl of night, maiden of dusk

began questioning the craft:
'Where are you off to, Väinämöinen
heading for, bridegroom of Calm Waters
and where, land's choice, making for?'

Well, that old Väinämöinen
    speaks up from his craft:
'I am off to hunt salmon
    to catch trout spawning
down in Tuoni's black river
    the deep sedgy ditch.'*

Annikki, she of good name
    put this into words:
'Don't tell empty lies, for I
too know about fish spawning!
Differently my father, my
honoured parent differently
used to go hunting salmon
    trying for sewin:
he had a boatful of nets
    a ship full of traps;
in it were seines, in it lines
water-beaters on the side
fishing spears under the thwart
    long poles in the stern.
Where are you off to, Väinämöinen
roving to, Calm Waters man?'

The old Väinämöinen said:
'I am off in search of geese
    to sport for bright-wings
    to bag slobber-chops
upon the deep German straits*
on the open expanses.'

Annikki, she of good name
uttered a word and spoke thus:

'I know one who speaks the truth;
I can spot a fraud as well!
Differently my father, my
honoured parent differently
used to drive off after geese
busy himself with red-mouths:
he had a big crossbow strung
    a handsome bow drawn
    a black dog chained up
the chain bound fast to the bow;
the cur ran along shore-roads
the pups scampered over rocks.
Tell the truth, Väinämöinen:
where after all are you bound?'

The old Väinämöinen said:
'And what if I were going
    to those mighty wars
    to those well-matched fights
in which blood reaches the shin
    redness is knee-deep?'

But Annikki keeps saying
    the tin-breast persists:
'I know warmongering too!
When my father used to go
    to those mighty wars
    to those well-matched fights
he'd a hundred men rowing
a thousand sitting about
crossbows bristling at the prow
    swords bare at the thwarts.
    Now tell me the truth
without lying or fooling:
where are you off to, Väinämöinen,
heading for, Calm Waters man?'

Then the old Väinämöinen
uttered a word and spoke thus:

'Come, girlie, into my craft
maid, into my little boat:
    then I'll tell the truth
without lying or fooling!'

But Annikki says a word
    the tin-breast rebuked:
'May the wind fall on your craft
the gale on your little boat!
I will overturn your craft
and topple your bows, if I
do not get to hear the truth
    where you mean to go
to hear the truth told with care
    and the end of lies.'

Then the old Väinämöinen
uttered a word and spoke thus:
'All right, I will tell the truth
if I did lie a little:
I am off to woo the maid
    to beg for the lass
    out in dark Northland
in dreary Sariola
    the man-eating, the
    fellow-drowning place.'

Annikki, she of good name
girl of night, maiden of dusk
    when she knew the truth
without lying or fooling
    left her veils unrinsed
    and her clothes unsoaked
    on the broad landing
at the end of the red stair.
In her hands she scooped her clothes
in her fists she grasped her hems
    then she was away

she broke straight into a run
and she comes to the smith's home
she steps into the workshop.

'Twas the smith Ilmarinen
the everlasting craftsman
was forging an iron bench
one of silver was working
an ell of dust on his head
a fathom of coal on his shoulders.
Annikki stepped to the door
uttered a word and spoke thus:
'Brother, smith Ilmarinen
O everlasting craftsman:
forge me a little shuttle
    forge me some fine rings
two or three pairs of earrings
    five or six belt chains
    and I'll tell the truth
without lying or fooling!'

The smith Ilmarinen said:
    'If you tell good news
I will forge you a shuttle
    I'll forge some fine rings
I'll forge a cross for your breasts
    your ringlets I'll mend;
    if you tell bad news
I will smash your old ones too
thrust them from you in the fire
shove them down into my forge.'

Annikki, she the good-named
    put this into words:
    'Smith Ilmarinen
look, you think of marrying
her who once you pledged with gifts
set aside to be your wife.

You're always tapping away
and all the time hammering;
all summer you shoe a horse
all winter you work iron
all night you repair your sleighs
and all day you make bobsleighs
    to go off wooing
    to get to Northland:
now smarter ones are leading
cleverer ones are ahead
    taking your own girl
    snatching your darling
who you looked for two years long
    three years long you wooed.
Väinämöinen's on his way
    on the blue high seas
in the stern of a gold-prow
with a paddle of copper
    bound for dark Northland
for dreary Sariola.'

A pain assailed the smith, a
heavy moment the blacksmith:
the tongs slipped out of his grasp
from his hand the hammer dropped.
The smith Ilmarinen said:
'Annikki, my dear sister
I will forge you a shuttle
    I'll forge some fine rings
two or three pairs of earrings
    five or six belt chains:
heat the honey-sweet bath-hut
stoke up the mead-sweet sauna
    with faggots chopped fine
    with little splinters!
    Make a bit of ash
    and some lye stir up
    to wash my head with

whiten my body
from autumn-hued coal
winter-hued forging!'

Annikki, she the good-named
slyly heated the sauna
with wood the wind had snapped off
a thunderstorm had beaten;
rocks she fetched from a rapid
brought them for stirring up steam
waters from a pleasant spring
from a trickling mire; she broke
a bath-whisk off from the scrub
a pleasant whisk from the grove
softened the honey-sweet whisk
on a honey-sweet rock's tip;
she made some ash sweet as curds
some soap sweet as bone marrow
soap that was sparkling
sparkling, lathering
for washing the bridegroom's head
for pouring on his body.

He, the smith Ilmarinen
the everlasting craftsman
forged the things the maid needed
mended her ringlets
while one bath-hut was prepared
and one sauna made ready;
thrust them into the girl's hand.
The girl put this into words:
'I have stoked up the sauna
heated the misty bath-hut
softened the bath-whisks ready
steeped the pleasant whisks.
Brother, bathe your fill
pour all the water you want

wash your head till it is flax
your eyes till they are snowflakes!'

Then the smith Ilmarinen
    himself went to bathe
    and he bathed his fill
    he doused himself white—
washed his eyes till they glistened
his eyebrows until they bloomed
his neck till it was hen's eggs
    all his body white.
He came in from the sauna
came unrecognizable
with his face mighty handsome
    with his cheeks flushing
and he put this into words:
'Annikki, my dear sister
bring now a shirt of linen
    fetch hard-wearing clothes
and with them I'll get ready
and fit to be a bridegroom!'

Annikki, she of good name
brought then a shirt of linen
    for his sweat-free skin
    for his naked flesh;
    then narrow breeches
    (those his mother stitched)
    for his grime-free flanks
    whose bones none could feel;
then she brought soft stockings, woven
by his mother as a lass
    for his study legs
    for his slender calves;
    then well-fitting shoes
    the best German boots
to cover the soft stockings
knitted by his mother as a maid;

and she fetched a blue cloth coat
with a liver-hued lining
to cover the linen shirt
    which is all of lawn;
on that a homespun caftan
trimmed with four strips of broadcloth
to cover the blue cloth coat
    and this is brand new;
a new thousand-buttoned fur
adorned with hundreds of adornments
over the homespun caftan
and this is trimmed with broadcloth;
and more, a belt for his waist—
a gold-bright cummerbund,* woven
by his mother as a lass
clicked when she was braid-headed;
    and then bright mittens
    gloves gold at the wrist
    made by Lapp children
    for fair hands to wear;
    then a tall helmet
    for his golden curls—
this was bought by his father
got when he was a bridegroom.
Then the smith Ilmarinen
clothed himself, prepared himself
dressed himself and decked himself
and then he said to his serf:
'Harness now a splendid foal
    before the bright sleigh
    for me to drive off
for me to go to Northland!'

The serf put this into words:
    'We have six stallions
    horses that eat oats.
Which of them should I harness?'

The smith Ilmarinen said:
    'Take the best stallion:
stick the foal into harness
the bay in front of the sledge;
    put on six cuckoos*
    seven bluebird-bells
to drone on the collar-bow
to thud against the traces
so that the fair ones will stare
    the lassies admire;
    take a bear-skin there
    for me to sit on
bring another, a sea beast's*
skin, to cover the bright sleigh!'

    That perpetual serf
the hireling bought for money
stuck the foal into harness
the bay in front of the sledge;
    put on six cuckoos
    seven bluebird-bells
to drone on the collar-bow
to thud against the traces;
    took a bear-skin there
for his master to sit on
brought another, a sea beast's
skin, to cover the bright sleigh.

He, the smith Ilmarinen
the everlasting craftsman
    prays to the Old Man
and worships the Thunderer:
    'Old Man, drop new snow
    fling down fine fresh snow—
snow for the sleigh to slide on
fresh snow for the sledge to skim!'

And the Old Man dropped new snow
    flung down fine fresh snow;

it covered the heather stalks
hid berry stalks on the ground.
Then the smith Ilmarinen
seats himself in the steel sledge;
    he says with this word
    he spoke with this speech:
'Go now, luck, upon my reins
God, into my little sledge!
Luck will not snap the reins, God
    will not break the sledge.'

He took the reins in one hand
seized the thong in the other
he hit the horse with the thong
    put this into words:
'Gee up, blaze-brow, off with you
    hemp-mane, get moving!'

    He drives it leaping
along sandy sea ridges
beside mead-sweet straits, across
an alder ridge's shoulders;
he drove clattering on shores
    jingling on shore sands:
gravel flew into his eyes
the sea splashed upon his chest.
He drove one day, he drove two
    soon he drives a third
    till on the third day
he startles Väinämöinen.
He uttered a word, spoke thus
    he declared, chattered:
    'Old Väinämöinen
    let us make a pact
in case we compete in gifts
    compete in wooing—
not to take the maid by force
marry her against her will.'

The old Väinämöinen said:
'I for one will make a pact
not to take the maid by force
marry her against her will.
To him the maid shall be given
    who takes her fancy
without long yearning, without
bearing a grudge for ages.'

    They drove on from there
    each on his journey:
the craft ran, the shore rumbled
the stallion ran, the ground shook.
    A little time passed
    a moment sped by.
    Now a grey dog barked
    and the stronghold's hound
    bayed in dark Northland
in murky Sariola;
it whined at first more softly
    more fitfully growled
its rump nudging the field edge
and its tail sweeping the ground.

The master of Northland said:
    'Just go, girl, and see
why the grey dog was barking
    the flop-ear yapping!'

The girl skilfully answered:
'I've no time, my dear father:
there's a big byre to muck out
a big herd to be seen to
there's a thick grindstone to turn
    and fine grains to sift;
the grindstone's thick, the grains fine
    the grinder puny.'

Soft the stronghold's demon barked
fitfully the grey one growled.
The master of Northland said:
'Just go, hag, and see
why the grizzled one barks, why
the stronghold's floppy one yaps!'

The hag put this into words:
'I've no time, nor intention:
there's a big household to feed
breakfast to be got ready
thick bread to be baked
dough to be patted;
the bread's thick, the grains are fine
the baker puny.'

The master of Northland said:
'Hags are always in a rush
daughters are always busy—
even roasting on the stove
seat, even stretched out in bed.
You go, son, and see!'

The son put this into words:
'I've no time to look:
there's a blunt axe to sharpen
a thick log to hew
a big stack to cleave
and faggots chopped fine to stow;
the stack's big, the faggots fine
the cleaver puny.'

The stronghold's tyke kept barking
the stronghold's hound bayed
the fierce pup bow-wowed
and the island's guard complained
its rump hard against the field
and its tail curled round.

The master of Northland said:
'No hoary one barks a lie
no aged one speaks idly;
it does not snarl at fir trees.'

He went to see for himself—
    steps across the yard
    to the furthest field
to the outermost barnyard.
He looked along the dog's snout
where its nose pointed he watched
towards the windy hilltop
the alder ridge's shoulders.
    Now he saw the truth—
why the grey dog was barking
and the land's choice was at work
and the fluffy-tail lilting:
there was a red boat sailing
on the sea side of Love Bay
there is a bright sleigh speeding
on the land side of Meadwood.
He, the master of Northland
    quickly goes indoors
under the roofs makes his way;
he uttered a word, spoke thus:
    'Strangers are coming
    on the blue high seas—
driving up in a bright sleigh
upon that side of Meadwood
sailing up in a big ship
upon this side of Love Bay!'

The mistress of Northland said:
    'How shall lots be cast
about the coming strangers?
    O my little wench
put rowan twigs on the fire

the choice wood into the flame!
    If it oozes blood
    then war is coming;
but if it oozes water
    we'll live on in peace.'

The tiny wench of the North
    the meek serving-maid
stuck rowan twigs on the fire
the choice wood into the flame;
it oozes no blood at all
    not blood, nor water:
    it oozed out honey
    it was trickling mead.
A crone spoke from a corner
an old hag under a cloak:
'If the wood oozes honey
    and is trickling mead
then those strangers arriving
are a great bridal party.'

Then the mistress of Northland
the hag, the girl of the North
quickly slipped out to the yard
tripped out into the farmyard
casting their eyes seaward and turning
their heads to below the sun.
There they saw what was coming—
    a new craft sailing
a hundred-planked one tacking
on the sea side of Love Bay;
    the vessel shone blue
and red the side of the craft;
a clear-skinned man in the stern
with a paddle of copper.
They saw a stallion running
and a red sledge careering
    a bright sleigh speeding

on the land side of Meadwood—
it had six golden cuckoos
on the collar-bow calling
    seven bluebird-bells
upon the traces singing;
a full-blown man in the back
a fine fellow at the reins.

The mistress of Northland said
    she declared, spoke thus:
'Which will you care to marry
when they come desiring you
to be a friend for ever
and a hen under their arm?
He who comes in the vessel
who sails up with the red boat
on the sea side of Love Bay—
that is old Väinämöinen:
    he brings wealth by ship
    and treasures on board.
He who drives up in the sleigh
    speeds in the bright one
on the land side of Meadwood—
that's the smith Ilmarinen:
    he brings empty lies
    a sleighful of spells.
    When they come indoors
bring mead in a flagon, fetch
some in a two-handled one;
put the flagon in the hand
of him you care to marry!
Give to Väinö-land's old man
    who brings goods by boat
    and treasures on board!'

Well, that fair girl of the North
    knew how to say this:
    'Mamma who bore me

O mother who brought me up
    I'll not marry goods
    nor sense in a man:
    I'll marry good looks
    beauty all over.
Never was the maid before
ever sold to property:
the maid shall be given free
to Ilmarinen the smith
    who forged the Sampo
    beat out the bright-lid.'

The mistress of Northland said:
    'Ah, child, lamb! You will
marry the smith Ilmari
to care for a frothy-brow
to rinse out a smith's burlap
to be a smith's head-washer!'

    The girl answers that
uttered a word and spoke thus:
'I'll not marry Väinö-land's old man
to care for an ancient one:
woe would come from an old one
boredom from someone aged.'

Then the old Väinämöinen
    was first to arrive:
    he drove his red craft
    sailed his blue vessel
up on to the steel rollers
up to the copper moorings;
    he pushes indoors
under the roofs makes his way.
There he declared from the floor
at the door, beneath the beam
    he says with this word
    he spoke with this speech:

'Will you marry me, maiden
to be my friend for ever
a lifelong mate on my knee
and a hen under my arm?'

Well, that fair girl of the North
    she hastened to say:
'Have you carved the little boat
and have you built the big ship
from the bits of my spindle
the pieces of my drawknife?'

The old Väinämöinen said
    he declared, chattered:
'I have built a good ship too
and carved a tough little boat
that is steady in the wind
and stable in bad weather
    to drive through billows
    ride high sea waters:
    as bubbles it bobs
as water lilies it glides
    over the waters
of Northland, the froth-capped waves.'

Well, that fair girl of the North
uttered a word and spoke thus:
'I will not praise a seaman
a billow-sailing fellow:
the wind tugs his mind at sea
his brains are cracked by the gale;
    nor yet can I come
to you, cannot marry you
to be your friend for ever
and a hen under your arm
    to lay out your bed
    to place your pillow.'

19. *Vipers, Beasts, Pike*

Then the smith Ilmarinen
the everlasting craftsman
    himself pushed indoors
edged his way under the roof.
A flagon of mead was brought
a jug of honey was borne
into smith Ilmarinen's hand.
The smith put this into words:
    'Never, nevermore
not in a month of Sundays
    shall I drink these drinks
before I can see my own—
whether my love is ready
ready the one I watch for.'

Well, that mistress of Northland
uttered a word and spoke thus:
'Big trouble your love is in
trouble the one you watch for:
    one foot is half shod
the other still less than half.
Your love will be ready, fit
the one you will take, only
if you plough the viper-field*
turn the snaky one over
without a plough trampling it
without tines disturbing it.
For the Demon ploughed it once
the Devil himself tilled it
    with tines of copper
with a plough of fiery share;
    my own luckless son
    left it half unploughed.'

Then the smith Ilmarinen
went into his maid's cabin
and he put this into words:
'Girl of night, maiden of dusk!
    Do you remember
when I shaped the new Sampo
    beat out the bright-lid?
You swore an oath for ever
before the God known to all
beneath the Almighty's face
and promised you would marry
    me, a good husband
to be my friend for ever
and a hen under my arm:
now your mother will not give
not bestow her girl on me
with the viper-field not ploughed
the snaky one turned over.'

    And the bride gave help*
    the maid encouraged:
    'Smith Ilmarinen
O everlasting craftsman
    shape a plough of gold
work one of silver! With it
you will plough the viper-field
turn the snaky one over.'

Well, that smith Ilmarinen
    put gold in the forge
his silver in the bellows
    from it forged a plough
    and he forged iron
    footwear, steel leggings
    and he puts them on
    sets them on his legs;
dresses in an iron shirt
and belts himself with steel belts;

he took his iron gauntlets
    fetched mittens of stone;
got then the fiery gelding
    harnessed the good horse
and went off to plough the field
    to till the acre.
    He saw writhing heads
    skulls that were rattling.
    He says with this word:
    'O worm, God's creature!
    Who raised your nose up
    who told, compelled you
    to hold your head stiff
    your neck erect? Shove
    out of the way now
    into the grass, wretch
    down into the scrub
    weave, sway in the hay!
    If you bob up there
    God will crack your head
    with steel-tipped arrows
    with iron hailstones.'

Then he ploughed the viper-field
he tilled the land full of worms
raised vipers on the ploughed soil
snakes on the soil turned over.
He said when he came from there:
'Now I've ploughed the viper-field
I've tilled the land full of worms
turned the snaky one over.
Will the girl be now bestowed
    my matchless one given?'

Well, that mistress of Northland
uttered a word and spoke thus:
    'The maid will be given
the girl here bestowed, only

if you bring me Tuoni's bear
quell the wolf of the Dead Land
from Tuonela's backwoods there
the Dead Land's furthest abode;
a hundred went to quell it
    but not one came back.'

Then the smith Ilmarinen
went into his maid's cabin
and uttered a word, spoke thus:
'A task has been set me—to
quell the wolves of the Dead Land
    and bring Tuoni's bears
from Tuonela's backwoods there
the Dead Land's furthest abode.'

    And the bride gave help
    the maid encouraged:
    'Smith Ilmarinen
O everlasting craftsman
out of steel make a bridle
forge a headstall of iron
    upon one rock wet
with the foam of three rapids:
with them you'll bring Tuoni's bears
quell the wolves of the Dead Land.'

Then the smith Ilmarinen
the everlasting craftsman
out of steel formed a bridle
forged a headstall of iron
    upon one rock wet
with the foam of three rapids.
He went then to the quelling
and he put this into words:
    'Mist-girl, Fog-daughter:
    sift mist with a sieve

waft some fog about
where the wealth wanders
so it does not hear my step
nor flee before me!'

And he got the wolf bridled
and the bear in iron chains
from Tuoni's heath there
from within the blue backwoods.
He said when he came from there:
'Give your daughter, hag
for I have brought Tuoni's bear
quelled the wolf of the Dead Land.'

Well, that mistress of Northland
uttered a word and spoke thus:
'The calloo will not be given
the mallard handed over
till you have got the great scaly pike
the quick fleshy fish
from Tuonela's river there
from the dale of the Dead Land
without taking up a seine
without turning a hand-net;
a hundred went to hunt it
but not one came back.'

Well, now things become painful
things turn out more troublesome.
He went to his maid's cabin
and he put this into words:
'A task has been set me, one
even better than before—
to get the great scaly pike
the quick fleshy fish
out of Tuoni's black river
the Dead Land's eternal brook

without a net or a seine
without any other trap.'

And the bride gave help
the maid encouraged:
'Smith Ilmarinen
don't worry at all!
Now, forge a fiery eagle
a wivern of flame:
with it you'll get the great pike
the quick fleshy fish
out of Tuoni's black river
from the dale of the Dead Land.'

Smith Ilmarinen
the everlasting craftsman
forges an eagle of fire
a wivern of flame;
the feet he shaped of iron
of steel the talons
for wings the sides of a boat.
Up on to the wings he climbed
on its back he placed himself
on the eagle's wingbone tips.
There he advised his eagle
and the wivern he counselled:
'My eagle, my little bird!
Go flying where I tell you—
towards Tuoni's black river
to the dale of the Dead Land:
strike the pike great and scaly
the quick fleshy fish!'

That eagle, a splendid bird
flaps off on its way
flew to hunt the pike, to seek
the one with terrible teeth
in Tuonela's river there

in the dale of the Dead Land:
one wing ruffled the water
    the other reached heaven
    its feet scooped the sea
and its beak clattered on crags.
Then the smith Ilmarinen
    goes off to harrow
that river of Tuonela
with the eagle standing guard.

An elf reared from the water
fastened on Ilmarinen:
the eagle leapt on its neck
twisted the water-elf's head
and rammed the head further down
    towards the black mud.
    Now comes Tuoni's pike
the water-dog veers along—
not a tiny little pike
    nor a great big pike
with a tongue two axe-hafts long
    teeth one rake-haft long
jaws the size of three rapids
its back long as seven boats:
it wanted to meet the smith
eat the smith Ilmarinen.
The eagle came winging along
the bird of the air beating—
no tiny little eagle
nor a really great big one
with a mouth a hundred fathoms wide
    jaws six rapids wide
    tongue six spear-shafts long
    claws long as five scythes.
It spied the great scaly pike
    the quick fleshy fish
    lunges at that fish
    battered at its scales

and then the great scaly pike
    the quick fleshy fish
    drags the eagle's claw
down below the clear waters.
    The eagle rises
up into the air it goes:
    it lifted black mud
on top of the clear waters.

    It glides, it hovers;
yes, it tries a second time.
It sank one of its claws in
the terrible pike's shoulders
in the water-dog's hooked bones;
sank another of its claws
    in a steel mountain
    a cliff of iron.
But the claw bounced off the rock
    it glanced off the cliff:
    the pike thrashed about
    the water-hulk slipped
out of the eagle's clutches
    from the wivern's toes
with claw marks upon its ribs
with gashes on its shoulders.

Then the iron-foot eagle
    made one more effort;
    its wings flashed as flame
    its eyes as clear fire:
it got the pike in its claws
the water-dog in its grasp
and raised the great scaly pike
    hauled the water-hulk
from below the deep billows
on top of the clear waters.
Well, the iron-foot eagle
    the third time it tries

    yes, gets Tuoni's pike
    the quick fleshy fish
from that Tuonela river
from the dale of the Dead Land:
water felt unlike water
because of the great pike's scales
air smelt unlike air because
of the great eagle's feathers.
Then the iron-foot eagle
carried the great scaly pike
to the bough of a stout oak
to a shock-headed pine's top
and there it tasted the taste
slashed the pike's belly across
    ripped the breast open
    hacked the head clean off.
The smith Ilmarinen said:
    'You wretched eagle!
What kind of bird may you be
    and what sort of fowl
that now you've tasted the taste
slashed the pike's belly across
    ripped the breast to boot
    hacked the head clean off!'

Well, the iron-foot eagle
at that flared up into flight—
up into the sky it soared
on to a long bank of cloud:
the clouds squirmed, the heavens mewed
the lids of the sky tilted
    the Old Man's bow snapped
so did the moon's horny points.

Then the smith Ilmarinen
carried the fish-head himself
to be mother-in-law's gift.
He uttered a word, spoke thus:

'Here is a long-lasting chair
for the good Northland cabin.'
Then he put this into words
    he declared, chattered:
'Now I've ploughed the viper-fields
I've tilled the lands full of worms
quelled the wolves of the Dead Land
shackled the bears of Tuoni;
I've got the great scaly pike
    the quick fleshy fish
from that Tuonela river
from the dale of the Dead Land.
Will the maiden now be given
    the girl here bestowed?'

The mistress of Northland said:
'But you did wrong even so
    to hack the head off
cut the pike's belly across
    rip the breast as well
    taste the taste to boot.'

Then the smith Ilmarinen
    put this into words:
'There is no catch without hurt
from even better places
let alone from Tuonela's river
from the dale of the Dead Land.
So is my love ready now
ready the one I watch for?'

The mistress of Northland said
    she declared, uttered:
'Yes, your love is ready now
ready the one you watch for!
My dear calloo will be given
my duckling handed over
to Ilmarinen the smith

to sit for ever, to be
a lifelong mate on his knee
and a hen under his arm.'

There was a child on the floor
and the child sang from the floor:
'Now to these cabins has come
one more bird for our stronghold.
The eagle flew from north-east
    the hawk across heaven;
one wing struck at the sky's rim
and the other swept the wave
    its tail skimmed the sea
    and its head reached heaven.
    It looks, it turns round
it glides, it hovers, and it
settled on the men's stronghold
    rattles with its beak;
the men's stronghold had an iron roof*
so it could not get inside.
    It looks, it turns round
it glides, it hovers, and it
sat on the women's stronghold
    rattles with its beak;
the women's stronghold was copper-roofed
so it could not get inside.
    It looks, it turns round
it glides, it hovers, and it
settled on the maids' stronghold
    rattles with its beak;
the maids' stronghold had a hempen roof
so now it could get inside!

'It settled on the stronghold chimney
from there dropped on the roof ridge
slid back the stronghold shutter
sat at the stronghold window
at the wall the green-plumed one

hundred-plumed at the wall joint.
It looks over the braid-heads
the plait-heads it sounded out
the best of the flock of maids
of the braid-heads the fairest
the brightest of the bead-heads
of the flower-heads the best known.
And then the eagle pounces
    the hawk-bird snatches—
it seized the best of the flock
comeliest of the duck-crowd
the brightest, the softest, the
most full-blooded, the whitest:
'tis she the bird of the air
    seized, the long-claw scratched
who was upright of bearing
    and choice of body—
as to her plumes the sweetest
the finest as to feathers.'

Then the mistress of Northland
uttered a word and spoke thus:
'How did you know, blessed one
and how hear, golden apple
that this maid was growing up
this flaxen-haired one moving?
Did the maid's silver glitter
was the maid's gold heard of there
    did our suns shine there
    and did our moons gleam?'

The child declared from the floor
and the one still growing crooned:
'From this the blessed one knew
the lucky dog found his way
    to the maid's famous
    home, to her fair farm:
father was well spoken of

after launching a great ship
    mother still better
after baking a thick loaf
after making a wheat loaf
and providing for a guest.
From this the blessed one knew
and the utter stranger grasped
that a young maid had risen
that a lassie had sprung up:
when once he walked by the yard
    stepped down by the sheds
right early in the morning
quite betimes on the morrow
soot was rising like a thread
smoke was thickly escaping
    from the maid's famous
home, from the growing one's farm;
the maid herself was grinding
swaying at the quern handle:
the quern handle as a cuckoo called
as a bean goose the quern bridge
the quern disc as a bunting
the quern as a bead rattled.
He went from there once more, stepped
along the edge of the field:
the maid on maddery ground
was tripping on yellow heaths
brewing potfuls of red dye
boiling pans of yellow dye.
He went a third time as well
passed below the maid's window
and he heard the maid weaving
the reed in her hand slamming
and the little shuttle whizzed
like a stoat in a rock-hole
the reed-teeth were tapping like
a woodpecker on a tree

and the breast beam was whirring
like a squirrel on a bough.'

Then the mistress of Northland
uttered a word and spoke thus:
'So there, so there, little maid!
Haven't I always told you:
in the spruces don't cuckoo
and don't sing in the valleys
or show your neck's curviness
    or your arm's whiteness
the ripeness of your young breast
or the rest of your glory!
All autumn I hurled it forth
I dinned it in this summer
    through the fleeting spring
    the next sowing-time:
let us build a secret hut
    small secret windows
for a maiden to weave cloth
squeak away with four heddles
unheard by Finnish bridegrooms—
by Finnish bridegrooms, the land's suitors!'

The child declared from the floor
and the fortnight-old piped up:
''Tis easy to hide a horse
to cover up a coarse-hair
but 'tis wrong to hide a maid
to keep secret a long-hair.
Though you build a stone stronghold
    amid the high seas
    there to hold wenches
    to rear hens of yours
they will be no secret there
nor will the lassies grow up
out of reach of great bridegrooms

great bridegrooms, the land's suitors
    men with tall helmets
    horses with steel hoofs.'

As for old Väinämöinen
his head down, in bad spirits
    as he went homeward
he uttered a word, spoke thus:
'Woe is me, a weary man
    for I did not know
    to marry young, to
seek at the time of my life!
    He regrets his all
who regrets a young marriage
having a child when a child
founding a family when small.'

There Väinämöinen forbade
the man of Calm Waters banned
the old from seeking the young
    trying for the fair;
forbade swimming recklessly
    and rowing rashly
and competing for a maid
with another, younger man.

20. *Slaughtering and Brewing*

What shall we sing about now
    which tale shall we lilt?
    We'll sing about this
    and we'll lilt this tale—
    of that Northland feast
those revels of the godly.*
Long the wedding was laid in
and the goods were made ready
in those cabins of Northland
in Sariola's buildings.
    And what was brought there
    and which was taken
    to the North's long feast
    the great crowd's revels
    to nourish the folk
    to feed the great crowd?

There grew an ox in Karelia
in Finland a bull fattened;
it was neither great nor small
but 'twas a calf and a half!*
Down in Häme its tail waved
its head swayed up at Kemi River*
horns a hundred fathoms long
muzzle half as thick again.
For a week a stoat turned round
in the space of one tether;
for a day a swallow flew
between the horns of the ox—
it only just reached the tip
with no rest in the middle;
for a month a summer squirrel ran
from the withers towards the tail-tip—

did not even reach the tip
nor in the next month make it.
That unmanageable calf
    that great Finnish bull
from Karelia was fetched
to the edge of the North's field:
by the horns a hundred men
by the muzzle a thousand
held the ox as it was led
    and brought to Northland.
And the ox lumbered about
at Sariola's strait-mouth
    browsing in a mire
    its back flicking clouds;
but there was no one to strike
down, to fell the land's grim one
in the ranks of the North's sons
    in all the great kin
among the youngsters rising
nor indeed among the old.

There came an old man, a foreigner,
Virokannas,* a Karelian
and he put this into words:
'Hold on, hold on, hapless ox
for I'm coming with a club
and with my rod I will thump
you, mean one, upon your skull:
not for another summer
will you fiercely turn your snout
    gape with your muzzle
at the edge of this field, nor
at Sariola's strait-mouth!'

The old man went to strike it
Virokannas to touch it
the Worshipful to hold it.
    The ox waved its head
    rolled its black eyes round:

the old man jumped up a spruce
Virokannas into brush
the Worshipful into a willow!
They sought one to strike
one to knock the great bull down
in Karelia the fair
on the great farms of Finland
in Russia's mild land
in the bold land of Sweden
in Lapland's broad distances—
the mighty land of Turja;
they sought one in Tuonela
the Dead Land, underground too—
they sought but they did not find
they searched but they did not see.
They sought one to strike
they looked for someone to fell
on the clear high seas
upon the vast waves.

A black man rose from the sea
a fellow burst from the waves
straight from the clear main
the open expanse.
He was not of the greatest
nor yet quite of the smallest:
he could lie beneath a bowl
stand beneath a sieve—
an iron-fisted old man
iron-hued to look upon;
on his head a rock helmet
on his feet stone shoes
a golden knife in his hand
with a bright copper handle.
So they got one to strike it
so found one to slaughter it—
Finland's bull one to knock it
down, to fell the land's grim one.

The moment he saw his prey
he dealt its neck a quick blow:
he brought the bull to its knees
    made it slump over.
Did he make much of a catch?
Oh no, not much of a catch—
a hundred pails of meat, a
hundred fathoms of sausage
and of blood seven boatfuls
and of grease six barrelfuls
    for that Northland feast
that Sariola blowout.

A cabin had been built in Northland
a huge cabin, a great hut
nine fathoms along the side
and seven wide at the top.
When a cock crowed on the roof
the sound does not reach the ground;
a pup barking at the back
cannot be heard at the door.
Well, that mistress of Northland
shifted at the floor seam, paced
in the middle of the floor;
    she thinks, considers:
'Now, what shall we get beer from
and skilfully brew the ales
to lay in for this wedding
    this feast to be held?
I don't know how ale is made
nor the Origin of beer.'

An old man sat on the stove.
The old man spoke from the stove:
'Barley is beer's Origin
hop that of the well-known drink
though not born without water
    nor without harsh fire.
    Hop, son of hubbub

was stuck in the ground when small
was ploughed in as a viper
was tossed in as a nettle
down by Kaleva's well-side
on the bank of Osmo's field:
from it a young seedling rose
    a green shoot came up;
it rose on a tiny tree
and towards the top it climbed.
    Lord Luck sowed barley
on top of Osmo's new field:
barley grew beautifully
came up exceedingly well
on top of Osmo's new field
in Kaleva's son's clearing.
    A little time passed.
Now hop called out from the tree
barley spoke from the field-top
water from Kaleva's well:
"When shall we get together
at what time meet each other?
    Life alone is dull;
twosomes, threesomes are nicer."

'Osmo-daughter the beer-smith
    the brewer woman
    took grains of barley
    six grains of barley
    seven hop catkins
of water eight ladlefuls;
she put a pot on the fire
and brought the stew to the boil.
Out of barley she stewed beer
on a fleeting summer day
on the misty headland's tip
at the foggy island's end
in a grooved cask of new wood
    inside a birch tub.

She got the beer brewed, but she
did not get it fermented.
    She thinks, considers
she uttered a word, spoke thus:
    "What may be brought here
and which thing may be looked out
for the beer, to ferment it
for the brew, to make it rise?"

'Kaleva-daughter, fair maid
    the sweet of fingers
the ever brisk of movement
    ever light of shoe
shifted at the floor seam, skipped
in the middle of the floor
busy with one, the other
    betwixt the two pans;
saw a splinter on the floor
picked the splinter off the floor.
She looks, she turns it over:
"What would even this become
in the fair woman's hands, at
the good lass's fingertips
if I bore it to her hand
the good lass's fingertips?"

'Well, she bore it to her hand
the good lass's fingertips.
The woman with her two palms
    squeezed it in both hands
    against both her thighs
and a white squirrel was born.
And thus she advised her son
she instructed her squirrel:
"Squirrel, darling of the mound
flower of the mound, earth's delight:
    run where I tell you
    tell and compel you—

into pleasant Forestland
to careful Tapiola
and run up a tiny tree
skilfully up a bush-top
lest the eagle should snatch you
the bird of the air strike you;
    bring cones from the spruce
    and husks from the pine
bear them to the woman's hand
into Osmo-daughter's beer!"

'The squirrel knew how to run
the bushy-tail how to rush
how to run a long way fast
how to range afar swiftly
across one wood, along two
through a third somewhat athwart
into pleasant Forestland
to careful Tapiola.
It saw three forest spruces
    four tiny pine trees
climbed up a spruce in a marsh
up a pine tree on the heath;
nor did the eagle snatch it
the bird of the air strike it.
It broke some cones from the spruce
some foliage off the pine
and hid the cones in its claws
    wrapped its paws round them
bore them to the woman's hand
the good lass's fingertips.
And she stuck them in her brew
Osmo-daughter in her beer;
but the beer will not ferment
for the young drink to grow up.
Osmo-daughter the beer-smith
    the brewer woman

keeps considering:
"What may be brought here
for the beer, to ferment it
for the brew, to make it rise?"

'Kaleva-daughter, fair maid
the sweet of fingers
the ever brisk of movement
ever light of shoe
shifted at the floor seam, skipped
in the middle of the floor
busy with one, the other
betwixt the two pans;
saw a shaving on the floor
picked the shaving off the floor.
She looks, she turns it over:
"What would even this become
in the fair woman's hands, at
the good lass's fingertips
if I bore it to her hand
the good lass's fingertips?"

'Well, she bore it to her hand
the good lass's fingertips.
The woman with her two palms
squeezed it in both hands
against both her thighs:
a gold-breast marten was born.
So she advised her marten
instructed her orphan child:
"My marten, my little bird
my fair precious-pelt:
go where I tell you
tell and compel you—
to the bruin's rocky den
to the forest bear's farmyard
where the bears fight, the
bruins live it up;

with your claws gather some yeast
in your hands scoop up some froth
bear it to the woman's hand
bring it to Osmo-daughter's shoulder!"

'Well now, the marten could run
the gold-breast could dash along
and it ran a long way fast
ranged afar swiftly, across
one river swam, along two
through a third somewhat athwart
to the bruin's rocky den
    the bear's craggy cell:
    there the bears fight, the
    bruins live it up
    on an iron cliff
    a mountain of steel.
Froth poured out of a bear's mouth
yeast from a massive one's jaws:
in its hands it scooped some froth
with its claws gathered some yeast
bore it to the woman's hand
the good lass's fingertips.
Osmo-daughter in her beer
dropped it, tipped it in her brew;
but the beer will not ferment
nor the juice of men bubble.
Osmo-daughter the beer-smith
    the brewer woman
    keeps considering:
    "What may be brought here
for the beer, to ferment it
for the brew, to make it rise?"

'Kaleva-daughter, fair maid
the girl that's sweet of fingers
the ever brisk of movement
    ever light of shoe

shifted at the floor seam, skipped
in the middle of the floor
busy with one, the other
    between the two pans;
saw a pea plant on the ground
picked the pea plant off the ground.
She looks, she turns it over:
"What would even this become
in the fair woman's hands, at
the good lass's fingertips
if I bore it to her hand
the good lass's fingertips?"

'Well, she bore it to her hand
the good lass's fingertips.
The woman with her two palms
    squeezed it in both hands
    against both her thighs
and a bee was born from it.
And so she advised her bird
    instructed her bee:
    "O bee, bird so brisk
    king of the turf flowers:
    fly where I tell you
    tell and compel you—
to an island on the main
    a crag in the sea!
There a maid has gone to sleep
a copper-belt slipped away
with mead-sweet grass at her side
honey-sweet grass on her hem.
Bring some mead upon your wing
bear some honey on your cape
    from a bright grass-top
from a golden flower petal;
bear it to the woman's hand
bring it to Osmo-daughter's shoulder!"

'The bee, bird so brisk
it both flew and sped
and it flew a long way fast
shortened distances swiftly
across one sea, along two
through a third somewhat athwart
to the island on the main
the crag in the sea.
It saw the maid gone to sleep
the tin-breast who'd pined away
on the nameless turf
the edge of the honey-field
with golden grass at her waist
with silver grass at her belt.
It dipped its wings in the mead
its feathers in the melted honey
on a glittering grass-top
a golden flower-tip
bore it to the woman's hand
the good lass's fingertips.
Osmo-daughter in her beer
stuck it, put it in her brew:
now the beer chose to ferment
the young drink grew up
in the grooved cask of new wood
inside the birch tub;
it foamed high as the handles
roared up to the brims
wanted to steer for the ground
to head for the floor.

'A little time passed
a moment sped by.
The fellows hurried to drink—
Lemminkäinen most of all:
Ahti got drunk, Farmind got
drunk, the full-blooded rogue got
drunk on Osmo-daughter's beer

on Kaleva-daughter's brew.
Osmo-daughter the beer-smith
    the brewer woman
at that put this into words:
"Woe, luckless me, for my days
    for brewing bad beer
    making wayward ale
that has climbed out of the tub
and ripples upon the floor!"
A red bird sang from a tree
and a thrush from the eaves' end:
    "It is no bad sort;
it is a good sort of drink
to tip into a barrel
to mature in a cellar
    in an oak barrel
inside one with copper hoops."

'That's the Origin of beer
how Kaleva's brew began;
that's how it got its good name
    its famous honour—
    being a good sort
a good drink for the well-bred:
it put smiles on women's lips
    men in good spirits
the well-bred making merry
but the mad leaping about.'

Then the mistress of Northland
when she heard beer's Origin
fetched a great tub of water
one of new wood to her side
in it put enough barley
and a lot of hop catkins;
she began to stew the beer
to stir the strong water round

in the grooved cask of new wood
    inside the birch tub.
For months the stones were heated
whole summers the water stewed
backwoodsfuls of trees were burned
wellfuls of water were brought:
the backwoods ran short of trees
waters grew less at the springs
as the beer was being brewed
    and the brew made up
    for the North's long feast
    the good crowd's revels.

Smoke burns upon the island
and fire at the headland's point;
    thick smoke billowed up
a haze rose into the air
from the harsh places of fire
    the plentiful flames:
    it filled half the North
blinded all Karelia.
    All the people glance
    they glance, long to know:
'Where is the smoke coming from
the haze rising in the air—
too small for the smoke of war
too big for a herdsman's fire?'

Now, Lemminkäinen's mother
quite early in the morning
went for water from the spring;
    she sees the thick smoke
    in the northern skies.
She uttered a word, spoke thus:
    'That is war-smoke, those
    are flames of battle!'

He, Ahti the Islander
    that one, fair Farmind

takes a look, turns round;
he thinks, considers:
'Suppose I wade out to look
inspect from close by to see
where that smoke is coming from
and the haze filling the air—
whether that is war-smoke, those
are flames of battle?'

Farmind did wade out to look
for the birthplace of the smoke:
there were no war-fires
nor flames of battle;
no, they were beer-fires
flames of a brew being stewed
at Sariola's strait-mouth
under the headland's cape's arm.
At that Farmind looks . . .
An eye squints in Farmind's head—
squints, the other looks askance
the mouth twists the slightest bit.
At last he spoke as he looked
from across the strait he says:
'O my dear mother-in-law
kindly mistress of the North:
make excellent beer
and stew a grand brew
fit for the great crowd to drink
Lemminkäinen most of all
at that wedding of his own
with your young daughter!'

The beer was getting ready
the juice of men drinkable:
the brown beer was being brewed
the fair brew was maturing
lying underground

in a stone cellar
in an oak barrel
behind a bung of copper.
Then the mistress of Northland
she brought the stew to the boil
the pans to rumbling
the stewpans to clamouring;
then she baked great loaves
and great dumplings she patted
to take care of the good folk
to feed the great crowd
at the North's long feast
at Sariola's revels.
Well, the loaves were baked
the dumplings patted.
A little time passed
a moment sped by:
the beer throbbed in the barrel
the brew stirred in the cellar:
'If now my drinker would come
and my lapper were prepared—
my rightful cuckoo-caller
my proper singer!'

A singer was sought
a proper singer
a rightful cuckoo-caller
and a fair crooner:
a salmon was brought to sing
a pike to call rightfully.
But a salmon cannot sing
nor can a pike croon:
a salmon's jaws are agape
and a pike's teeth are spaced out.
A singer was sought
a proper singer
a rightful cuckoo-caller
and a fair crooner;

and a child was brought to sing
    to call rightfully.
    But no child can sing
no slobber-chops can cuckoo:
    a child's tongue is shrill
and the root of the tongue stiff.
    The brown beer threatened
    and the young drink cursed
    in the cask of oak
behind the bung of copper:
'If you don't find a singer
    a proper singer
a rightful cuckoo-caller
    and a fair crooner
I will kick my hoops away
my bottom I will force out!'

Then the mistress of Northland
sent the invitations out
the heralds on their errands
and she put this into words:
    'Hey there, tiny wench
    my perpetual serf:
call the folk together, the
crowd of men to the revels;
call the wretched, call the poor
the blind, even the troubled
the lame and the sledge-cripples;
    row the blind in boats
drive the lame here on horseback
drag the cripples here by sledge;
call all of the North's people
and all Kaleva's people
invite old Väinämöinen
to be the proper singer—
but do not invite Farmind
that Ahti the Islander!'

Well, that tiny wench
uttered a word and spoke thus:
'And why not invite Farmind
Ahti the Islander too?'

Well, that mistress of Northland
she says a word in answer:
'You shall not invite Farmind
that wanton Lemminkäinen
because by all accounts he
quarrels, picks fights on purpose;
he's brought shame on weddings too
at feasts he has done great crimes
disgraced pure wenches
in their Sunday clothes.'

Well, that tiny wench
uttered a word and spoke thus:
'How shall I know 'tis Farmind
to leave him uninvited?
I do not know Ahti's home
the farm of Farmind.'

The mistress of Northland said
she declared, uttered:
'You will know Farmind all right
that Ahti the Islander:
Ahti lives on an island
the rogue by waters
at the broadest bay's
side, under Far Headland's arm.'

Well, that tiny wench
the bought drudge carried
the invitations six ways
and the summonses eight ways:
she called all the North's people
and all Kaleva's people—

those thin cotters too
and gipsies* in tight caftans;
only matchless Ahti boy
him she left uninvited.

21. *The Wedding*

Now, that mistress of Northland
old wife of Sariola
    was outside awhile
    busy with her chores.
From the swamp came a whip-crack
from the shore a sledge-rattle.
She cast her eyes north-west, turned
her head to below the sun
    she thinks, considers:
'What's this band lying in wait
for poor me upon my shores?
Is it a mighty war-band?'

And she waded out to look
to inspect it from close by:
    it was no war-band
but a great wedding party
the son-in-law in the midst
    among the good folk.
When the mistress of Northland
old wife of Sariola
saw her son-in-law coming
she uttered a word, spoke thus:
'I thought the wind was blowing
    the woodstack toppling
    the seashore rumbling
    the gravel crooning
and I waded out to look
to inspect it from close by:
it was not the wind blowing
was not the woodstack toppling
was not the seashore yielding
was not the gravel crooning—

my son-in-law's band comes, by
the hundred in pairs they turn!
    How shall I pick out
my son-in-law from the band?
The son-in-law stands out from the band
the bird cherry from the other trees
the oak tree from the saplings
the moon from the stars of heaven:
he is on a black stallion
as on a ravening wolf
on a raven bearing prey
upon a flying griffin
    with six gold buntings
calling on the collar-bow
    seven bluebird-bells
singing upon the traces.'

The noise is heard in the lane
the shaft-din on the well-path:
now the son-in-law reaches
the yard, his party the farm.
The son-in-law's in the midst
    among the good folk—
he's for sure not the foremost
    nor quite the hindmost.
'Away, boys, outside, fellows,
into the yard, tallest men
to tear away the breast straps
to pull away the traces
    to let down the shafts
to bring in the son-in-law!'

The son-in-law's stallion runs
    and the bright sleigh speeds
along father-in-law's yard.
The mistress of Northland said:
    'Hey you, serf, hireling
    fine village gipsy:

take the son-in-law's stallion
let the braze-brow out
from the harness of copper
the breast straps of tin
the leather traces
from the sapling collar-bow;
lead the son-in-law's stallion
guide it skilfully
by the silk bridle
by the silver-tipped headstall
to soft places for romping
to the level ground
to some fine fresh snow
to some milk-hued land;
water my son-in-law's foal
at the spring nearby
that stands unfrozen
and courses trickling
beneath the gold spruce's root
and the sprouting pine;
fodder my son-in-law's foal
from the gold basket
the box of copper
with washed barley, with white bread
with cooked summer wheat
with crushed summer rye;
lead the son-in-law's stallion
then to the snuggest manger
to the highest place
the furthest barnyard;
tie the son-in-law's stallion
with the golden band
to the iron ring
to the post of curly birch;
give the son-in-law's stallion
a gallon of oats
and one of hay husks
and a third of chaff;

comb the son-in-law's stallion
with a comb of walrus bone
    that no hair may split
and no coarse hair come away;
drape the son-in-law's stallion
in the silver-trimmed blanket
    in the gold-trimmed hood
in the copper-trimmed padding!

    'Village lads, sweet doves:
lead the son-in-law indoors
with no hat upon his hair
no mitten on his hand! Wait—
I'll see to the son-in-law
whether he will fit indoors
without taking the door off
and pulling the doorpost down
    raising the lintel
and lowering the threshold
knocking out the corner wall
and moving the bottom beam:
no, he can't be got indoors
the godsend beneath the roof
without taking the door off
and pulling the doorpost down
    raising the lintel
and lowering the threshold
knocking out the corner wall
and moving the bottom beam
for he's taller by a head
    higher by an ear.
Let the lintels be lifted
so that his cap's not knocked off
let the thresholds be lowered
so that his shoe heel's not touched
let the doorposts be dislodged
and let the doors swing open
as the son-in-law comes in

the real man steps inside!
    Thanks to the fair God
the son-in-law has got in!
Wait, I'll look to the cabin
keep an eye on its inside:
have the tables here been washed
the benches sluiced with water
    and the smooth boards wiped
    and the plank floors swept?

'I will look to this cabin
    but I cannot tell
what trees the hut was made from
what the shelter was got from
what the walls were put up from
    and the floors laid down:
the side wall's of hedgehog bones
the rear wall of reindeer bones
the door-wall of glutton bones
and the lintel of lamb bones;
the beams are from apple trees
the post from curly birch trees
the stove sides out of water lilies
    the roof of bream scales;
the seat was built of iron
the benches of German planks
the table adorned with gold
and the boards polished with silk;
the stove was cast in copper
the stove seat of good boulders
    the hearth of sea rocks
the inglenook from Kaleva's trees.'

The bridegroom pushes indoors
under the roofs makes his way.
He uttered a word, spoke thus:
    'Welcome here too, God

under the famous roof beam
    under the fair roof!'

The mistress of Northland said:
    'Hail, hail and welcome
    to this small cabin
    to this squat abode
    to this room of fir
    to this nest of pine!
Hey there, my little serf wench
    you village hireling:
bring fire on a birchbark scrap
snatch some on a tar-wood tip
for me to look at the son-in-law
and to see the bridegroom's eyes—
whether they are blue or red
    or else white as cloth!'

    The tiny serf wench
    the village hireling
    brought fire on birchbark
    snatched fire on tar-wood.

    'Birchbark fire crackles
    tar-wood smoke is black;
'twould soil the son-in-law's eyes
and blacken his handsome looks:
now, bring fire on a candle
    flame on one of wax!'

    The tiny serf wench
    the village hireling
brought some fire on a candle
    flame on one of wax:
    the white waxen smoke
    the bright candle fire
lightened the son-in-law's eyes
brightened the son-in-law's face.

'Now I can see my son-in-law's eyes:
they're not blue, not red
nor yet white as cloth;
they're white as sea froth
brown as a sea reed
and fair as a sea bulrush.
Village lads, sweet doves:
lead this son-in-law
to the greatest seats
the topmost places
with the blue wall to his back
the red table to his front
facing the invited guests
amid the folk's din!'

Then the mistress of Northland
fed the guests, gave them to drink:
mouthfuls of melted butter
and fistfuls of cream pancakes
she fed those invited guests—
her son-in-law most of all.
There was salmon on the plates
and beside it pork
the cups were brimming
the bowls up to the bulwarks
for the guests to eat—
the son-in-law most of all.
The mistress of Northland said:
'Hey you, tiny wench:
bring beer in a flagon, fetch
some in a two-handled one
for all those invited guests—
my son-in-law most of all!'

Well, that tiny wench
the money-bought drudge
let the flagon do its job

and the five-hoop circulate
    the hop soak the beards
and the froth whiten the beards
of all those invited guests—
the son-in-law most of all.
And what now could the beer do
what did that in five hoops say
when it was with its singer
its rightful cuckoo-caller?
It was old Väinämöinen
age-old wielder of a tale
who was the proper singer
    the best cunning man.

    First he takes some beer
then he put this into words:
    'Dear beer, darling drink:
don't moisten a man in vain
but set the men singing, the
golden-mouths cuckoo-calling!
    The masters marvel
and the mistresses wonder:
have the songs gone out of tune
    the joy-strings come loose
or did I prepare bad beer
make a wretched drink to drink
that our singers do not sing
    nor our good bards hum
nor our welcome guests cuckoo
nor our joy-cuckoos rejoice?
Now, who here will cuckoo-call
and who will sing with his tongue
    at this Northland feast
these Sariola revels?
The benches here will not sing
if the bench-sitters do not
and the floors will not declare
if the floor-treaders do not

nor will the windows rejoice
if the window-masters don't
nor will the table-rims boom
if those at table do not
those smoke-holes will make no din
if those beneath them do not.'

There was a child on the floor
a milk-beard on the stove seat.
The child declared from the floor
from the seat the boy chattered:
    'I'm of no great age
    no mighty stature;
    be that as it may
if others, plump ones, won't sing
and men, fatter ones, won't chant
nor fuller-blooded ones lilt
then I, a lean boy, will sing,
a skinny boy, I'll warble;
    I'll sing from lean flesh
    from unfattened flanks
to cheer this evening of ours
to honour the famous day.'

An old man was on the stove
and he put this into words:
'There's nothing in children's songs
in the cooing of wretches:
    children's songs are lies
and daughters' tales are empty!
Let a shrewd man tell a tale
a bench-sitter sing a song!'

Then the old Väinämöinen
    put this into words:
'Is there among these youngsters
    in all the great kin
someone to put hand in hand
and clasp in another clasp

and to begin reciting
    to burst out singing
to gladden the closing day
honour the famous evening?'

The old man said from the stove:
    'Here there has been heard
    either heard or seen
    ever in this world
    no better singer
no more careful cunning man
    than when I cooed, I
carolled as a younger man
sang upon the bay's waters
and echoed upon the heaths
cuckoo-called in the spruces
recited in the backwoods.
My voice was great and graceful
    my tone very fair:
as a river then it ran
    as a stream it flashed
travelled like a ski on snow
a sailing ship on the waves.
But now I cannot recite
nor this can I rightly tell—
what has stifled my great voice
laid my sweet voice low: now it
does not as a river run
nor as waves ripple, but it
is like a harrow among
treestumps, a pine on hard snow
like a sledge on seashore sands
    a boat on dry rocks.'

Then the old Väinämöinen
    put this into words:
    'If no one else will
    come and sing with me

I will launch into poems
and burst out singing alone:
since I've been made a singer
and turned out a reciter
I'll not ask others the way
a stranger to start a tale.'

Then the old Väinämöinen
age-old wielder of a tale
sat down for merrymaking
to song-work applied himself
with the joy-tales at his side
with the words at the ready
and old Väinämöinen sang
he both sang and worked wisdom:
words are not lacking in words
tales in the telling don't fail;
    cliffs sooner lack rocks
and still pools water lilies.
And there Väinämöinen sang
the whole evening rejoiced:
all the wives with smiling lips
and the men in good spirits
    listened, wondered at
Väinämöinen's turn of phrase
for 'twas a wonder to the hearer
and a marvel to the idler too.

The old Väinämöinen said
uttered when his tale ended:
'But still, what is there in me
of singer, of cunning man!
I can do nothing, am not
capable of anything.
Were the Creator singing
with a sweet mouth reciting
    he would sing a song
he would sing and work wisdom:

he'd sing the seas to honey
    the sea sands to peas
    the sea's soil to malt
and to salt the sea's gravel
the broad groves to lands of bread
the glade-sides to lands of wheat
    the hills to puddings
    the stones to hen's eggs;
he would sing, practise his craft:
he would recite and call forth
    he'd sing for this house
    byrefuls of heifers
    lanefuls of hook-heads
    glades of milk-givers
a hundred bearers of horns
a thousand udder-bringers;
he would sing and work wisdom:
he would recite and call forth
coats of lynx fur for masters
broadcloth cloaks for mistresses
and fancy shoes for daughters
    and red shirts for sons.

    'Grant always, O God
and again, true Creator
that this may be thus lived up
    may be done again—
    this, a Northland feast
and Sariola revels:
beer running as a river
honey flowing as a stream
in these cabins of Northland
in Sariola's buildings
that by day there may be song
at evening merrymaking
all the days of this master
the lifetime of this mistress!
    God give a reward

and the Creator their due
to the master at table
to the mistress in her shed
to the sons at their fishing
at their looms to the daughters
that they may never regret
nor another year bewail
    this long-lasting feast
    the great crowd's revels!'

22. *Laments*

When the wedding was well drunk
  and feasted that feast
the wedding in the cabins
of Northland, the Darkland feast
the mistress of Northland said
to Ilmarinen the son-in-law:
'What do you sit, well-born one
  land's choice, gaping at?
Is it at father's goodness
  or mother's sweetness
or else at the room's whiteness
the wedding party's beauty?
No, not at father's goodness
  nor mother's sweetness
nor yet at the room's cleanness
the wedding party's beauty:
at your lass's goodness you
gape, at the young maid's sweetness
  at your love's whiteness
  your braid-head's beauty.

'Bridegroom, my splendid brother
you have waited long, wait still
for your love is not ready
your lifelong spouse not prepared:
half of her head is in plaits
  half is unplaited.
Bridegroom, my splendid brother
you have waited long, wait still
for your love is not ready
your lifelong spouse not prepared:
  one sleeve has been sleeved
the other has yet to be.

Bridegroom, my splendid brother
long you have waited, wait still
for your love is not ready
your lifelong spouse not prepared:
only one foot has been shod
the other has yet to be.
Bridegroom, my splendid brother
long you have waited, wait still
for your love is not ready
your lifelong spouse not prepared:
    one hand has been gloved
the other has yet to be.
Bridegroom, my splendid brother
long you've waited unweary:
now your love is ready, your
duckling has prepared herself.

    'Go along, sold maid
    with him now, bought hen!
    Now your hour is close
right at hand your time to leave
for your leader is by you
your dear taker at the doors
and the stallion champs the bit
and the sledge awaits a maid.
Since you were keen on money
    quick to give your hand
eager to become betrothed
    to try on the ring
keenly now get in the sledge
eagerly in the bright sleigh
    quickly get away
and like a good girl be off!
    Young maid, you scarcely
    glanced to either side
or puzzled your head if you'd
done a deal you regretted
to weep over for ever

to whimper over for years
when you left your father's home
shifted from your birthplaces
from your kindly mother, from
the farmyards of your parent.

'What a life was yours
on these farms of your father's!
You grew in the lanes a flower
a strawberry in the glades;
you rose from bed to butter
and from lying down to milk
to buns from being outstretched
from the straw to churn-scrapings;
when you could not eat butter
you sliced off some pork.
You had no care whatever
and never a thought:
you left worry to fir trees
thinking to fence poles
sorrowing to a swamp-pine
to a birch upon the heath
while you fluttered as a leaf
as a butterfly you twirled
as a berry on your mother's lands
as a raspberry on the acre.

'Now you are leaving this house
going to a different house
to a different mother's rule
to a strange household.
One way here, another there
different in a different house:
differently the trumps* sound there
and differently the doors creak
and differently the gates squeak
and the iron hinges speak.
You'll not be able to go

through the doors, stroll through the gates
like a daughter of the house;
you will not know how to blow
the fire, to heat the fireplace
as the man of the house likes.
Did you really, young maid
did you really know or think
you'd be going for a night
coming back the next day? Look—
you'll not be gone for a night
not for one night nor for two:
you'll have slipped off for longer
for always you'll have vanished
for ever from father's rooms
and for life from your mother's.
By a pace the yard will be
longer, the threshold higher
by a timber, when you come
again, the time you return.'

The hapless maid sighed
she sighed and she gasped;
grief weighed on her heart
tears loaded her eyes
but she got this into words:
'This I knew and this I thought
this I thought throughout my days
said through all my growing-time:
You, maid, will not be a maid
within your own parent's care
upon your own father's grounds
within your old mother's rooms.
You would only be a maid
going to a husband's house
with one foot on the threshold
and one in a suitor's sleigh:
you'd be taller by a head
higher by an ear.

This I hoped for all my days
looked for all my growing-time
waited as for a good year
looked as for summer's coming
and now my wish has come true
my going has come closer:
one foot is on the threshold
and one in a suitor's sleigh.
But I cannot tell at all
    what has changed my mind:
I am not going gladly
nor with joy am I parting
    from this precious home
where all my young days I sat
from these farmyards where I grew
these dwellings my father made;
I go, thin and full of cares
full of longings I depart
as into an autumn night's embrace
on a sheet of ice in spring
leaving no track on the ice
no footprint on the surface.
    How might others feel
    and how other brides?
Surely others do not feel
sorrow, bear a yearning heart
    as I, mean one, bear—
    bearing black sorrow
a heart that looks like coal, care
    the hue of charcoal.
This is how the lucky feel
    how the blessed think—
    like daybreak in spring
the sun on a spring morning.
    But how do I feel
    in my gloomy depths?—
like the flat brink of a pool
like the dark bank of a cloud

like a dark night in autumn
    a black winter day;
    no, blacker than that
gloomier than an autumn night.'

There was an old charwoman
who always lived in the house
and she put this into words:
'So there, so there, young maiden!
Don't you recall what I said
and said hundreds of times too?
Don't be charmed by a bridegroom
    by a bridegroom's mouth
don't trust the look in his eyes
or gaze upon his fine feet!
    Sweetly he'll hold forth
turn his eyes gently, although
in his jawbones the Devil
in his mouth Doom were to dwell.
I've always advised a maid
instructed my charge like this:
    When great bridegrooms come
great bridegrooms, the land's suitors
    you tell 'em straight back
    speak up for yourself
    and say with this word
    and speak with this speech:
    "There's nothing in me
not a thing worth leading off
to be a daughter-in-law
taking off to be a serf:
no maiden who looks like me
knows how to live as a serf
will think of going along
keeping under someone's thumb.
Should the other say a word
    I'd answer with two;
and should he come at my hair

trespass among my tresses
from my hair I would twist him
from my tresses I'd yank him!"

'But no, you took no notice
you didn't hear what I said:
you've walked aware into fire
knowing into boiling tar
dashed into the fox's sledge
gone off on the bear's runners
for the fox to drag off in its sledge
for the bear to carry far away
to be a master's serf for ever
and a mother-in-law's serf for life.
You have gone from home to school
from father's yards to torment;
hard the school you will attend
long the torment you will bear:
there the reins have been bought, there
the irons have been laid in—
    not for anyone
    except hapless you.
Soon you'll come to suffer, wretch
to suffer, ill-fated one
father-in-law's bony jaw
mother-in-law's stony tongue
a brother-in-law's cold words
sister-in-law's tossing head.

'Listen, maid, while I'm talking
while I'm talking and speaking!
At home you have been a flower
in your father's yards a joy:
your father called you moonlight
    your mother sunshine
your brother water-sparkle
and your sister blue broadcloth.

You go to a different house
    a strange mother's rule:
no stranger is worth mother
no other woman worth a parent!
A stranger seldom scolded
fairly, seldom taught rightly:
father-in-law will dub you doormat
and mother-in-law slowcoach
brother-in-law rock bottom
and sister-in-law trollop.
The only time you would be
good, would measure up would be
when as mist you went outside
when as smoke you reached the yard
when as a leaf you fluttered
    when as sparks you sped;
but you are no bird to fly
    and no leaf to flit
    not a spark to speed
    smoke to reach the yard.

'Oh, maid, my little sister
you've exchanged, and what exchanged!
You've exchanged your dear father
for a bad father-in-law
exchanged your kindly mother
for a stern mother-in-law
exchanged your splendid brother
for a brutish-necked brother-in-law
exchanged your decent sister
for a mocking-eyed sister-in-law;
you've exchanged your hempen beds
    for sooty log fires
you've exchanged your white waters
    for mucky oozes
you've exchanged your sandy shores
    for black muddy holes

you've exchanged your darling glades
    for heathery heaths
and your hills full of berries
    for rough burnt treestumps!

'Did you really think, young maid
did you really, growing hen
that cares were done, work was less
by spending this evening, that
you'd be led there to lie down
you'd be taken there to sleep?
You'll not be led to lie down
not taken to sleep at all:
henceforth you must stay awake
henceforth you'll be full of care
    you'll be made to think
you'll be put in bad spirits.
While you fluttered kerchiefless
    you fluttered carefree;
while you moved without a veil
you moved without too much grief.
Only now will a kerchief
bring care, linen bad spirits
    hemp too many griefs
    flax no end of them.

'At home a maid has it made!
In her father's house she is
like a king in his castle
with only a sword missing.
But a poor daughter-in-law!
In her husband's house she is
like a Russian prisoner
with only a guard missing:
she has worked at work-time, put
    her back into it
    her skin bathed in sweat
    her brow white with froth;

come another time
to fire she is doomed
driven to the forge
given into that one's hand
and she is supposed to have
(luckless wench) to have
a salmon's mind, a ruff's tongue
a pond-perch's thought
a roach's mouth and a bleak's belly
and to be wise as a goldeneye.
Not one knows, even
nine don't understand
of the girls a mother has
their parent cares for
where the eater will be born
the gnawer grow up
the flesh-eater, bone-biter
who'll strew their hair on the wind
scatter their tresses
give them to the gale.

'Weep, weep, young maiden;
when you weep, have a good cry!
Weep your tears in fistfuls, your
grief-waters in cupped palmfuls
drops on father's yards
pools on papa's floors
weep the cabin into floods
and into waves the floorboards!
If you don't when you're made to
you will weep when you visit
when you come to father's home
and you find your old father
dead from smoke in the sauna
a dry whisk under his arm.
Weep, weep, young maiden;
when you weep, have a good cry!
If you don't when you're made to

you will weep when you visit
when you come to mother's home
and you find your old mother
suffocated in the byre
dead with an armful of straw.
    Weep, weep, young maiden;
when you weep, have a good cry!
If you don't when you're made to
you will weep when you visit
when you come into this home
find your full-blooded brother
    laid low in the lane
    felled in the farmyard.
    Weep, weep, young maiden;
when you weep, have a good cry!
If you don't when you're made to
you will weep when you visit
when you come into this house
and find your decent sister
dropped down on the wash-place path
an old club under her arm.'

    The hapless maid sighed—
    she sighed and she gasped
    she fell to weeping
    turned to shedding tears:
she wept tears in fistfuls, wept
grief-waters in cupped palmfuls
on her father's well-washed yards
    pools on papa's floor.
Then she put this into words
    she declared, chattered:
'O sisters, buntings of mine
former comrades of my age
all my growing-companions:
listen while I am talking!

I cannot now tell at all
    what could have struck me
    with this great longing
and loaded me with this care
    brought me this yearning
burdened me with this sorrow.
Differently I knew, I thought
differently hoped through my time—
meant to go as a cuckoo
    to call on hilltops
    when I'd reached these days
and come to these thoughts; but now
I'll not go as a cuckoo
not call on hilltops: I am
like a calloo on billows
or a teal in a broad bay
swimming in chilly water
disturbing icy water.

'Woe my father, my mother
woe, woe my honoured parents!
    Why did you make me
and what bear this mean one for—
    to weep these laments
    to bear these yearnings
    to care with these cares
    and grieve with these griefs?
You might sooner, poor mamma
you might, fair one who bore me
dear one who gave milk to me
lovely one who suckled me
    have swaddled treestumps
    have washed little stones
    than wash this daughter
    swaddle your fair one
    just for these great griefs
    for these low spirits!
    Many elsewhere say

  and several think:
  The fool has no care
  no worry ever.
  Do not, good people
  oh do not say it!
  For I have more care
  than rapids have rocks
  bad land has willows
  the heath has heather.
  A horse could not draw
  an iron-neck jerk
without the shaft-bow shifting
the collar-bow shaking off
these cares of this skinny one
and these black sorrows of mine.'

A child sang from the floor, one
growing from the inglenook:
'What lamenting by a maid
  and what great grieving!
Let a horse do the caring
and a black gelding sorrow
and an iron-mouth pity
  and a big-head wail!
A horse has a better head—
a better head, firmer bone;
the arch of its neck bears more
its whole body is larger.
There is nothing to weep for
  greatly grieve about.
You'll not be led to a swamp
taken to a ditch: they will
lead you from a corn-hummock
lead you to one fatter yet
and take you from beer-cabins
take you to some flusher still.
  When you look to your
  flank, to your right side

there's a bridegroom to keep you
a full-blooded man by you—
a good husband, a good horse
everything to set up house;
    grouse-bells parading
on the collar-bow chirping
    thrush-bells rejoicing
upon the traces singing
    six gold cuckoo-bells
    on the hames bobbing
    seven bluebird-bells
on the sledge-prow cuckooing.
    Don't worry at all
mother's offspring, about that!
You're not set for worsening
no, you're set for bettering
beside a ploughman husband
beneath a furrower's cloak
beneath a breadwinner's chin
under a fisherman's arm
amid an elk-chaser's sweat
in a bear-hunter's sauna.
You've a man of the finest
of fellows the most handsome:
his crossbows won't be idle
quivers won't hang on their pegs;
his dogs will not lie at home
nor his pups rest on the straw.
    Full three times this spring
quite betimes on the morrow
he's risen from a camp fire
woken on a bed of sprigs
    and three times this spring
dew has dripped upon his eyes
    sprigs have brushed his head
    twigs combed his body.
The man is a flock-rearer

the fellow a herd-raiser:
    this bridegroom of ours
has wilds full of foot-walkers
sandbanks full of leg-runners
scourers of a marsh's depth
a hundred bearers of horns
a thousand udder-bringers;
he has ricks in every glade
he has bins at every brook
alder groves are his bread-lands
ditch sides are his barley-lands
sides of rock are his oat-lands
riversides are his wheat-lands
    all cairns* are his coins
    little stones his pence.'

23. *Instructions and a Warning*

Now is the maid's advising
the bride's instructing: well, who
shall be the maid's adviser
and the lassie's instructor?
Osmo-daughter, plump woman
Kaleva-daughter, fair lass—
    she'll advise the maid
    instruct the orphan
    how to be prudent
    and remain blameless
prudent in a husband's house
blameless in a mother-in-law's house.
    She said with these words
    spoke with these phrases:
'Bride, little sister of mine
    heartsease, my darling:
listen while 'tis me talking
my tongue telling differently!
Now, flower, you're going away
strawberry, creeping away
plush one, you're bowling away
velvet one, wandering off
    out of this famous
    home, from this fair farm;
you'll come to a different house
    to a strange household.
Different in a different house
otherwise in strange others—
    thoughtfully stepping
    cautiously working;
not as on your father's ground
on your own mother's mainland
    in valleys singing

in lanes cuckooing.
When you leave this house
remember to take all your
other things, but leave at home
three—your daytime naps
your mother's dear words
your scrapings from every churn!
Remember all your chattels
but leave out your weariness
for the daughters still at home
still at the home-stove corner!
Leave the songs upon the bench
the joy-tales at the windows
girlhood on the whisk handle
your wildness on burlap hems
on the stove seat your bad ways
your laziness on the floor;
or else offer them to your bridesmaid
tuck them underneath her arm
for her to bear to the brush
to carry to the heather!

'There's a new way to take on
and the old one to forget—
father-love to leave
father-in-law-love to take
and lower to bow
and good words to give.
There's a new way to take on
and the old one to forget—
mother-love to leave
mother-in-law-love to take
and lower to bow
and good words to give.
There's a new way to take on
and the old one to forget—
brother-love to leave

brother-in-law-love to take
    and lower to bow
    and good words to give.
There's a new way to take on
and the old one to forget—
    sister-love to leave
sister-in-law-love to take
    and lower to bow
    and good words to give.

    'Never in this world
not in a month of Sundays
wed if you have no manners
marry if you have no skills!
A house expects good manners
    even a good house
and a husband tries you out
even the best husband does;
you need only be careful
if a house is ill-mannered
and you have to be steadfast
if a husband is worthless.
Though master's a wolf in the corner
mistress a bear in the inglenook
brother-in-law as threshold vipers
sister-in-law as nails in the yard
there's the same respect to give
    and lower to bow
than once beside your mother
in your own father's cabins
there was father to bow to
and your mamma to respect.

    'And you are to keep
a careful head, common sense
your judgement always strict, your
    understanding sound

your eyes watchful at evening
  to see to the fire
your ears sharp in the morning
to listen for the cockcrow:
the first time the cock has sung
and has not yet uttered twice
that's the young folk's rising-time
and the old folk's resting-time.
If the cock does not sing, if
the master's bird does not crow
treat the moon as your cockerel
the Great Bear as your model:
  go outside often
  and look at the moon
  observe the Great Bear
  and study the stars!
When the Great Bear is set right
its horns pointing straight southward
and its tail pointing due north
then 'tis time for you to rise
from beside the young bridegroom
from the full-blooded one's side
to get fire from the cinders
flame out of the little box
to blow the fire at a stick
taking care not to spread it.
If no fire's in the cinders
no flame in the little box
tickle your darling for some
  tackle your fair one:
  "Give me fire, my dear
  some flame, my berry!"
You will get a tiny flint
quite a small piece of tinder:
  strike fire, make a spark
kindle the splint at the door
and go and muck out the byre
  fodder the cattle;
  mother-in-law's cow

lows, father-in-law's horse neighs
    brother-in-law's cow
stirs, sister-in-law's calf mews
for someone to toss fine grass
    to hold out clover.
    Tread the lanes crouching
    and the byres stooping
    feed the cows meekly
    and the sheep mildly;
hold out the straw to the cows
the drink to the poor things' calves
to the foals the chosen stalks
to the lambs the fine grasses;
    do not scold the pigs
    don't kick the piglets:
take a troughful to the pigs
the piglets their mangerful!

    'Don't rest in the byre
and don't laze in the sheep-fold:
when you have mucked out the byre
    seen to all the herd
    hurry back from there
    whirl indoors as snow!
    A child's crying there
a small one inside the quilts
and the poor child cannot speak
neither can the infant say
whether 'tis cold or hungry
or what else is the matter
before the one it knows comes
and it hears its mother's voice.
    But when you come in
    come in as four—with
a water-pail in your hand
a bath-whisk under your arm
a fire-stick between your teeth

and yourself making the fourth.
    Start wiping the boards
    sweeping the plank floors:
toss water upon the floor—
don't chuck it over a child!
Should you see a child upon the floor
even if 'tis sister-in-law's child
lift the child on to a bench
wash its eyes and smooth its hair
put some bread into its hand
spread some butter on the bread;
if there's no bread in the house
put a wood-chip in its hand.

'When 'tis table-washing time
after a week at the most
wash the tables, remember
the sides, don't forget the legs;
sluice the benches with water
wipe the walls with a duster
the benches and all their sides
along the walls and their chinks;
what dust is on the table
and what dirt on the windows—
well, flick them with a duster*
run a wet rag over them
so the dirt won't fly about
nor the dust swirl to the roof;
shake the muck down from the roof
and sweep the soot off the hearth
and keep the doorpost in mind
and do not forget the beams
that it may seem a cabin
may be reckoned a dwelling!

'Listen, maid, while I'm talking
while I'm talking and speaking!
Do not rush about vestless

and don't loaf about shirtless
don't move about kerchiefless
and don't pad about barefoot:
your bridegroom would be angry
your young husband would grumble.
Be very wary of those
rowans in the yard: holy
are the rowans in the yard
holy are the rowans' boughs
holy the boughs' foliage
the berries still holier
with which a maid is advised
    an orphan is taught
what pleases a young husband
what touches a bridegroom's heart.
Keep the sharp ears of a mouse
and the neat feet of a hare:
    lean down your young nape
    bend down your fair neck
like a sprouting juniper
or a green bird cherry top;
    you must stay awake—
always awake, wary that
you don't end up on your bum
or full length on the stove seat
    or sink on the sheets
    drag yourself to bed.

'Brother-in-law comes in from sowing
father-in-law from building fences
your fellow from outdoor work
your fair one from slash-and-burn:
there is a bowl of water
to take, a hand towel to bring
    and low down to bow
    and kind words to say.
Mother-in-law comes in from the shed
the grain-box under her arm:

run to meet her in the yard
    bow down low, ask for
the box from under her arm
that you may take it indoors.
    If you cannot guess
nor puzzle out for yourself
    which task to take on
    which job to start on
find out from the mistress thus:
"O my dear mother-in-law
    how are tasks done here
    how are chores assigned?"
The mistress will answer, yes
mother-in-law say the word:
"This is how tasks are done here
    how chores are assigned:
there is pounding and grinding
swaying at the quern handle
then there's water to carry
    there is dough to mix
there are faggots to bring in
    for heating the stove;
and then there are loaves to bake
    and thick rolls to make
and there are dishes to soak
    wooden plates to rinse."

'When you've heard your tasks from the mistress
your chores from mother-in-law
take the grains from the hearthstone
hurry to the grinding-hut;
    then, when you've got there
and come to the grinding-hut
do not cuckoo with your throat
    nor shriek with your neck:
cuckoo with the quern's rumble
    with the bridge's song

and don't groan loudly
or puff at the quern
lest father-in-law should think
mother-in-law consider
you are groaning in anger
shoving in a bad temper!
Sift the flour lightly
bring it indoors on the lid;
take the loaves gently
knead them with great care
that here no flour may remain
nor there the leaven be loose.

'You'll see a tub on its side:
take the tub on your shoulder
the bucket under your arm
start stepping to the water;
bear the tub beautifully
carry it on a cowlstaff.
Come back as the wind
step along as the gale does
not lingering long at the water
not getting lost at the well
lest father-in-law should think
mother-in-law consider
that you stare at your likeness
and admire yourself
your full-bloodedness in the water
and your beauty in the well!

'You'll go out to the long stack
to haul in faggots:
don't look down on a faggot—
take one even of aspen;
drop a faggot quietly
without making a racket
or father-in-law would think
mother-in-law consider

that you toss it in your hate
make a racket out of spite!

'When you step into the shed
and go off to fetch the flour
don't hang about in the shed
linger long on the shed path
or father-in-law will think
mother-in-law consider
that you're sharing out the flour
giving to the village hags!

'You'll go off to wash a dish
    to rinse wooden plates:
wash the jugs with their handles
and the flagons with their grooves;
rinse the bowls—think of the sides;
the spoons—think of the handles!
    Keep count of the spoons
    and check your dishes
lest the dogs sneak off with them
or the cats carry them off
or the birds too shift them, or
the children spread them around:
there are plenty of children
in the village, lots of little heads
who would carry off the jugs
    spread the spoons around.

'When evening sauna-time comes
draw the water, bring the whisks
soften the bath-whisks ready
in the sauna rid of smoke
not lingering long and not
vanishing in the sauna
or father-in-law would think
mother-in-law consider
you were lazing on the planks

and romping at the bench end!
When you come indoors from there
tell father-in-law to bathe:
"O my dear father-in-law
now the sauna is prepared
the water drawn, the whisks got
and all the boards have been swept;
    go and bathe your fill
douse yourself all that you want!
I shall raise the steam myself
under the planks I shall stay."

'When spinning-time comes
and cloth-weaving time, don't go
to the village for wrinkles
beyond the ditch for guidance
to the next house for warp-thread
to a stranger for reed-teeth:
spin the yarn yourself, and with
your own fingertips the weft
    make the yarn lightweight
the thread always tightly spun;
wind it into a firm ball
    on the reel toss it
on to the warp beam fit it
then set it out on the loom.
    Strike the reed smartly
and raise the heddles nimbly
    weave homespun caftans
    and make woollen skirts
    from one strip of wool
the fleece of a winter sheep
from the coat of a spring lamb
the down of a summer ewe.

'So listen while I'm talking
    telling something more:
    brew the barley beer

the tasty malt drink
from one barley grain
half a tree's charred wood.
When you steam barley
when you sweeten malt
do not stir it with a hook
do not turn it with a branch:
always stir it with your fist
turn it with your palm;
visit the sauna often
don't let a shoot spoil
nor a cat sit on the shoots
nor a puss lie on the malt;
and don't grieve for wolves
nor fear forest beasts
as you make for the sauna
as you walk there at midnight!

'Whenever a stranger comes
don't hate the stranger:
a good house always
keeps supplies for a stranger
lots of bits of meat
beautiful biscuits.
Tell the stranger to sit down
and chat politely:
feed the stranger with words till
the soup is ready.
Again, when he leaves the house
and makes his farewells
do not lead your guest
out through the door, for
the bridegroom would be angry
your fair one would grow ugly.

'Whenever the urge takes you
to go visiting yourself
ask if you may go

and say you want to go out;
    then while you are out
    tell skilful stories:
don't you find fault with home, don't
run down your mother-in-law!
Daughters-in-law where you go—
that is, other wives will ask:
"Did mother-in-law give you butter
as mother used to at home?"
Never say: "Mother-in-law
    gives me no butter"
but always say it is given
brought in a dipper, though you
get it but once in summer
and that from two winters back!

'Listen still while I'm talking
    telling one thing more:
when you go out from this house
and come to the other house
    don't forget mother
or dishearten your mamma
for 'twas mother who kept you
her lovely breasts suckled you
    from her lovely self
    from her white body;
many sleepless nights she spent
    many meals she missed
    lulling you, caring
    for her little one.
Whoever forgets mother
and disheartens her mamma
may she not go towards Death
cheerfully to Tuonela:
the Dead Land gives bad payment
Tuonela a rough reward
to one who forgets mother

who disheartens her mamma.
    Tuoni's daughters scold
    and Death's maids quarrel:
"How could you forget mother
dishearten your own mamma?
Mother has taken great pains
your parent has known hardship
lying on the sauna earth
    staying on the straw
    giving birth to you
    bearing the mean one."'

There was a hag on the floor
an old hag with a cloak on
one who trod village thresholds
one who knew the parish* roads
and she put this into words
    she declared, held forth:
'The cock has sung to his love
the hen's child to his fair one
and the crow has sung in March
in the spring month it has swung.
It ought to be me singing
    and them not singing:
they have their loved one at home
always with them their darling;
I am loveless and homeless
all the time with no darling.
Listen, sister, while I talk:
when you too go to a husband's house
do not mark your husband's will
    as I, luckless, marked
a husband's will, a lark's tongue
    my great bridegroom's heart!

'I was a flower in my day
in my growing was heather
a young shoot in my rising

a bud in my coming up
a honey-berry* talked of
a darling whispered about
a teal in my father's yards
a bean goose on mother's floors
a water-bird beside my brother
a finch beside my sister
and I walked the lanes a flower
the field as a raspberry
skipped upon the sandy shores
tripped upon the flowery knolls;
I sang in every valley
on every mound I cuckooed
and the groves were my playground
and the glades my constant joy.

'Mouth drew fox into the trap
tongue drew stoat into the snare
will a maid into marriage
wish into another house:
so a maid even at birth
a daughter is lulled to be
daughter-in-law in a husband's house
a serf in a mother-in-law's house.
I, a berry, fell on other lands
a bird cherry, on different waters
a cowberry to be bit
a strawberry to be cursed:
    every tree bit me
    every alder cut
    every birch hurt me
    every aspen snapped.
I was wed, led to a husband's house
taken to a mother-in-law's house:
    I was told that there
    once the maid was wed
would be six cabins of spruce
and twice as many chambers

the glade sides would be shed-lands
and the lane sides blossom-lands
and the ditch sides barley-lands
    the heath sides oat-lands
    binfuls of threshed grain
other binfuls to be threshed
    a hundred coins got
a hundred more to be got;
but when I, fool, got married
and, madcap, struck the bargain
the cabin was on six poles
    upon seven stakes
the glades full of unkindness
the groves full of lovelessness
lanefuls, poor me, of my cares
forestfuls of low spirits
    binfuls of threshed hate
other binfuls of unthreshed
    a hundred words got
a hundred more to be got.

    'I took no notice
but tried to live blamelessly:
    I hoped for respect
    I strove to win love
by bringing the fire indoors
by picking up splint-ends; I'd
poke my brow in at the door
my head in at the doorpost:
in the doorway were strange eyes
narrowed in the inglenook
looking askance in mid-floor
at the far end full of hate
and fire would flash from a mouth
firebrands from beneath a tongue
from the wicked master's mouth
from beneath his unkind tongue.
    I took no notice

but still tried to carry on
    to keep in with them
    meekly obedient:
I hopped upon a hare's feet
went about on a stoat's paws
went to bed dreadfully late
got up woefully early;
but I, wretch, got no respect
    luckless, won no love
though I were to roll mountains
    and break rocks in two.

'In vain I pounded the groats
uselessly sifted the meal
for my stern mother-in-law to eat
for the fire-throat to nibble
at the long deal table's head
from a gold-rimmed dish, while I—
I ate, poor daughter-in-law
I gobbled flour off the quern
the fireplace seat my table
a wooden dipper my spoon.
Often in my gloom as a
daughter-in-law in a husband's house
I brought mosses from the swamp
baked them for my bread, water
from the well in a bucket
tippled that for my tipple.
Cheerless, I only ate fish
hapless, only ate smelt when
I stooped at the seine-poles, rocked
in the middle of the boat;
I got not one fish from what
my mother-in-law gave me
that would serve for a day, be
    good for its one meal.

'Summers I gathered fodder
winters wielded a pitchfork

just like a gipsy of old
or else a serf, a hireling
for in mother-in-law's house
    I was always given
the thickest flail in the kiln
the sauna's heaviest brake
the hardest club on the shore
the barnyard's biggest pitchfork.
No one believed me worn out
nor worried when I sank down
though the fellows got worn out
and the horse's foals sank down.
    So I, luckless wench
    worked at working-time
and put my back into it;
    come another time
    to fire I was doomed
delivered into its hand.

'Groundless gossip was started
    and idle tongues wagged
    against my good ways
against my famous honour:
the words rained upon my head
    the stories pattered
    like harsh sparks of fire
    or iron hailstones.
But that did not put me off:
I would have gone on living
as a help to the stern hag
as the fire-throat's companion;
    but what got me down
    what made things worse, was
that my bridegroom turned wolfish
my fair one became a bear—
faced me to eat, turned his back
to sleep and to do his work.
For that I wept by myself

I considered in my shed;
I recalled my other days
my earlier way of life
    in father's long yards
    fair mother's farmyard
and then I started saying
    I uttered, chattered:
    "She knew, my mother
knew how to get an apple
she could raise a shoot, but she
did not know how to plant it:
she planted the lovely shoot
    in wicked places
    set it in bad spots—
    upon hard birch roots
    to weep all its days
    to moan for ever.
    I would have been fit
    for better places
    and for longer yards
    and for wider floors
right for a better body
worth a more full-blooded man;
but I was stuck with this lout
landed with this layabout
who had got a crow's body
and had grabbed a raven's nose
his mouth from a ravening wolf
and all his looks from a bear.
I would have got such a one
if I'd just gone up a hill
got from there a tarry stump
an alder log from a grove
made a muzzle out of sward
a beard from bad beard-mosses
a mouth from rock, head from clay
    eyes out of hot coals
    birch gnarls for his ears
a goat willow fork for legs."

'That's what I sang in my woes
    and sighed in my cares;
but my fair one chanced to hear
to be standing by the wall!
    When he came from there
    walked up the shed steps
I knew it was him coming
recognized his step: his hair
whirled although there was no wind
his locks tossed although there was
no draught; his gums were agape
his eyes were out of kilter
a warped rowan in his grip
a bent rod under his arm
which he keeps beating me with
clobbering me on the head.
    Then come the evening
    when he went to bed
he took a lash at his side
a leather whip off its peg
    not for anyone
    except hapless me.
    Well, I also went
    to bed at evening
lay down beside my bridegroom:
he let me snuggle up, then
he gave me enough elbow
and plenty of hateful hand
a lot of thick willow sticks
some walrus-bone whip handle.
I got up from his cold side
    from the chilly bed:
my bridegroom chased after me
    threw me out with threats!
A hand moves among my hair
    fumbles my tresses
shared my hair out to the wind
    gives it to the gale . . .

'What was my best plan?
What plan to follow?
I had shoes made out of steel
shoelaces shaped of copper
in which I stood beside walls
and listened at lane-ends for
the wrathful one to calm down
the stern one to settle down;
but he calms down not at all
he settles down at no time!
At last I got cold
wandering hated
standing beside walls
stuck behind a door.
I thought, considered:
there's no point in my
bearing a long grudge
a lasting contempt
in this devil's crew
this nest of demons.
I left the charming cabins
my darling abodes
and, though not strong, went roaming.
I roamed swamps, roamed lands
I roamed fleet waters
roamed to my brother's field-end:
there the dry spruces cuckooed
and the shock-headed pines sang
all the crows cawed, all
the magpies cackled:
"This is not your home
nor is your birthplace!"

'I took no notice
but roamed to my brother's yard.
Now the gates uttered to me
and all the acres complained:
"What are you coming home for

and what, wretch, to hear about?
Your father's long dead, long gone
is the fair one who bore you;
brother's a stranger to you
his wife is like a Russian."
    I took no notice
    but went straight indoors.
I put my hand on the latch:
the latch was cold to my hand.
    When I got indoors
in the doorway I stood still:
    the haughty housewife
    doesn't embrace me
nor does she offer her hand;
    I'm haughty as well
    and don't embrace her
nor do I offer my hand.
I stick my hand on the hearth:
the stones are cold on the hearth;
I turn my hand to the fire:
embers are cold in the fire.

'Brother's lazing on the bench
gaping upon the stove seat
a fathom of coal on his shoulders
a span on the rest of him
an ell of dust on his head
half a foot of solid soot.
Brother asked of the stranger
inquired of the newcomer:
"Where is the foreigner from?"
    I merely answered:
"Do you not know your sister
who was once your mother's child?
We are one mother's children
    rocked by the same bird
    hatched by the same goose
    from one grouse's nest!"

At that, brother made to weep
and his eyes to run with tears . . .
Brother uttered to his wife
he whispered to his darling:
"Fetch some food for my sister!"
Brother's wife with mocking eyes
brought from the cook-house some cabbage soup
whose fat the cur had eaten
whose salt the dog had licked, which
Blackie had breakfasted on.
Brother uttered to his wife
he whispered to his darling:
    "Bring beer for the guest!"
Brother's wife with mocking eyes
brought some water for the guest
but it was no clean water:
it was the sisters' eye-wash
the sisters-in-law's hand-rinse.

'I roamed on from my brother
I shifted from my birthplace:
I fell, a wretch, to walking
I took, a wretch, to rambling
poor one, to skirting the shores
woebegone, to wandering
    always to strange doors
    and to foreign gates
the poor one's children abroad
woebegone to village care . . .
    Many now I have
    and a lot there are
who talk with angry voices
who with harsh voices attack;
I do not have many who
    offer a kind word
    chat with a sweet mouth
    bid me to a hearth
when I've come out of the rain

and made it out of the cold
    with frosty skirt hems
with coat hems weather-beaten.
    When I was younger
I would not have believed them
though a hundred had said it
and a thousand tongues had told
that I would sink to these ways
that I would fall on these days—
the days I have fallen on
the ways I have sunk into.'

24. *Departure*

Now the maid has been advised
  the bride instructed.
Next I'll address my brother
to my bridegroom speak by mouth:
'Bridegroom, my splendid brother
better still than a brother
dearer than my mother's child
milder than my father's child:
listen while 'tis me talking
'tis me talking and speaking
about this hemp-bird of yours
  this hen you have got!
  Bridegroom, thank your luck
for the good catch you have made;
  when you thank, thank well!
Good you got and good you found
good your Creator promised
good the merciful one gave:
tell out thanks to the father
to the mother even more
  who lulled such a girl
  such a bride as this!
  Pure the maid you have
  bright the maid you wed
  white the one you hold
  fair the one you keep
strong the daughter at your side
and full-blooded beside you
strong the daughter, a thresher
charming winnower of hay
a superb washerwoman
a lively bleacher of clothes
an able spinner of thread

a nimble weaver of cloth.
    Her reed slammed out loud
like a cuckoo on a hill
    and her shuttle whizzed
like a stoat in a wood-stack
    and her spool whirred like
a cone in a squirrel's mouth:
the village could not sleep tight
nor could the townsfolk slumber
for the tap of the maid's reed
for the buzz of her shuttle.

    'Bridegroom, dear youngster
    fair husband-to-be:
forge a scythe that's sharp, fit it
into a handle that's good—
    carve in the gateway
    hammer on a stump;
    and when daylight comes
lead the maid on to the turf:
you will see how the hay snaps
    the tough hay crackles
    the sedge swishes down
    the sorrel tumbles
    a hummock goes too
    and a sapling breaks.
    When the next day comes
    fetch a fit shuttle
    a decent batten
    a proper breast beam
    cut handsome treadles
    fetch all weaving-tools
put the maiden to the loom
the batten into her grasp:
only then will the reed slam
the loom thud, the clanking be
    heard in the village
the reed's rattle further off.

The hags will think about that
the village women will ask:
    "Who is weaving cloth?"
It will suit you to answer:
"My own darling is weaving
my sweetheart is clattering.
    Has the cloth rucked up
    the reed missed a thread?"
"No, the cloth has not rucked up
nor has the reed missed a thread:
'tis as though woven by Moon-daughter
    spun by Sun-daughter
wrought by the Great Bear's daughter
finished off by Star-daughter."

    'Bridegroom, dear youngster
    fair husband-to-be:
    now that you're leaving
    and driving from here
    with your young maiden
    beside your fair hen
    don't drag your sparrow
    this hemp-bird of yours
    into the bank, or
drive her into fence corners
or spill her upon a stump
or tip her over on rocks!
Never in her father's home
in her fair mother's farmyards
was the maid dragged into banks
driven into fence corners
    spilt upon a stump
    tipped over on rocks.
    Bridegroom, dear youngster
    fair husband-to-be:
    don't lead your maiden
    convey your darling

to grumble in nooks
to grouse in crannies!
Never at her father's home
in her mother's cabins did
she grumble in nooks
or grouse in crannies:
she always sat at windows
tripped in the middle of floors
at evenings her father's joy
at mornings mother's darling.
Just don't, poor bridegroom
don't you lead this hen
to the hunger-bread mortar
don't set her pounding bark-bread
or baking straw-bread
or beating pine-bread!
Never at her father's home
in her fair mother's farmyard
was she led to that mortar
set pounding bark-bread
or baking straw-bread
or beating pine-bread.
No, you lead this hen
lead her to a corn-hummock
to unload a bin of rye
to take a bin of barley
to make a thick loaf
skilfully brew beer
to bake a wheat loaf
and to knead the dough!

'Bridegroom, my splendid brother
don't you make this hen
don't make our little
goose weep with longings!
If a heavy hour should come
the maid feel longing

stick the bay between the shafts
or the white into harness
bring her to her father's home
to her dear mother's cabins!
Don't you use this little hen
    don't use our little
    hemp-bird as your serf
don't treat her as a hired wench
don't bar her from the cellar
and from the shed don't ban her!
Never at her father's home
in her fair mother's farmyard
was the maid used like a serf
or treated as a hired wench
never barred from the cellar
and from the shed never banned:
she was always slicing buns
    looking for hen's eggs
    around the milk vat
    beside the beer keg
mornings opening the sheds
evenings locking up the loft.
    Bridegroom, dear youngster
    fair husband-to-be:
if you treat the maiden well
    you'll be well thought of:
when you come to father-in-law's house
to matchless mother-in-law's
    you will be well fed—
    fed, given to drink
your horse will be unharnessed
    led to the stable
    fed, given to drink
a box of oats will be brought.
Don't say of our little maid
this little hemp-bird of ours
    that she has no kin

don't declare she has no kind
    for this maid of ours
has great kin, has mighty kind:
were a gallon of peas sown
    each would get a grain
were a gallon of flax set
    each would get a stalk.

    'Just don't, poor bridegroom
    ill-treat the maiden
    guide her with serf-whips
with leather whips make her mew
with five lashes make her squeal
at the hut-end make her yell!
Never was the maid before
never at her father's home
    guided with serf-whips
with leather whips made to mew
with five lashes made to squeal
at the hut-end made to yell.
Stand as a wall before her
    stay as a doorpost:
don't let mother-in-law smite
nor father-in-law scold her
don't let a stranger hate her
another house slander her!
The household has told you to
beat, other folk to punch her;
but surely you wouldn't harm
your poor one, hurt your sweetheart
you heard about for three years
and were always begging for!

'Bridegroom, advise your maiden
    and teach your apple
advise the maiden in bed
and teach her behind the door

for a whole year in each place—
    one by word of mouth
    two by a tipped wink
three by putting your foot down!
    If she doesn't care
    then, takes no notice
take a reed from the reed-bed
or a horsetail from the heath:
with it advise your maiden
advise her for a fourth year
dress her down with the horsetail
with the sedge's edge goad her;
don't yet whack her with a thong
nor thrash the maid with a switch!
But if then she doesn't care
    still takes no notice
fetch a lash from the thicket
a birch out of a wild dell—
bring it under your coat hem
without the next house knowing:
    show it to your maid
    wave it but don't whack!
And if she still doesn't care
chooses to take no notice
advise the maid with the lash
instruct her with the birch bough;
advise her between four walls
speak in a room caulked with moss
do not bash her on the turf
nor beat her at the field edge:
the noise would reach the village
and the uproar the next house
the wife's weeping the neighbours
and the great row the forest.
Always warm up her shoulders
    soften her buttocks—
    don't chastise her eyes
and don't box her ears: a lump

would come up on the eyebrow
a blueberry on the eye.
Brother-in-law would ask about it
father-in-law would wonder
the village ploughmen would see
the village women would laugh:
    "Has she been to war
    mixed up in a fight
or was she torn by a wolf
or mauled by a forest bear—
or is the wolf her bridegroom
    the bear her partner?"'

There was an old man on the stove top
    a tramp at the hearth
and the old man spoke from the stove top
    the tramp from the hearth:
    'Just don't, poor bridegroom
    mark a woman's will
a woman's will, a lark's tongue
as I did, a luckless boy!
    I bought meat, bought bread
    bought butter, bought beer
    bought fish of all kinds
relishes of many sorts
    beer from my own lands
    wheat from foreign lands
but I got no good with it
    found no benefit:
when the woman came indoors
she came like a hair-tearer
    with her face bulging
    and her eyes rolling;
she raved on in her fury
in her hatred talked away
    called me a fat-arse
and blamed me for a blockhead.
Now I thought up a new dodge

yes, hit on a different road:
when I stripped a birch bough clean
she hugged me, called me her bird;
when I lopped a juniper
she yielded, called me her dear;
and then, when I laid on with willows
she flung herself on my neck.'

    The hapless maid sighs—
    she sighs and she gasps
    she burst into tears;
she uttered a word, spoke thus:
'Others' leaving-time is near
and others' hour has come close:
my leaving-time is nearer
    my hour is closer
though it is hard too to leave
    difficult the hour
of parting from this famous
    village, this fair farm
where I grew beautifully
    rose up gracefully
    all my growing-time
    my years of childhood.
    I had neither thought
    nor ever believed—
    thought I would give up
    believed I would part
from the border of this hill
from the shoulder of this ridge.
Now I both think and give up
I both believe and depart:
the parting-flagons are drained
the parting-beer has been drunk
soon the sleighs will have been turned
to face outward, backs to the cabin
    sides to father's barn
    flanks to the cowshed.

'With what now as I depart
as I, mean one, leave
shall I pay for mother's milk
and for my father's goodness
with what my brother's kindness
and my sister's tenderness?
I thank you, father
for the meals I've had
for breakfasts of old
for the best morsels;
I thank you, mother
for lulling me as a babe
for holding me when little
for feeding me with your breasts;
next I thank my dear brother
my dear brother, dear sister
I repay the whole household
all those I grew up
with and lived among
grew with in my growing-time.
Do not now, my good father
do not, my kindly mother
or others of my great kin
of my illustrious people
don't give way to care
or yield to great grief
even though I go
to other lands, move somewhere:
the Creator's sun will shine
the Creator's moon will gleam
the stars of heaven will glitter
and the Great Bear will stretch out
further off too in the world
elsewhere too in the wide world—
not only in father's yards
in these farmyards where I grew.

'Now I'm really leaving here
leaving this dear home

the hall father made
mother's full cellar:
I leave my swamps, leave my lands
leave my grassy yards
leave my white waters
leave my sandy shores
to the village hags to bathe
and to the herdsmen to splash;
I leave the swamps to squelchers
the lands I leave to laggards
and the alders to idlers
and the heather to strollers
the fence sides to those who step
lane-edges to those who walk
yards to those who run along
the wall sides to those who stand
the board-planks to those who wipe
and the floors to those who sweep;
fields I leave for the reindeer to run
backwoods for the lynx to roam
the glades for the geese to dwell
the groves for the birds to rest.
I am really leaving here
with another who's leaving
for an autumn night's embrace
for a sheet of ice in spring
so there's no track on the ice
no footprint on the surface
on the crust no skirt's pattern
no hem's brush-mark on the snow.

'Then, when I've come back
visiting my home
mother will not hear a voice
nor father notice weeping
though I moan on their eyebrows
and sing on their scalps: young turf
will already have risen

a juniper bush have grown
on her skin who suckled me
on her face who carried me.
    And when I come back
    into these long yards
the others will not know me
    but these two things will—
    the lowest fence-lash
    the furthest field-stake:
those I stuck in when little
    and lashed as a maid.
And my mother's barren cow
    I watered when young
    cared for as a calf
    will keep on lowing
    within the long yards
    on the wintry grounds:
    that one will know me
for the daughter of the house.
My father's aged stallion
    which I fed when small
    foddered as a maid
    will keep on neighing
    within the long yards
    on the wintry grounds:
    that one will know me
for the daughter of the house.
And my brother's ageless dog
    I fed as a child
    taught as a maiden
    will keep on barking
    within the long yards
    on the wintry grounds:
    that one will know me
for the daughter of the house.
Those others will not know me
    when I have come home
though they are my old moorings

places where I used to live—
in their places whitefish-straits
    in their stead seine-coves . . .

    'Fare you well now, room—
    room with your plank roof
good for me to come back to
fair for me to frolic to!
    Fare you well now, porch—
    porch with your plank floor
good for me to come back to
fair for me to frolic to!
    So fare you well, yard—
    yard with your rowans
good for me to come back to
fair for me to frolic to!
    I bid all farewell—
lands, forests with their berries
    lane sides with their flowers
    heaths with their heather
lakes with their hundreds of isles
the deep straits with their whitefish
the good mounds with their spruces
the wild dells with their birches.'

Then the smith Ilmarinen
grabbed the maid into his sleigh
struck the courser with the lash
uttered a word and spoke thus:
    'Fare you well, lakeshores—
    lakeshores and field banks
all you firs upon the hill
you tall trees in the pinewood
bird cherries behind the house
junipers on the well-path
all berry stalks on the ground—
    berry stalks, grass stems
    willow shrubs, spruce roots
alder foliage, birchbark!'

There the smith Ilmarinen
went from the yards of Northland
but the children kept singing
the children sang and declared:
'This way a black bird has flown
through the wilds it has glided
has enticed the duck from us
has lured the berry from us
taken that apple from us
    led the fish astray
cheated her with little coins
with silver coins tempted her.
Who'll now lead us to water
go with us to the river?
The pails will have to stand still
and the cowlstaves to clatter
    the boards stay unwiped
    and the floors unswept
    the tankard rims clogged
the flagon handles tarnished.'

He, the smith Ilmarinen
    with his young maiden
    hurtles on his way
along those shores of the North
    by the mead-sweet straits
across the ridge of fine sand:
the gravel rang, the sand clinked
the sledge rolled, the road flashed past
the iron traces rattled
the runner of birch clattered
the curly-birch strut thudded
the bird cherry collar-bow
quivered, the shaft-lashes squealed
    the copper rings shook
    as the good horse ran
as the good blaze-brow galloped.
He drove one day and then two

soon he drove a third as well
one hand on the stallion's rein
one hand under the maid's arm
one foot over the sledge side
the other beneath the rug.
Courser ran and journey sped
the day rolled, the road shortened
    till on the third day
as the sun is going down
    the smith's home appears
the cabins of Ilma loom:
soot was rising as a thread
smoke was thickly escaping
it billowed from the cabin
up into the clouds it rose.

25. *Homecoming*

Now, long they waited—
they waited, looked out
for the maid's escort to come
to the smith Ilmari's home:
the eyes of the old ones stream
sitting at windows
the knees of the young ones sag
waiting at the gates
children's feet were cold
standing beside walls
the shoes of the middle-aged
wore out roving on the shores.
One morrow among others
and one day among many
comes a noise from the backwoods
a sledge-rattle from the heath.
Lokka the gentle mistress
Kaleva-daughter, fair wife
uttered a word and spoke thus:
'That is my son's sledge!
He is coming from Northland
with his young maiden!
Head now for these lands
and for these farmyards
the cabins your father made
your parent laid out!'

Smith Ilmarinen
soon he arives home
in the yards his father made
his parent laid out:
grouse-bells are cooing
on the sapling collar-bows

cuckoo-bells are cuckooing
on the prow of the bright sleigh
and squirrels are scurrying
upon the shaft of maple.
Lokka the gentle mistress
Kaleva-daughter, fair wife
at that put this into words
    she declared, spoke thus:
'The village waited for the new moon
the young ones for the sunrise
children for a land of strawberries
water for a tarry boat;
I not even a half-moon
    no sun whatever:
I waited for my brother—
my brother, daughter-in-law.
I looked morning, looked evening
did not know where he'd vanished
if he was raising a little one
or fattening a lean one
since he did not come at all
though he certainly promised
to come while his tracks were there
to arrive before they cooled.
I kept looking out mornings
for days he was on my mind
since brother's sled does not roll
nor does brother's sleigh clatter
    to these little yards
    these narrow farmyards.
Had I a stallion of straw
    a sledge with two struts
even that I'd call a sled
    promote to a sleigh
if it drew my brother here
    brought my fair one home.
So I spent my time hoping
    I looked out all day—

looked till my head was askew
till my topknot was awry
and my straight eyes were oval
hoping my brother would come
    to these little yards
    these narrow farmyards.
    Now at last he comes
    for once he makes it—
with him a full-blooded face
one with red cheeks at his side!

'Bridegroom, my splendid brother
    let the blaze-brow go
and let the good horse be led
to the hay it had before
to the oats it used to have
    and give us greeting—
    give us, give others
    give all the village!
When you have done the greetings
    tell us your stories:
did you travel untalked of
did you go your way healthy
bound for your mother-in-law
matchless father-in-law's home?
Did you get the maid, defeat
the might, crush the gate of war
flatten the maiden's stronghold
demolish the upright wall
step on mother-in-law's boards
sit upon the master's bench?
Now I see without asking
and guess without questioning:
yes, he fared well on his way
sweetly upon his journey;
he brought the goose, defeated
the might, crushed the gate of war
laid low the stronghold of planks

flattened the wall of limewood
while he was with mother-in-law, in
matchless father-in-law's home
and the scaup is his to keep
the hen is under his arm
the pure maid is his to have
the white one is his to hold.

'But who brought this lie, who bore
the wrong news that the bridegroom
was coming empty-handed
the stallion was running light?
He's not come empty-handed
the stallion has not run light:
there's something for it to draw
    the hemp-mane to move
for the good horse is sweating
and the choice foal is frothing
from bringing the chicken here
drawing the full-blooded one.

'Rise now from the sleigh, fine one
good gift, out of the bobsleigh!
    Rise, do not be raised
get up, do not be helped up
though one to raise you is young
one to help you up is proud!
When you are up from the sleigh
and let out of the sledge-back
step along the well-swept road
    the liver-hued earth
    trodden smooth by pigs
    trampled by piglets
    stamped on by a sheep
rubbed down by a horse's mane!
Step with the steps of a goose
pad with the feet of a teal
    upon these washed yards
    on these level grounds

the yards father-in-law made
and mother-in-law set out
the banks where the brother carves,
sister's meadows of blue dye;
    set foot on the steps
and shift on to the porch boards
and step through the mead-sweet porch;
    from there shift inside
under the famous roof beam
    under the fair roof!

'Here through this very winter
    through the summer past
the boards of duck bones have rung
for someone to stand on them
the ceiling of gold has boomed
for someone to step beneath
and the windows have rejoiced
for someone to sit at them;
here through this very winter
    through the summer past
the latches have been creaking
for a ringed hand to shut them
the thresholds have been writhing
for a charmer with fine hems
the doors have kept opening
for someone to open them;
here through this very winter
    through the summer past
the room has been in a whirl
for someone to sweep the room
the porch has been making space
for someone to wipe the porch
and the huts have been moaning
for a hand to brush the huts;
here through this very winter
    through the summer past
the yard has secretly turned

for someone to pick up chips
the sheds have lowered themselves
for someone to step inside
the beams have sagged, the joists bowed
for the clothes of a young wife;
here through this very winter
    through the summer past
the lanes have been cooing forth
for someone to walk in them
the byres have been drawing near
for someone to muck them out
and the barnyards have drawn back
for a teal to toil in them;
here throughout this very day
    throughout yesterday
the big cow has kept lowing
for its morning feed-giver
the foal has been whinnying
for someone to pitch its hay
and the spring lamb has whimpered
for someone to feed it more;
here throughout this very day
    throughout yesterday
the old have sat at windows
the children have roved on shores
the women have stood by walls
and the boys in the doorways
attending a young woman
    waiting for a bride.

'Hail now, yard with all you hold
you out there with your fellows
hail, you hut with all you hold
    hut with your strangers
hail, you porch with all you hold
birchbark roof with your people
hail, you room with all you hold

hundred-planked with your children
    hail, moon and hail, king
    and hail, young escort!
Here there has not been before
not before nor yesterday
a crowd as well-turned as this
nor people as fair as these.

'Bridegroom, my splendid brother
strip away the red kerchiefs
    snatch off the silk hoods:
show that dear marten of yours
the one you sought five years long
    eight years long looked for!
Have you brought her you tried for?
You tried to bring a cuckoo
choose a white one from the earth
get one full-blooded from the waters.
Now I see without asking
and guess without questioning:
you've brought the cuckoo with you
the mallard in your keeping
    the greenest shoot-top
    of many green shoots
the freshest bird cherry sprig
of many fresh bird cherries.'

There was a child on the floor
and the child spoke from the floor:
'Brother, what are you dragging?—
one fair as a tarry stump
one tall as a tar-barrel
lofty as a winding-frame!
So there, so there, poor bridegroom!
This you hoped for all your days
said you'd get one worth hundreds
you'd bring a maid worth thousands:
now you've got a right one worth

hundreds, that lump worth thousands—
one like a crow from a swamp
a scare-magpie from a fence
a bird-scarer from a field
like a black bird from fallow!
What has she done all her days
and what through the summer past?
No mitten she's woven, no
stocking even started on!
Empty-handed she's come in
without gifts to father-in-law's house:
in her basket mice have been
rustling, big-ears in her box!'

Lokka the gentle mistress
Kaleva-daughter, fair wife
    heard the weird story
and uttered a word, spoke thus:
'What did you say, wretched child
and what prattle, ne'er-do-well?
About others let wonders
be heard, and let insults waft—
    not about this maid
not about those in this house!
Now you have said a bad word
an evil word spoken from
the mouth of a night-old calf
the head of a day-old pup!
A good maid the bridegroom's got
brought from the land the land's best—
like a half-ripe cowberry
a strawberry on a hill
or a cuckoo in a tree
a small bird in a rowan
in a birch one fine-feathered
bright-breasted in a maple.
Not even from Germany would he
have got, from beyond Estonia

have found this maid's handsomeness
    this calloo's sweetness
    this beauty of face
    glory such as this
    nor this arm's whiteness
this slender neck's curviness.
She's not come empty-handed
either: she had furs to bring
    cloaks to bargain with
    broadcloth to carry.
    This maid has plenty
of work from her own distaff
spun on her own spinning-wheel
goods from her own fingertips—
    garments all of white
    laundered in winter
    bleached in the spring sun
    dried in summer moons:
good bedsheets are fluttering
    pillows are plumping
    silk scarves are flapping
and woollen cloaks are flashing.

'O good woman, fair woman—
    woman in full bloom
you were well renowned at home
as a girl in father's home:
be well renowned all your days as a
daughter-in-law in your husband's house!
    Don't start worrying
    don't be full of cares!
You've not been led to a swamp
taken to a ditch: you've been
led from off a corn-hummock
led towards one fatter yet
and taken from beer-cabins

taken to some flusher still.
    Good maid, fair woman
    I will ask you this:
as you came here did you see
some stacks coiled at the bottom
    some plump-topped corn ricks?
    All are of this house
    this bridegroom's ploughing—
    ploughing and sowing.
Little maid, little young one
    now I'll tell you this:
as you knew how to come here
so know how to behave here!
A woman's life here is good
fair a daughter-in-law's growth—
a bowl of curds in your grip
a dish of butter all yours.
A maiden's life here is good
and fair a little hen's growth:
here the sauna planks are broad
and wide the cabin floorboards
the masters are good as your father
the mistresses good as your mother
the sons good as your brother
daughters good as your sister.
    When the lust takes you
and you have a mind for those
    fish your father caught
those grouse your brother hunted
don't ask your brother-in-law
nor beg your father-in-law:
    ask your bridegroom straight
bother the one who brought you!
There's nothing in the forest
    running on four legs
nor are there birds of the air
    flapping on two wings

nor even in the water
    the best shoal of fish
that your catcher will not catch—
catcher catch nor bringer bring.
A maiden's life here is good
and fair a little hen's growth:
there is no fret for the quern
nor worry for the mortar—
water here has ground the wheat
a rapid has stirred the rye
the billow washes the bowls
and the sea froth bleaches them.

    'O darling village
mine the best place in the land!
Meadows below, fields above
and the village in between;
below it the sweet lakeshore
at the shore the dear water
just right for the duck to swim
the water-bird to wallow.'

The crowd was given to drink
was fed, was given to drink—
    lots of bits of meat
    beautiful biscuits
    beer made from barley
    wort made out of wheat.
Yes, there was enough ready
enough to eat and to drink
    in vessels of red
    in handsome dishes—
    pies to put about
    butter-bits to bite
    whitefish to dish out
    salmon to share out
    with a silver knife
    a golden dagger.

Beer flowed that had not been bought
honey no marks had paid for
booze from the top of the beam
and mead from within the bungs
    beer to steep the lips
    honey to turn wits.

Now, who here was to be the
cuckoo, the proper singer?
Steady old Väinämöinen
the everlasting singer—
    he started the song
set about the job of tales;
    he says with this word
    he spoke with this speech:
'Dear brothers, my kid brothers
    my fellow-mouthers
    my tongue-companions:
listen now while I'm talking!
Seldom are geese face to face
little sisters eye to eye
seldom brothers side by side
mother's children cheek by jowl
    on these poor borders
the luckless lands of the North;
so shall we launch into song
set about the job of tales?
Singing is a job for bards
calling for the spring cuckoo
pressing is for dye-daughters
weaving is for loom-daughters.

'Even Lapland's children sing
    the hay-shod pitch notes
    after scraps of elk
    flanks of small reindeer;
so why don't I sing too, why
    don't our children sing

from a meal of rye
from a well-stuffed mouth?
Even Lapland's children sing
the hay-shod strike up
when they've drunk a bowl
of water, bitten bark bread;
so why don't I sing too, why
don't our children sing
from drinks made of grain
beer made of barley?
Even Lapland's children sing
the hay-shod strike up
from sooty camp fires
from beds full of grime;
so why don't I sing too, why
don't our children sing
under a famous roof beam
under a fair roof?

'For the men's life here is good
sweet the women's dwelling too
beside a beer keg
round a honey vat
at our side straits of whitefish
by us seine-shores of salmon
where the food does not run out
and the drink does not run short.
For the men's life here is good
sweet the women's sojourn too:
here is no eating with grief
no sojourning among care;
here is eating without grief
sojourning carefree
in the days of this master
the lifetime of this mistress.

'Which one here shall I praise first—
the master or the mistress?

Fellows before have always
    praised the master first
who got shelter from the swamp
gathered a home from the wilds—
    brought tough firs base first
    pines lopped at the top
put them down on a good spot
    set them somewhere firm
for big family-size cabins
    and for fair farmyards;
bolted walls from the backwoods
timbers from the frightful hill
rafters from the rocky ground
battens from the berry-heath
bark off the bird cherry slope
mosses from unfrozen swamps.
The cabin was built aright
the shelter put in its place:
a hundred men joined the walls
a thousand worked on the roof
    building this cabin
    laying down the floor.
But still, while this master was
    making this cabin
many winds his locks have seen
his hair terrible weather:
many times the good master's
mitten was left on a rock
his hat was snagged on a twig
his stocking sunk in a swamp;
many times the good master
quite betimes on the morrow
before others had got up
and the village folk could hear
has got up from the log fire
woken in his huts of sprigs
and a sprig has brushed his hair

and dew has washed his quick eyes.
    Then the good master
brings indoors people he knows—
a whole benchful of singers
windows of merrymakers
floorboards full of soothsayers
inglenooks full of crooners
wall sides full of folk standing
fence sides full of folk stepping
yards of folk walking along
lands of travellers across.

'I have praised the master first;
and now the kindly mistress
for making the food ready
for filling the long table.
'Tis she has baked the thick loaves
has patted the great dumplings
    with her nimble palms
    with ten bent fingers;
she has raised the loaves gently
she has fed the guests promptly
    with plenty of pork
    with crusty fish pies:
the blades of our knives have slipped
the tips of our dirks have dulled
    chopping salmon heads
    cutting off pike heads.
Many times the good mistress
    this careful housewife
learned to rise without the cock
leap up without the hen's child
while this wedding was prepared
    pies were being made
and the yeast was got ready
    and the beer was brewed;

full well has the good mistress
    this careful housewife
    known how to brew beer
got the tasty drink flowing
    from fomented shoots
    and out of sweet malt
which she worked on with no wood
    scooped with no cowlstaff
    but stirred with her fists
    and turned with her arms
in the sauna rid of smoke
    on the well-swept planks.
Neither does this good mistress
    this careful housewife
    beat the shoots to pulp
spill the malt upon the earth;
she's often in the sauna
at dead of night on her own—
she does not care about wolves
fear the beasts of the forest.

'Now the mistress I have praised;
wait while I praise my best man!
Who has been made the best man
who taken to run the show?
The village best is best man
the lucky one runs the show.
    See, our best man is
    decked out in cogware
well-fitting under the arm
comely in the gut region;
    see, our best man wears
    a narrow caftan—
    the hems sweep the sand
    the back parts the ground;
a little of his shirt shows
a tiny bit peeps out—'tis
as though Moon-daughter wove it

the tin-breast made it jingling;
    see, our best man has
at his waist a fine-wove belt
woven by the sun's daughter
brightened by the bright-nailed one
at a time when no fire was
    when fire was unknown;
    see, our best man has
stockings of silk on his feet
    stocking bands of silk
    and garters of lawn—
    they're woven with gold
    and worked with silver;
    see, our best man has
    real German shoes
like swans upon a river
    wigeon on the banks
    or geese on a bough
birds of passage on felled trees;
    see, our best man has
    curls of gold ringlets
    a beard of gold plaits—
on his head a tall helmet
    that pokes through the clouds
that glitters through the forest
and can't be got for hundreds
nor bought for thousands of marks.

'Now I have praised my best man;
wait while I praise the matron!
Where was the matron got from
and the lucky one taken?
There the matron was got from
and the lucky one taken—
    the back of Tallinn
the far side of Novgorod.
But no, not even from there—
    not a bit of it!

There the matron was got from
and the lucky one taken—
the White Sea of Archangel
from the open* expanses.
But no, not even from there—
    not a bit of it!
On the earth there grew a strawberry
a cowberry on the heath
    in a field bright grass
a golden flower in a glade:
there the matron was got from
and the lucky one taken.
The matron's mouth is comely
as a Finnish shuttle is;
    the matron's quick eyes
are like the stars in the sky;
the matron's famous eyebrows
like the moon above the sea.
    See, our matron has
a neck full of golden locks
a head full of golden coils
    hands with gold bracelets
    fingers with gold rings
    ears with golden beads
    brows with golden knots
    eyelashes with pearls.
I thought the moon was gleaming
when her golden buckle gleamed;
I thought the sun was shining
when her shirt collar shone out;
I thought a ship was flashing
when the cap flashed on her head.

'Now, I have praised the matron;
let me look at everyone
to see whether they are fair—
    the old folk hearty

the youngsters comely
the whole crowd well-turned!
I have looked at everyone—
perhaps I knew already:
here there has not been before
nor indeed will be again
a crowd as well-turned as this
nor people as fair as these
old folk as hearty
youngsters as comely:
everyone is in cloth coats
like a forest in hoarfrost
from below like the dawn glow
from above like the daybreak.
Cheap the silver coins
free the gold coins at the feast
the money-bags in the yards
and the purses in the lanes
were for these invited guests
to honour the feast!'

Steady old Väinämöinen
age-old wielder of a tale
then shifted into his sledge
and sets off homeward;
and he sings, rapt in his tales
he sings, practises his craft.
He sang one tale, he sang two
till at the third tale
a runner clonked on a rock
a strut caught on a stump top:
the bard's sledge smashed, the
singer's runner broke
the strut came off with a crack
the planks crunched apart.
The old Väinämöinen said
he uttered a word, spoke thus:
'Is there among these youngsters

among the people growing
or else among these old ones
among the folk shrinking, one
who would go to Tuonela
would set out for Death's abodes
would bring a spike from Tuoni
  a drill from Death's folk
for me to make a new sledge
for me to build a sleigh with?'

  Both the younger say
  and the old answer:
'There's not among these youngsters
nor indeed among the old
  in all the great kin
  a fellow so brave
as would go off to Tuoni
would set out for Death's abodes
would bring a spike from Tuoni
and a drill from Death's abodes
for you to make a new sledge
for you to build a sleigh with.'

Then the old Väinämöinen
the everlasting singer
went again to Tuonela
and travelled to Death's abodes;
brought a spike from Tuonela
and a drill from Death's abodes.
At that old Väinämöinen
  sings the blue backwoods
into them a shapely oak
  and a fit rowan;
he built them into his sleigh
pressed them into his runners
  from them looked out struts
  turned out collar-bows:

he finished building the sleigh
   making the new sledge.
He stuck the foal in harness
the bay in front of the sledge
and he sat down in the sledge
settled down in the bobsleigh.
Though unlashed the courser ran
unsmitten by beads the horse
to the mash it had before
the fodder it used to have;
it brought old Väinämöinen
the everlasting singer
to his own door's openings
in front of his own threshold.

26. *A Perilous Journey*

Ahti dwelt on the island
underneath Far Headland's arm;
    was ploughing a field
    tilling an acre.
    His ear was most keen
very alert of hearing:
he hears noise from the village
a din from beyond the lakes
the stamp of feet on the ice
a sledge-rattle on the heath.
    It occurred to him
    the thought came to him:
Northland's holding a wedding
    the sly crowd revels!
He twisted his mouth, he turned his head
he twisted his black whiskers
    the blood drained away
    from his luckless cheeks;
at once he left his ploughing
the tilling in mid-acre
jumped straight on the horse's back
    and sets off homeward
    to his dear mother
towards his honoured parent
and he said when he got there
    explained when he came:
'O my mother, old woman
    put out food quickly
for a hungry man to eat
for one who wants it to bite;
heat the sauna this minute
burn the fire down in the room

where a man makes himself clean
the best fellow grooms himself!'

That Lemminkäinen's mother
    put out food quickly
for the hungry man to eat
for him who wanted to bite
while the bath-hut got prepared
and the sauna made ready;
then wanton Lemminkäinen
    took food quickly, went
to the sauna that minute
    walked to the bath-hut
and there the chaffinch washes
the snow bunting cleans himself
his head into a handful
    of flax, his neck white.
He came in from the sauna
and uttered a word, spoke thus:
'O my mother, old woman
step to the shed on the hill
bring from there my comely gear
carry the hard-wearing clothes
    for me to put on
    to kit myself out!'

The mother hastened to ask
the old woman to inquire:
'Where are you bound, my offspring?
Are you off to hunt the lynx
or else to ski after elk
    or to shoot squirrel?'

Wanton Lemminkäinen spoke
    the fair Farmind said:
'O my mother who bore me
I'm not off to hunt the lynx

neither to ski after elk
    nor to shoot squirrel:
I am off to Northland's feast
    the sly crowd's revels.
Bring my comely gear to me
    my hard-wearing clothes
to show off at the wedding
    to wear at the feast!'

The mother forbade her son
and the woman banned her man;
    two maidens banned him
three nature-daughters forbade
Lemminkäinen to go off
    to good Northland's feast.
The mother said to the son
the eldest spoke to her child:
    'Don't go, my offspring—
my offspring, my dear Farmind
    to that Northland feast
    the great crowd's revels!
You were not invited there
simply not wanted at all.'

That wanton Lemminkäinen
uttered a word and spoke thus:
'Wretches go when invited—
a good one leaps up when not!
Summoners old as the moon
and perpetual heralds stand
in a sword of fiery blade
    in a sparkling brand.'

That Lemminkäinen's mother
    still tried to forbid:
    'Just don't, my offspring
    go to Northland's feast!
Many the wonders on your journey

great on your road the marvels—
    three of the worst dooms
    three deaths for a man.'

Wanton Lemminkäinen spoke
    the fair Farmind said:
'Hags are always full of dooms
    of deaths everywhere;
no fellow frets about them—
no, he'll not beware at all.
    Be that as it may
say so that my ears may hear:
    what is the first doom—
the first, and the last as well?'

Lemminkäinen's mother spoke
and the old woman answered:
I'll tell the dooms as they are
not as a man would have them.
    I'll tell the first doom—
this doom is the foremost doom.
You will go a little way
you'll finish a day's journey:
you'll meet a fiery river
    over against you;
in the river a fiery rapid
and in the rapid a fiery crag
on the crag a fiery peak
and on the peak a fiery eagle
by night sharpening a tooth
and by day whetting a claw
for the stranger who comes, for
    one on his way there.'

Wanton Lemminkäinen spoke
    the fair Farmind said:
'That doom is a woman's doom—
'tis no death for a fellow.

Yes, I'll spot a way round that
think up something good:
I'll sing a horse of alder
sing a fellow of alder
to shift past my side
to walk before me
while I as a duck will dive
as a calloo I'll go down
beyond the eagle's clutches
past the wivern's toes.
O my mother who bore me
tell the midmost doom!'

Lemminkäinen's mother said:
'This doom is the second doom.
You will go a little way
just a second day's journey:
you'll meet a fiery ravine
that's across the road
stretching eastward for ever
north-west without end
full of red-hot rocks
of burning boulders;
in it hundreds have landed
thousands have piled up—
a hundred swordsmen
a thousand iron stallions.'

Wanton Lemminkäinen spoke
the fair Farmind said:
'That is no man's doom
nor a death for a fellow.
I'll think of a dodge round that—
think of a dodge, spot a way:
I'll sing a man out of snow
from hard snow fudge a fellow
I'll thrust him amid the fire
press him hard into the flame

to bathe in the hot sauna
with a bath-whisk of copper
while I shift aside
and squeeze through the fire
so that my beard will not burn
and my curls will not be singed.
O my mother who bore me
tell the latest doom!'

Lemminkäinen's mother said:
'This doom is the third of dooms.
You will go a bit further
you'll finish a day from there
heading for Northland's gateway
through the narrowest region:
a wolf will pounce upon you
a bear will attack you next
at Northland's gateway
in the smallest lane;
they've eaten a hundred men
destroyed a thousand fellows
so why should they not eat you
destroy one with no defence?'

Wanton Lemminkäinen spoke
the fair Farmind said:
'Let a ewe be eaten young
be torn apart fresh
but not even the worst man
the sleepiest of fellows!
I'm belted with a man's belt
fixed with a man's pin
tied with a fellow's buckles
so that I shall not fall yet
into the Dreamer's wolves' mouths
the jaws of the cursed maids.
I will think of a dodge for the wolf
spot a way round the bear too:

the wolves I'll bridle with song
sing the bears in iron chains
or I'll flatten them to chaff
    I'll sift them piecemeal.
That's how I'll get free of that
    reach my journey's end.'

Lemminkäinen's mother said:
'You have not reached the end yet!
While you were on your way there
    they were great marvels
    three grievous wonders
three ways for a man to die;
    when you arrive there
will be the worst wonders yet.
You'll travel a tiny way
and you'll come to Northland's yard:
an iron fence has been built
a steel pen has been fashioned
from the earth up to the sky
from the sky down to the earth;
with spears it has been staked out
with earthworms it has been fenced
with snakes it has been lashed up
    and with lizards bound;
the tails have been left to wave
    the blunt heads to sway
    and the skulls to spit—
heads outside and tails inside.
On the ground are other worms
a line of vipers, of snakes
with their tongues seething above
with their tails waving below:
one more dreadful than others
lies across before the gate
longer than cabin timber
thicker than a lane doorpost
with its tongue seething above

with its mouth above hissing
    not for anyone
    except hapless you.'

Wanton Lemminkäinen spoke
    the fair Farmind said:
'That doom too is a child's doom—
'tis no death for a fellow.
I know how to bewitch fire
    and how to tame flame
I know how to banish worms
    and turn snakes away.
    Only yesterday
I ploughed land full of vipers
    I turned snaky land
    quite with my bare hands;
held the vipers with my nails
    in my hands the snakes;
I killed about ten vipers
    a hundred black worms:
viper-blood is on my nails
still, and snake-fat on my hands.
So I don't think I'll become
oh no, not yet come to be
    a great worm's mouthful
    a snake's handiwork:
    I'll seize the scoundrels
    wring their wicked necks
sing the vipers further on
move the snakes along the road
and I'll step from Northland's yard
and slip inside the cabin.'

Lemminkäinen's mother said:
    'Just don't, my offspring
go into Northland's cabin
to Sariola's buildings!
Men there have swords at their belts

fellows have weapons of war
    men are mad from hops
    bad from much drinking:
they will sing you, luckless, on
to a sword of fiery blade;
    better have been sung
greater ones overcome too.'

Wanton Lemminkäinen spoke
    the fair Farmind said:
'I have been before, you know
in those cabins of Northland.
No Lapp sings at me, no man
of Turja shoves me around;
I'll sing at the Lapp myself
I'll shove the man of Turja—
    sing through his shoulders
    talk right through his chin
till his shirt collar's in two
    till his breastbone breaks.'

Lemminkäinen's mother said:
    'Ah, my luckless boy
still you think of how it was—
you boast of your last visit!
You have been before, I know
in those cabins of Northland—
    swum all the still pools
    sampled weed-choked ponds
    shot rapids roaring
    currents in a flash
come to know Tuoni's rapids
and sounded the Dead Land's streams—
and you'd still be there today
but for your poor old mother.
Now, think of what I'm saying!
You'll come to Northland's cabins:
the hill is bristling with stakes

the yard is bristling with poles
and they bristle with men's heads:
one stake is a headless stake
and for the tip of that stake
it will be your head chopped off!'

Wanton Lemminkäinen spoke
    the fair Farmind said:
    'A fool may worry
about them, a knave foresee
    five, six battle-years
    seven war-summers!—
but no fellow will heed them
nor avoid them in the least.
    Bring me my war-gear
    my old battledress!
I will fetch my father's sword
my papa's blade I'll look out;
long it has been in the cold
for ages hidden away
    weeping out its days
there, longing for a wearer.'

At that he got his war-gear
    his old battledress
his father's long-lasting sword
that war-comrade of papa's
and he stuck it in the boards
thrust its blade into the floor
and the sword turned in his hand
like a fresh bird cherry top
or a growing juniper;
wanton Lemminkäinen said:
'Hardly in Northland's cabins
in Sariola's buildings
is there one to measure this
sword, one to defy this blade.'

The crossbow off the wall he
snatched, the strong bow off the peg;
    he says with this word
    he spoke with this speech:
    'Him I'd call a man
    reckon a fellow
    who'd draw my crossbow
    fasten my curved one
in those cabins of Northland
in Sariola's buildings.'

Then wanton Lemminkäinen
    he, the fair Farmind
fitted himself in war-gear
    put on battledress
and he declared to his serf
uttered a word and spoke thus:
    'O serf I have bought
my toiler got for money:
make ready my war stallion
harness up the battle foal
for me to go to the feast
to the Devil-crowd's revels!'

The serf, meekly obedient
slipped straight out into the yard
thrust the foal into harness
between shafts the fiery red
and he said when he came back:
    'I have done my task—
prepared that stallion of yours
and harnessed the splendid foal.'

Then wanton Lemminkäinen's
    hour comes to be off:
one hand bade, one hand forbade
but sinewy fingers forced
and he went just as he meant—

off he went, did not beware.
The mother advised her son
and the eldest warned her child
at the door, beneath the beam
    by the pan cupboards:
'My offspring, my matchless one
my child and my steadfastness!
If you get to the revels
wherever you happen on
    drink half your flagon
    half way down your bowl;
let another have the other half
and a worse one the worse half:
a worm lies in the bowl, a
maggot in the flagon's depths.'

And still she advised her son
certainly assured her child
    at the furthest field's
    end, at the last gate:
'If you get to the revels
wherever you happen on
    sit on half a seat
    and step half a step;
let another have the other half
and a worse one the worse half:
that way you'll become a man
you'll come out a bold fellow
    for going through court
settling disputes openly
    among the fellows
    in a crowd of men.'

Then Lemminkäinen set off
sitting in the stallion's sledge—
struck the courser with the lash
hit it with the beaded whip

and off the courser careered
 and the horse dashed off.
He drove for a little time
a good while he jogged along.
On the road he saw a flock
of black grouse: the black grouse whirled
into flight, the flock of birds
flapped before the running horse.
Just a few feathers remained
some black grouse plumes on the road.
Lemminkäinen gathered them
stuffed them into his pocket:
you never know what might come
might happen on a journey;
all is handy in a house
useful in emergency.

He drove forward a little
went a tiny bit of road;
now the horse pricks up its ears
 the flop-ear fidgets.
That wanton Lemminkäinen
 he, the fair Farmind
 leapt out of his sleigh
 leant over to look:
it is as his mother said
as his own parent assured!
Yes, there's a fiery river
across in front of the horse;
in the river a fiery rapid
and in the rapid a fiery crag
on the crag a fiery peak
and on the peak a fiery eagle:
it had a throat spewing fire
 a mouth pouring flame
feathers as a fire whirling
 and as sparks sparkling.
It sees Farmind from afar

Lemminkäinen from further:
'Where is Farmind going, where
are you off to, Loverboy?'

Wanton Lemminkäinen spoke
    the fair Farmind said:
'I am off to Northland's feast
    the sly crowd's revels.
    Move aside a bit
give way, away from the road
let a travelling man pass—
Lemminkäinen most of all—
    to shift past your side
    to walk beyond you!'

The eagle managed to say
and the fire-throat to whisper:
'I'll let a traveller pass—
Lemminkäinen most of all—
    to roam through my mouth
to make his way down my throat:
that's where the road goes for you—
to go from there for its sake
    down to that long feast
those everlasting sessions.'

What did Lemminkäinen care!
He did not then greatly fret
for he groped in his pocket
    dipped into his purse
    took some black grouse plumes;
    he rubs them slowly
    between his two palms
and betwixt his ten fingers:
out sprang a flock of black grouse
a whole bevy of capercaillies.
He flung them into the eagle's mouth
gave them to the gobbler's jaws

down the fiery eagle's throat
between the bird of prey's gums.
That's how he got free of that
    finished the first day.

    He lashed the courser
whacked it with the beaded lash:
the stallion set off headlong
    the horse galloped off.
He drove a bit of a way
    traced a tiny way;
    now the stallion is
    startled, the horse snorts.
He got up out of his sleigh
    craned his neck to look:
it is as his mother said
as his own parent assured!
In front's a fiery ravine
    that's across the road
stretching eastward for ever
    north-west without end
    full of red-hot rock
    a burning boulder.

What did Lemminkäinen care!
He beseeches the Old Man:
    'O Old Man, chief god—
that is, heavenly father:
raise a bank of cloud from the north-west
another send from the west
set a third out of the east
lift one out of the north-east
shove them edge-on together
knock them against each other;
rain a ski-stick's depth of snow
    run up a stake's depth
    on those red-hot rocks
    those burning boulders!'

That Old Man, chief god
the old heavenly father
raised a bank of cloud from the north-west
another sent from the west
reared a cloud out of the east
lifted air from the north-east
and he joined them together
knocked them against each other;
rained a ski-stick's depth of snow
ran up a stake's depth
on those red-hot rocks
those burning boulders
and there came a pool of snow
and a lake of slush was formed.
Then wanton Lemminkäinen
sang on it a bridge of ice
across the pool of
snow from bank to bank.
Thus he escaped that danger
and finished the second day.

He lashed the courser
whacked it with the beaded belt
and the courser flashed away
the horse trotted off.
The courser ran a mile, two
and the land's best fled a bit;
then it suddenly
stopped, will not flee from its place.
He, wanton Lemminkäinen
started, jumped to look:
there's a wolf in the gateway
a bear in the lane ahead
in the gateway of Northland
at the end of the long lanes.

Then wanton Lemminkäinen
he, the fair Farmind

groped in his pocket
fumbled in his purse;
took scraps of ewe wool
and softly rubs them
in the midst of his two palms
and betwixt his ten fingers.
He blew once upon his palm:
the ewes fluffed into a run—
a whole flock of sheep
of lambs quite a herd.
The wolves rushed that way
and the bears attacked with them;
he, wanton Lemminkäinen
drove forward on his journey.

He went but a tiny way
till he came to Northland's yard:
an iron fence had been built
and a steel pen made
a hundred fathoms earthward
a thousand fathoms skyward;
with spears it had been staked out
with earthworms it had been fenced
with snakes it had been fastened
and with lizards bound;
the tails had been left to wave
the blunt heads to sway
the powerful heads to quiver—
heads outside and tails inside.
That wanton Lemminkäinen
thereupon now considers:
'It is as my mother said
as the one who bore me moaned:
that is quite a fence
set from the earth to the sky!
A viper crawls low

but the fence is set lower;
    a bird has flown high
but the fence is set higher.'

Well, at that Lemminkäinen
did not care to fret greatly:
he drew the knife from its sheath
from its holder harsh iron;
with it he slashed at the fence
    broke the poles in two;
the iron fence he opened
he unwound the pen of snakes
leaving a gap five withes high
    and seven stakes wide
    and forward he drives
before the gate of Northland.

A snake writhes upon the road
lies across before the gate
longer than cabin timber
and thicker than a gatepost:
a hundred eyes the worm has
a thousand tongues the snake has
its eyes the size of sieve holes
its tongue long as a spear shaft
its fangs the size of rake teeth
its back long as seven boats.
There wanton Lemminkäinen
    dare not lay hands on
    the hundred-eyed worm
    the thousand-tongued snake;
wanton Lemminkäinen spoke
    the fair Farmind said:
    'Black worm on the ground
    Tuoni-hued maggot
    mover in dry grass
    in Devil-leaf roots
    goer through hummocks

threader of tree roots!
Who raised you from grass
roused you from hay roots
to crawl on the ground
to thrash on the road?
Who raised your nose up
who told, compelled you
to hold your head stiff
your neck erect—did
your father or your mother
the eldest of your brothers
the youngest of your sisters
another of your great kin?
Sweeten now your mouth, cover
your head, hide your nimble tongue
coil up in a coil
curl up in a curl
give way, half the way, one side
for the traveller to go;
or shift off the road
move, wretch, into scrub
wade into heather
slink off into moss
slip off as a tuft of wool
as an aspen log roll off
thrust your head into the sward
stuff it inside a hummock
for in sward is your cabin
beneath a hummock your house:
if you bob up there
God will crack your head
with steel-tipped needles
with iron hailstones.'

That's what Lemminkäinen spoke
but the worm took no notice:
it keeps on spitting

rears with tongue seething
with mouth hissing rears
poised for Lemminkäinen's head.
Then wanton Lemminkäinen
thought of some old words
the dame had advised
his mother had taught;
wanton Lemminkäinen said
fair Farmind uttered:
'If you'll heed not even that
nor yield with a little word
you'll grow bloated with your pains
swell with your days of suffering
you'll split, villain, into two
scoundrel, into three pieces
if I seek out your mother
and fetch your honoured parent.
I know, coiled one, of your birth
earth's grim one, of your growing:
the Ogress was your mother
an elf your parent.

'On the waters the Ogress
spat, dropped slobber on the waves
and the wind lulled it
and the water-breeze rocked it
lulled it for six years
seven summers too
on the clear high seas
on the rippling waves;
the water stretched it out long
and the sun roasted it soft
and the surf pushed it to land
the billow drove it ashore.
Three nature-daughters
walked on the plashy seashore
the coast of the roaring sea

and they saw it on the shore
    and said with this word:
"Now, just what would come of that
if the Creator put breath
into it, blessed it with eyes?"
The Creator chanced to hear;
he uttered a word, spoke thus:
"Evil would come of evil
scoundrel from scoundrel-vomit
should I put breath into it
    bless its head with eyes."
But the Demon got to hear
the vicious man to take note:
he became a creator
the Demon gave breath to it—
the wicked scoundrel's slaver
    the Ogress's spit
and it turned into a snake
it changed into a black worm.

'What was breath for it got from?—
breath from the Demon's embers.
What was a heart tossed in from?—
    the Ogress's heart.
    What the brute's brains from?—
the froth of a powerful stream.
What were the rascal's wits from?—
foam of a fiery rapid.
What was the bad one's head from?—
its head was from a bad pea.
What were eyes for it made from?—
    the Devil's hemp seeds.
What were the scoundrel's ears from?—
    the Devil's birch leaves.
What was a mouth made up from?—
from the Ogress's buckle.
What a tongue in the wretch's mouth from?—
    from a fairy's spear.

What the vicious one's teeth from?—
the husks of Tuoni's barley.
What the wicked one's gums from?—
from the gums of the grave's lass.
What was its back stuck up from?—
    the Demon's charred stake.
What the tail set waving from?—
    the evil one's plait.
What were its guts knotted from?—
its guts were from Doom's belt chain.

    'So much for your kin
    your famous honour!
    Black worm on the ground
    Tuoni-hued maggot
    ground-hued, heather-hued
    all-the-rainbow-hued:
now leave the traveller's road
before the fellow who moves;
let the traveller go, let
Lemminkäinen trip along
    to that Northland feast
the blowout of the well-born!'

    Now the worm pushed off
and the hundred-eye shifted
and the fat snake turned away
changed its place along the road
let the traveller go, let
Lemminkäinen trip along
    to that Northland feast
    the sly crowd's revels.

27. *Magic and Mayhem*

I have now led my Farmind
brought Ahti the Islander
past the mouth of many dooms
past the reach of the grave's tongue
    to those Northland yards
    the sly folk's farmyards:
    now I have to say
    and tell with my tongue
how wanton Lemminkäinen
    he, the fair Farmind
came to the Northland cabins
the Sariola buildings
uninvited to the feast
heraldless to the revels.
That wanton Lemminkäinen
that boy, that full-blooded rogue
the moment he came inside
stepped to the midst of the floor
the boards of limewood juddered
    the spruce cabin boomed.
Wanton Lemminkäinen said
    he uttered, spoke thus:
    'Hail, I am welcome
    hail to one who hails!
Listen, master of Northland:
would there be within this house
barley for a horse to bite
beer for a fellow to drink?'

He, the master of Northland
sat at the long table's head
and that one answered from there
uttered a word and spoke thus:

'There may be within this house
ground for a stallion to stay
and you are not forbidden
if you behave well inside
    standing at the door—
at the door, beneath the beam
    between the two pans
    where the three hooks touch.'

There wanton Lemminkäinen
he twisted his black whiskers
that were the colour of pans
and uttered a word, spoke thus:
    'The Devil come here
    to stand at the door
    sweep away your soot
    and shake off the muck!
    My father did not
nor did my honoured parent
    stand upon that spot
at the door, beneath the beam
    for there was space then—
a barnyard for a stallion
a room washed for men's coming
    nooks for throwing gloves
    pegs for men's mittens
    walls for stacking swords;
so why is it not for me
as was once for my father?'

Then he shifted further up
he swept to the table head
he sat down at the seat end
at the head of the pine bench
    and the seat creaked back
    and the pine bench sagged.
Wanton Lemminkäinen said:

'I can't be a welcome guest
    if no beer is brought
    for the coming guest.'

Ilpo-daugher, good mistress
uttered a word and spoke thus:
'Ah, son of Lemminkäinen
    what a guest you'd be!
You've come to trample my head
    to bring down my brains!
Our beer is barley as yet
    our tasty drinks malt
    unbaked the wheat loaves
    the meat stews unstewed.
You ought to have come the night
before, or the day after.'

There wanton Lemminkäinen
twisted his mouth, turned his head
and twisted his black whiskers
and he put this into words:
'So the food's been eaten here
the wedding drunk, the feast held
the beer's been shared out, each man's
had his measure of honey
the jugs have been collected
    and the flagons stowed!
O you mistress of Northland
snarler of Darkland, you held
the wedding with wickedness
the feast with a dog's honour:
    you baked the great loaves
    brewed the barley beer
sent invitations six ways
    summoners nine ways;
called the wretched, called the poor
called the outcast, called the vile
    all the thin cotters

the gipsies in tight caftans;
you invited all the rest
but left me uninvited!
    Why do this to me
because of my own barley?
Others brought some in ladles
others dripped some in cupfuls
but I flung by the bushel
    squandered by the sack
    barley of my own
    grains of my sowing.
I can't be Lemminkäinen
now, not a guest of good name
    if no beer is brought
and no pot put on the fire
and no stew inside the pot
    no quarter of pork
for my eating, my drinking
    at my journey's end.'

Ilpo-daughter, good mistress
    put this into words:
    'Hey there, tiny wench
    my perpetual serf:
    put stew in a pot
    bring beer for the guest!'

The small girl, child with nothing
    the least dish-washer
    least wiper of spoons
    scraper of dippers
    put stew in a pot—
    meat bones and fish heads
    old tops of turnip
    and crusts from stale loaves;
brought then a flagon of beer
a jugful of the worst brew
for wanton Lemminkäinen to drink

for him who wanted it to gobble
and she put this into words:
'Are you really man enough
    to drink up this beer
    to tip up this jug?'

Lemminkäinen, wanton boy
looked then into his flagon:
a maggot is in the depths
    and snakes half way down
    on the rim worms crawled
    and lizards slithered.
Wanton Lemminkäinen said
Farmind blurted out: 'To Hell
with the flagon-bringers, Death
    to the jug-bearers
    before the moonrise
    the end of this day!'
Then he put this into words:
    'Ah, you mean beer, now
you have come to be idle
come to follow idle ways!
Beer shall be drunk with the mouth
rubbish cast upon the ground
    with the ring finger
    and with the left thumb!'

And he groped in his pocket
    fumbled in his purse;
took a hook from his pocket
an iron barb from his bag
and sank it in his flagon
began to angle the beer:
the worms got stuck on his hook
on his barb hateful vipers.
He fished up a hundred frogs
    a thousand black worms
cast them down for the ground's sake

dropped them all upon the floor;
    he drew his sharp knife
    that harsh sheathed iron
with it beheaded the worms
and snapped the snakes' necks, then drank
the beer to his heart's content
the black honey as he liked.
He uttered a word, spoke thus:
'I can't be a welcome guest
    if no beer is brought
    any better drink
with a more plentiful hand
    in a bigger bowl
neither is a ram struck down
    a great bull slaughtered
    an ox brought indoors
a hoof-shank into the room.'

He, the master of Northland
uttered a word and spoke thus:
'So why have you come here, who
invited you to the throng?'

Wanton Lemminkäinen spoke
    the fair Farmind said:
'An invited guest is fine;
uninvited is finer.
Listen, Northlander's son, you
    master of Northland:
    let me buy some beer
    some drink for money!'

Well, that master of Northland
at that was angry and wroth
very angry and furious:
he sang a pool on the floor
in front of Lemminkäinen
and uttered a word, spoke thus:

'There's a stream for you to drink
a pool for you to lap up!'

What did Lemminkäinen care!
He uttered a word, spoke thus:
'I am no wives' calf
no ox with a tail
to drink stream waters
to lap pool water.'

And he started singing charms
set about singing;
he sang a bull on the floor
a great gold-horned ox:
it slurped up the pool and drank
the stream to its heart's content.
The Northlander, a tall boy
brought forth a wolf from his mouth;
he sang it upon the floor
to slay the fat bull.
Lemminkäinen, wanton boy
he sang a white hare
to hop on the floor
before the wolf's mouth.
The Northlander, the tall boy
sang a dog with a hooked jaw
to slaughter the hare
to tear the squint-eye.
Lemminkäinen, wanton boy
sang a squirrel on a beam
to dart about on the beams
for the dog to bark at it.
The Northlander, the tall boy
sang a gold-breasted marten:
the marten grabbed the squirrel
sitting on the beam.
Lemminkäinen, wanton boy
sang a brown fox: it

ate the gold-breasted marten
    lost the fine-haired one.
The Northlander, the tall boy
brought forth a hen from his mouth
    to strut on the boards
in front of the fox's mouth.
Lemminkäinen, wanton boy
brought forth a hawk from his mouth
one with quick claws off his tongue
    and it seized the hen.

The master of Northland said
    he declared, spoke thus:
'Here the feast will not improve
if there are not fewer guests—
house to work, guest on the road
after even good revels:
go from here, Demon's outcast
from all company of men;
    head off home, scoundrel
run off, bad man, to your land!'

Wanton Lemminkäinen spoke
    the fair Farmind said:
'No man is got by cursing
    no worse man either
    to shift from his place
to run off from where he is.'

Then the master of Northland
seized a sword from off the wall
    snatched his fiery blade
and uttered a word, spoke thus:
'You Ahti the Islander—
    that is, fair Farmind:
    let's size up our swords
let's look to our brands and see

whether mine's the better sword
or Ahti the Islander's!'

Wanton Lemminkäinen said:
'As for my sword, it
has split among bones
and smashed among skulls!
Be that as it may
since this feast will not improve
let us size up, look and see
whose sword is keener!
My father never
feared to size up swords:
has the stock changed with the son
the strain dwindled with the child?'

He took his sword, bared the iron
snatched the one of fiery blade
out of the holder of hide
out of the belt of leather.
They sized up, looked down
the length of those swords:
a tiny bit longer was
the sword of Northland's master
by one fingernail's black speck
by half a knuckle.
Ahti the Islander said
the fair Farmind spoke:
'See, yours is the longer sword
so you should strike first.'

Then the master of Northland
slashed away and lunged away;
he reached for but could not reach
Lemminkäinen's scalp.
Once he hit a beam
clouted a lintel:
the beam broke off with a crack

the lintel flew into two.
Ahti the Islander said
    the fair Farmind spoke:
'What wrong have the beams done, what
    foul deed the lintel
that you hit out at the beams
    clout at the lintel?
Listen, Northlander's son, you
    master of Northland!
'Tis hard to quarrel indoors
to argue among women:
we will spoil the new cabin
we will stain the floors with blood.
Let's go out into the yard
out to the field to quarrel
    to the ground to fight:
in the yard blood is better
fairer out in the farmyard
more natural in the snow.'

They went out into the yard;
    a cowhide was fetched
and was spread out in the yard
    for them to stand on.
Ahti the Islander said:
'Listen here, son of the North!
Now, yours is the longer sword
your brand is the more dreadful—
perhaps you will need it too
    before we part, or
    your neck is broken:
you strike first, son of the North!'

The son of the North struck first:
    he struck once, struck twice
and soon a third time he thrashed;
    but he scores no hit
does not even graze the flesh

does not take off the top skin.
Ahti the Islander said
    the fair Farmind spoke:
    'Let me have a go;
    now it is my turn!'

Well, that master of Northland
was not going to heed that:
still he struck, did not waver
    aimed but could not reach.
And the harsh iron flashed fire
the blade—yes—flame in the hand
of wanton Lemminkäinen;
    the gleam fared further
    crashed down upon the
neck of that Northlander's son.
    The fair Farmind said:
'Aha, master of Northland:
    your neck, wretched man
    is like the dawn—red!'

    That Northlander's son
    master of Northland
    then shifted his gaze
    towards his own neck.
That wanton Lemminkäinen
    thereat slashed away:
he struck the man with his sword
    bashed him with his brand.
    Now, he cracked down once—
took the head off the shoulders
the skull he smacked from the neck
like the top off a turnip
or the head off a cornstalk
or a fin from any fish:
the head rolled on to the yard
the man's skull on the farmyard

as picked off by an arrow
a capercaillie drops from a tree.

There were a hundred stakes on the hill
a thousand stood bristling in the yard
with hundreds of heads upon the stakes.
One stake is without a head:
that wanton Lemminkäinen
took up the worthy boy's head
bore the skull from the farmyard
on to that very stake's tip.
Then Ahti the Islander
    he, the fair Farmind
when he had returned indoors
uttered a word and spoke thus:
'Bring water, hateful wench, that
    I may wash my hands
of the evil master's blood
    the vicious man's gore!'

The hag of the North was wroth—
she was wroth, she was angry
    and she sang swordsmen
    fellows with weapons
    a hundred swordsmen
a thousand bearers of brands
out for Lemminkäinen's head
to fall upon Farmind's neck.
Now the time comes, to be sure
the day slips towards the hour
indeed, things grow too painful
things turn out too troublesome
for the boy Ahti to stay
Lemminkäinen to dawdle
    at that Northland feast
    the sly crowd's revels.

28. *Into Hiding*

Now Ahti the Islander
he, wanton Lemminkäinen
    slips into hiding
    and takes to his heels
    out of dark Northland
the murky house of Sara:
he whirled out of doors as snow
arrives as smoke in the yard
    to flee from bad deeds
    to hide from his crimes.
When he comes into the yard
he looks around, turns around
sought the stallion he once had:
he does not see the stallion
but a boulder in the field
a willow shrub at the edge.

    What is the best plan
    what plan to follow
    lest his head go ill
    his locks come to grief
    and his fine hair fall
    in these Northland yards?
Now a noise was heard from the village
a hubbub from the other houses
a light winked in the village
eyes were staring from windows.
There wanton Lemminkäinen
he, Ahti the Islander
had to become someone else
    he must change his shape:
as an eagle he swept up

wanted to soar heavenward;
  the sun burnt his cheeks
  the moon lit his brows.
There wanton Lemminkäinen
  prays to the Old Man:
  'O Old Man, good god
  careful man of heaven
  keeper of stormclouds
and governor of vapours:
  make misty weather
and create a tiny cloud
in whose shelter I may go
  wend my way homeward
back to my kindly mother
towards my honoured parent!'

  And away he flaps
  looked once behind him
  spotted a grey hawk:
its eyes burned as fire like those
of the Northerner's son, who
had been master of the North.
  The grey hawk said: 'Hey
Ahti my little brother
do you remember the war
of old and the well-matched fight?'

Ahti the Islander said
  the fair Farmind spoke:
'O my hawk, my little bird
  turn around homeward!
  Say when you get there
in dark Northland: "It is hard
to catch an eagle by hand
to eat a quill-bird with nails."'

  Soon he arrived home
back to his kindly mother

with a sad look on his face
    and a gloomy heart.
    He meets his mother
as she walks along the lane
    steps beside the fence;
his mother hastened to ask:
'My offspring, my younger one
    my child, my baby!
Why are you in bad spirits
as you come back from Northland?
Was there cheating with tankards
    at that Northland feast?
If they cheated with tankards
you'll get a better tankard
got by your father from war
    fetched back from a fight.'

Wanton Lemminkäinen said:
'O my mother who bore me
who would cheat me with tankards?
I would cheat masters myself
I'd cheat a hundred fellows
a thousand men I'd take on.'

Lemminkäinen's mother said:
'Why are you in bad spirits?
Were you beaten with stallions
shamed with the foals of a horse?
If they beat you with stallions
buy a stallion that's better
with the goods your father got
    your parent laid up!'

Wanton Lemminkäinen said:
'O my mother who bore me
who would shame me with horses
    or beat me with foals?

I would shame masters myself
    beat stallion-drivers
    stout men with their foals
and fellows with their stallions.'

Lemminkäinen's mother said:
'Why are you in bad spirits
and wherefore gloomy of heart
    coming from Northland?
Were you disgraced with women
    or mocked with wenches?
    If you were disgraced
with women, mocked with wenches
others will be mocked again
women will be disgraced back.'

Wanton Lemminkäinen said:
'O my mother who bore me
who'd disgrace me with women
or would mock me with wenches?
I'd disgrace masters myself
all the wenches I would mock
I'd disgrace a hundred women too
and a thousand other brides.'

Lemminkäinen's mother said:
'What's the matter, my offspring?
Has something happened to you
on your visit to Northland
or after eating too much—
eating and drinking too much—
    have you had strange dreams
    where you spent the night?'

Then wanton Lemminkäinen
    managed there to say:
    'Let hags think about
    those dreams in the night!

I remember my night-dreams
but my day-dreams more clearly.
O my mother, old woman
lay provisions in a sack
put meal in a linen cloth
stow salt in a rag! It is
time for a boy to be off
    and to take a trip
    abroad from this dear
    home, from this fair farm:
    men are honing swords
    and sharpening spears.'

The mother hastened to ask
the pains-taker to question:
'But why are they honing swords
    and sharpening spears?'

Wanton Lemminkäinen spoke
    the fair Farmind said:
'For this they are honing swords
    and sharpening spears—
for the head of luckless me
for this mean one's neck. There was
a deed, something has happened
    in those Northland yards:
I've killed the Northerner's son—
him, the master of Northland.
Northland has risen for war
the pest yonder for a fight
against me, the woebegone
all around me on my own.'

The mother put this in words
the eldest spoke to her child:
'I have already told you
and already warned you too

and still tried to forbid you
    to go to Northland.
You could have stayed in the right
and lived in mother's cabins
in your own parent's care, at
the farm of her who bore you
and there would have been no war
and no fight would have happened.
Where now, my son, luckless boy
    where, mean one I bore
will you go to hide from crime
    flee from the bad deed
    lest your head go ill
    and your fair neck break
    your locks come to grief
    and your fine hair fall?'

Wanton Lemminkäinen said:
    'I don't know where I
    could take to my heels
    to hide from my crimes.
O my mother who bore me
where do you tell me to hide?'

Lemminkäinen's mother said
    she declared, spoke thus:
'I don't know where to tell you—
where to tell and compel you.
Go, be a pine on a hill
a juniper on the heath:
even there ruin will come
    hard luck will meet you
for often a hilltop pine
    is cut down for splints
often a juniper heath
    is cleared to make stakes.
Rise, be a birch on a marsh
or in a grove an alder:

even there ruin would come
    hard luck would find you
for often a marshland birch
    is chopped for stacking
often a grove of alders
    is hewn for sowing.
Go and be a berry on a hill
a cowberry on the heath
on these lands be strawberries
bilberries on other lands:
even there ruin would come
    hard luck would meet you
for the young maids would pluck you
the tin-breasted would tear you.
Go, be a pike in the sea
be a whitefish in the smooth river:
even there ruin would come
    a hard end would strike
for a young, a sooty man
would take his net to waters
haul the young ones in the seine
catch the old ones in his net.
Go and be a wolf in the forest
bruin in the wilderness:
even there ruin would come
    hard luck would meet you
for a young sooty-faced man
    would sharpen his spear
    for slaughtering wolves
    felling forest bears.'

Then wanton Lemminkäinen
uttered a word and spoke thus:
'But I know the wickedest
can work out the worst places
    where doom would bite hold
    a hard end would strike.
    Mother who fed me

mamma who gave milk to me!
Where do you tell me to hide—
where do you tell and compel?
Doom stares me right in the face
the evil day at my beard
one day left for a man's head—
hardly a whole one at that.'

Then Lemminkäinen's mother
 uttered and spoke thus:
'I will say quite a good place
one very sweet I will name
for hiding from a bad deed
for a culprit to flee to:
I recall a tiny spot
I know a bit of a place
with no eating, no beating
no meeting of a man's sword.
You, swear an oath for ever
without lying or fooling
that for six, for ten summers
 you'll not go to war
even for greed of silver
 or for need of gold!'

Wanton Lemminkäinen said:
'I swear an oath—no fooling—
that not for the first summer
nor yet for the next either
shall I get into great wars
into those clashes of swords;
my shoulders still bear the wounds
and my chest the deep gashes
from merrymakings before
 from clashes gone by
 on the great war-hills
on the killing-grounds of men.'

Then Lemminkäinen's mother
uttered a word and spoke thus:
'All right: take your father's craft
    go yonder and hide—
    right over nine seas
    and half a tenth sea
to the island on the main
    the crag in the sea
    where your father hid—
    both hid and kept safe
in the great summers of war
in the hard years of battle;
'twas good for him to be there
sweet for him to tarry there.
Hide there for one year, for two
and come home during the third
to father's cabins you know
    your parent's moorings!'

29. *Conquests*

Lemminkäinen, wanton boy
    he, the fair Farmind
gets provisions in a sack
summer butter in his box
butter to eat for his year
    and pork for the next;
then he went into hiding—
    he both went and sped.
He uttered a word, spoke thus:
'So now I'm off, on the run
for the whole of three summers
    for five little years;
I leave lands for worms to eat
groves for lynxes to rest in
fields for reindeer to romp in
and glades for geese to dwell in.
Farewell, my good mother! When
the people of the North come
and the large crowd of Darkland
    asking for my head
    say I wandered off
went from here after felling
    the very clearing
whose crop has just now been reaped!'

With a jerk he launched the boat
let the ship go to the waves
    off rollers of steel
    from copper moorings;
he hoisted sails up the pole
    canvas on the mast;
    he sits in the stern
    got himself going

with the birch prow's help
the long paddle's aid.
He uttered a word, spoke thus
he declared, chattered:
'Blow, wind, on the sail
gale, drive the vessel;
let the wooden craft
run, the pine boat go
to the island with no word
to the headland with no name!'
The wind lulled the little boat
the sea surf pushed it along
over the clear main
on the open expanses;
lulled it along for two months
soon for a third month as well.

And there sat the headland maids
on the shore of the blue sea;
they are looking and turning
their eyes towards the blue sea.
One waited for her brother
hoped her father was coming;
but that one truly waited
who waited for her bridegroom.
Far away Farmind appears
Farmind's ship further away:
'tis like a small bank of cloud
between the water and heaven.
The headland maids think
and the island lassies say:
'What's that strange thing on the sea
what wonder is on the waves?
If you are a ship of ours
if an island sailing-craft
turn yourself homeward
towards the island's moorings:
we would get to hear the news

the tidings from foreign lands
whether shore-folk are at peace
or else living in battle.'

The wind is veering the craft
the billow driving the ship;
soon wanton Lemminkäinen
brought the craft up to the crag
ran the ship to the isle's end
the tip of the isle's headland.
He said when he arrived there
    inquired when he came:
'Is there space on the island
land on the island's mainland
to beach a boat, overturn
    a craft on dry land?'

    The island lassies
say, the headland maids answer:
'Yes, there's space on the island
land on the island's mainland
to beach a boat, overturn
    a craft on dry land:
here the moorings are roomy
the shores are full of rollers
though you arrived in a hundred boats
and came in a thousand craft.'

Then wanton Lemminkäinen
beached the boat and hauled the craft
on to the wooden rollers
and he put this into words:
'Is there room on the island
land on the island's mainland
for a tiny man to hide
for a puny one to flee
from the great thunders of war
from the clashes of sword blades?'

The island lassies
say, the headland maids answer:
'Yes, there's room on the island
land on the island's mainland
for a tiny man to hide
for a puny one to flee:
we have many strongholds here
grand farms to dwell in
though a hundred fellows should arrive
and a thousand men should come.'

Then wanton Lemminkäinen
uttered a word and spoke thus:
'Is there room on the island
land on the island's mainland
a small corner of birchwoods
and a bit of other land
for me to fell a clearing
a good spot for pioneering?'

The island lassies
say, the headland maids answer:
'There's no room on the island
land on the island's mainland
not one space broad as your back
not a bushel's worth of land
for you to fell a clearing
no good spot for pioneering:
the isle's lands are parcelled out
the fields measured with yardsticks;
for the glades lots have been cast
for the turf courts have been held.'

Wanton Lemminkäinen spoke
the fair Farmind asked:
'Is there space on the island

land on the island's mainland
    for me to sing my
    songs, to lilt long tales?
The words unfreeze in my mouth
on my gums they are sprouting.'

    The island lassies
say, the headland maids answer:
'Yes, there's space on the island
land on the island's mainland
    for you to sing your
    songs, to lilt good tales
groves for you to play games in
ground for you to dance upon.'

Then wanton Lemminkäinen
    set about singing:
he sang rowans in the yards
oaks in the midst of barnyards
upon an oak shapely boughs
upon each bough an acorn
upon the acorn a golden whorl
upon the golden whorl a cuckoo;
    when the cuckoo calls
gold gushes out of its mouth
and copper flows from its jaws
    silver comes foaming
    on a golden knoll
    on a silver hill.
And still Lemminkäinen sang
still he sang and recited—
    sang the sands to beads
all the rocks till they glistened
all the trees till they glowed red
the flowers till they were gold-hued;
and then Lemminkäinen sang—
sang a well in the farmyard
a golden lid on the well

a golden pail on the lid
from which brothers drink water
    sisters wash their eyes;
he sang a pool on the ground
    on the pool blue ducks
their brows gold, their heads silver
and all their toes of copper.

The island lasses marvelled
and the headland maids wondered
at Lemminkäinen's singing
    at the fellow's skill.
Wanton Lemminkäinen spoke
    the fair Farmind said:
'I would sing quite a good tale
quite a fair one I'd bellow
if I were under a roof
at a long deal table's head.
If there's no cabin to spare
and no floor to yield, I'll take
the words off to the backwoods
tip the tales in the thicket.'

    The island lassies
say, the headland maidens think:
'We have cabins to come to
    grand farms to dwell in
to bring your tales from the cold
get the words in from outside.'

Then wanton Lemminkäinen
the moment he came indoors
he sang flagons from beyond
to the long deal table's head
sang the flagons full of beer
    the jugs fair with mead
the bowls up to the bulwarks
    the cups to the brim:

flagonfuls of beer, jugfuls
of honey had been brought in
and butter laid in ready
    pork to go with it
for wanton Lemminkäinen
to eat, Farmind to enjoy.
But Farmind is most haughty:
no, he will not start eating
without a silver-tipped knife
without a golden dagger.
He got a silver-tipped knife
he sang a golden dagger;
    then he eats his fill
drank beer to his heart's content.

Then wanton Lemminkäinen
    went out visiting
making merry with the isle's lasses
amid braided heads' beauty:
wherever he turned his head
    there his mouth is kissed
wherever he reached his hand
    there his hand is touched.
    He stayed out all night
    in the pitch darkness:
    there was no village
where there were not ten houses
    there was not a house
where there were not ten daughters
    nor yet a daughter
    not a mother's child
by whose side he did not stretch
and whose arm he did not tame.
A thousand the brides he knew
a hundred widows he laid:
there were not two out of ten

three out of a whole hundred
    wenches left unheld
    widows left unlaid.

So wanton Lemminkäinen
relishes a quiet life
    for three whole summers
in the isle's great villages
delighted the isle's lasses
all the widows too he soothed.
    One remained unsoothed
    one wretched old lass
who's at the long headland's end
in a tenth village; by now
he had a mind to travel
to go off to his own lands
but the wretched old lass came
and she put this into words:
'Wretched Farmind, handsome man!
If you don't remember me
I will as you go from here
run your craft upon a rock.'

But he did not hear to rise without
the cock, leap up without the hen's child
to enjoy that lassie too
disgrace the wretched woman;
so one day among others
one evening among many
he set on an hour to rise
before the moon, the cock too
and he rose before his hour
before his appointed time
    and straight off he went
roaming through the villages
to enjoy that lassie too
disgrace the wretched woman.
As by night alone he went

his way through the villages
there to the long headland's end
    to the tenth village
    he saw not one house
in which were not three dwellings
    he saw no dwelling
in which were not three fellows
    he saw no fellow
who was not honing a sword
not sharpening a hatchet
meant for Lemminkäinen's head.
Then wanton Lemminkäinen
uttered a word and spoke thus:
'Woe, darling day has broken
and the dear sun has risen
    on me, luckless boy
    on this mean one's neck!
    Will the Devil shield
but one fellow in his clothes
    keep him in his cloaks
    guard him in his capes
    as hundreds arrive
as thousands set upon him!'

The maids remained unembraced
and the embraced unfondled.
He strolled to the boat rollers
now, the luckless to his craft:
the craft has been burnt to ash
    and reduced to dust!
He felt his ruin coming, his
day of trouble catching up.
He began to carve a boat
    work on a new craft
but the craft-smith needed trees
    the boatbuilder planks:
he gets wood, a tiny bit
and planking, very little—

five pieces of a distaff
six fragments of a bobbin.
Out of that he carves a boat
    works on a new craft:
he built the boat with knowledge
    on stocks of wisdom:
he struck once—one side emerged;
he struck twice—two sides were born;
he struck a third time as well—
from that the whole boat arrived.
    Now he launched the boat
let the ship go to the waves.
He uttered a word, spoke thus
    he declared, chattered:
'Be bubbles, boat, on waters
water lilies on the waves!
Eagle, three of your feathers
eagle, three and raven, two
    for the small boat's sake
    the slight craft's handrails!'

He steps into his vessel
he scrambled to the boat's stern
his head down, in bad spirits
    helmet all askew
for he could not stay the nights
    nor dally the days
making merry with the isle's lasses
capering with braided heads.
Wanton Lemminkäinen spoke
    the fair Farmind said:
    "Tis time for a boy to go
on his way from these abodes
from making merry with these lasses
capering with these fair ones;
but for sure when I have left
    when I've gone from here
lassies will not make merry

nor braided heads skip about
    in these dull cabins
    in these mean farmyards.'

Now the island lasses wept
    the headland maids groaned:
'Why, Lemminkäinen, have you
left, departed, best of men?
Were the wenches too proper
or were the women too few?'

Wanton Lemminkäinen spoke
    the fair Farmind said:
'The wenches weren't too proper
nor were the women too few:
why, I'd have a hundred wives
could hold a thousand wenches.
Here's why I, Lemminkäinen
left, departed, best of men:
I have felt a keen longing—
a longing for my own lands
for my own lands' strawberries
for my own slope's raspberries
for my own headland's maidens
    my own farmyard's hens.'

Then wanton Lemminkäinen
let his ship go further out:
    a wind came, blew it
and a billow came, drove it
out upon the blue high seas
upon the open expanse.
The wretches remained ashore
the soft ones on a wet rock
the island lasses weeping
and the golden ones moaning:
the isle's lasses only wept
and the headland maids cried woe

while the mast is visible
and the iron-rowlocked looms;
they do not weep for the mast
yearn for the iron-rowlocked
but for him below the mast
for the keeper of the sheet.
Lemminkäinen himself wept
but he only wept and grieved
while the island's lands are visible
and the island's ridges loom;
he does not weep for the island's lands
yearn for the island's ridges
but for the island lassies
for those goslings of the ridge.

Then wanton Lemminkäinen
fared forth upon the blue sea;
he fared one day, he fared two
  till on the third day
  there sprang up a wind
  the skyline flared up—
a great wind, nor'westerly
a hard wind, a nor'easter:
it took one side, it took two
  capsized the whole boat.
Then wanton Lemminkäinen
turned his hands to the water
rowed away with his fingers
  paddled with his feet.
When he had swum night and day
when he'd paddled quite a lot
he beheld a tiny cloud
a cloud bank to the north-west—
and lo, it changed into land
altered into a headland.

He climbed ashore to a house
and found the mistress baking

the daughters patting the loaves:
    'O kindly mistress!
If you could see my hunger
could guess how it is with me
you'd go running to the shed
swirl as snow to the beer-hut;
you'd bring a flagon of beer
    and a slice of pork
you would put it on to roast
you would spread butter on it
for a weary man to eat
for a fellow who has swum to drink.
I've been swimming nights and days
on the open sea's billows
with every wind my refuge
the sea's billows my mercy.'

    That kindly mistress
went to the shed on the hill
cut some butter from the shed
    and a slice of pork
and she puts it on to roast
for the hungry man to eat
she brings beer in a flagon
for the fellow who has swum to drink;
she gave him then a new craft
    a boat quite ready
for the man to go to other lands
    to make his way home.

Then wanton Lemminkäinen
    when he arrived home
knew the lands and knew the shores
both the islands and the straits
    knew his old moorings
places where he used to live;
the hills he knew with their pines
all the mounds with their spruces—
but he does not know where his

cabin is, where his wall stands:
there instead of the cabin
young bird cherries were rustling
pines upon the cabin-hill
junipers on the well-path!
Wanton Lemminkäinen spoke
    the fair Farmind said:
'There is the grove where I moved
    the rocks I rocked on
    the turfs I played on
the field edges where I romped.
What took the cabins I knew
    and who the fair roofs?
The cabin's been burnt to ash
the wind's swept up the cinders!'

At that he began to weep—
he wept one day, he wept two;
he wept, not for the cabin
nor for the shed did he yearn
but for her he knew indoors
for his dear one in the shed.
He beholds a bird flying
    an eagle gliding
and set about asking it:
'O eagle, my little bird
could you not manage to say
where is the mother I had
where the fair one who bore me
the sweet one who suckled me?'

But the eagle remembers
the stupid bird knows nothing:
the eagle swore she was dead
the raven that she was lost
    dispatched with a sword
    killed with a hatchet.

Wanton Lemminkäinen spoke
    the fair Farmind said:
'Alas, fair one who bore me
and sweet one who suckled me:
now you who bore me are dead
and gone, my kindly mother
your flesh rotted into mould
and spruces have grown on top
junipers upon your heels
willows at your fingertips!
    Vainly I, a wretch
    in vain, ill-fated
    I sized up my sword
    bore a fair weapon
    in those Northland yards
    Darkland's field edges
to the doom of my own kin
the loss of her who bore me!'

He looks around, turns around:
he saw a bit of a track
    crumpled in the grass
and broken in the heather.
He trod the road to find out
    trod the path to learn:
into the forest the road
    leads, the path takes him.
He strolled from there one mile, two
he ran off a little way
into gloomiest backwoods
a hollow in the dim wilds:
he sees a hidden sauna
    a small secret hut
between two cliffs and beneath
a corner of three spruces—
sees there his kindly mother
that honoured parent of his.
Then wanton Lemminkäinen

was utterly delighted;
    he says with this word
    he spoke with this speech:
    'Ah, my dear mamma
    mother who kept me!
Mother, you are still alive
    my parent, awake
when by now I thought you dead
    by all accounts lost
    dispatched with a sword
    picked off with a spear!
I wept away my sweet eyes
    my fair face I lost.'

Lemminkäinen's mother said:
'Oh yes, I am still alive
    though I had to flee
    slip into hiding
here into gloomy backwoods
a hollow in the dim wilds.
    Northland waged a war
the crowd yonder picked a fight
against you, the woebegone
and on you, the ill-fated:
they burnt the cabins to ash
    all our farm they felled.'

Wanton Lemminkäinen said:
'O my mother who bore me
    don't worry at all—
    at all about that!
    New cabins will be
built, and better ones gone for;
Northland will be made war on
the Devil's folk will be felled.'

Then Lemminkäinen's mother
    put this into words:

'Long you've lingered, my offspring,
far, my Farmind, you have been
    in those foreign lands
    always at strange doors
on the headland with no name
on the island with no word.'

Wanton Lemminkäinen spoke
    the fair Farmind said:
''Twas good for me to be there
pleasant for me to flit there:
    the trees there shone red
the trees red and the lands blue
    silver the fir boughs
gold the flowers of the heather;
there the hills were full of mead
and the cliffs full of hen's eggs;
honey oozed from dry spruces
    milk from rotten pines
from fence corners butter dripped
    from the stakes beer poured—
'twas good for me to be there
sweet for me to tarry there.
    Then 'twas bad to live
then 'twas strange for me to be:
they were afraid their wenches
    they thought their sluts, those
    pot-bellied wretches
    Old Harry's waddlers
would get ill-treatment from me
spend too many nights with me;
but I hid from the wenches
kept clear of woman's daughters—
as the wolf hides from the pigs
the hawks from the village hens!'

30. *Jack Frost*

Ahti boy, the matchless boy
wanton boy Lemminkäinen
quite early in the morning
quite betimes on the morrow
stepped out to his boathouses
set out for his ship moorings.
And there a wooden craft wept
one with iron rowlocks moaned:
'What of me who have been built
wretched me who have been formed?
Ahti has not rowed to war
    these six, ten summers
even for greed of silver
nor even for need of gold.'

That wanton Lemminkäinen
struck the craft with his mitt, his
    brightly trimmed mitten
and he put this into words:
'Never mind, floating fir tree
one with bulwarks, don't complain!
You'll get off to war again
    trudge off to a fight:
you will be full of oarsmen
    from tomorrow on.'

He steps up to his mother
and he put this into words:
'You'll not weep now, my mother
    complain, my parent
    if I go somewhere

head for the places of war.
    It occurred to me
    the thought came to me
to fell the folk of the North
    punish the mean ones.'

The mother tried to hinder
    the old woman warned:
    'Do not go, my boy
    to those Northland wars!
    There your doom will come
    you will meet your death.'

What did Lemminkäinen care!
He was determined to go
he intended to set out;
he uttered a word, spoke thus:
'Where could I get a second
    man, both man and sword
as a war-help to Ahti
one more for the well-to-do?
Now, there's Tiera I know of
Snowy I have heard about!
That's where I'll get a second
    man, both man and sword
as a war-help to Ahti
one more for the well-to-do.'

He goes there through villages
down the roads to Tiera's farm
and he said when he got there
    explained when he came:
    'Tiera, my old mate
    my friend, my buddy!
Do you recall how we were
    how we used to live
when once the two of us walked

in the great places of war?
    There was no village
where there were not ten houses
    there was not a house
where there were not ten fellows
    there was no fellow
nor a man to reckon with
    who we did not fell
and the two of us cut down.'

Father was at the window
    whittling a spear shaft
mother on the shed threshold
    was rattling a churn
the brothers in the gateway
    were building bobsleighs
the sisters at the quay end
    were fulling some cloaks.
Father spoke from the window
mother from the shed threshold
the brothers from the gateway
the sisters from the quay end:
'Tiera has no time for war
Tiera's ice-pick for a fight!
Tiera's made a famous deal
struck a bargain for ever:
he's just wedded a young wife
taken on his own mistress;
    the nipples are yet
unfingered, the breasts unworn.'

Tiera who was at the hearth
Snowy at the stove corner
put on one shoe at the hearth
the other at the seat's edge
at the gate puts on his belt
and outside paces about.
    Tiera snatched his spear;

it is not a great big spear
nor a little tiny spear
but a spear of middle size:
a horse stood upon the edge
a foal frolicked on the side
a wolf howled upon the joint
a bear growled where the peg went.
    He brandished his spear—
    brandished it, yanked it
hurled the spear shaft a fathom
deep into the clayey field
the turf where nothing would grow
the land where no hummock was;
    Tiera thrust his spear
    in with Ahti's spears
    he both went and sped
as a war-help to Ahti.
Then Ahti the Islander
    he pushed the boat out
like a viper in the grass
    or a snake alive
    and struck out north-west
    on that Northland sea.

Then the mistress of Northland
sent Jack Frost the evil one
    on that Northland sea
upon the open expanse
and she put this into words
    both told and declared:
    'Jack Frost, little boy
my own fair one I brought up:
    go where I tell you—
    tell and compel you!
    Chill the rogue's small boat
wanton Lemminkäinen's craft
    upon the high seas
upon the open expanse

and chill the master himself
freeze the rogue on the waters
so that he'll never get out
never in this world be free
unless I get to letting him out
get round to relieving him!'

  Jack Frost of bad kin
  an ill-mannered boy
  went to chill the sea
  to fix the billows
  and on his way there
  going overland
  bit the trees leafless
  the grasses huskless;
  then, when he got there
to the edge of the North's sea
to the brink of the boundless
  right on the first night
  he chilled bays, chilled pools
  struck seashores rigid
but did not yet chill the sea
nor fix the billows. There is
a small chaffinch on the main
a wagtail upon the waves:
its claws are not chilled either
its small head has not felt cold.
Only two nights after that
  he sprang to full size
cast about him shamelessly
and grew to be quite dreadful:
he chilled then with all his might
  the force of frost bit—
chilled with ice a cubit thick
  snowed a ski-pole deep
  and chilled the rogue's boat
Ahti's ship upon the waves.
He meant to chill Ahti too

to freeze the mighty fellow;
he asked for his nails
went for his toes from below.

Then Lemminkäinen
was angry, took it badly;
he thrust Jack Frost into fire
pushed him into a furnace.
He laid hands upon Jack Frost
seized the hard weather;
he says with this word
he spoke with this speech:
'Jack Frost, son of Blast
winter's slushy son:
do not chill my nails
don't demand my toes
and don't touch my ears
do not bite my head!
There's enough for you to chill
a lot too to bite
without man's skin, the body
of one borne by a mother:
chill swamps and chill lands
and chill chilly rocks
bite weeping willows
take gnarls of aspen
make bark of birch ache
nibble young spruces—
not man's skin, the hairs
of one made by a woman!
If that's not enough for you
chill other, more wondrous things:
chill some red-hot rocks
some burning boulders
some cliffs of iron
some mountains of steel
the steep rapid of Vuoksi
wicked Imatra

the mouth of the whirlpool's throat
    the frightful eddy!

'Shall I tell you now your kin
    make your honour known?—
for I know about your kin
all about your growing up:
Jack Frost was born on willows
hard weather among birches
deep inside a Northland tent
down in a Darkland cabin
of an ever rascally
father, a useless mother.
    Who suckled Jack Frost
    moistened hard weather
when mamma was without milk
    mother without dugs?
A viper suckled Jack Frost—
a viper suckled, a snake
fed with nipples without tips
    with a withered dug;
    the north wind lulled him
the chilly air dandled him
upon evil willow streams
upon overflowing mires.
The boy became ill-mannered
    he grew destructive;
    but he had no name
    yet, the worthless boy.
The bad boy was called a name:
    he was called Jack Frost.
Then along fences he dashed
among brushwood he rustled;
summers he darted in mires
on the largest open swamps;
winters he throbbed among firs
    pounded among pines
slammed about among birches

among alders flapped about
    chilled trees and hay stalks
    levelled out bare ground
    bit the trees leafless
    the heather flowerless
    stripped the pines of bark
    the firs of slivers.

'Now you have sprung to full size
come up to be most handsome
do you intend to chill me
    to inflame my ears
go for my feet from below
ask for my nails from above?
    But you'll not chill me
nor bite me badly either:
I'll thrust fire in my stocking
    firebrands in my shoe
fine embers into my hems
and beneath my shoelaces—
a blaze Jack Frost cannot bite
and hard weather will not touch.

    'There I banish you—
    to the furthest North;
    then, when you get there
    when you reach your home
chill the pans upon the fire
the embers in the fireplace
the woman's hands in the dough
the boy on the maid's bosom
the milk in the ewe's udder
the foal in the mare's belly!

'If you pay no heed to that
yonder I will banish you—
among the Demon's embers
    to the Devil's hearth:

there thrust yourself in the fire
set yourself on the anvil
for the smith to beat with his
sledgehammer, to bash with his hammer
beat hard with his sledgehammer
painfully with his hammer!

'If you'll not heed even that
and not yield even a bit
I recall still somewhere else
I can think of one region:
I'll take your mouth to the south
and your tongue to summer's home
from where you'll never get out
never in this world be free
unless I get to free you
and turn up to unloose you!'

    Jack Frost, son of Blast
felt ruin coming, and he
began to beg for mercy;
he uttered a word, spoke thus:
    'Let us make a pact
not to hurt one another
    ever in this world
not in a month of Sundays!
If you hear I'm chilling things
or up to mischief again
thrust me into the fireplace
    tame me in the flame
down among the smith's embers
down in Ilmarinen's forge
or take my mouth to the south
and my tongue to summer's home
so that I'll never get out
never in this world be free!'

Then wanton Lemminkäinen
    left the ship frozen

and the war-craft stuck
and goes on; at that
Tiera as the second man
strode after the rogue.
He tramped on the level ice
over its smoothness he slid:
he stepped one day and then two
till on the third day
Hunger Headland now appears
and the wretched village looms.
He stepped below its stronghold
and uttered a word, spoke thus:
'Is there meat in the stronghold
and fish at the farm
for fellows who are weary
for men who are tired?'
No meat was in the stronghold
no fish at the farm.
Wanton Lemminkäinen spoke
the fair Farmind said:
'Fire, burn the stupid stronghold
may water take such a place!'
He fares further on
up into the wilds he went
on ways where no dwelling was
and on roads unknown.
Then wanton Lemminkäinen
that one, fair Farmind
wound scraps of wool off a rock
tore hairs off a cliff
fashioned them into stockings
improvised mittens
for the great places of cold
the bites of Jack Frost.
He trod the road to find out
trod the path to learn:
into the forest the road
leads, the path takes him.

Wanton Lemminkäinen spoke
    the fair Farmind said:
'Tiera my little brother
now we've ended up somewhere
    to roam night and day
on the skyline for ever!'

Tiera put this into words
    he declared, spoke thus:
    'Vainly, poor wretches
vainly we, the ill-fated
    came to a great war
    here in dark Northland
    just to waste our lives
to lose ourselves for ever
in these places of evil
    on these roads unknown.
    We don't know at all—
we don't know, we've no idea
    what road will lead us
    which track will take us
    to die in the wilds
    to fall on the heath
    on the ravens' homes
    on the crows' acres.
There the ravens will shift us
the wicked birds bear us off:
the little birds will get meat
the crows hot blood, the ravens
something to moisten their beaks
    from our poor corpses;
our bones they'll cast on a cairn
    bear off to a reef.
My luckless mother does not
nor the mean one who bore me
know where her flesh is moving
where her own blood is rolling—

whether 'tis in a great war
    in a well-matched fight
or else on the mighty main
    upon the vast waves
or treading a piny hill
wandering scrubby backwoods.
    Mother knows nothing
    of her luckless son:
mother has learnt that he's dead
she who bore him that he's lost.
This is how my mother weeps
    my parent complains:
"There's the son of luckless me
there, woe is me, my support—
    in Tuoni's corn crop
the harrow-lands of the grave;
    now my son's, my child's
    crossbows, hapless me
    will be left idle
the mighty bows to dry out
the little birds to grow fat
the grouse in the grove to strut
the bruins to live it up
the reindeer to romp afield!"'

Wanton Lemminkäinen spoke
    the fair Farmind said:
'That's right, yes, luckless mother
that's right, mean one who bore me!
You brought up a brood of chicks
    a whole crowd of swans:
the wind came and scattered us
the Devil came and strewed us—
    some this way, some that
and a third lot somewhere else.
I well recall long ago
I think of a better time
when we went about as flowers

as berries on our own lands:
    many looked at our
    forms, stared at our stems.
    Not like nowadays
in this evil age: there is
of our friends only the wind
the sun of those we once saw;
    even this the clouds
    cover, the rain hides.
But I do not care to care
    nor greatly to grieve
though the lasses should live well
the braided heads skip about
the wives all with smiling lips
and the brides in honeyed mood
not weeping out of longing
    giving way to care.

'Witches won't bewitch us yet
witches bewitch nor seers see
    to die on these roads
    to sink on these ways
    to fall asleep young
to roll over full-blooded.
Whoever witches bewitch
    whoever seers see
    may he make it home
and moulder in his dwelling—
and may they bewitch themselves
may they sing at their children
    may they slay their kin
    may they curse their clan!
    My father did not
nor did my honoured parent
    heed a witch's will
    give gifts to a Lapp;
    thus said my father
    and thus say I too:

Keep me, steadfast Creator
    guard me, fair God, keep
me with your merciful hand
    with your mighty power
    from the whims of men
    from the wiles of hags
the chatter of bearded mouths
the chatter of the beardless;
    be a constant help
and a steadfast protector
lest a son should turn away
one borne by a mother stray
from the trail the Creator
has blazed, God has brought about!'

Then wanton Lemminkäinen
    he, the fair Farmind
made his cares into horses
sorrows into black geldings
headstalls out of evil days
saddles out of secret hates:
he leapt on a good one's back
upon a good blaze-brow's flanks
and he thunders on his way
    with his friend Tiera
and he clattered along shores
he swished along sandy shores
back to his kindly mother
towards his honoured parent.

There I will leave my Farmind
out of my tale for some time
sending Tiera down the road
    on his way homeward
    and I'll switch the tale
set it on another track.

31. *Feud and Serfdom*

A mother reared chicks
a great crowd of swans;
she set the chicks on the fence
brought the swans to the river.
An eagle came, snatched them up
a hawk came and scattered them
a winged bird strewed them:
one it bore to Karelia
one it took to Russian soil
and the third it left at home.
The one it took to Russia
grew to be a trading man
the one borne to Karelia
grew up to be Kalervo
and the one it left at home
sprang up to be Untamo
who would blight his father's days
who would break his mother's heart.

Untamo let down his nets
in Kalervo's fishing-ground;
Kalervo looked to the nets
gathered the fish in his bag.
Untamo, a lively man
he was angry and furious:
he made war from his fingers
from his palm-ends a lawsuit
raised a quarrel from fish guts
a row from perch fry.
They quarrelled, they fought
but neither beat the other:
whichever slanged the other
got back as good as he gave.

Another time after that
at the end of two, three days
    Kalervo sowed oats
behind Untamo's cabin;
Untamo-land's fine ewe ate
    Kalervo's oat-crop;
    Kalervo's fierce dog
tore Untamo's ewe to bits.
    Untamo threatens
    to slaughter the kin
of Kalervo his brother
to smite the great, smite the small
to strike down all the people
to burn the cabins to ash:
he put swords in the men's belts
weapons in the fellows' hands
pikes in the little boys' belts
billhooks on striplings' shoulders
and he went to a great war
    with his own brother.

Kalervo's handsome daughter-in-law
was sitting by the window;
she looked out of the window
uttered a word and spoke thus:
    'Is that thick smoke, or
    is it a dark cloud
    on those furthest fields
    at the new lane's end?'
But it was no hazy haze
    nor was it thick smoke:
it was Untamo's fellows
    approaching for war
and Untamo's fellows came
the sword-belted men arrived
and they felled Kalervo's crowd

and the great kin they slaughtered
burnt the house to ash
razed it to the ground.
One Kalervo lass remained
who had a heavy belly:
Untamo's fellows
took her home with them
to clean a small room
and to sweep the floor.

A little time passed
and a small boy-child was born
to the unhappy mother.
What shall he be named?
Mother called him Kullervo
but Untamo Warrior.
The small boy was put
and the orphan child was laid
in a cot to sway
and in a cradle to rock.
The child rocked in the cradle
the child rocked, his locks wafted:
he rocked one day, he rocked two
till soon by the third
when that boy kicked out—
kicked out, tensed himself
he burst through his swaddling bands
got on top of his cover
smashed the rocker of limewood
ripped up all his rags.
A promising one was seen
a fit one spotted.
Untamo-land waits
for this one to grow from this
into a good mind, a man
a right fellow, to become
a serf worth a hundred, to
turn out one worth a thousand.

He grew two, three months
till by the third month
the boy at knee-height
began to think for himself:
'Would I were to get bigger
to grow stronger in body
I'd avenge my father's knocks
I'd pay back my mother's tears!'

Untamo happened to hear
and he put this into words:
'From this my kin's doom will come
from this Kalervo will grow!'
And the fellows consider
all the hags think where
the boy shall be put
and where meet his doom:
he's put in a kilderkin
thrust into a barrel, then
he's taken to the water
dropped into the wave.
They go out to see
after two, three nights, whether
he has drowned in the water
and died in the kilderkin:
he's not drowned in the water
not died in the kilderkin!
He's escaped the kilderkin
was sitting on the billows
a copper rod in his hand
a silken line on the end;
he is angling for sea fish
measuring the seawater:
there's quite a lot of water
for he has two ladlefuls;
were he to measure it right
he would get part of a third.

Untamo considers: 'Where
shall the boy be put
where will this one be destroyed
and where meet his doom?'
He told his serfs to gather
birches, hardwood trees
firs with sprigs by the hundred
lumps of tar-wood they knew of
for the burning of one boy
the losing of Kullervo.
They collected, they gathered
birches, hardwood trees
firs with sprigs by the hundred
lumps of tar-wood they knew of,
birchbark, a thousand sledgefuls,
ashwood, a hundred armfuls
and the wood was set on fire
the pile set ablaze:
into it the boy was hurled
right into the burning fire.
It burned one day and then two
it burned a third day as well.
They went out to check: the boy
was in ash up to his knees
in dust up to his forearms
with a charred hook in his hand
with which he stirs up the fire
rakes the embers together
without a hair being lost
without a curl being crimped!

And Untamo rages: 'Where
shall the boy be put
where will this one be destroyed
will doom come to him?'
The boy is hanged on a tree
strung up on an oak.
Two or three nights passed

the same number of days too
and Untamo considers:
'It is time to go and see
whether Kullervo is lost
the boy's dead on the gallows.'
    He made a serf look.
    The serf brought word back:
'No, Kullervo is not lost
he's not dead on the gallows!
The boy's drawing on the wood
with a small thorn in his hand;
the whole tree's full of pictures
the oak is full of drawings:
    here are men, here swords
    here spears at the side.'

Well, what could Untamo do
    with this wretched boy!
Whatever dooms he arranged
whatever deaths brought about
the boy will not fall into doom's mouth
nor will he die anyway.
In the end he had to tire
of arranging dooms for him
had to bring up Kullervo
raise the serf as his own son
and Untamo said his say
he uttered a word, spoke thus:
    'If you live nicely
    always behave well
you may remain in this house
    and do a serf's jobs.
Wages are paid in arrears
    earnings are assigned—
a handsome belt for your waist
or else a belt on the ear.'

When Kullervo had grown up
put on a span of body
    he was set to work
    he was put to toil
looking after a small child
rocking one with small fingers:
'Look after the child nicely
feed the child, eat too yourself;
rinse out its rags in the stream
    wash its little clothes!'

He looked after the child one day, two—
broke its hand, gouged out its eye;
soon after, on the third day
he killed the child with disease
flung its rags for the stream to bear off
and burnt its cradle with fire.
And Untamo considers:
'He is not cut out for this—
looking after a small child
rocking one with small fingers!
I don't know where to put him
    what work to set him.
Shall I make him slash-and-burn?'
And he made him slash-and-burn.

Kullervo, Kalervo's son
at that put this into words:
    'I'll not be a man
till I get an axe in hand
much better to look upon
sweeter than I was before:
then I'll be a man worth five
a fellow wondrous as six.'

He went to the smith's workshop
and uttered a word, spoke thus:

'O smith my little brother
    forge me a hatchet
forge an axe fit for a man
iron right for a toiler!
I am off to slash-and-burn
to cut down a sturdy birch.'

The smith forges what he needs
produces an axe, and out
came an axe fit for a man
iron right for a toiler.
Kullervo, Kalervo's son
    then honed his axe: he
spends a day honing the axe
an evening making a haft.
He set off to slash-and-burn
into the high wilderness
up to the best timberland
to massive standing timber.
He struck a tree with the axe
he lunged with the even blade:
at a stroke good timbers go
and bad ones at half a stroke.
Furiously he felled five trees
    by all accounts eight;
then he put this into words
    he declared, spoke thus:
'To the Devil with this toil!
Let the Demon fell timbers!'
He bashed the top of a stump
    he shouted out loud
    he whistled, he shrilled
he uttered a word, spoke thus:
'Let the slash-and-burn be done
let the sturdy birch be cut
as far as my voice is heard
as far as the whistling rolls!
    Let no sapling stretch

let no stem spring up
    ever in this world
not in a month of Sundays
in Kalervo's son's clearing
on the excellent man's plot!
Should the earth take on a shoot
    should a young crop rise
if a stem should come stemming
and a stalk should come stalking
let it not bring forth a blade
nor the stalk produce an ear!'

Untamo the lively man
    went to look at that
clearing of Kalervo's son
the cutting of the new serf:
the clearing seemed no clearing
    cut by a young man.
And Untamo considers:
'He is not cut out for this!
Good timber he has ruined
and felled the best timberland!
I don't know where to put him
    what work to set him.
Shall I make him build fences?'
And he made him build fences.

Kullervo, Kalervo's son
    starts building a fence:
lofty firs from their places
    he sets for fence poles
and whole spruces of the wild
    he sticks in for stakes;
    lashed them fast with withes
from the tallest of rowans;
he built a fence with no gap
knocked up one without a gate.

Then he put this into words
    he declared, spoke thus:
    'Unless as a bird
he can soar, flutter two wings
let nobody get over
the fence of Kalervo's son!'

    Untamo chances
    to come and look at
that fence of Kalervo's son
what the war-serf has cut down:
he saw that the fence had no
opening, no slit, no hole—
had been built from mother earth
pointed up into the clouds.
He uttered a word, spoke thus:
'He is not cut out for this!
He's built a fence with no opening
knocked up one without a gate
and he's raised it to the sky
lifted it into the clouds:
I cannot get over it
    nor in through a hole!
I don't know where to put him
    what work to set him.
Shall I put him to thresh rye?'
And he put him to thresh rye.

Kullervo, Kalervo's son
    was threshing rye now—
and he threshed the rye to chaff
the straw he reduced to bran.
Well, the master came along
    went himself to look
at Kalervo's son's threshing
Kullervo's beating:
    the rye is now chaff
and the straw was rustling bran!

Untamo rages:
'Nothing comes of this toiler!
Whatever work I set him
he stupidly spoils.
Shall I take him to Russia
or trade him in Karelia
to Ilmarinen the smith
to wield the smith's sledgehammer?'

Then he sold Kalervo's son
traded him in Karelia
to Ilmarinen the smith
the skilful craftsman.
What did the smith give for him?
The smith gave a lot for him—
two pans with holes in
three hooks snapped in half
five scythes quite worn out
six hoes past their prime
for a man of no account
for a serf who was worthless.

32. *To Guard a Herd*

Kullervo, Kalervo's son
the blue-stockinged gaffer's son
    yellow-haired, handsome
    fair of shoe-upper
straight away in the smith's home
asked for work in the evening
the master for evening work
the mistress for morning work:
'Let the jobs here be named, let
a job be given a name
what is the work to be set
    the toil made to do!'

The smith Ilmari's mistress
    she is thinking there
what work to set the new serf
    what toil the one bought:
she made the serf a herdsman
    guard of the big herd.
    That wicked mistress
    the smith's grinning hag
baked a loaf for the herdsman
    a thick roll she roasts:
below the oats and above the wheat
in between she works a stone.
She smeared the roll with melted butter
the crust she coated with fat
gave it for the serf's rations
a titbit for the herdsman
and she instructed the serf
uttered a word and spoke thus:
'Don't eat this before the herd
has gone towards the forest!'

At that Ilmari's mistress
drove the herd out to pasture;
    she says with this word
    she spoke with this speech:
'I send my cows to the grove
the milk-givers to the glade
the wide-horns to the aspens
the crook-horns to the birches;
    I set them to take
    grease, to fetch tallow
    from the wide glade-lands
    from the broad grove-lands
    from the tall birches
    from the squat aspens
    the golden spruces
    the silver backwoods.
Look after them, O fair God
keep them, steadfast Creator
and keep them out of harm's way
    guard them from all ills
    lest they come to grief
    get up to mischief!
As you looked in the cowshed
and in safekeeping watched them
so look where no cowshed is
care for them where none watches
that the herd may grow fair, that
the mistress's wealth may thrive
as a well-wisher would like
an ill-wisher would dislike!

'If my herdsmen are wretched
the herd-wenches very shy
make a willow a herdsman
an alder a cow-watcher
a rowan a keeper, a
bird cherry a bringer home
without the mistress searching

or other folk worrying!
If the willow will not herd
nor the rowan keep them well
nor the alder drive the cows
the bird cherry bring them home
    put your better ones
    set nature's daughters
    to cherish my wealth
    to watch all my herd
for you have many wenches
hundreds of order-takers
those who live beneath the sky
    good nature-daughters.

'Summer-daughter, choice woman
South-daughter, dame of nature
Fir-daughter, O good mistress
Juniper-daughter, fair maid
Rowan-daughter, little wench
Birdcherry-daughter, Tapio's girl
Mielikki, forest daughter-in-law
Tellervo, Tapio's maid:
    look after my herd
    and cherish my wealth
    all summer nicely
    in leaf-time softly
when the leaf waves on the tree
the grass ripples on the ground!
Summer-daughter, choice woman
South-daughter, dame of nature:
    cast off your fine hems
    your apron spread out
as a hood for my herd, a
cover for my little ones
unblown by the angry wind
unrained on by angry rain;
    guard my herd from ills

and keep them out of harm's way
    from those shaking swamps
    from those spilling springs
    from those moving mires
    from those round potholes
    lest they come to grief
    get up to mischief
a foot stumble in a swamp
    slither in a mire
    against God's wish, the
    blessed one's desire!
Bring a trump from beyond, from
the pole of heaven yonder
bring a honey-trump from heaven
a mead-trump from mother earth;
    blow that trump of yours
    blast your famous one:
blow the mounds into blossom
    the heath edges fair
    the glade edges sweet
the grove edges soft, the swamp
edges to melted honey
the mire edges into wort
    and then feed my herd
    fodder my cattle
    feed them honeyed food
    give them honeyed drink;
    feed them golden grass
    a silver hay-tip
    out of trickling mires
    out of spilling springs
    from roaring rapids
    from rushing rivers
    from the golden knolls
    from the silver glades!
    Form a golden well
on both sides of the herd-land
    for the herd to drink

water from, quaff mead
until udders burst
and until teats ache
so that veins may come to throb
and rivers of milk to run
and brooks of milk to break out
and rapids of milk to foam
and milk-tubes to pour
milk-channels to stream
every time to give
every turn to ooze
above even the hateful
past the ill-wisher's fingers
without the milk going lost*
the herd-gift going to waste!

'Many they are and evil
who make milk go lost
and the herd-gift go to waste
what a cow brings go elsewhere;
few they are and good
who save milk from loss
their curds from the village grasp
and their fresh milk from elsewhere.
My mother did not
ask the village for advice
nor the next house for know-how;
no, she saved her milk from loss
and her curds from the grasper
and her fresh milk from elsewhere.
She let it come from beyond
arrive from further away—
let it come from Tuonela
the Dead Land, lost underground
come by night all on its own
and in the dark secretly
unheard by the wicked one
by the bad one unspotted

by the hateful one unchecked
by the envious unenvied.
    Thus said my mother
    and thus say I too:
Where has my cow-wealth lingered
which way has my milk vanished?
Has it been taken abroad
tethered in the village yards
in the parish whores' bosoms
under envious folk's arms, or
in woods has it got tangled
in forests has it perished
has it been spilt on grove-lands
has it vanished upon heaths?
But the milk shall not go lost
nor the cow-wealth go abroad
to the parish whores' bosoms
under envious folk's arms, nor
in woods will it get tangled
in forests will it perish
nor in groves will it be spilt
nor will it fall on the heath.
The milk is needed at home
all the time it is longed for:
at home the mistress waits, a
juniper pail in her hand.

'Summer-daughter, choice woman
South-daughter, dame of nature:
come now and feed my Muncher
and give my Guzzler a drink
    make Nervy trickle
    and make Fresh One drip
    give milk to Sweetie
    to Apple new curds
    out of bright hay-tips
    fair dewy grasses

sweet mothers of earth
    honey-sweet hummocks
from turf thick with honey-plants
from land full of berry stalks
from flower-daughters of heather
    husk-daughters of hay
    curd-daughters of cloud
    pole-daughters of heaven
    bring milky drippers
forever bursting udders
for the nimble wife to milk
for the little wench to squirt!
    Rise, maid, from a marsh
    fine-hemmed from a mire
    warm maid from a spring
    clear-faced from the mud;
take some water from the spring
and sprinkle my herd with it
that the herd may grow fair, that
the mistress's wealth may thrive
before the mistress goes out
    and the herd-wench checks—
the mistress who is worthless
the herd-wench who's very shy.

'Mielikki, forest mistress
    broad-palmed herd-dame, set
the tallest of your wenches
and the best of your hirelings
    to cherish my wealth
    look after my herd
    this great summertime
the Creator's warm summer
    the God-granted one
given by the merciful!

'Tellervo, Tapio's maid
    buxom forest girl

delicate-shirted, fine-hemmed
    yellow-haired, handsome
you who guard the herd, you who
cherish the mistress's wealth
in delightful Forestland
in careful Tapiola:
    guard the herd nicely
and cherish the wealth briskly;
    guard them with fair hands
with comely fingers guide them
    brush them to lynx fur
comb them to a fish's fin
    to a mermaid's hair
    a forest ewe's down;
come evening, darkening night
    the dimming of dusks
    bring my herd homeward
in front of the good mistress
a moving mire on their backs
a pool of milk at their flanks!
As the sun goes to the sheds
as the evening bird warbles
    tell my herd yourself
    say to my horned line:
    "Home with you, crook-horns
milk-givers, towards the shed!
At home it is good for you to be
the ground is sweet for you to lie on;
the wilds are gloomy for you to walk
and the shore for you to trot.
    For your homecoming
the wives are lighting a fire
on turf thick with honey-plants
on ground full of berry stalks."

'Nyyrikki, Tapio's son
    blue-cloaked thicket boy:
stick tall spruces by the base

shock-headed pines by the top
for a bridge where there is dirt
for hardcore across bad lands
on unfrozen swamps and soils
    upon bobbing ponds;
    let a curve-horn walk
    a cloven-hoof trot
    and reach every smudge
    unhurt and unharmed
without sinking in the swamp
or falling flat in the dirt!

'If the herd does not take care
does not come home for the night
Rowan-daughter, little wench
Juniper-daughter, fair maid
cut down a birch from a grove
take a lash from a thicket
    use a rowan rod
a herd-whip of juniper
from the back of Tapio's stronghold
that side of Birdcherry Slope;
drive the herd towards the farm
where the sauna's being stoked
    homeward the home herd
the forest herd into Forestland!

'Beastie, forest apple, bear,*
    honey-pawed hunchback:
    let us make a pact
settle our border dispute
for our lifetime, for our world
for our age, for all our days
that you'll not crush a hoof-shank
    fell a milk-bearer
    this great summertime
the Creator's warm summer!

When you hear a bell sound, or
    the toot of a trump
crash down upon a hummock
on the turf to fall asleep
thrust your ears into the grass
press your head on the hummock
    or make for the wilds
get into a mossy hut
    go to other hills
    to other mounds move
so that no cowbell is heard
nor yet a herdsman's chatter!

'My Beastie, my precious one
honey-paw, my fair darling:
I don't forbid you to turn
nor ban you from wandering;
I forbid your tongue to touch
your ugly mouth to attack
    to scatter with your
    teeth, cuff with your paws.
    Swerve round the herd-lands
    hide from the curd-heaths
turn from the tinkle of bells
    flee the herdsman's voice!
When the herd is on the heath
    slink off to a swamp
when the herd has slithered on a swamp
    then make for the wilds
when the herd goes up a hill
    you step down the hill
when the herd goes down a hill
    go over the hill
when 'tis stepping in a glade
    stroll in a thicket
when it strolls in a thicket
    you step in a glade!

Go as a golden cuckoo
as a silver dove
shift aside as a whitefish
withdraw as a fish
roll as a bundle of wool
move as a sheaf of flax, hide
your claws in your hair
your teeth in your gums
lest the livestock scare
the little wealth shy;
give the cattle peace
the hoof-shanks quiet
let the herd wander nicely
neatly trot about
across swamps, across lands, through
the heaths of the wilds
so that you never touch them
nor ever get rough with them!
Remember your oath of old
there at Tuonela's river
at steep Claw Rapid
before the Creator's knees:
leave was given you
three times in summer to go
within earshot of a bell
on lands where cowbells tinkle
but it was not granted you
nor was leave given you to
start any rough stuff
get up to mischief.

'If you grow furious
your teeth desirous
fling your fury into a thicket
your evil desires into the firs;
strike some rotten wood
fell some blocks of birch
turn logs in the water round

grub among berry-hummocks!
When you are in need of food
and you have a mind to eat
eat mushrooms from the forest
    break up some ants' nests
roots of red angelica
Forestland's honey-titbits
but not my fodder grasses
not the hay I depend on!
Forestland's vat of honey
is fizzing as it ferments
    on a golden knoll
    on a silver hill:
there is food for the greedy
drink for the man who guzzles—
eating won't use up the food
nor will drinking shrink the drink.

'We'll make a pact for ever
peace unravel for ever
so that we may live kindly
    all summer nicely:
we'll have the lands in common
and the produce separate.
But if you should want to fight
to live on a war footing
let us fight in the winter
in the snow-time let us scrap;
come summer and swamp-melting
    when the pools warm up
don't ever come here, within
earshot of the darling herd!
If you do come to these lands
    chance on these backwoods
here there is always shooting;
when no shooters are at home
    we have clever wives

mistresses ever to hand
    who will spoil your road
    ruin your journey
so that you'll never touch them
nor ever get rough with them
    against God's will, the
    blessed one's pleasure.

    'O Old Man, chief god
when you hear himself coming
change my little cows and thump
my herd into something else
    my own into rocks
my fair darlings into stumps
as the horror treads the earth
    as the hulk wanders!

'If I were a Beast and went
about as a honey-paw
    I would not always
be under hags' feet like that
for there is land elsewhere too
a pen further away too
for an idle man to run
a free man to dash about
to walk till your paw-tips split
and your calf-flesh comes away
inside blue backwoods, under
the arm of the famous wilds.
The pine-heath's for your walking
the sand for your clinking step
the road's made for your going
the seashore for your running
    to the furthest North
the plains of Lapland: 'twill be
lucky for you to be there
sweet for you to tarry there

to walk shoeless in summer
    in autumn sockless
on the largest open swamps
    on the wide slime-lands.
If you'll not go there at all
    nor find the right way
take a path for your running
and a track for your tripping
there to Tuonela's backwoods
    or to the grave's heath!
There's a swamp there to trot on
    heather to wade through;
there is Brightie, there Flighty
    there other yearlings
    in iron traces
    upon ten tethers;
there even the lean grow fat
even the bones put on flesh.

'Sweeten, grove and soften, wilds
and be tender, blue backwoods:
    give the cattle peace
    the hoof-shanks quiet
    this great summertime
    the Lord's hot summer!
    Longneck, forest king
the forest's greybeard keeper:
    carry off your dogs
and clear away your curs! Stick
a mushroom in one nostril
in the other an apple
    so no scent is sniffed
    the herd-smell smelt out;
    bind their eyes with silk
and tie their ears with a tie
so they'll not hear them moving
    nor see them walking!

'Should not enough come of that
should he not yet take good care
    call away your son
    and ban your bastard:
see him off from these backwoods
    from these shores thrash him
far from these narrow herd-lands
    from these wide borders;
hide your dogs in a hollow
    and lash your curs fast
    to golden tethers
    to thongs of silver
    lest they do damage
    get up to mischief!

'Should not enough come of that
should he not yet be wary
    Old Man, golden king
    silver governor
    hear my golden words
    and my sweet phrases!
Press a rowan collar down
    around his snub nose:
if the rowan will not hold
have one cast out of copper;
if the copper is not firm
make a collar of iron;
but if he snaps the iron
    if he still goes wrong
wedge a golden cowlstaff from
    jawbone to jawbone
    jam the ends in hard
    fix them really fast
so the bad jaws cannot move
nor the few teeth part, unless
they are shattered with iron
    wrenched away with steel
    or bloodied with knives
    or jerked with an axe!'

Then Ilmari's mistress, that
careful wife of the craftsman
sent the cows out from the byre
let the herd out to pasture
put the herdsman in the rear
and the serf to drive the cows.

33. *The Broken Knife*

Kullervo, Kalervo's son
took provisions in a bag
drove the cows along the swamp
himself clambered on the heath
uttered a word as he strolled
    and told as he went:
'Woe is me, a luckless boy
woe, a boy down on his luck!
Now I have come to something
come to follow idle ways:
I'm herdsman to an ox-tail
    a keeper of calves
trampler upon every swamp
traveller on evil land!'

He sat down on a hummock
stopped on a sunny hillside
uttered there as he told tales
and as he sang thus set forth:
    'Shine, sunlight of God
    wheel of the Lord, blaze
on the guard of the smith's herd
upon the luckless herdsman—
not on Ilmari's cabins
on the mistress not at all!
    The mistress lives well:
    she slices up buns
    stuffs herself with pies
    spreads butter on them;
    the hapless herdsman
    gnaws dry bread, dry crust
    grooves out an oat cake
    cuts a loaf of grits

holds out one of straw
crunches pinebark bread
with a cone of birchbark scoops
water off a wet hummock.
Go, sun, roll, precious
sink down, time of God;
move, sun, towards the spruces
roll, precious, towards the brush
flee towards the junipers
fly level with the alders:
let the herdsman go home, to
scrape the butter dish
rip unleavened bread
dig into biscuits!'

Meanwhile Ilmari's mistress
as the herdsman was chanting
and Kullervo cuckooing
had now scraped her butter dish
ripped her own unleavened bread
dug into her own biscuits;
made watery gruel, cold
cabbage soup for Kullervo
whose fat the cur had eaten
Blackie breakfasted on, Spot
eaten as much as he liked
Hoary gulped what he wanted.

A bird sang out from a grove
a little bird from a bush:
''Tis time for the serf to eat
for the fatherless to sup.'
Kullervo, Kalervo's son
looked up at the long sunlight
and he put this into words:
'Now 'tis time to take a meal
time to start on food
to seek out the provisions.'

And he drove his cows to rest
the herd to lie on the heath;
himself sat on a hummock
    upon a green sward.
He slipped his pack off his back
took the loaf out of his pack
looks at it, turns it over;
then he put this into words:
'Many rolls are fair on top
    very smooth of crust
    but have husks within
    chaff beneath the crust.'

He drew his knife from the sheath
    to cut up the loaf:
the knife skidded on the stone
stubbed against the piece of rock
and the blade sheered off the knife
    snapped off the dagger.
Kullervo, Kalervo's son
    looks at his dear knife
    and fell to weeping;
he uttered a word, spoke thus:
    'One knife was brethren
    one iron was love—
    goods my father got
    my parent laid up
and I broke it on a stone
scrunched it on a piece of rock
on the bad mistress's loaf
baked by the evil woman!
How shall I repay the wife's laughter
wife's laughter and wench's taunts
the wicked hag's provisions
what the evil whore has baked?'

A crow cawed out of the scrub
a crow cawed, a raven croaked:

'O wretched gold-buckled one
matchless son of Kalervo
why are you in bad spirits
    with a gloomy heart?
Take a lash from the thicket
a birch out of the wild dell
drive the dung-shanks to a swamp
in the ooze scatter the cows—
half for the great wolves and half
for the bruins of the wild;
    round up the wolves, all
    the bears together;
turn the wolves into Tiny
knock the bears into Whiteback
drive them as a herd homeward
as brindled ones to the farm!
Thus you will repay the wife's laughter
the evil woman's insults.'

Kullervo, Kalervo's son
    put this into words:
'Hold on, hold on, demon's bitch!
If I weep my father's knife
    you too will weep yet—
    you'll weep your milch cows.'
He took a lash out of the thicket
a herd-whip of juniper;
he sank the cows in a swamp
in a windfall he smashed the oxen—
half for the wolves to eat, half
for the bruins of the wild;
the wolves he spelt into cows
made the bears into a herd
turned this one into Tiny
knocked that one into Whiteback.

The sun veered south-west
swung round half way to evening

dropped level with the spruces
flew to the cows' milking-time.
That poor wretch of a herdsman
Kullervo, Kalervo's son
    drove the bruins home
the herd of wolves to the farm
and then he advised his bears
to his wolves he spoke by mouth:
    'Rip the mistress's
    thigh, bite half her calf
    when she comes to look
    and crouches to milk!'
He made a pipe from cow-bones
from an ox-horn a hooter
a trump from Birdcherry's leg
a whistle from Brightie's hock
and he peeped upon his pipe
he tooted upon his trump
three times upon the home hill
six times at the lanes' entrance.

That mistress of Ilmari
the smith's hag, the fine woman
    long lolls without milk
sprawls without summer butter.
She heard playing from the swamp
    ringing from the heath;
    she says with this word
    she spoke with this speech:
    'Be praised, God: a trump
    sounds, the herd comes! But
where did the serf get a horn
and the toiler find a trump
    that he comes playing
    he trumpets tooting
    blowing through my ears
    going through my head?'

Kullervo, Kalervo's son
uttered a word and spoke thus:
'From the swamp the serf has got a horn
brought a trump out of the slime.
Now your herd is in the lane
the cows at the byre-field's end:
    come and light the smudge
    go and milk the cows!'

    Ilmari's mistress
told the old mother to milk:
'Just go, old mother, and milk
    deal with the cattle!—
for I cannot spare the time
    from kneading the dough.'

Kullervo, Kalervo's son
uttered a word and spoke thus:
    'Now, good mistresses
and skilful housewives always
themselves used to milk the cows
themselves deal with the cattle.'

At that Ilmari's mistress
herself came and lit the smudge
and then comes to the milking.
    She glanced at her herd
    she eyed her livestock;
she uttered a word, spoke thus:
'It is a fine-looking herd
    the livestock smooth-haired
all with the coat of a lynx
the down of a forest ewe
considerable udders
    teats full to bursting.'

She stooped to milk, set about
    making a trickle;

she tugged once, then twice
soon a third time tried:
a wolf pounces upon her
a bear bears down upon her.
The wolf rips her face to shreds
the bear yanked her foot sinews
it bit half her calf
broke her heel off her leg bone.
Kullervo, Kalervo's son
thus avenged the wench's taunts
wench's taunts, woman's laughter
paid the evil wife's wages.

But Ilmari's proud mistress
she burst into tears;
she uttered a word, spoke thus:
'Poor herder, you have done wrong:
you have driven bruins home
wolves to the great yards!'

Kullervo, Kalervo's son
this one answered that:
'I, poor herdsman, have done wrong
but you, poor mistress, have not done right!
You baked a stone loaf
you roasted a roll of rock:
I took my knife to the stone
and upon the rock
scrunched my matchless father's knife
my kinsfolk's dagger!'

And Ilmari's mistress said:
'O you herder, dear herder
reverse your meaning
speak your speech backwards:
free me from the wolf's snappers
and from the bear's claw save me!
I'll make you look good with shirts

with breeches make you handsome
I'll feed you butter and buns
I'll give you fresh milk to drink—
feed you one year without toil
two without having to work.
If you will not set me free
nor straight away unloose me
    I shall soon fall dead
    and change into mould.'

Kullervo, Kalervo's son
uttered a word and spoke thus:
'If you are dying, then die
vanish if you're vanishing!
The earth has room for those gone
and the grave for those vanished
for the mightiest to lie
and for the largest to rest.'

But Ilmari's mistress said:
    'O Old Man, chief god
make ready your great crossbow
    look out your best bow
    fit a copper bolt
upon that fiery crossbow;
send forth the fiery arrow
    shoot the copper bolt
    shoot through his armpits
    cleave his shoulder flesh
fell that son of Kalervo
    and shoot the wretch dead
with the arrow of steel tip
    with the copper bolt!'

Kullervo, Kalervo's son
    put this into words:
    'O Old Man, chief god
    do not shoot at me:

shoot at Ilmari's mistress
    lose the mean woman
without her shifting her place
without moving anywhere!'

Then Ilmari's mistress, that
wife of the careful craftsman
    soon rolled over dead
    fell to be pan-soot
in her own cabin yard, in
    her narrow farmyards.
That was how the young wife went*
and with her the fair mistress
who had been long watched for, six
years long asked after, to be
Ilmari's joy for ever
and the famous smith's honour.

34. *Father and Mother*

Kullervo, Kalervo's son
the blue-stockinged gaffer's child
    yellow-haired, handsome
    fair of shoe-upper
    made his getaway
from the smith Ilmarinen
before the master could get
    wind of his wife's death
could sink into bad spirits
    and could pick a fight.
With music he left the smith
rejoicing left Ilma's lands
    trilling on the heath
shrilling upon the burnt ground:
the swamp jarred and the land quaked
    the heath echoed back
    Kullervo's music
the wicked one's merriment.

'Twas heard in the smith's workshop:
the smith stopped in the workshop
went to the lane to listen
to the yard to see what was
the music in the backwoods
the trilling upon the heath.
    Now he saw the truth
without lying or fooling:
saw a woman gone to sleep
    his fair one fallen—
    fallen in the yard
keeled over upon the lea.
    At that the smith stopped
    with a gloomy heart;

he settled down for the night
weeping, for long shedding tears
his mood no better than tar
his heart no whiter than coal.

As for Kullervo, he walked
    stepped forward somewhere
    all day through hard wilds
heaths of demon's timber-trees.
Come evening, darkening night
he halted on a hummock;
on it sits the fatherless
the unloved one considers:
'What could have created me
and who could have shaped this wretch
    to roam night and day
all my life under the sky?
    Homeward others go
to their dwellings they travel:
I have my home in the wilds
    on the heath my farm
out in the wind my fireplace
in the rain my sauna steam.
    Do not, O good God
do not ever in this world
create an unlucky child
    nor one quite unloved
fatherless under the sky
motherless—that least of all—
as you created me, God
shaped wretched me, created
like one of a flock of gulls
like a sea-mew on a reef!
    Day comes to swallows
    whitens for sparrows
joy for the birds of the air;
    but never for me
does day come in a lifetime

nor joy ever in this world!
I do not know who made me
nor who brought me here: could a
goldeneye have made me on a road
a duck formed me on a swamp
a teal shaped me on a shore
a smew in a rock crevice?
Small I was left fatherless
lowly without my mamma:
father died and mother died
the rest of my great kin died—
    left me shoes of ice
forgot with stockings of slush
    left on icy tracks
    on steps where snow whirls
to sink into every swamp
    fall flat in the dirt . . .
But I shall not in this world
I shall not yet come to be
    a causeway on swamps
boards on dirty places, nor
shall I sink into a swamp
    while I bear two hands
    line up ten fingers
    raise ten fingernails.'

Now it came into his mind
the thought lodged in his brain, to
go to Untamo's village
and avenge his father's knocks
father's knocks and mamma's tears
    his own ill-treatment;
he uttered a word, spoke thus:
    'Wait, wait, Untamo
    hold on, my kin's doom:
when I come for war, won't I
bring the cabins to cinders
and the farmyards to firebrands!'

He came upon a hag, a
    blue-cloaked thicket-dame
and she put this into words
    she declared, spoke thus:
'Where are you bound, Kullervo
where wading, Kalervo's son?'
Kullervo, Kalervo's son
uttered a word and spoke thus:
'It has come into my mind
the thought has lodged in my brain
to set out somewhere else, to
go to Untamo's village
    avenge my kin's doom
father's knocks and mamma's tears
burn the cabins to cinders
    reduce them to dust.'

The hag put this into words
    she declared, spoke thus:
'But your kin has not been slain
Kalervo's not fallen yet.
You have a father alive
a mamma on earth and well.'
    'O my dear gammer!
    Say, my dear gammer:
    where is my father
where the fair one who bore me?'
    'There is your father
there the fair one who bore you—
upon Lapland's wide border
at the edge of a fish-pool.'
    'O my dear gammer!
    Say, my dear gammer:
    how shall I get there
    which way can I go?'
''Tis good for you to get there
though a stranger, to make it
to walk a nook of the wilds
to run on a riverbank:

you will step one day, then two
soon you'll step a third as well.
    You will head north-west
and you'll come upon a slope:
    step below the slope
walk to the left of the slope.
Then you'll come to a river
    over on your right:
walk that side of the river
past the foam of three rapids.
You'll come to a headland's tip
reach the end of a long cape;
there's a cabin on the headland's tip
a fish-hut at the cape's end:
that's where father is living
there the fair one who bore you
there your sisters are as well—
    the two fair daughters.'

Kullervo, Kalervo's son
    then stepped on his way:
he stepped one day and then two
soon he stepped a third as well.
    He headed north-west
and he came upon the slope:
    he stepped below it
skirted the slope on the left.
He reaches the river then:
he steps by the riverside
follows the river leftward;
he passed by the three rapids
came to the headland's tip, reached
the end of the long headland;
the cabin was on the headland's tip
the fish-hut at the cape's end.
He entered the cabin then
but he is not known indoors:
'Where is the foreigner from

where is the wanderer's home?'
    'Don't you know your son
    not know your own child—
the one Untamo's fellows
took off home with them when he
was big as his father's span
tall as his mother's distaff?'

The mother hastened to say
the old woman to declare:
    'Ah, my luckless boy
ah, wretched gold-buckled one!
    So with eyes alive
you are travelling these lands
when I have been weeping you
    dead and long since lost!
    Two sons I had once
    and two fair daughters:
    of them I, hapless
    lost the two eldest—
lost the boy in a great war
the girl I do not know where.
    My boy has come back
but the girl won't come at all.'

Kullervo, Kalervo's son
    he hastened to ask:
    'Where was your girl lost
which way did my sister go?'
The mother put this in words
    she declared, spoke thus:
    'There my girl was lost
there your sister went—set out
for berries in the forest
raspberries under the slope;
that is where the hen was lost
the bird died untimely, went

to a doom without a word
    with a name unknown.
    Who mourned for the girl?
Who else if not her mother!
Mother was the first to search
mother searched and mother missed.
I set out, luckless mother
    in search of my girl;
ran the wilds as a bruin
as an otter roamed the woods.
I searched one day and then two
soon I searched a third as well;
at the end of the third day
after a week at the most
    I climbed a high hill
    up a lofty peak.
There I shouted for my girl
    pined for the one lost:
"Where are you, my little girl?
    Come home now, my girl!"
Thus I shouted for my girl
    longed for the one lost
    but the slopes talked back
    and the heaths echoed:
    "Don't shout for your girl
    don't shout or yell out!
She'll never come in this world
not return in her lifetime
to her one-time mother's crofts
to her old father's moorings."'

35. *Brother and Sister*

Kullervo, Kalervo's son
the blue-stockinged gaffer's child
    came at that to live
    watched by his parents
but did not come to grasp things
have a man's understanding
for he'd been crookedly reared
stupidly lulled as a child
with someone crooked rearing
with someone stupid lulling.
    The boy sets to work
    puts himself to toil
and he waded out to fish
    row out the big seine;
    there he speaks like this
thinks with the oar in his hand:
'Shall I pull with all my strength
and row as hard as I can
or pull as the tools allow
row as much as is needed?'

The cox declared from the stern
uttered a word and spoke thus:
'If you pull with all your strength
and row as hard as you can
you'll not pull the craft apart
    nor wreck the rowlocks.'

Kullervo, Kalervo's son
    hauled with all his strength
and rowed as hard as he could:
he rowed the wooden rowlocks apart

snapped the ribs of juniper
    wrecked the aspen boat.
Kalervo came, took a look
and uttered a word, spoke thus:
'You'll never make a rower!
You've rowed the wooden rowlocks apart
snapped the ribs of juniper
    and wrecked the whole boat!
Go fish-beating with the seine:
perhaps you'll be a better beater.'

Kullervo, Kalervo's son
went fish-beating with the seine;
    there while beating he
uttered a word and spoke thus:
'Shall I beat with might and main
lay it on as a man can
or lay as the tools allow
beat as much as is needed?'

The dragger uttered his word:
'What use is a beater who
does not beat with might and main
lay it on as a man can!'

Kullervo, Kalervo's son
battered then with might and main
laid it on as a man can:
the water he stirred to gruel
    beat the seine to tow
and the fish he mashed to scum.
Kalervo came, took a look
and uttered a word, spoke thus:
'You'll never make a beater!
You've beaten the seine to tow
to chaff you've pounded the floats
the head ropes you've chopped to bits!
Go and take in the taxes

and pay in the rents: perhaps
you'll be better travelling
more skilful on a journey.'

Kullervo, Kalervo's son
the blue-stockinged gaffer's child
    yellow-haired, handsome
    fair of shoe-upper
went to take in the taxes
    to pay in the tithes.
When the dues were taken in
    and the tithes paid in
in his sledge he flings himself
    settles in his sleigh
    and started for home
travelling to his own lands.
    He rumbles along
    paces his journey
upon those heaths of Väinö
in the glades tilled long before
    and he meets a maid
a golden-haired one skiing
upon those heaths of Väinö
in the glades tilled long before.
Kullervo, Kalervo's son
    there now he holds in;
began chatting up the maid
    chatting up, tempting:
'Get up, maid, into my sleigh
    lie back on my furs!'

But the maid says from her skis
she gives tongue from her skiing:
'May doom come into your sleigh
disease lie back on your furs!'

Kullervo, Kalervo's son
the blue-stockinged gaffer's child

struck the courser with the lash
whacked it with the beaded belt:
courser ran and journey sped
the road rolled, the sledge clattered.
    He rumbles along
    paces his journey
    on the clear high seas
upon the open expanse
    and he meets a maid
a leather-shod one wading
    on the clear high seas
upon the open expanse.
Kullervo, Kalervo's son
    he holds in his horse
    he adjusts his mouth
    he orders his words:
'Come into my sleigh, fine one
the land's choice, on my travels!'

    But the maid says back
    the leather-shod raps:
'Tuoni come into your sleigh
and Death upon your travels!'

Kullervo, Kalervo's son
the blue-stockinged gaffer's child
struck the courser with the lash
whacked it with the beaded belt:
courser ran and journey sped
the sledge rolled, the road shortened.
    He rumbles along
    paces his journey
upon those heaths of the North
the broad borders of Lapland
    and he meets a maid
a tin-breasted one strolling
upon those heaths of the North
the broad borders of Lapland.

Kullervo, Kalervo's son
he reins in his horse
he adjusts his mouth
he orders his words:
'Step, maiden, into my sledge
dear, under my quilt
to eat some of my apples
to nibble some nuts!'

But the maid says back
and the tin-breast snaps:
'I spit, wretch, upon your sled
tramp, upon your sleigh!
'Tis chilly under the quilt
dismal in the sleigh.'

Kullervo, Kalervo's son
the blue-stockinged gaffer's child
grabbed the maid into his sleigh
and snatched her into his sledge
dumped her on his furs
and rolled her under the quilt.
There the maid says this
the tin-breast quarrels:
'Let me get out, give
a child her freedom
from heeding a worthless one
from serving an evil one
or I'll kick the bottom through
I'll lay low your planks
your sleigh to splinters
into bits the toboggan!'

Kullervo, Kalervo's son
the blue-stockinged gaffer's child
opened a chest full of wealth
slammed the bright lid back

and showed off his silver coins
    spread out strips of cloth
    gold-topped stockings, his
    belts trimmed with silver:
    the cloth lured the maid
    the wealth changed the bride
the silver overwhelms her
    and the gold takes hold.
Kullervo, Kalervo's son
the blue-stockinged gaffer's child
    there flattered the maid
    he took hold, tickled
one hand on the stallion's reins
the other on the maid's tits:
there he sported with the maid
    touched up the tin-breast
under the copper-bright cloak
on top of the speckled fur.

    Now God gave morning
    God brought the next day
and the maid put into words
    she asked and she talked:
    'What kin are you of
    bold one, of what stock?
You are surely of great kin
    and of grand background.'

Kullervo, Kalervo's son
uttered a word and spoke thus:
    'I'm of no great kin
    neither great nor small
    but only middling—
a mean son of Kalervo
a boy with no wits, a waif
    a poor child, a stray.*
But tell me of your own kin
    of your own bold stock—

whether you are of great kin
    and of grand background!'

And the maid indeed answers
uttered a word and spoke thus:
    'I'm of no great kin
    neither great nor small
    but only middling—
mean daughter of Kalervo
a girl with nothing, a waif
    a poor child, a stray.
Once when I was a child in
my kindly mother's dwellings
I went for berries to the forest
raspberries under the slope;
picked strawberries off the ground
raspberries under the slope
picked by day, by night rested.
I picked one day, I picked two
    till by the third day
I did not know the way home:
the road led into forest
the track took me to backwoods.
    There I sat and wept
I wept one day and then two
    till on the third day
    I climbed a high hill
    up a lofty peak:
there I shouted and yelled out.
    The backwoods talked back
    and the heaths echoed:
    "Do not shout, mad girl
mindless one, don't make a din!
It won't be heard anyway
the shout won't be heard at home."
    After three days, four
    five, six at the most
    I prepared to die
I gave myself up for lost.

I did not die even so
cheerless one, I was not lost!
    Had I died, poor wretch
and been broken off, mean one
then only two years later
    but three summers on
I'd have been waving as grass
bobbing as a flowery head
on the land a good berry
    a red cowberry
without hearing these horrors
    learning these sorrows.'

She just managed to say this
and to tell it once: at once
she tumbled out of the sledge
then ran into a river
into a rapid's steep foam
into a smoking whirlpool.
There she brought about her doom
    there she met her death
found refuge in Tuonela
mercy among the billows.
Kullervo, Kalervo's son
    dashed out of his sleigh
began to weep greatly, to
    lament grievously:
'Woe, luckless me, for my days
and woe, wretch, for my horrors
that I have used my sister
and spoilt her my mother bore!
Woe my father, my mother
woe, woe my honoured parents!
What did you create me for
and why carry this mean one?
I would have been better off
had I not been born, not grown

not been brought into the world
not had to come to this earth;
    doom did not deal straight
disease did not act aright
when it did not kill me, not
lose me as a two-night-old.'

With a knife he cut his hames
with iron split his traces
leapt upon the good one's back
upon the good blaze-brow's flanks
rides across a bit of land
a tiny bit he covers
and comes to his father's yards
    his own papa's ground.
Mother comes into the yard:
'O my mother who bore me!
Had you, my hapless mother
as I was being given birth
but filled the sauna with smoke
    shot the sauna bolt
and smothered me in the smoke
lost me as a two-night-old
brought me in burlap to the water
sunk me in the bed curtain
cast the cot into the fire
thrust the rocker into the fireplace!
    Had the village asked:
"Where has the cabin's cot gone
why is the sauna bolted?"—
    you would have answered:
"The cot I've burnt in the fire
burnt the rocker in the fireplace flame;
in the sauna I have been
making shoots, sweetening malt."'

The mother hastened to ask
and his parent to inquire:
'What is the matter, my boy

what horror is in the wind?
'Tis as though you came from Tuonela
and travelled from the Dead Land!'

Kullervo, Kalervo's son
uttered a word and spoke thus:
'Horrors have been in the wind
rascally things have happened:
I have used my own sister
and spoilt her my mother bore!
I came from taking in the taxes
    paying in the rents
    when I met a maid.
    I sported with her:
she was my little sister
    my own mother's child!
She has brought about her doom
    and has met her death
within a rapid's steep foam
within a smoking whirlpool.
As for me, I don't know now
cannot guess nor grasp at all
where to bring about my doom
and where, wretch, to cause my death—
in the mouth of howling wolf
    in growling bear's jaws
or the belly of a whale
    or a sea-pike's teeth?'

Mother put this into words:
    'Do not go, my boy
to the mouth of howling wolf
    to growling bear's jaws
nor the belly of a whale
nor a terrible pike's teeth!
There's lots of room in Finland
and within murky Savo*
for man to hide from his crimes

to feel shame for evil deeds
to hide for five years, for six
  for nine years in all
  till time brings mercy
  and the years ease care.'

Kullervo, Kalervo's son
uttered a word and spoke thus:
'I'll not go into hiding
this evil one will not flee!
I will go before doom's face
to the doors of the grave's farm
to the great places of war
to the killing-grounds of men:
Untamo is still upright
the mean man is still unfelled
still unavenged father's knocks
mamma's tears still unpaid for—
not to think of other woes
  my own well-treatment.'*

36. *The Cowbone Whistle*

Kullervo, Kalervo's son
the blue-stockinged gaffer's child
then fits himself for battle
gets ready for the war-path—
for one moment honed his sword
for the next sharpened the spear.
Mother put this into words:
    'Don't, my luckless boy
get into a great war, don't
go to a sword-clash! He who
gets into war without cause
into a fight on purpose
    in war will be slain
    and killed in the fight:
by swords he will be dispatched
by his brands he will be felled.
You'll go to war on a goat
to fight on a nanny-goat;
soon the goat will be beaten
the nanny felled in the dirt
and you'll come home on a dog
on a frog you'll reach the yard.'

Kullervo, Kalervo's son
uttered a word and spoke thus:
'I'll not then sink in a swamp
    nor fall on the heath
    in the ravens' homes
on the crows' acres, when I
sink down in places of war
    drop on battlefields.
It is sweet to die in war
fair to die in a sword-clash!

War is a pleasant disease:
a boy comes off suddenly
goes off without suffering
falls down without growing thin.'

Mother put this into words:
'When you die in war
what will be left your father
to keep him in his old age?'
Kullervo, Kalervo's son
uttered a word and spoke thus:
'Let him die on the midden
let him fall in the farmyard!'
'What will be left your mamma
to keep her in her old age?'
'Let her die with an armful
of straw, and choke in the byre!'
'What will be left your brother
to keep him in days to come?'
'In the forest let him be
dispatched, on the acre drop!'
'What will be left your sister
to keep her in days to come?'
'On the well-path let her fall
on the wash-place path sink down!'

Kullervo, Kalervo's son
left home straight away;
he says a word to father:
'Fare you well, my good father!
Will you weep for me
when you hear that I am dead
lost to the people
sunk down from the kin?'

Father put this into words:
'I'll not weep for you
if I hear that you are dead:

another son will be had
    a much better son
    a lot cleverer.'

Kullervo, Kalervo's son
uttered a word and spoke thus:
'And I shall not weep for you
should I hear that you are dead:
I'll get a papa like this—
a mouth from clay, head from rock
eyes out of swamp cranberries
a beard out of dry grasses
legs out of goat willow forks
other flesh from rotten wood.'

He spoke then to his brother:
'Farewell, my little brother!
    Will you weep for me
when you hear that I am dead
    lost to the people
    sunk down from the kin?'

Brother put this into words:
    'I'll not weep for you
if I hear that you are dead:
another brother will be
got, a much better brother
    one twice as handsome.'

Kullervo, Kalervo's son
uttered a word and spoke thus:
'And I shall not weep for you
should I hear that you are dead:
I'll get a brother like this—
a head from rock, mouth from clay
eyes out of swamp cranberries
    hair from dry grasses

legs out of goat willow forks
other flesh from rotten wood.'

He said then to his sister:
'Farewell, my little sister!
    Will you weep for me
when you hear that I am dead
    lost to the people
    sunk down from the kin?'

Sister put this into words:
    'I'll not weep for you
if I hear that you are dead:
another brother will be
got, a much better brother
    a lot cleverer.'

Kullervo, Kalervo's son
uttered a word and spoke thus:
'And I shall not weep for you
should I hear that you are dead:
I'll get a sister like this—
a head from rock, mouth from clay
eyes out of swamp cranberries
    hair from dry grasses
ears out of pond lily flowers
a body from a maple sapling.'

He said then to his mother:
'My dear mother, my darling
    fair one who bore me
precious one who carried me!
    Will you weep for me
when you hear that I am dead
    lost to the people
    sunk down from the kin?'

Mother put this into words
    she declared, spoke thus:
'You can't grasp how a mother
feels, nor guess a mother's heart.
    Yes, I'll weep for you
when I hear that you are dead
    dwindled from the folk
    sunk down from the kin:
I'll weep our cabin to floods
    the floorboards to waves
crouching down in all the lanes
    stooping in the byres;
snows I'll weep to sheets of ice
    ice sheets to soft soils
    soft soils till they bloom
    and blooms till they fade.
    What I dare not weep
    cannot cry woe for
weep among people, I'll weep
in the sauna secretly—
the loft to running waters
and the sauna planks to waves.'

Kullervo, Kalervo's son
the blue-stockinged gaffer's child
went to war making music
to a fight making merry:
he played on swamp, played on land
    echoed on the heath
    blared among the grass
    skirled among the hay.
A message rolled after him
    and news reached his ears:
'Your father at home has died
your honoured parent has dropped
    so go and see to
the burial of the dead one!'

Kullervo, Kalervo's son
    indeed he answered:
'If he is dead, let him die!
We have a gelding at home:
with it let him be taken
earthward, covered in the grave!'

He played as he trod the swamp
    shrilled on the burnt ground.
A message rolled after him
    and news reached his ears:
'Your brother at home has died
your parent's child has dropped down
    so go and see to
the burial of the dead one!'

Kullervo, Kalervo's son
    indeed he answered:
'If he is dead, let him die!
    There's a stallion there:
with it let him be taken
earthward, covered in the grave!'

He played as he walked the swamp
he trilled among the spruces.
A message rolled after him
    and news reached his ears:
'Your sister at home has died
your parent's child has dropped down
    so go and see to
the burial of the dead one!'

Kullervo, Kalervo's son
    indeed he answered:
'If she is dead, let her die!
    We've a mare at home:
with it let her be taken
earthward, covered in the grave!'

Squealing through the grass he stepped
    pealing through the hay.
A message rolled after him
    and news reached his ears:
'Your kindly mother has died
your sweet mamma has fallen
    so go and see to
her burial by the parish!'

Kullervo, Kalervo's son
uttered a word and spoke thus:
'Woe is me, a luckless boy
that my mother has died, my
curtain-maker has wearied
dropped down my cloak-adorner
    spinner of long thread
drawer of the big distaff;
nor was I near at her end
at hand when she breathed her last!
Could she have died of a chill
or else for want of bread? Let
the dead one be washed at home
in water with German soap
and let her be wound in silk
    and put in linen
and then let her be taken
earthward, covered in the grave—
    taken with laments
    and let down with song!
I cannot yet make it home:
Unto is not yet repaid
    the mean man not felled
the wicked man not destroyed.'

With music he went to war
rejoicing to Unto-land;
he uttered a word, spoke thus:
    'O Old Man, chief god

if you'd get me now a sword
    the fairest brand too
that would hold for a whole crowd
    see off a hundred!'
Well, he got a sword he liked
    the best brand of all:
with it he felled all the folk
and destroyed Untamo's crowd.
The cabins he burnt to ash
    reduced them to dust;
the stones he left on the hearths
a tall rowan in the yards.

Kullervo, Kalervo's son
now turned from there and went home
to his late father's cabins
his parent's acres: empty
the cabin at his coming
deserted when he opened;
nobody embraces him
    or offers a hand.
He put his hand to the fire:
embers were cold in the fire.
By that he knew when he came:
his mother is not alive.
He stuck his hand on the hearth:
the stones were cold on the hearth.
By that he knew when he came:
his father is not alive.
He cast his eyes to the floor
and the floor is all unswept.
By that he knew when he came:
his sister is not alive.
He strolled to the home-waters:
no boat was at the mooring.
By that he knew when he came:
his brother is not alive.
At that he burst into tears;

he wept one day, he wept two
and he put this into words:
'Alas, my kindly mother!
What did you leave here for me
when you lived upon this earth?
But you don't hear me, mother
though I'm sobbing on your eyes
    moaning on your brows
    talking on your scalp!'

The mother woke from the grave
reminds from under the mould:
'Well, I've left Blackie the dog
so that you can go hunting:
    take your dog with you
    go hunting yonder
    up into the wilds
to where the forest girls live
the yard of the blue wenches
to the pine stronghold's edges
    to seek provisions
    and to beg for game!'

Kullervo, Kalervo's son
    took his dog with him
    trudged off up the road
    up into the wilds
and he went a little way
stepped a tiny bit of road
and he came to that islet
he happened upon the place
where he had ravished the wench
and spoilt her his mother bore:
there the fair turf was weeping
the dearest glade complaining
the young grasses were grieving
the heather flowers crying for
that ravishing of the wench

spoiling of the mother-borne
    and no young grass sprang
    no heather flower grew
    came up in the place
    on that evil spot
where he had ravished the wench
and spoilt her his mother bore.

Kullervo, Kalervo's son
    snatched up the sharp sword
looks at it, turns it over
    asks it, questions it;
he asked his sword what it liked:
    did it have a mind
    to eat guilty flesh
to drink blood that was to blame?
The sword followed the man's drift
it guessed the fellow's chatter
and answered with this word: 'Why
should I not eat what I like
    not eat guilty flesh
not drink blood that is to blame?
I'll eat even guiltless flesh
I'll drink even blameless blood.'

Kullervo, Kalervo's son
the blue-stockinged gaffer's child
pushed the hilt into the field
pressed the butt into the heath
turned the point towards his breast
rammed himself upon the point
and on it he brought about
    his doom, met his death.
And that was the young man's doom
the Kullervo fellow's death—
the end for the fellow, death
    for the ill-fated.

Then the old Väinämöinen
when he heard that he was dead
    Kullervo was lost
uttered a word and spoke thus:
'Do not, folk of the future
bring up a child crookedly
with someone stupid lulling
a stranger sending to sleep!
A child brought up crookedly
or a son lulled stupidly
    won't come to grasp things
have a man's understanding
though he should live to be old
or should grow strong in body.'

37. *The Golden Bride*

Smith Ilmarinen
wept his wife evenings on end
nights he wept without sleeping
days without eating
mornings betimes he complained
and morrows he sighed
that the young woman was dead
the fair covered in the grave
nor in his hand did
the copper hammer shaft turn
no clatter from the workshop
came though one month passed.
The smith Ilmarinen said:
'I, luckless boy, do not know
how to be, which way to live.
I sit all night or I lie
there's much night, the hour heavy
many troubles, might is low.
Full of longing my evenings
low-spirited my mornings
only staler in the night
sadder on waking.
Not for evenings the longing
low spirits for my mornings
nor grief for my other times:
for my lovely the longing
the low spirits for my dear
the grief for my black-browed one.
Now these days only
often in my gloom
in dreams at midnight
my fist gropes empty

my hand strokes a lie
along both my loins.'

The smith lives without a wife
without a mate he grows old.
He wept two, three months
till in the fourth month
he picked gold coins from the sea
some silver coins from the waves;
he gathered a stack of wood
thirty sledges full;
his wood he burnt to embers
pushed the embers in the forge.
Of those gold coins of his he
took, of his silver he chose
an autumn ewe's worth
worth a winter hare
thrust the gold into the heat
pushed in the forge the silver
set the serfs puffing
the hirelings pressing:
the serfs puffed and flapped
and the hirelings pressed away
with no mittens on their hands
with no hoods over their heads;
as for smith Ilmarinen
he stokes up the forge
tried for a golden figure
for a silver bride.

But the serfs do not puff well
neither do the hirelings press
so the smith Ilmarinen
himself set about puffing:
he puffed away once and twice
until the third time
he looked down into his forge
at the brims of his bellows

what pushes out of the forge
squeezes out of the fireplace.
A ewe pushes from the forge
sends itself from the bellows
one hair gold and one copper
and the third a silver hair.
The others are delighted
but Ilmarinen is not;
the smith Ilmarinen said:
'The wolf hoped for one like you!
I hope for a golden spouse
    for a silver mate.'

Then the smith Ilmarinen
thrusts the ewe into the fire
and he added more gold coins
silver coins to top it up
and he set the serfs puffing
    the hirelings pressing:
    the serfs puffed and flapped
and the hirelings pressed away
with no mittens on their hands
with no hoods over their heads;
as for smith Ilmarinen
    he stokes up the forge
tried for a golden figure
    for a silver bride.

But the serfs do not puff well
neither do the hirelings press
so the smith Ilmarinen
himself set about puffing:
he puffed away once and twice
    until the third time
he looked down into his forge
at the brims of his bellows
what pushes out of the forge
sends itself from the bellows.

A foal pushes from the forge
sends itself from the bellows
its mane gold, its head silver
and all its hoofs of copper.
The others were very pleased
but Ilmarinen is not;
the smith Ilmarinen said:
'The wolf hoped for one like you!
I hope for a golden spouse
    for a silver mate.'

Then the smith Ilmarinen
thrusts the foal into the fire
and he added more gold coins
silver coins to top it up
and he set the serfs puffing
    the hirelings pressing:
    the serfs puffed and flapped
and the hirelings pressed away
with no mittens on their hands
with no hoods over their heads;
as for smith Ilmarinen
    he stokes up the forge
tried for a golden figure
    for a silver bride.

But the serfs do not puff well
neither do the hirelings press
so the smith Ilmarinen
himself set about puffing:
he puffed away once and twice
    until the third time
he looked down into his forge
at the brims of his bellows
what pushes out of the forge
sends itself from the bellows.
A maid pushes from the forge
goldilocks from the bellows

her head silver, her braids gold
all her body beautiful.
The others were badly scared
but Ilmarinen was not!
Then the smith Ilmarinen
forged a golden figure, forged
    without a night's rest
without a day's breathing-space:
feet he made for the maiden—
feet he made, hands he formed, but
a foot would not lift at all
nor the hands turn to embrace;
he forged ears for his maid, but
the ears would not hear at all;
so he fitted a fine mouth—
a fine mouth, quick eyes, but he
got no word into the mouth
into the eye nothing sweet.
The smith Ilmarinen said:
    'She'd be a fine maid
if she were able to talk
if she had a will, a tongue.'

    Then he brought the maid
to a fine-wove bed curtain
    and to soft pillows
    and to silken beds;
then the smith Ilmarinen
    heated a fine bath
prepared a soapy sauna:
he made whisks of twigs ready
and three tubfuls of water
with which the chaffinch washes
the snow bunting cleans himself
    of that golden dross.
    The smith bathed his fill
doused himself all he wanted;
by the maid's side he stretched out

within the fine-wove curtain
    in a tent of steel
    in iron netting.

There the smith Ilmarinen
straight away on the first night
certainly needs a cover:
    he makes cloaks ready
    two or three bear hides
    five, six woollen cloaks
    to lie with his mate
that golden figure of his.
That side certainly was warm
which was against his cloaks, but
the one against the young maid
against the golden figure
that side was growing cold, was
    stiffening to slush
    freezing to sea ice
    hardening to rock.
The smith Ilmarinen said:
'This is no good to me! I'll
take the maid to Väinö-land
to care for Väinämöinen
for a lifelong mate upon his knee
for a hen under his arm.'

And he takes the maid to Väinö-land.
    Then, when he got there
he uttered a word, spoke thus:
'Hullo, old Väinämöinen!
    Here's a girl for you
a maid fair to look upon
nor is she a chatterbox
not all that wide in the jaws.'

Steady old Väinämöinen
    glanced at that figure

casts his eyes upon the gold;
he uttered a word, spoke thus:
'Why have you brought this to me—
    this golden bugbear?'

The smith Ilmarinen said:
    'Why else than for good?
For a lifelong mate upon your knee
for a hen under your arm.'

The old Väinämöinen said:
'O my little smith brother!
Thrust your maid into the fire
    forge from her all tools
or take her to Russia, bring
your figure to Germany
for rich men to be rivals
great men to fight over her!
'Tis not fitting for my kin
    not for me myself
to woo a woman of gold
to work on one of silver.'

Then Väinämöinen forbade
the Calm Waters bridegroom banned
forbade the people growing
    banned those coming up
    from bowing to gold
    scraping to silver;
    he says with this word
    he spoke with this speech:
    'Do not, luckless boys
    fellows just growing
    whether you're wealthy
    even if you're not
    ever in this world
not in a month of Sundays
don't woo a woman of gold

or work on one of silver
for the gleam of gold is cold
and silver's glitter is chill.'

38. *Girl into Gull*

Now, that smith Ilmarinen
the everlasting craftsman
cast out his golden figure
 his silver maiden.
He stuck the foal in harness
the bay in front of the sledge
 he sits in the sledge
 settles in his sleigh:
he promised he would set off
 and he thought he would
 go to ask Northland
for Northland's other daughter.
He managed one day's driving
then another day's rolling
 till on the third day
he arrived in Northland's yard.

Louhi, mistress of Northland
 comes into the yard
and there she started talking
 she turned round to ask
 how her own child was
and her darling getting on
as daughter-in-law in husband's house
as wife in a mother-in-law's house.
 Smith Ilmarinen
his head down, in bad spirits
 helmet all askew
uttered a word and spoke thus:
'Don't, my dear mother-in-law
 don't ask about that—
how your daughter is living

your darling is getting on!
    Doom has savaged her
    a hard end has struck:
in the earth is my berry
in the heath my beautiful
my black-browed one in the grass
my silver one in the hay.
I've come for your other girl
    for your younger maid:
give, my dear mother-in-law
and put your other daughter
    where my late wife lived—
    in her sister's place!'

Louhi, mistress of Northland
uttered a word and spoke thus:
    'I, luckless, did wrong
I, down on my luck, was wrong
when I pledged my child, bestowed
even the other on you
    to fall asleep young
to roll over full-blooded—
gave as into a wolf's mouth
into a bear's growling jaws.
I'll not now give the other
    I'll not put my girl
    to sweep up your soot
    to scrub off your muck:
I'll sooner put my daughter
    place my baby child
into a roaring rapid
into a smoking whirlpool
in the Dead Land's burbot's mouth
on the teeth of Tuoni's pike!'

Then the smith Ilmarinen
twisted his mouth, turned his head

and twisted his black whiskers
    shook his curly head
    and he pushed indoors
under the roofs made his way;
he uttered a word, spoke thus:
    'Right, come with me, girl
    in your sister's place
    where my late wife lived
    to bake honey-bread
    and to brew the beer!'

But a child sang from the floor
both sang and declared: 'Be off
extra one, from our stronghold
    strange man, from these doors!
You destroyed a block of the stronghold
you damaged a bit of the stronghold
    when you came before
    when you reached the doors.
    Maiden, you sister
don't be charmed by the bridegroom
by the bridegroom's speeches, nor
    yet by his fine feet!
The bridegroom has a wolf's gums
fox's legs in his pocket
a bear's claws under his arm
and a blood-drinker's knife at his belt
    with which he will slash
    your head, cut your back.'

The maid herself talked like this
to Ilmarinen the smith:
'I will not go off with you
nor do I care for birdbrains!
You killed the wife you wedded
    you slew my sister:
you'd go on to kill me too
    you'd slay me as well.

Look, this maid has it in her
to deserve a better man
to wed a fairer body
to fill a handsomer sleigh
to go to better places
    and to grander seats—
not to a smith's coal-holes, to
    a stupid man's fires.'

    Smith Ilmarinen
the everlasting craftsman
twisted his mouth, turned his head
and twisted his black whiskers;
he grabbed the girl that minute
    wrapped his paws round her
    whirled outdoors as snow
hurled himself towards his sledge
thrust the girl into the sledge
    dumped her in his sleigh
    and straight off he went
    prepared to depart
one hand on the stallion's rein
and one on the maid's nipples.
    The maid wept and groaned
uttered a word and spoke thus:
'I went to the swamp for cranberries
for arum to the water
and there I, a hen, am lost
I, a bird, untimely die!
Listen, smith Ilmarinen:
if you will not let me go
I shall kick your sleigh to bits
smash your sledge to smithereens
kick it apart with my knees
    smash it with my shanks!'

    Smith Ilmarinen
    put this into words:

'That is why a smith's sledge sides
    are built of iron—
    to withstand the kicks
the writhing of a good lass.'

    And the maiden moans
the copper-belted complains
    she twists her fingers
    wrings her little hands;
she uttered a word, spoke thus:
'If you will not let me go
I'll sing myself into a sea fish
to a whitefish of the deep billow.'
    Smith Ilmarinen
    put this into words:
    'You will not get there:
I'll pursue you as a pike.'

    And the maiden moans
the copper-belted complains
    she twists her fingers
    wrings her little hands;
she uttered a word, spoke thus:
'If you will not let me go
I'll dispatch myself to the forest
be a stoat in a rock hole.'
    Smith Ilmarinen
    put this into words:
    'You will not get there:
I'll chase you as an otter.'

    And the maiden moans
the copper-belted complains
    she twists her fingers
    wrings her little hands;
she uttered a word, spoke thus:
'If you will not let me go
    as a lark I'll soar

hide behind a cloud.'
Smith Ilmarinen
put this into words:
'You will not get there:
I'll chase you as an eagle.'

He went a bit of a way
drove a tiny bit of road
till the horse pricks up its ears
the flop-ear fidgets.
The maid raised her head
saw a footprint in the snow
and she asked, she talked:
'What has just run across here?'
The smith Ilmarinen said:
'A hare has run across there.'

The hapless maid sighs
she sighs and she gasps;
she uttered a word, spoke thus:
'Woe is me, poor wretch:
better it would be for me
and better it were
in a running hare's footprints
on a crook-knee's stamping-grounds
than within this suitor's sledge
under the quilt of this wrinkle-face
for a hare's coat is fairer
a hare's muzzle more comely!'

Smith Ilmarinen
bit his lip and turned his head;
he hurtles along.
He drove a bit of a way
and the horse pricks up its ears
again, the flop-ear fidgets.
The maid raised her head

saw a footprint in the snow
    and she asked, she talked:
'What has just run across here?'
The smith Ilmarinen said:
'A fox has run across there.'

    The hapless maid sighs—
    she sighs and she gasps;
she uttered a word, spoke thus:
    'Woe is me, poor wretch:
better it would be for me
    and better it were
in a bustling fox's sledge
an ever-moving one's sled
than within this suitor's sledge
under the quilt of this wrinkle-face
for a fox-coat is fairer
a fox-muzzle more comely!'

    Smith Ilmarinen
bit his lip and turned his head;
    he hurtles along.
He drove a bit of a way
and the horse pricks up its ears
again, the flop-ear fidgets.
    The maid raised her head
saw a footprint in the snow
    and she asked, she talked:
'What has just run across here?'
The smith Ilmarinen said:
'A wolf has run across there.'

    The hapless maid sighs—
    she sighs and she gasps;
she uttered a word, spoke thus:
    'Woe is me, poor wretch:
better it would be for me
    and better it were

in a panting wolf's footprints
the steps of one low-snouted
than within this suitor's sledge
under the quilt of this wrinkle-face
for a wolf's coat is fairer
a wolf's muzzle more comely!'

    Smith Ilmarinen
bit his lip and turned his head;
    he hurtles along
to lodge in a new village.
    Tired from the journey
    the smith sleeps soundly . . .
and someone else seduces
the wife of the sleepy man.

Then the smith Ilmarinen
when he woke in the morning
twisted his mouth, turned his head
and twisted his black whiskers;
the smith Ilmarinen said
    he thought and spoke thus:
    'Shall I start to sing
    and sing such a bride
to the forest for the forest's own
or to water for the water's own?
I'll not sing her for the forest's own:
all the forest would take it amiss;
nor yet for the water's own:
the fishes would sheer away.
I will sooner fell her with my brand
and dispatch her with my sword.'

The sword followed the man's drift
it guessed the fellow's chatter
and uttered a word, spoke thus:

'Surely I have not been shaped
to dispatch women
or to fell the mean.'

Smith Ilmarinen
now started to sing
was wroth enough to recite—
sang his woman to a gull
to perch on a crag
to screech on a water-reef
to mew at tips of headlands
to wheel in head winds.
Then the smith Ilmarinen
into his sledge flings himself
and hurtles along
his head down, in bad spirits;
he travelled to his own lands
he came to the lands he knew.

Steady old Väinämöinen
meets him on the road
and begins to say:
'Brother, smith Ilmarinen!
Why are you in bad spirits
helmet all askew
as you come back from Northland?
What is life in Northland like?'

The smith Ilmarinen said:
'What a life 'tis in Northland!
There the Sampo is grinding
the bright-lid is swivelling:
one day it ground things to eat
the second day things to sell
the third things to store at home.
To say what I say
I'll tell it again:
what a life 'tis in Northland

with the Sampo in Northland!
There is ploughing, there sowing
there are all kinds of growing
there is good luck for ever.'

The old Väinämöinen said:
'Brother, smith Ilmarinen
where have you left the young wife
in what place the famous bride
that you come empty-handed
driving still without a wife?'

    Smith Ilmarinen
uttered a word and spoke thus:
'I sang a woman like that
to a gull on a sea crag:
now as a gull she sprawls out
as a sea-mew she cackles
    she growls on wet rocks
    and on reefs she yells.'

39. *Sailing to Northland*

Steady old Väinämöinen
  put this into words:
'Look here, smith Ilmarinen:
let us be off to Northland
to get the good Sampo, to
  look for the bright-lid!'

  Smith Ilmarinen
uttered a word and spoke thus:
'There's no getting the Sampo
and no bringing the bright-lid
  out of dark Northland
from dreary Sariola!
There the Sampo's been taken
  the bright-lid carried
into Northland's rocky hill
inside the slope of copper
  locked behind nine locks;
in there roots have been rooted
to a depth of nine fathoms
with one root in mother earth
and one in a riverbank
and a third in the home-hill.'

The old Väinämöinen said:
'Brother smith, my dear brother
let us be off to Northland
  to get that Sampo!
Let's build a big ship in which
the Sampo will be taken
  the bright-lid carried
out of Northland's rocky hill

from inside the copper slope
and from behind the nine locks!'

The smith Ilmarinen said:
'Travel by land is safer.
Let the Devil go to sea
and Doom to the mighty main!
There the wind would swill us round
    there a squall would toss
and fingers would serve for oars
    and palms for paddles.'

The old Väinämöinen said:
'Travel by land is safer—
safer but more difficult
still more dodgy than others.
'Tis merry on the waters
for a boat, a craft to cruise
to make the wide waters gleam
    to sail the clear main:
    the wind lulls the craft
and the billow drives the ship
and the west wind makes ripples
the south wind takes it forward.
    Be that as it may
since it seems you're no sailor
    let's travel by land
    struggle along shores!
Forge for me now a new sword
make a sword of fiery blade
with which I'll harry the hounds
drive out the folk of the North
when we come for the Sampo
yonder to the cold village
    into dark Northland
to dreary Sariola!'

    Smith Ilmarinen
the everlasting craftsman

thrust some iron in the fire
some steel among the embers
a whole handful of gold coins
a fistful of silver coins;
    he made the serfs puff
    and the hirelings press.
    The serfs puffed and flapped
    the hirelings pressed well:
the iron as gruel stretches
    the steel bends as dough
the silver as water gleamed
the gold rippled as a wave.
Then the smith Ilmarinen
the everlasting craftsman
    looked down in his forge
at the brim of his bellows:
he saw a sword being born
a gold-tipped one taking shape.
He took the stuff from the fire
    snatched the good matter
from the forge to the anvil
the hammers, the sledgehammers;
he forged the sword as he liked
    the best brand of all—
    he shaped it with gold
    worked it with silver.

Steady old Väinämöinen
came to look at it and he
took the sword of fiery blade
    into his right hand.
He looks, he turns it over;
he uttered a word, spoke thus:
'Is the sword fit for a man
the brand right for a bearer?'

The sword was fit for a man
the brand right for a bearer

for the moon shone from its point
and the sun shone from its side
and the stars flashed from the hilt
a horse neighed upon the blade
a cat mewed on the rivet
a dog snarled on the scabbard.
    He brandished his sword
in an iron mountain's cleft
and he put this into words:
'Now with this blade I could smite
even the mountains apart
    split the cliffs in two!'

    Smith Ilmarinen
uttered a word and spoke thus:
'But with what shall I, luckless
with what, harsh one, shield myself
    bolt up and belt up
for land, for water? Shall I
spell myself into armour
    put on iron shirts
    buckle on steel belts?
In armour a man's tougher
in an iron shirt better
in a steel belt more powerful.'

    The hour comes to be
off, the time is ripe to go:
first the old Väinämöinen
next the smith Ilmarinen
set off in search of a horse
listening for a grass-mane, a
yearling's bridle at their belt
shouldering a foal's harness.
The two seek a horse, they look
for a head amid the trees
    carefully they watch
    round the blue backwoods:

they found a horse in a grove
a grass-mane among spruces.
Steady old Väinämöinen
next the smith Ilmarinen
pressed the golden headstall on
    bridled the yearling.
    They struggle along—
the two men, along the shore:
from the shore moaning was heard
a complaint from the mooring.
Steady old Väinämöinen
uttered a word and spoke thus:
    'There's a lass weeping
    there's a hen whining!
Shall we go over to look
to inspect her from close by?'

    He steps up closer
    he went up to look;
but it was no lass weeping
nor a little hen whining:
    'twas a craft weeping
a little boat complaining.
Old Väinämöinen uttered
    when he reached the craft:
'Why do you weep, wooden craft
strong-rowlocked boat, why complain?
Do you weep your woodenness
brood over your rowlocks' strength?'

But the craft of wood answers
the boat with strong rowlocks says:
'A boat's will is for waters
though its rollers be tarry;
a maid's will is for a husband's house
though her own home be lofty.
This is why I weep, poor craft
woeful boat, why I complain:

I weep for a waterman
for a launcher on the waves.
It was said as I was made
sung as I was being built
that a war-boat would be got
and a battle-craft worked on
to bring my full load of spoils
my hold full of treasure; but
there's been no getting to war
not upon spoil-roads at all!
Other craft, even bad craft
they are always off to wars
    trudging off to fights:
    three times in summer
they bring their full load of coins
their hold full of treasure; but
I, a well-carved little boat
well built with a hundred planks
here rot upon my shavings
and stretch out upon my stocks
and the very worst earthworms
    dwell beneath my ribs
and the air's wickedest birds
    nest upon my mast
and all the wild's very frogs
    hop upon my prow.
    'Twould be twice more fair
twice, three times better to be
as a fir tree on a hill
as a pine upon the heath
for a squirrel to run on my boughs
for a dog to roll beneath.'

Steady old Väinämöinen
at that put this into words:
    'Don't weep, wooden craft
boat with strong rowlocks, don't fuss!

Soon you will be off to wars
    trudging off to fights.
If you, craft, are the Lord's work—
the Lord's work, the giver's gift
edge-on you'll rush into water
broadside into the billows you'll plunge
without a fist touching you
with no hand laid upon you
with no shoulder guiding you
no arm taking care of you!'

But the wooden craft answers
the boat with strong rowlocks says:
'My other great kin will not
neither will my brother boats
go without being pushed out
being launched upon the waves
    unless they are touched
    by fists, turned by arms.'

The old Väinämöinen said:
    'If I push you out
    will you run unrowed
    not helped with oars, not
    backed with a tiller
    your sail not blown on?'

But the wooden craft answers
the boat with strong rowlocks says:
'My other great kin will not
nor will the next of my crowd
run without fingers rowing
    not helped with oars, not
    backed with a tiller
    their sail not blown on.'

Steady old Väinämöinen
at that put this into words:
    'Will you run when rowed

when helped with oars, when
backed with a tiller
your sail blown upon?'

And the wooden craft answers
the boat with strong rowlocks says:
'Certainly my other kin
all my brother boats
have run with fingers rowing
when helped with oars, when
backed with a tiller
their sail blown upon.'

At that old Väinämöinen
left the horse upon the sand
fixed the halter to a tree
fastened the reins to a bough
shoved the boat in the waters
sang the craft on to the waves
and he asked the wooden craft
he uttered a word, spoke thus:
'O you strong-ribbed little boat
wooden craft with tough rowlocks
are you fair at carrying
as you're fair to look upon?'

And the wooden craft answers
the boat with strong rowlocks says:
'Yes, I'm fair at carrying
and roomy below:
a hundred fellows can row
and a thousand sit about.'

At that old Väinämöinen
sings under his breath—
sang first one side full
of bristle-headed bridegrooms
bristle-headed, flint-fisted

great ones with boots on their feet
and he sang the other side
full of tin-headed daughters
tin-headed, copper-belted
comely ones with gold fingers;
Väinämöinen sang on, sang
    the thwarts full of folk—
    and they are old folk
    forever sitting
where a little room was left
by the youngsters who were first.
He himself sits in the stern
    behind the birch prow
    and let his ship go;
he uttered a word, spoke thus:
'Run, craft, where there are no trees
boat, over the wide waters;
ride as bubbles on the sea
water lilies on the waves!'

He put the bridegrooms to row
and the maids to sit about:
the bridegrooms rowed, the oars sagged
but they got nowhere at all.
He put the maidens to row
the bridegrooms to sit about:
the maids rowed, their fingers sagged
but they got nowhere at all.
He moved the old in to row
    the young to look on:
the old rowed, their heads trembled
but again they got nowhere.
At that smith Ilmarinen
    himself sat to row
and now the wooden craft ran—
the craft ran, the journey sped.
Far off the oar-splash was heard

far away the rowlocks' whirr.
    He rows with gusto:
the thwarts bent and the sides sagged
    the rowan oars slammed
the oar handles squealed as grouse
and the blades as black grouse cooed
and the bow droned as a swan
the stern croaked as a raven
and the rowlocks swished as geese.
    Old Väinämöinen
    goes full speed ahead
in the stern of the red craft
in charge of the large paddle.

A headland looms on the way
and a wretched village gleams:
Ahti dwells on the headland
Farmind underneath its arm.
Farmind wept a lack of fish
Lemminkäinen lack of bread
Ahti his shed's littleness
the rogue his rations' smallness.
He was carving a boat's sides
and the keel of a new craft
on the long hunger-headland
on the mean village's beach.
    He was keen of ear
and of eye even better:
he cast his eyes north-west, turned
his head to below the sun
and sees a rainbow far off
further off a bank of cloud.
But it was no rainbow, nor
was it a small bank of cloud:
it was a craft on the move
a little boat travelling
    on the clear high seas
upon the open expanse

a clear-skinned man in the stern
a handsome man at the oars.
Wanton Lemminkäinen said:
'I don't know that craft, I don't
recognize that splendid boat;
rowing from Finland it comes
its oar striking from the east
its paddle heading north-west.'

He shouted out loud
he hallooed, hollered, the man
shouted from the headland tip
the full-blooded across the waters:
'Whose boat is on the waters
whose ship on the waves?'

The men in the craft
speak and the women answer:
'What are you, forest-dweller
tree-thumping yokel
that you don't know this craft, don't
recognize Väinö-land's boat
don't know the fellow astern
nor yet the oarsman?'

Wanton Lemminkäinen said:
'Now I know the helmsman, now
I see who the oarsman is:
steady old Väinämöinen
he is the helmsman
Ilmarinen the oarsman.
So where are you going, men
which way bound, fellows?'

The old Väinämöinen said:
'Northward we're sailing
towards the steep foam
and the froth-capped waves

to try and get the Sampo
    to look the bright-lid
out of Northland's rocky hill
from inside the copper slope.'

Wanton Lemminkäinen said:
'Ahoy, old Väinämöinen!
    Do take me, a man
for a third fellow, if you're
going to raise the Sampo
    bear off the bright-lid!
I shall count as a man too
should the need arise to fight:
I'll give orders to my palms
instructions to my shoulders.'

Steady old Väinämöinen
took the man on his travels
and the rogue into his boat.
That wanton Lemminkäinen
    now comes panting, makes
    his roundabout way
bringing a board as he comes
into Väinämöinen's boat.
The old Väinämöinen said:
'Surely there's wood in my craft
    and boards in my boat
to ballast it for the best
so why do you put your board
    add wood to the craft?'

Wanton Lemminkäinen said:
'Care will not capsize a boat
nor a prop destroy a rick.
Often on the Northern sea
    a wind demands boards
    a head wind bulwarks.'

But old Väinämöinen said:
'That is why the war-boat's breast
  is built of iron
and is tipped with steel, so that
it will not be overwhelmed
by a wind, tossed by a squall.'

40. *The Pike*

Steady old Väinämöinen
    goes full speed ahead
from that long headland's end, out
of earshot of the wretched village;
he sailed the waters singing
    the waves rejoicing.
The maids on the headlands' tips
    look on and listen:
'What could be the joy at sea
what the song upon the waves—
the joy better than before
song more fitting than others?'

The old Väinämöinen sailed—
sailed one day on land-waters
the next day on swamp-waters
a third on rapid-waters.
Then wanton Lemminkäinen
thought of a few of his words
on the fiery rapid's brink
in the holy stream's whirlpool;
    he says with this word
    he spoke with this speech:
'Leave off, rapid, your foaming
mighty water, your stirring!
Girl of the rapid, foam-maid
sit upon a teeming rock
get on a teeming boulder:
with your arms stay the billows
with your hands bundle them up
with your fists control the foam
so they'll not spurt on our breasts
    nor spray upon us!

Hag below the billows, old
    wife at the foam's brink
rise fists first upon the foam
breasting the billows come up
    to gather the foam
to take care of the froth-crests
so they'll not shove the guiltless
    roll on the blameless!
Let the rocks in mid-river
the boulders at the foam's peak
    lower their foreheads
    and press down their scalps
from the way of the red craft
the path of the tarry boat!

'Should not enough come of that
Rocky Horror, son of Dread*
drill a hole now with a drill
    pierce with a borer
the heart of the rapid's rock
    the bad boulder's side
for the craft to run unjammed
    and the boat unharmed!

'Should not enough come of that
water-master, undertow
turn the rocks into mosses
into a pike's air bladder the boat
as the foam is ridden, as
the wave-crests are gone over!
Maid upon the rapid's brink
lass at the edge of the stream
    spin now a fine yarn
out of a fine bunch of flax:
take your yarn to the water
your bluish stuff to the wave
for the craft to run along
the tar-breast to dash along

for a man to reckon with to go
for an utter stranger to know how!
Paddle-daughter, sweet woman
    take your sweet paddle
with which you will hold the stern
through enchanted streams ease it
before an envious Lapp's tent
below a witch's window!

'Should not enough come of that
    Old Man, heaven's god
hold the stern with your sword, keep
    watch with it unsheathed
for the wooden craft to run
for the boat of pine to go!'

    Old Väinämöinen
    goes full speed ahead:
he let it go between reefs
    over that steep foam;
nor did the wooden craft jam
the wise man's boat run aground.
Only when he had got there
    to those wide waters
did the craft jam, stop running
the little boat stop speeding—
    and the craft jams hard
    the boat will not budge.
    Smith Ilmarinen
next wanton Lemminkäinen
stuck a paddle in the sea
a spruce sliver in the wave:
patiently they work to free
    that craft from the jam;
but the little boat won't run
nor will the wooden craft shift.
Steady old Väinämöinen
uttered a word and spoke thus:

'O you wanton Loverboy
    lean over and see
what the craft is jammed upon
the little boat tangled with
    on these wide waters
    on this quiet stretch—
whether a rock or a log
or something else in the way!'

That wanton Lemminkäinen
    spun round to look. He
looks below the little boat;
he uttered a word, spoke thus:
'The boat is not on a rock—
not a rock and not a log:
the boat's on a pike's shoulders
on a water-dog's haunches!'

Steady old Väinämöinen
uttered a word and spoke thus:
'Anything's in a river—
it may be logs, may be pike.
If we're on a pike's shoulders
on a water-dog's haunches
drag the water with your sword
    chop the fish in two!'

That wanton Lemminkäinen
the boy, the full-blooded rogue
he draws the sword from his belt
the bone-biter from his flank;
he dragged the sea with the sword
below the side he sweeps it—
and toppled in the water
fists first plunged in the billow.
At that smith Ilmarinen
seized the fellow by the locks
hoisted the man from the sea

and he put this into words:
'All has been fashioned into
a man, made to wear a beard
to add up to a hundred
to fill out to a thousand!'

He draws the sword from his belt
from its sheath the harsh iron
with which he slashed at the fish
below the side thwacked at it:
the sword broke into bits, but
the pike knew nothing at all.
Steady old Väinämöinen
at that put this into words:
'Between you's not half a man
of a fellow not a third!
Whenever there is a need
and a man's mind is required
then the mind is anyhow
all the sense is somewhere else.'

He hauled out his sword himself
    snatched the sharp iron
thrust his sword into the sea
below the side brought it down
on the fishy pike's shoulders
on the water-dog's haunches
    and the sword stuck hard
    in the gills fastened.
At that old Väinämöinen
hoisted up the fish, he dragged
the pike out of the water:
    the pike broke in two;
the tail sank to the bottom
the head jumped into the skiff.
Now the little boat could run
the craft got free of the jam;
steady old Väinämöinen

brought the craft towards a crag
    hustled it ashore.
He looks at, he turns over
the head portion of the pike
and he put this into words:
'The oldest of the bridegrooms
is the one to split the pike
    to slice up the fish
to hack the head to pieces!'
But the men speak from the craft
women declared from the sides:
'The catcher's hands the sweetest
the hunter's fingers the holiest.'

Steady old Väinämöinen
drew the knife from its holder
from his flank the cold iron
with which he splits up the pike
and hacks the fish to pieces
and he puts this into words:
'The youngest of the maidens
is the one to cook the pike
    for breakfast titbits
    for fishy lunches!'

    The maids came to cook—
as many as ten raced up;
    then the pike is cooked
breakfasted on in titbits.
Some bones were left on the crag
    fishbones on the rock.
Steady old Väinämöinen
    at that looks at them—
looks at them, turns them over;
he uttered a word, spoke thus:
    'I wonder what these—
    these pike-teeth, this wide
    jawbone—could become

were they in a smith's workshop
with a skilful craftsman, in
    a mighty man's hands?'

The smith Ilmarinen said:
'What's nothing becomes nothing
    a fishbone no tool
even in a smith's workshop
with a skilful craftsman, in
    a mighty man's hands.'

Steady old Väinämöinen
    put this into words:
'But surely these could become
a kantele* of fishbones
were there someone who knew how
who could make an instrument of bones.'

When no one else came forward
and there was none who knew how
who could make an instrument of bones
steady old Väinämöinen
made of himself a maker
took the shape of a shaper:
he made an instrument of pike bones
produced a joy for ever.

What was the kantele's belly from?—
'twas from the big pike's jawbone.
What the kantele's pegs from?—
they were made from the pike's teeth.
What the kantele's strings from?—
from the hairs of the Demon's gelding.

Now the instrument was made
and ready the kantele
the great pikebone instrument
the kantele of fish-fins:

the young men came up to it
and the married fellows came
    the half-grown boys came
and the little wenches too
    young girls and old wives
    middle-aged women
to look at the kantele
to inspect the instrument.
Steady old Väinämöinen
told a young one, told an old
told one too of middle age
to play with their fingers that
    sounding thing of bones
the kantele of fishbones.
The young played and the old played
    the middle-aged played:
the young played, their fingers sagged
the old tried, their heads trembled;
but joy did not rise to joy
nor instrument to music.

Wanton Lemminkäinen said:
'O you half-witted sons, you
    silly daughters too
    and other mean folk:
among you there's no player
no one who rightly knows how!
Bring the instrument to me
and carry the kantele
to two upright kneecaps, to
the tips of ten fingernails!'

Then wanton Lemminkäinen
took the kantele in hand
the joy closer to himself
the instrument beneath his fingers:
he tunes the instrument, turns
    the kantele round;

but the instrument won't play
the joy won't rejoice at all.

The old Väinämöinen said:
'There's not among these youngsters
among the people growing
nor among the old, any
player of this instrument
one to make this joy rejoice.
    Might Northland better
    play this instrument
    make this joy rejoice
if I sent it to Northland?'

He sent it to Northland, to
Sariola had it brought:
the boys in Northland played it
both lads and lasses played it
and the men with wives played it
the women with husbands too;
the mistress herself played it
    turned it and tried it
she put her fingers to it
plucked it with ten fingernails.
The boys in Northland played, all
    sorts of people played;
but joy did not sound like joy
nor the music like music:
    the strings went awry
    the hairs twanged badly
    the sound rang out wrong
the instrument hoarsely hummed.
A blind man slept in a nook
an old man on a stove top;
the old man on the stove woke
    at the hearth started
    growled from the sleep-place
    snarled from his corner:

'Have done and leave off
give over, stop it!
It is blowing through my ears
it is going through my head
making all my hair stand up
robbing me of hours of sleep!
If the Finnish folk's music
will not move to joy
or wear down to sleep
persuade to slumber
then chuck it in the water
and sink it in the billows
or else take it back
have the instrument brought there—
to the hands of him who shaped,
its tuner's fingers!'

The instrument finds its tongue
the kantele struck up words:
'I'll not hit the water yet
nor dwell below the billows!
I'll play first with a player
whine with one who's taken pains.'
So it was carried with care
borne beautifully
to the hand of its maker
the knees of him who fetched it.

41. *The Pikebone Kantele*

Steady old Väinämöinen
the everlasting singer
    prepares his fingers
    rubs his thumbs ready;
he sits on the rock of joy
on the song-boulder settles
    on the silver hill
    on the golden knoll;
he fingered the instrument
turned the curved thing on his knees
the kantele in his hands;
he uttered a word, spoke thus:
'Now, let him come and listen
who may not before have heard
the joy of eternal bards
the sound of the kantele!'

At that old Väinämöinen
began to play prettily
the sounding thing of pike-bones
the kantele of fishbones;
his fingers rose nimbly, his
    thumb lifted lightly:
    now joy waxed joyful
delight echoed like delight
music sounded like music
song had the effect of song;
    the pike's tooth tinkled
    the fish-tail poured forth
    the stallion's hairs called
the hairs of the steed rang out.
As old Väinämöinen played

there was none in the forest
    running on four legs
    or hopping on foot
that did not come to listen
marvel at the merriment:
the squirrels reached from leafy
    twig to leafy twig
    and the stoats turned up
    sat down on fences;
the elk skipped upon the heaths
and the lynxes made merry.
The wolf too woke on a swamp
and the bear rose on the heath
    from a den of pine
    from a spruce thicket;
the wolf ran long distances
the bear ranged over the heaths
sat down at last on a fence
and fling themselves at a gate:
the fence fell upon the rock
the gate toppled in the glade;
then they scrambled up a spruce
    they swung up a pine
to listen to the music
marvel at the merriment.

Tapiola's careful lord
Forestland's master himself
and all Tapio's people
    both lasses and lads
    climbed a mountain peak
to take note of the music;
the forest's mistress herself
Tapiola's careful wife
dresses up in blue stockings
    puts on red laces
squatted in a birch's crook
perched on an alder's warp, to

listen to the kantele
to take note of the music.

What birds of the air there were
    wheeling on two wings
    they too came whirling
    and speeding they sped
to listen to the delight
marvel at the merriment:
when the eagle at home heard
the fine music of Finland
it left its brood in the nest
    and took wing itself
to the sweet fellow's music
the strains of Väinämöinen;
from on high the eagle flew
    through the clouds the hawk
calloos from the deep billows
and swans from unfrozen swamps;
even little chaffinches
    and twittering birds
    buntings in hundreds
    nigh a thousand larks
    admired in the air
chattered upon his shoulders
as the father made merry
as Väinämöinen played on.

Yes, the air's nature-daughters
and the air's lovely lassies
marvelled at the merriment
listened to the kantele;
one on the sky's collar-bow
shimmered upon a rainbow
one on top of a small cloud
bloomed upon the russet edge.
That Moon-daughter, handsome lass

the worthy maid Sun-daughter
   were holding their reeds
   raising their heddles
   weaving golden stuff
   and jingling silver
on the rim of the red cloud
upon the long rainbow's end;
   when they got to hear
the sound of that fine music
the reed slipped out of their grasp
the shuttle dropped from their hand
   the golden threads snapped
and the silver heddles clinked.

   There was no creature
not in the water either
   moving with six fins
   the best shoal of fish
that did not come to listen
marvel at the merriment:
   the pike slink along
the water-dogs veer along
the salmon roamed from the crags
and the whitefish from the depths;
the little roach, the perch too
pollans and other fish too
drift side by side to the reeds
   wend their way shoreward
to listen to Väinö's tale
to take note of the music.

Ahto, king of the billows
the water's grass-bearded lord
draws himself to the surface
glides on a water lily;
there he listened to the joy
and he put this into words:

'I have not heard such before
    ever in this world
as Väinämöinen's music
as the eternal bard's joy!'
The scaup-daughter sisters, the
shore's reedy sisters-in-law
    were smoothing their hair
    brushing their tresses
with a brush of silver tip
    with a comb of gold;
they got to hear the strange sound
    and that fine music:
the comb slid in the water
the brush vanished in the wave
and the hair was left unsmoothed
    the locks half undone.
The water's mistress herself
the water's reed-breasted dame
now rises out of the sea
jerks herself out of the wave;
at the reedy edge she reared
she turns upward on a reef
    to hear that sound, the
music of Väinämöinen
for it was a wondrous sound
and the music very fine
and there she fell fast asleep
she sank down on her belly
on the back of a bright rock
the side of a thick boulder.

Then the old Väinämöinen
played for one day, played for two;
    there was no fellow
    nor any brave man
there was no man nor wife, nor
one who wore her hair in braids

who did not fall to weeping
    whose heart did not melt:
the young wept and the old wept
and the unmarried men wept
and the married fellows wept
    the half-grown boys wept
    both boys and maidens
and the little wenches too
for it was a wondrous sound
and the old man's music sweet.
Even from Väinämöinen
    a tear tumbled down:
the trickles dripped from his eyes
    the water-drops rolled
bigger round than cranberries
    and thicker than peas
    rounder than grouse eggs
and larger than swallows' heads.
The waters rolled from his eye
others oozed from the other
    dropped upon his cheeks
    upon his fair face
    down from his fair face
    upon his wide jaws
    down from his wide jaws
    upon his stout breast
    down from his stout breast
    to his sturdy knees
    from his sturdy knees
upon his handsome insteps
down from his handsome insteps
to the ground beneath his feet
    through five woollen cloaks
    through his six gold belts
    seven blue waistcoats
    eight homespun caftans;
    the water-drops rolled
down from old Väinämöinen

to the shore of the blue sea
from the shore of the blue sea
down below the clear waters
    upon the black mud.

Then the old Väinämöinen
    put this into words:
'Is there among these youngsters—
    these youngsters so fair
    among this great kin
    these of grand background
one to gather up my tears
from below the clear waters?'

    The young there speak thus
    and the old answer:
'There's not among these youngsters—
    these youngsters so fair
    among this great kin
    these of grand background
one to gather up your tears
from below the clear waters.'

The old Väinämöinen said
    he uttered, spoke thus:
'Whoever brought back my tears
gathered up the water-drops
from below the clear waters
would get from me a coat of feathers.'

A raven came flapping up
and old Väinämöinen said:
    'Raven, fetch my tears
from below the clear waters
and I'll give you a coat of feathers.'
But the raven got nothing.

A blue scaup heard that
so the blue scaup came
and old Väinämöinen said:
'Blue scaup, you often
dive down with your beak
and cool off in the water
so go, gather up my tears
from below the clear waters!
You will get the best wages:
I will give you a coat of feathers.'

The scaup went to gather up
Väinämöinen's tears
from below the clear waters
from the top of the black mud;
gathered the tears from the sea
carried them to Väinö's hand.
They had changed to other things
had grown to things that are fair:
into beads they had swollen
into pearls they had ripened
to be the delights of kings
and rulers' joys for ever.

42. *Stealing the Sampo*

Steady old Väinämöinen
next the smith Ilmarinen
third the wanton Loverboy
    he, the fair Farmind
went off upon the clear sea
    upon the vast waves
yonder to the cold village
    into dark Northland
    the man-eating, the
    fellow-drowning place.
Now, who there would be rower?
First the smith Ilmarinen:
yes, he there would be rower
    at the foremost oars;
next wanton Lemminkäinen
    at the hindmost oars.
Steady old Väinämöinen
    sat down at the stern
and he goes full speed ahead
    cutting through the waves
    through all that steep foam
    through the froth-capped waves
headed for the North's moorings
for the rollers known of old.

    Well, when they got there
reached the end of their voyage
they dragged the boat up on land
    they hauled the tar-breast
up on to the steel rollers
    the copper moorings;
then they came to the cabins
    and pushed straight inside.

The mistress of Northland asked
inquired of the newcomers:
'What message do the men have
    what news the fellows?'

Steady old Väinämöinen
    this one answers that:
'The men's message concerns the Sampo
the fellows' news the bright-lid:
we've come to share the Sampo
to look out for the bright-lid.'

She, the mistress of Northland
uttered a word and spoke thus:
'No grouse can be shared by two
nor a squirrel by three men.
'Tis good that the Sampo hums
and the bright-lid churns away
within Northland's rocky hill
and inside the copper slope;
it is good too that I am
keeper of the great Sampo.'

Steady old Väinämöinen
uttered a word and spoke thus:
'If you'll not give a part, that
other half of the Sampo
we shall carry off the lot
we shall take it to our boat.'

Louhi, mistress of Northland
    she took that badly.
She called Northland together
    young men with their swords
and fellows with their weapons
out for Väinämöinen's head.

Steady old Väinämöinen
    seized his kantele
    he sat down to play
began to play prettily;
and they all stopped to listen
marvel at the merriment—
    men in good spirits
    wives with smiling lips
fellows with tears in their eyes
and boys kneeling on the ground.
    He wears the folk down
    he tires the people:
all the listeners fell asleep
    the watchers sank down;
the young slept and the old slept
at Väinämöinen's music.
Then the shrewd Väinämöinen
the everlasting wise man
    groped in his pocket
    fumbled in his purse;
    he takes sleep-needles
    smeared their eyes with sleep
    knits up the lashes
    and locked up the lids
    of the weary folk
of the slumbering fellows:
into a long sleep, into
a longer slumber he put
the whole household of Northland
and all the village people.

He went to get the Sampo
    to look the bright-lid
out of Northland's rocky hill
from inside the copper slope
    from behind nine locks
and an inner bolt the tenth;

and there old Väinämöinen
    sings under his breath
in the copper slope's doorways
at the rocky stronghold's rims:
    now the stronghold's gates
moved, the iron hinges shook.
As for smith Ilmarinen
he was there as second man:
with butter he smeared the locks
    the hinges with fat
    lest the doors should creak
and the hinges mew. The locks
he eased loose with his fingers
the bolts he slipped with a hoe:
now as though in bits the locks
turned, the strong doors swung open.

At that old Väinämöinen
    put this into words:
'O you wanton Loverboy
    foremost of my friends
    go, take this Sampo
    and tug the bright-lid!'

That wanton Lemminkäinen
    that is, fair Farmind
quite prompt without being told
quick without being extolled
went off to get the Sampo
    to tug the bright-lid
and he said as he went there
    boasted on his way:
'What of man there is in me
what of fellow in the Old Man's son
by it may the Sampo be
shifted, and the bright-lid turned
with the help of my right foot
with the touch of my shoe heel!'

Lemminkäinen made to shift—
made to shift and made to turn
gripped the Sampo in his arms
strove with his knees on the ground;
but the Sampo will not move
the bright-lid will not swivel
for its roots had been rooted
to a depth of nine fathoms.

There's a good ox in Northland
 that is strong of frame
 very tough of flank
and of sinews most handsome;
its horns are a fathom long
one and a half thick its snout.
He took the ox from the hay
and a plough from a field edge;
with it ploughed the Sampo's roots
 the bright-lid's fasteners:
the Sampo started to move
and the bright-lid to swivel.
At that old Väinämöinen
next the smith Ilmarinen
third wanton Lemminkäinen
led away the great Sampo
out of Northland's rocky hill
from inside the copper slope
and they took it to their boat
and stowed it aboard their ship
got the Sampo in their craft
the bright-lid upon its ribs
launched the boat on the waters
the hundred-planked on the waves;
the boat splashed in the water
set off broadside on the wave.
The smith Ilmarinen asked
he uttered a word, spoke thus:
'Where shall the Sampo be brought

which way shall it be conveyed
    from these bad places
    from luckless Northland?'

Steady old Väinämöinen
    uttered and spoke thus:
'There shall the Sampo be brought
    and the bright-lid fetched—
to the misty headland's tip
to the foggy island's end
that it may be lucky there
    and dwell there always.
There is a little room there
    just a bit of space
with no eating, no beating
no meeting of a man's sword.'

At that old Väinämöinen
went away out of Northland
    went in good spirits
gladly towards his own lands
and then he recited thus:
    'Turn, craft, from Northland
    turn yourself homeward
and your back to foreign lands!
    O wind, lull the craft
    water, rock the boat
    give help to the oars
    ease to the tiller
    on these wide waters
on these open expanses!
    If the oars are small
    the rowers puny
    the helmsmen little
    the pilots children
Ahto, give oars of yours, a
boat of yours, water-master
    new and better oars

another, firmer paddle
apply yourself to the oars
    settle down to row:
    let the wooden craft
run, let the iron-rowlocked
    cleave through the steep foam
    and the froth-capped waves!'

At that old Väinämöinen
    goes full speed ahead.
As for smith Ilmarinen
and wanton Lemminkäinen
    they are there rowing
rowing and speeding along
over the main's clear waters
    over the vast waves.
Wanton Lemminkäinen said:
    'Once upon a time
as a rower had water
so a singer had a tale;
    but not nowadays
    do we ever hear
    lilting in a boat
    singing on the waves.'

Steady old Väinämöinen
uttered a word and spoke thus:
'No lilting on the waters
and no singing on the waves!
    Song keeps you lazy
    tales delay rowing.
Precious day would pass and night
would overtake us midway
    on these wide waters
    upon these vast waves.'

The wanton Lemminkäinen
uttered a word and spoke thus:

'The time will pass anyway
 the fair day will flee
and the night will come panting
and the twilight will steal in
if you don't sing while you live
 nor hum in this world.'

 Old Väinämöinen
 sailed the blue high seas
 sailed one day, sailed two
 till on the third day
that wanton Lemminkäinen
a second time declared: 'Why
won't you sing, Väinämöinen
and hum, man of Good Waters
now you've got the good Sampo
 and set your course straight?'

Steady old Väinämöinen
 for sure he answers:
''Tis too early for singing
too betimes for merriment.
'Twould only be right to sing
and proper to make merry
if our own doors were in sight
and our own gates were creaking.'

Wanton Lemminkäinen said:
'If it were me at the stern
I would sing out all I could
I'd cuckoo with all my strength;
we may not be able to
again, not have strength enough.
If you'll not promise to sing
I will start a song myself.'

Then wanton Lemminkäinen
 he, the fair Farmind

he adjusts his mouth
he pitches his tone
and began to hum
the wretch burst out cuckooing
with his surly voice
with his rasping throat.
Wanton Lemminkäinen sang
Farmind bellowed out:
his mouth moved and his beard shook
and his jaws quivered.
The song was heard further off
the trill across the waters
was heard in six villages
over seven seas.

A crane sat upon a stump
on top of a wet hummock
counting its toe bones
lifting up its feet.
Now, it was greatly startled
by Lemminkäinen's singing:
the crane let out a weird croak
blurted out an evil note
and took off at once
flew off to Northland.
Then, when it got there
and arrived on the North's swamp
it was still screeching harshly
and shrilly yelling:
that way it awoke Northland
roused the evil power.
The mistress of Northland rose
after lying long asleep.
She went into her cowshed
she ran to her store
looks over her herd
checks her property:
none of the herd had vanished

of her goods none had been snatched.
She went to the rocky hill
the door of the copper slope
and she said when she got there:
'Woe, luckless me, for my days!
A stranger has been here, made
    all the locks quiver
    moved the stronghold gates
broken the iron hinges!
Could the Sampo have been got
from here, taken without leave?'

Yes, the Sampo had been got
from there, and snatched the bright-lid
out of Northland's rocky hill
from inside the copper slope
    from behind nine locks
and an inner bolt the tenth.
Louhi, mistress of Northland
    she took that badly
    saw her power sinking
her authority failing
and she prays to Mist-daughter:
    'Mist-girl, fog-maiden
    sift mist with a sieve
    waft some fog about
    drop slime down from heaven
let a haze down from the sky
    on the clear high seas
upon the open expanse
to cut Väinämöinen off
stop the man of Calm Waters!

'Should not enough come of that
Sea-monster, the Gaffer's son
raise your head out of the sea
    your scalp from the wave;
fell the men of Kaleva

and drown those of Calm Waters
destroy the vicious fellows
underneath the deep billows;
bring the Sampo to Northland
without rolling from the boat!

'Should not enough come of that
    O Old Man, chief god
    the sky's golden king
    silver governor
    make stormy weather
    raise a great air force:
create wind, send a billow
    right against the boat
to cut Väinämöinen off
block the man of Calm Waters!'

The mist-girl, maid of the fog
breathes a mist upon the sea
brought forth a fog in the air
and kept old Väinämöinen
    for all of three nights
    amid the blue sea
so that he could not get on
not go anywhere at all.
When for three nights he'd rested
    amid the blue sea
old Väinämöinen uttered
    he declared, spoke thus:
'Not even a worse man, a
    sleepier fellow
is to be drowned in a mist
    overcome by fog!'

He dragged the water with his
brand, smacked the sea with his sword:
mead swished forth from the brand's path

and honey from the sword-splash;
the slime rose to heaven
the mist went up to the sky
and the sea was clear of fog
and the sea's billow of haze
and the sea sprang to full size
the world filled out big.

A little time passed
a moment sped by;
and now a loud roar was heard
at the rim of the red boat;
foam rose high against
Väinämöinen's craft.
Then the smith Ilmarinen
was truly greatly startled:
the blood drained from his
face, the red fell from his cheeks
and he pulled a quilt over his head
over his ears he drew it
covered his face handsomely
and his eyes that much better.
Old Väinämöinen
looked aside at the waters
cast his eyes at the craft's side
saw something of a wonder:
Sea-monster, the Gaffer's son
at the rim of the red boat
raised his head out of the sea
his scalp from the wave.
Steady old Väinämöinen
got hold of him by the ears
and by the ears he hoists him;
he asked him, he talked
uttered a word and spoke thus:
'Sea-monster, the Gaffer's son
why did you rise from the sea

why come up from the billow
    in front of mankind—
let alone Kaleva's son?'

Sea-monster, the Gaffer's son
neither is he pleased at that
nor is he very frightened
nor indeed does he answer.
Steady old Väinämöinen
carefully inquired again
    three times loudly asks:
'Sea-monster, the Gaffer's son
why did you rise from the sea
why come up from the billow?'

Sea-monster, the Gaffer's son
    at the third time now
he says a word in answer:
'For this I rose from the sea
and came up from the billow:
    I had it in mind
to slay Kaleva's kin, to
get the Sampo to Northland.
But if you will drop me in the waves
now, and spare a rascal's life
I will never come again
    in front of mankind.'

Then the old Väinämöinen
threw the rascal in the waves
and he put this into words:
'Sea-monster, the Gaffer's son
don't you rise out of the sea
don't come up from the billow
    in front of mankind
    from this day forward!'
And not since that day has the

Monster risen from the sea
    in front of mankind
nor will he rise while there is
moon and sun, and the day good
and the world a joy to see.

Then the old Väinämöinen
    eased his ship forward.
    A little time passed
    a moment sped by;
now the Old Man, the chief god
he, the master of the skies
    told the winds to blow
the stormy weather to rage.
    The winds rose to blow
the stormy weather to rage:
loudly the west wind blustered
and the north-west wind flared up;
    more so the south wind
the east whistled wickedly;
dreadfully the south-east roared
    the north loudly screamed;
and they blew the trees leafless
the conifer trees coneless
    the heather flowerless
    the grasses huskless
    raised black mud on top
    of the clear waters.
    Hard then the winds blew
the billows rammed the vessel:
they bore the harp of pike-bones
the kantele of fish-fins
for the Wave-wife's people's good
Ahto-land's joy for ever.
Ahto noticed it on the billows
Ahto's children on the waves:
they took the fine instrument
    carried it off home.

At that old Väinämöinen's
    tears sprang to his eyes
and he put this into words:
'So much for what I have done:
there goes my best instrument
my joy for ever is lost!
    No more shall I have
    ever in this world
    joy of a pike's tooth
    fishbone melody.'

As for smith Ilmarinen
    he was sorely pained;
he uttered a word, spoke thus:
'Woe, luckless me, for my days
that I set out on these seas
on these open expanses
    trod on whirling wood
    on a trembling twig!
    My locks have seen wind
and my hair frightful weather
    my beard evil days—
seen on these very waters;
seldom can a man have known
wind before that looks like this
    foam as steep as this
    froth-capped waves like these.
Now the wind is my refuge
the sea's billow my mercy!'

Steady old Väinämöinen
    at this point he thinks:
    'No crying aboard
    shrieking in the craft!
Tears won't free us from trouble
nor will screams from evil days.'
Then he put this into words
    he declared, spoke thus:

'Water, forbid your
son, wave, ban your child,
Ahto, settle the billows
and Wave-wife, the water-folk
so they don't splash the handrails
or reach the top of my ribs!
Rise, wind, to the sky
up into the clouds begone
to your kin, your tribe
your clan, your household!
Do not fell the wooden craft
or capsize the boat of fir;
sooner fell trees to be cleared
overturn spruces on mounds!'

The wanton Lemminkäinen
he, the fair Farmind
uttered a word and spoke thus:
'Come, O eagle of Lapland
and bring three of your feathers
eagle, three and raven, two
to take care of the small boat
be the wretched craft's handrail!'

He added some boards
he prepared bulwarks;
he joined on the extra boards
a full fathom high
to stop the billow coming
over, splashing the handrails.
Now there were quite enough boards
on the boat enough bulwarks
for the harsh wind to flare up
for the stern billow to push
as the foam was ridden, as
the wave-crests were gone over.

43. *Battle at Sea*

Louhi, mistress of Northland
called Northland together: she
armed the crowd with their crossbows
equipped the men with their swords;
she made ready the North's craft
    prepared the war-boat
mustered the men in her ship
    prepared the warriors
    as a scaup its young
as a teal musters its chicks—
    a hundred swordsmen
a thousand fellows with bows;
    she erected masts
    fitted canvas-trees
hoisted sails upon the mast
    canvas on the trees
    like a long cloud-bank
a mass of cloud in the sky
    and then she cast off
    she both went and sped
to try and get the Sampo
out of Väinämöinen's boat.

Steady old Väinämöinen
is sailing on the blue sea
and he put this into words
spoke from the stern of his craft:
'O you wanton Loverboy
    foremost of my friends:
    climb to the masthead
scramble up the canvas-tree
glance at the weather ahead
check the sky astern, to see

whether the skyline is clear
whether clear or overcast!'

That wanton Lemminkäinen
the boy, the full-blooded rogue
quite prompt without being told
quick without being extolled
    climbed to the masthead
scrambled up the canvas-tree.
    He looked east, looked west
    looked north-west and south
looked across to the North's shore;
then he put this into words:
'All clear the weather ahead
but gloomy the sky astern:
there is a small cloud northward
a cloud-bank to the north-west.'

The old Väinämöinen said:
    'Surely you have lied!
    That's no cloud at all
a cloud-bank it cannot be:
    that's a craft with sails.
Look again more carefully!'

He looked again, looked with care
and says with this word: 'Far off
an island heaves into view
out there it is looming, with
aspens full of hawks, birches
of speckled capercaillies.'

The old Väinämöinen said:
    'Surely you have lied!
    Hawks those cannot be
nor speckled capercaillies:
    they're sons of the North.
Look carefully a third time!'

The wanton Lemminkäinen
    looked a third time too;
    he says with this word
    he spoke with this speech:
'Now the North's craft is coming
the hundred-rowlocked cleaving!
There's a hundred men at oars
a thousand sitting about!'

Then the old Väinämöinen
    realized the truth;
he uttered a word, spoke thus:
'Row, you smith Ilmarinen
row, wanton Lemminkäinen
    row, the lot of you
that the little boat may run
    the craft make headway!'

The smith Ilmarinen rowed
wanton Lemminkäinen rowed
and the whole lot of them rowed.
    The hardwood oars bent
and the rowan rowlocks slammed
and the boat of fir shuddered;
the prow flung spray as a seal
the stern as a rapid roared
the water boiled in bubbles
and the froth flew up in balls.
The fellows vied in tugging
and the men strove in pulling;
but they got nowhere at all
the wooden craft would not flee
from before the craft with sails
    that boat of Northland.
Then the old Väinämöinen
felt his ruin coming, his
day of trouble catching up;
    he thinks, considers

how to be, which way to live
and he put this into words:
'I can still think of a dodge
for this: I've hit on a trick.'

He groped among his tinder
fumbled among his fire-tools
took a tiny bit of flint
quite a small piece of tinder;
into the sea he tosses
them, over his left shoulder.
    He says with this word
    he spoke with this speech:
'Let this become a reef, grow
into a hidden island
for the North's craft to run on
the hundred-rowlocked to split
    where the sea-storm chafes
    where the wave scratches!'

Then it grew into a reef
it turned into a sea-crag
with its longer side eastward
    and crossways northward.
The North's craft came hurtling on
    through the billow cleaves
    and it hits the reef
    jammed hard on the crag.
The wooden craft flew apart
    the hundred-ribbed smashed;
the masts went splat in the sea
and the sails came tumbling down
to be swept off by the wind
    driven by the gale.
Louhi, mistress of Northland
runs on foot in the water
    went to raise the craft
    to lift up the ship;

but the boat will not come up
    nor will the craft budge:
    all its ribs had snapped
all its rowlocks splintered too.
    She thinks, considers
and she put this into words:
    'What is the best plan?
    What is to be done?'

    Now she changed her shape
dared to become someone else.
    She took up five scythes
    six hoes past their prime:
she fashioned them into claws
fitted them to be her feet;
the shattered part of the craft
    she put under her;
the sides she slapped into wings
the rudder to be her tail;
put a hundred men under a wing
a thousand at her tail tip—
    the hundred swordsmen
the thousand fellows who shot.
And she spread her wings to fly
as an eagle lifted off
    and she flaps along
heading for Väinämöinen:
    one wing flicked the clouds
and one swerved off the water.

The water-mother, fair wife
    put this into words:
    'Old Väinämöinen
turn your head from underneath the sun
    cast your eyes north-west
look behind you a little!'

Steady old Väinämöinen
turned his head from underneath the sun
    cast his eyes north-west
looked behind him a little:
now the North's dame is coming
the wondrous bird glides along—
as for shoulders, like a hawk
a wivern as for body!
She startles Väinämöinen.
She flew on to the masthead
to the canvas-tree rustled
on top of the post she perched
and the craft all but capsized
the ship nearly keeled over.

Then the smith Ilmarinen
casts himself upon his God
and in his Creator trusts;
    he says with this word:
'Keep us, steadfast Creator
    and guard us, fair God
lest a boy should come away
and a mother's child should fall
short of the Creator's toll
of the span decreed by God!
O Old Man, God known to all
    heavenly father
bring me a fiery fur coat
put on me a blazing shirt
shielded by which I may make
war, and behind which may fight
lest my head should come to grief
and my locks should go to waste
in the sport of bright iron
upon the point of harsh steel!'

As for old Väinämöinen
he uttered a word, spoke thus:
    'Mistress of Northland!

Now will you share the Sampo
on the misty headland's tip
at the foggy island's end?'

The mistress of Northland said:
'No, I'll not share the Sampo
    with you, mean one, not
    with Väinämöinen!'
She tried to get the Sampo
out of Väinämöinen's boat.
Then wanton Lemminkäinen
snatched the sword out of his belt
    wrenched the sharp iron
    from his left side; he
lunges at the eagle's feet
    and pounds the webbed toes.
Wanton Lemminkäinen struck
    he both struck and spoke:
'Down with the men, with the swords
down with the sleepy fellows—
hundreds from under a wing
dozens from a feather tip!'

At that the North's dame declared
    from the masthead spoke:
'O you wanton Loverboy
    poor Farmind, mean man!
You deceived your own mother
    lied to your parent—
said you would not go to war
    for six, ten summers
not even for need of gold
even for greed of silver!'

Steady old Väinämöinen
the everlasting wise man
    saw that it was time
knew the moment had come. He

drew his paddle from the sea
the oak sliver from the wave:
with it he bashed the woman
struck the claws off the eagle;
the other claws fell to bits
but there was one talon left.
And the boys fell from the wings
the men went splosh in the sea—
a hundred men from under a wing
and a thousand fellows from the tail.
The eagle herself plumped down
clattered upon the rib beams
like a capercaillie from a tree
a squirrel from a spruce bough.
Then she reached for the Sampo
with her ring finger: she dropped
the Sampo in the water
    felled all the bright-lid
down over the red craft's side
in the midst of the blue sea;
there the Sampo came to bits
and the bright-lid to pieces.

So some of those bits, those great
fragments of the Sampo went
below the quiet waters
    down to the black mud;
they were left for the water
treasures for Ahto-land's folk.
That's why never in this world
not in a month of Sundays
will the water go without
or its Ahto lack treasures.
    But some other bits
some smaller fragments were left
    on the blue high seas
    on the broad sea's waves
    for the wind to lull

the billows to drive;
and the wind lulled them
the sea-swell rocked them
on the blue high seas
on the broad sea's waves
and the wind nudged them to land
the billow drove them ashore.
Steady old Väinämöinen
saw the surf pushing
and the spray washing landward
the billow driving ashore
those bits of the dear Sampo
those pieces of the bright-lid.
He was delighted
and uttered a word, spoke thus:
'Out of this a seed will spring
constant good luck will begin;
from this, ploughing and sowing
from this, every kind of growth
out of this the moon to gleam
the sun of good luck to shine
on Finland's great farms
on Finland's sweet lands!'

Louhi, mistress of Northland
uttered a word and spoke thus:
'I can still think of a dodge for this
think of a dodge, spot a way
for your ploughing, your sowing
for your herds, your things growing
for your gleaming moons
for your shining suns:
I'll thrust the moon in a rock
the sun I'll hide in a cliff;
I'll let the frost bite
the chilly weather delay
your ploughing, sowing
your harvests, your corn;

I'll bring iron hail
steel hail I'll hurl down
upon your good crops
upon your best fields;
I'll raise a bear from the heath
a gap-tooth from the pine sprigs
to crush your geldings
and to kill your mares
and to fell your herds
and lay the cows low;
people I'll kill with disease
I'll slay all your kin
so that nevermore
are they heard of in the world.'

Then the old Väinämöinen
put this into words:
'No Lapp sings at me, no man
of Turja shoves me around!
God holds the heavens' mantle
the Creator the keys of good luck:
they're not under envy's arm
not at hatred's fingertip.
If I trust my Creator
and take refuge in my God
he'll keep maggots from my corn
and foes from my wealth
my corn from being grubbed up
and my growing things from being felled
my shoots from being taken
and my wealth from being hurt.
Mistress of Northland:
thrust ruin into a rock
evils press into a cliff
expel pains to a mountain—
but never the moon
not the sun ever!
Let the frost bite, let

the chilly weather
delay your own shoots
the grains you have sown!
Rain down iron hail
steel hail rattle down
upon your own tilth
upon the North's furthest fields
and raise a bear from the heath
from a thicket a fierce cat
from the wilds a hollow-hand
and from beneath a sprig a gap-tooth
for Northland's furthest lane, for
where the North's herd treads!'

Then the mistress of Northland
uttered a word and spoke thus:
'Now the power has drained from me
my authority has failed:
my property has foundered
the Sampo smashed in the waves!'
She set off homeward weeping
northward bewailing her luck.
From all the Sampo she got
nothing to speak of for home;
but she did take a little
with her ring finger:
she bore the lid to Northland
brought the handle to Sariola.
And that's why Northland is poor
life in Lapland is breadless.

Steady old Väinämöinen
when he made landfall
found bits of the dear Sampo
and pieces of the bright-lid
upon the shore of the sea
upon the fine sands; he brought
the bits of the dear Sampo

the pieces of the bright-lid
to the misty headland's tip
to the foggy island's end
    to grow, to increase
    to turn, to thicken
    into barley beer
    into loaves of rye.
At that old Väinämöinen
    put this into words:
'Grant, Creator, vouchsafe, God
grant that we may be lucky
that we may live well always
that we may die with honour
    in Finland the sweet
in Karelia the fair!
Keep us, steadfast Creator
    and guard us, fair God
    from the whims of men
    from the wiles of hags;
overturn the earth-envious
defeat the water-wizards;
be on the side of your sons
always your children's helper
always a support by night
and a protector by day
that the sun may not shine ill
that the moon may not gleam ill
that the wind may not blow ill
that the rain may not rain ill
    nor may the frost bite
    nor hard weather touch!
    Build an iron fence
construct a stronghold of stone
    round my property
on both sides of my people
from the ground up to the sky
from the sky down to the ground
for my protection alone

for my support, my refuge
that no foe may eat too much
no enemy steal the wealth
    ever in this world
not in a month of Sundays!'

44. *The Birch Kantele*

Steady old Väinämöinen
    ponders in his brain:
'Now some music would be good
and some merrymaking right
for this new state of affairs
    upon these fair farms;
but the kantele is lost
my joy has gone for ever
to the farm of the fishes
to the crags of the salmon
to the sea-trough's keepers, to
the Wave-wife's eternal folk
nor will it be brought again
nor will Ahto give it back.
    Smith Ilmarinen
you forged once, forged yesterday
    so forge today too:
    forge an iron rake
on the rake a mass of prongs—
a mass of prongs, a long shaft
with which I can rake the waves
    fluff up the billows
the sea's reed beds into cocks
all the shores into windrows
to get back the instrument
to reach for the kantele
from the haunt of the fishes
from the crags of the salmon!'

    Smith Ilmarinen
the everlasting craftsman
    forged an iron rake
with a copper shaft; he forged

prongs a hundred fathoms long
a shaft of five he prepared.
Then the old Väinämöinen
    took the iron rake
and he stepped a tiny way
went a bit of a journey
to the rollers of steel, to
    the copper moorings.
    There were craft, two craft
    two boats were ready
on the rollers of steel, at
    the copper moorings:
one craft was a new craft, the
other craft was an old craft.
The old Väinämöinen said
he uttered to the new boat:
'Off now, boat, on the waters
craft, begone on the billows
    unturned by an arm
    unheld by a thumb!'
And the boat was off on the waters
the craft gone on the billows.
Steady old Väinämöinen
    sat down at the stern;
off he went to broom the sea
    and to sweep the wave.
He gathers water lilies
he rakes rubbish on the shore
    heaped up shreds of reed—
shreds of reed, scraps of bulrush
every trough he raked as well
and all the reefs he harrowed
but did not get, could not find
his instrument of pike-bones
    joy gone for ever
    the lost kantele.
Steady old Väinämöinen
    trudges off homeward

his head down, in bad spirits
helmet all askew;
he told this in words:
'No more will be that
joy of a pike's tooth
fishbone melody!'

As he trod a glade
skirted the edge of backwoods
he heard a birch tree weeping
a curly birch shedding tears.
He went up to it
drew nearer to it
he asked it, he talked:
'Why do you weep, lovely birch
green tree, why do you go on
white-belt, why do you complain?
You'll not be taken to war
not be wanted for battle.'

The birch skilfully answered
the green tree uttered:
'Well, some people say
certain people think
that I live in joy
in delight revel;
but lean in my cares
in my longings I ring out
set forth in my suffering-days
in sorrows murmur. Empty
for my silliness I weep
for my shortcomings complain
that I am hapless, wretched
utterly woeful, helpless
in these evil spots
on these vast pastures.
The happy and the lucky
are always hoping

for a fair summer to come
a great summertime to warm
    but not silly me:
    woe is me, I dread
    having my bark stripped
my leafy twigs taken off!
    Often in my gloom
and often, a gloomy wretch
children of the fleeting spring
    come up close to me
    and with five knives slash
my sappy belly open;
evil herdsmen in summer
take my white belt—one for a
drinking-cone, one for a sheath
one for a berry basket.
    Often in my gloom
and often, a gloomy wretch
    girls stand under me
    and romp beside me
    cut off foliage
and bind twigs into bath-whisks.
    Often in my gloom
and often, a gloomy wretch
I am felled for slash-and-burn
    for firewood chopped up:
    three times this summer
    this great summertime
men have stood under me, have
    whetted their axes
to dispatch my luckless head
    to end my weak life.
So much for the summer's joy
the great summertime's delight;
but winter is no better
the snow season no sweeter:
    always early on

sorrow alters how I look
    my head weighs heavy
    and my face goes pale
    recalling black days
    thinking of bad times.
    Then the wind brings pains
    the frost saddest cares:
the wind takes off my green coat
    the frost my fair skirt.
    So I with small means
    a poor wretched birch
    am left quite naked
    utterly undressed
    to quake in the chill
    to howl in the frost.'

The old Väinämöinen said:
    'Do not weep, green tree
leafy sapling, don't go on
    white-belt, don't complain!
You'll get good luck in plenty
    a new, sweeter life;
soon you'll be weeping for joy
with delight you will echo.'

Then old Väinämöinen formed
from the birch an instrument
carved it through a summer day
hammered at a kantele
on the misty headland's tip
at the foggy island's end
carved a belly for the kantele
a soundboard for the new joy
a belly out of tough birch
a soundboard of curly birch.
The old Väinämöinen said
    he declared, spoke thus:
'Here's a belly for the kantele

a soundboard for the eternal joy;
but where shall the pegs be got
    the screws be fetched from?'

An oak grew in a barnyard
a tall tree at a yard's end;
on the oak were shapely boughs
on each bough was an acorn
on the acorn was a golden whorl
on the golden whorl was a cuckoo.
    When the cuckoo calls
    and utters five words
    gold wells from its mouth
    and silver pours forth
    on a golden knoll
    on a silver hill:
from there the kantele's pegs
the screws for the curly birch!
The old Väinämöinen said
    he uttered, spoke thus:
'I've got the kantele's pegs
the screws for the curly birch
but still something is missing:
five strings the kantele lacks.
Where should I get the strings from
for it, put on the voices?'

He went in search of a string.
    He steps through a glade:
a lassie sat in the glade
a young maiden on the marsh.
The lass was not weeping, nor
indeed was she rejoicing
but just singing to herself:
she sang to pass her evening
hoping a bridegroom would come
thinking about her lover.
Steady old Väinämöinen

yonder crept with no shoes on
without toe-rags* he tiptoed;
    then when he got there
he began to beg tresses
and he put this into words:
'Lass, give some of your tresses
    damsel, of your hair
    for kantele strings
voices of eternal joy!'

The lass gave of her tresses
    some of her fine hair;
    gave tresses five, six
    even seven hairs:
from there the kantele strings
sounders of eternal joy.
The instrument was ready:
at that old Väinämöinen
sits down upon an outcrop
on a stepping-stone; he took
the kantele in his hands
the joy closer to himself;
the head he turned heavenward
propped the shoulder on his knees
    pitches the voices
    and checks the tuning;
he got the voices pitched, his
instrument in a fit state
turned it till it was under
his hands and across his knees;
he let his ten fingernails
go, he set his five fingers
to dart about on the strings
    to leap on the notes.

Then, when old Väinämöinen
    played the kantele

with small hands, slender fingers
    thumbs curving upward
the curly birch tree uttered
the leafy sapling lilted
    the cuckoo's gold called
and the lassie's hair rejoiced.
With his fingers Väinämöinen played
with its strings the kantele rang out:
mountains thundered, boulders boomed
    all the cliffs trembled
    rocks lapped upon waves
gravels on waters floated
    the pines made merry
    stumps leapt on the heaths.
Kaleva's sisters-in-law
while they were embroidering
they ran there as a river
    all rushed as a stream—
young women with smiling lips
mistresses in merry mood
to listen to the music
marvel at the merriment.
    What men were nearby
    were all cap in hand;
    what hags were nearby
    were all hand on cheek;
daughters with tears in their eyes
    sons down on their knees
listened to the kantele
marvelled at the merriment.
    They said with one voice
    found a single tongue:
    'Never before was
    such sweet music heard
    never in this world
not in a month of Sundays!'

It is heard, the fine music
was heard in six villages

and there was no animal
that did not come to listen
    to that sweet music
the sound of the kantele;
what beasts were in the forest
    crouched on their claws to
listen to the kantele
marvel at the merriment;
the flying birds of the air
    gathered upon twigs
and all manner of fishes
    crowded on the shore;
    the very earthworms
moved to the top of the mould—
    they turned, they listened
to that sweet music, to the
kantele's eternal joy
    Väinämöinen's tune.
There the old Väinämöinen
    played finely indeed
and rang out beautifully;
he played one day, he played two
    starting only once
after one morning's breakfast
one tying on of his belt
one putting on of his shirt.
    When he played at home
    in his room of fir
    the rafters echoed
    the floorboards thudded
the loft beams sang, the doors creaked
all the windows made merry
    the hearth of stone moved
the curly-birch post chanted;
when he walked among spruces
    and roamed among pines
    the spruces bowed down
the pines on the hill turned round

the cones rolled upon the lea
the sprigs showered down on the root;
when he wandered in a grove
    or tripped in a glade
    the groves played a game
the glades were glad all the time
    the flowers had a fling
the young saplings bobbed about.

45. *Death's Daughter Gives Birth*

Louhi, mistress of Northland
    got wind of the news
that Väinö-land was thriving
Kalevala flourishing
on the Sampo bits it got
the pieces of the bright-lid.
She was very envious
    and she keeps thinking
what doom she could bring about
which death she could carry out
on those folk of Väinö-land
those Kalevala people
and she prays to the Old Man
she worships the Thunderer:
    'O Old Man, chief god
strike down Kaleva's people
    with iron hailstones
    with steel-tipped needles;
or else with disease kill them
    and slay the mean kin—
the men in the long yards, the
women upon the byre floors!'

A girl there was of Tuonela, blind
Pit-daughter, an old woman
the worst of Tuoni's daughters
wickedest of death-daughters
    the source of all ills
    a thousand downfalls;
she had a swarthy face, a
    skin of loathsome hue.
Well, that black girl of Tuoni
the sightless one of the depths

made her bed upon a road
her litter on evil land
lay with her back to the wind
her side to the rough weather
her rear to the chilly blast
and her front to the daybreak.
There came a great gust of wind
out of the east a big squall
that blew the bad one with child
wetted her till her womb swelled
    in a barren glade
upon land without hummocks.
    She bore a hard womb
a difficult bellyful;
she bore it for two, three months
a fourth and a fifth as well
    for seven, eight months
    round about nine months
and by old wives' reckoning
    half of a tenth month.

    At the ninth month's end
the beginning of the tenth
    her womb becomes hard
    presses till it hurts;
    but no birth is born
no creatures are created.
    She shifted her place
she put herself somewhere else;
    the whore went to breed
the scarlet woman to teem
in a gap between two cliffs
a chasm between five mountains;
but no, there no birth is born
no creature is created.
She sought a place to give birth

land to unload her belly
 in a moving mire
 in a spilling spring;
but there she found no place, no
unloading for her belly.
She made to bring forth her brood
made to unload her belly
in a fiery rapid's foam
a swirl of mighty water
beneath a waterfall of
three rapids, beneath nine brinks;
and yet still no birth is born
the wretch's womb will not ease.
The nightmare began to weep
and the evil freak to scream:
she does not know where to go
which way she ought to walk, to
 unload her belly
 and to breed her sons.

Out of a cloud God spoke, the
Creator declared from heaven:
'There is a shack on a swamp
 hard by the seashore
 there in dark Northland
in murky Sariola:
 go that way to breed
 and to ease your womb!
 There you are needed
and your brood is awaited.'

Well, that black girl of Tuoni
wicked lass of the Dead Land
came towards Northland's cabins
Sariola's sauna-lands
 to bring forth her brats
 to have her offspring.
Louhi, mistress of Northland

the gap-toothed hag of the North
led her to the sauna secretly
stealthily to the bath-hut
unheard by the locals, with
no word reaching the village.
She heated the sauna secretly
hurriedly she settled her;
    with beer smeared the doors
wetted the hinges with ale
so that the doors did not creak
    nor the hinges squeal.

Then she put this into words
    she declared, spoke thus:
    'O dame, nature's girl
woman of gold, handsome one
who are the eldest of wives
    the first of matrons:
run knee-deep into the sea
up to your belt in the wave
    take a ruff's slaver
    slime from a burbot
    to smear between bones
    to stroke along sides
free a wench from a tight spot
a woman from belly-throes
    from this harsh pain, this
difficult belly-labour!

'Should not enough come of that
    O Old Man, chief god
come here when you are needed
go this way when you are called!
Here's a wench in a tight spot
a woman in belly-throes
amid smoke in the sauna
    the village bath-hut.
    Take up a golden

club in your right hand:
with it shatter bars
and break the doorposts
dislodge the Creator's locks
and snap off the inner bolts
for the great to go, the small
to go, the puny to pass!'

There that abomination
the sightless girl of Tuoni
unloaded her belly, brought
forth her hateful brats
beneath a copper-bright cloak
a fine-woven bed curtain:
she produced nine sons
in one summer night
with one stir of steam
one heating of the sauna
from one belly-brood
from one hard wombful.
And she named her sons
got her brats ready
as anyone would her young,
creatures she has hatched herself:
this one she stuck to be stitch
that one called to be colic
this she goaded to be gout
that to be rickets she raised
this bullied to be a boil
that screwed up to be a scab
this to be cancer she kicked
that she punched to be the plague.
One was left unnamed, the son
down at the litter's bottom:
him she bade yonder
thrust to be water-wizards
witches in the marshy depths
and the envious everywhere.

Louhi, mistress of Northland
bade the others go yonder
to the misty headland's tip
to the foggy island's end;
she inflamed the cross creatures
thrust the wayward diseases
against Väinö-land's folk, to
    slay Kaleva's kin.
And Väinö-land's sons sicken
Kaleva's people languish
with the wayward diseases
    whose names are unknown:
    beneath them floors rot
above the cover decays.

Then the old Väinämöinen
the everlasting wise man
    went to free their heads
    to ransom their lives
went forth to war with Tuoni
and to battle with disease:
he got the sauna heated
    and the stones steaming
    with wood that was clean
with faggots brought by water;
he took water in hiding
he brought bath-whisks underhand
he warmed the ready bath-whisks
the hundred-leaved he softened;
then he stirred up mead-sweet steam
honey-sweet steam he wafted
    up through the hot stones
    the burning boulders.
    He says with this word
    he spoke with this speech:
'Come now into the steam, God

sky-father, into the warm
    to bring about health
    and to make for peace;
wipe away the holy sparks
and the holy ills put out
    beat down wicked steam
    bad steam send away
so it will not scald your sons
    spoil those you have made!
    What water I fling
    upon these hot stones
may it change into honey
    trickle into mead;
may a honeyed river run
    a pool of mead splash
    up through the stone hearth
up through the mossy sauna!
We'll not be eaten without
cause, nor killed without disease
unless the great Creator
allows, unless God slays us.
Who would eat us without cause
into his mouth his own words
on his head his evil plans
and his thoughts back on himself!
If I am not man enough
nor fellow enough the Old Man's son
to take away jinxes, to
    free us from seizures
then the Old Man himself is—
    he who keeps the clouds
dwells in a fair-weather cloud
governs among the vapours.
    O Old Man, chief god
    god above the clouds
come here when you are needed
make your way when you are asked
    to feel out these pains

to oust these days of trouble
to take away these jinxes
and to relieve these attacks;
    bring me a fiery
sword, a sparkling brand bear me
with which I will hold off ills
set the wicked for ever
the pains along the wind's roads
aches into wide open glades!
    Yonder I drive aches
    yonder banish pains—
    into stone cellars
    into iron cairns
    to make the rocks ache
to make the boulders suffer:
    no rock weeps for aches
no boulder complains of woes
though much were put upon it
any amount dumped on it.

    'Ache-girl, Tuoni's maid
sitting upon the ache-rock
    where three rivers run
    where three waters part
    grinding the ache-quern
    making Mount Ache turn:
go and gather up the aches
in the jaws of the blue rock
or roll them in the water
hurl them into the sea's deep
where the wind will not find them
nor the sun shine upon them!

'Should not enough come of that
Ache-daughter, kindly mistress
Injury-daughter, choice wife
come along, go together
    to bring about health

and to make for peace;
make the aches acheless
the injuries untrembling
that the sick may get some sleep
the ill some rest free from care
the one in pain an hour's pause
the one hurt some exercise;
take the aches in a casket
the woes in a copper box
to carry the aches yonder
to lead the injuries tame
to the middle of Ache Hill
the peak of Mount Ache
and there cook the aches
in a tiny pan
in which one finger will go
and a thumb will fit!
There's a rock on the hillside
a hole in the rock
that has been drilled with a drill
pierced with a borer:
there the aches will be dragged off
the bad injuries confined
and the harsh pains will be thrust
and the days of suffering pressed
so that they can try nothing
by night, nor get out by day.'

At that old Väinämöinen
the everlasting wise man
went on to anoint the hurts
and to treat those injuries
with the nine ointments
the eight remedies;
he says with this word
he spoke with this speech:
'O Old Man, chief god
heavenly ancient

rear a cloud out of the east
raise a bank from the north-west
and from the west send a wisp:
rain honey, rain down water
to be ointments for the aches
treatments for the injuries!
I can do nothing if my
Creator will not allow:
may the Creator give help
    and may God bring help
to one I've seen with my eyes
to one I've laid my hands on
one I've talked to with sweet lips
one I've breathed on with my breath!
And where my hands are not laid
may the hands of God be laid;
where my fingers don't avail
may the Lord's fingers avail:
the Lord's are fairer fingers
the Creator's palms nimble.
Come now, Creator, to sing
charms, O God, to recite spells,
Almighty, to look after:
    make healthy by night
and hearty by day, so that
no pain will be felt above
no ache will ache in the midst
nor suffering weigh on the heart—
not even a tiny, not
    even a slight woe
    ever in this world
not in a month of Sundays!'

Steady old Väinämöinen
the everlasting wise man
with that took away jinxes
    and relieved attacks;
    he removed curses

he healed victims of ill-will
he freed the people from death
Kaleva's from being lost.

46. *The Bear*

The news reached Northland
the knowledge the cold village
that Väinö-land had pulled through
that Kalevala was free
from those hurts that had been raised
from those wayward diseases.
Louhi, mistress of Northland
the gap-toothed hag of the North
 she took that badly;
she uttered a word, spoke thus:
'I can still think of another way
I know yet a different road:
I'll raise a bear* from the heath
from the wilds a hollow-hand
against Väinö-land's livestock
the herd of Kalevala.'

She raised a bear from the heath
a bruin from the harsh lands
for those glades of Väinö-land
herd-lands of Kalevala.
Steady old Väinämöinen
 put this into words:
'Brother, smith Ilmarinen
 forge me a new spear
forge a spear of three edges
 with a copper shaft!
There's a Beast to be taken
a precious-pelt to be felled—
stopped from crushing my geldings
 going for my mares
 from felling my herd
 laying the cows low.'

And the smith forges a spear;
not a long nor a short one—
he forged one of middling sort:
a wolf stood upon its edge
a bruin where the blade was
an elk skied around the joint
a foal wandered on the shaft
a reindeer kicked on the handle's tip.

Then there was a fresh snowfall:
    somewhat fine flakes fell—
    an autumn ewe's worth
    worth a winter hare.
The old Väinämöinen said
    he uttered, spoke thus:
    'I have a good mind—
a mind to range Forestland
to visit the forest girls
the yards of the blue wenches.
I go from men forestward
from fellows to outdoor work:
take me, forest, for one of your men
for one of your fellows, Tapio;
    help me to have luck
to fell the forest's fair one!
Mielikki, forest mistress
Tellervo, Tapio's wife
    tie your dog up tight
    and put up your cur
in a honeysuckle lane
    in an oaken frame!

'Beast, apple of the forest
    chunky honey-paw
when you hear me coming, a
    real man stepping
tie your claws up in your fur
    your teeth in your gums

so that they never touch me
    when you make a lunge!
My Beastie, my matchless one
honey-paw, my handsome one
slump down upon a hummock
    upon a fair rock
with pines swaying overhead
spruces rustling overhead:
there, Beast, circle round and round
honey-paw, turn round and round
like the grouse upon its nest
    the goose on its brood!'

There the old Väinämöinen
    heard the dog barking
the pup holding forth out loud
the beady-eye in the yard
the smooth-snout in the barnyard.
He uttered a word, spoke thus:
'I thought it was the cuckoo
calling, the love-bird singing;
but it was not the cuckoo
calling, the love-bird singing:
here's my most splendid dog, my
most excellent animal
at the Beastie's cabin door
and in the fair man's farmyard!'

Steady old Väinämöinen
    there killed the Beastie;
the lawn beds he laid low, the
golden places overturned.
    He says with this word
    he spoke with this speech:
    'Be thanked, God, be praised
alone, Creator, that you
gave the Beast for my portion
the backwoods' gold for my catch!'

He looks at his golden one;
he uttered a word, spoke thus:
'My Beastie, my matchless one
honey-paw, my handsome one
don't be angry without cause!
It was not I that felled you:
you rolled off the collar-bow
yourself, toppled off the log
tearing your wooden breeches
    splitting your pine coat.
Autumn weather's slippery
and the cloudy days are dark:
golden forest cuckoo, fair
one with fur luxuriant
    leave your home cold now
the land where you live empty
    your home of birch boughs
your abode of basket twigs;
go, famous one, on your way
pride of the forest, step out
get moving, nimble of shoe
blue of stocking, on tiptoe
    from these little yards
    these narrow alleys
to be among the fellows
to be in a crowd of men!
No one there is ill treated
nor made to live like a wretch:
    mead is fed there, fresh
honey is given to drink
    to the guest who comes
to the would-be visitor.
Go now from here after all
from this little den, and go
under the famous roof beam
    under the fair roof;
float upon the snow, like

water lily on a pool
    flit upon a sprig
like a squirrel on a bough!'

Then the old Väinämöinen
the everlasting singer
stepped through glades making music
    on heaths echoing
    with his famous guest
his shaggy bundle, until
the music was heard indoors
under the roofs the echo.
The folk in the cabin spoke
and the fair people lilted:
'Listen to that noise, the words
of the player in the woods
the prattle of the crossbill
the forest wench's whistling!'

Steady old Väinämöinen
    made it to the yard.
The folk indoors blurted out
    the fair people talked:
'Is the golden one walking
the silver one wandering
the precious dear stepping, the
pennyworth picking his way?
Has the forest given Honeyman
the master of the backwoods
the lynx, that you come singing
    ski along humming?'

Steady old Väinämöinen
at that put this into words:
    'For words the otter
has been got, for tales God's wealth:
that is why we come singing
    ski along humming.

But 'tis no otter at all
not an otter nor a lynx:
'tis the famous one walking
the pride of the woods stepping
the ancient man wandering
the broadcloth-coated strolling.
If our guest is allowed in
    fling the doors open
but if the guest is hated
    slam them firmly shut!'

    The folk answering
say, the fair people lilted:
    'Hail, Beast, and welcome
    honey-paw, arrived
    in these well-washed yards
    in these fair farmyards!
This I've hoped for all my days
looked for all my growing-time—
that Tapio's trump would sound
that the forest's pipe would shrill
that the forest's gold would walk
that the woods' silver would come
    to these little yards
    these narrow alleys.
I've hoped as for a good year
looked as for summer's coming
just as a ski for new snow
a left ski for smooth going
a maid for a young bridegroom
one with red cheeks for a mate.
Evenings I sat at windows
mornings upon the shed steps
    at the gates for weeks
for months at the lanes' entrance
whole winters in the barnyards;
I stood till the snows gave way

to ground, the ground to soft soils
  soft soils to gravels
  gravels to fine sands
  fine sands till they bloomed.
I wondered mornings on end
whole days I puzzled my head
where the Beast so long lingered
the backwoods' dear one tarried:
had he strolled to Estonia
and trotted out of Finland?'

At that old Väinämöinen
  put this into words:
'Which way shall I lead my guest
  convey my darling;
shall I set him in the barn
put him in the litter-house?'

  The folk answering
say, the fair people lilted:
'Yonder you shall lead our guest
  convey our darling—
under the famous roof beam
  under the fair roof.
There foods have been made ready
and drinking vessels laid out
  and all the boards wiped
  and swept all the floors;
  all the women are
  dressed up in clean clothes
  in handsome headgear
  and in white dresses.'

At that old Väinämöinen
  uttered and spoke thus:
'My Beastie, my little bird
honey-paw, my little lump
there's still land for you to walk

heath for you to clamber on:
go now, darling, on your way
    dear one, tread the land
black of stocking, take a trip
broadcloth-breeches, take a stroll
down the paths of the tomtit
in the haunts of the sparrow
    under five rafters
    under six roof beams!

    'Beware, wretched wives
    lest your herd should scare
    your little wealth shy
the mistress's wealth be hurt
    as the Beast arrives
    Whiskers thrusts his way!
Boys, get out of the doorway
wenches, go from the doorposts
as the fellow comes indoors
the real man steps inside!

'Forest Beastie, apple, fair
chunky one of the forest
    don't fear the wenches
don't be scared of the braid-heads
and don't beware of the wives
don't grieve for wrinkled stockings!
    What hags are indoors
are all in the inglenook
    as the man comes in
as the big boy steps inside!'

The old Väinämöinen said:
    'Welcome here too, God
under the famous roof beam
    under the fair roof!—
Where shall I leave my charmer
put down my shaggy bundle?'

And the folk answering say:
    'Hail, hail and welcome!
Lay your little bird down here
    convey your darling
    to the pine bench end
    the iron seat's tip
for his coat to be fingered
for his fur to be looked at!

'Don't worry, Beast, about that
    and don't take it ill
if the hour of the coat comes
the looking-time of the fur!
Your coat won't be spoilt, your fur
won't be looked out to become
flounces for the flighty, clothes
    for the woebegone.'

Then the old Väinämöinen
had the Beast's coat taken off
put it up in the shed loft;
he laid the meat in a pan
    a gilded copper
in a copper-bottomed pot.
Now the pots were on the fire
the copper-brims on the flame;
    they were crammed, filled with
    lots of bits of meat.
Lumps of salt had been thrown in:
they'd been brought from further off—
the salt got from Germany
the White Sea of Archangel
    rowed through the Salt Straits
    let down off a ship.
    When the stew was stewed
and the pans got off the fire
    the catch was carried
    the crossbill conveyed

to the long deal table's head
    to golden dishes
    for a sip of mead
    for a draught of beer.
Of pine the table was made
and the bowls cast in copper
    the spoons in silver
    the knives wrought in gold;
the cups were all brimming, the
    bowls to the bulwarks
with the forest's pleasant gifts
with the dear backwoods' catches.

At that old Väinämöinen
    put this into words:
'Golden-breasted old mound-man
master of Tapio's house
Forestland's honey-sweet wife
the forest's kindly mistress
clear-skinned man, Tapio's son
clear-skinned man in the red cap
Tellervo, Tapio's maid
Tapio's other folk too:
come to your ox's wedding
to the feast of your long-wool!
Now there is enough ready—
enough to eat and to drink
enough to keep for yourselves
enough to give the village.'

Thereupon the folk speak thus
and the fair people lilted:
    'Where was the Beast born
where did the precious-pelt grow;
was he born on straw, or did he grow
in the sauna inglenook?'

Then the old Väinämöinen
    put this into words:

'The Beast is not born on straw
    nor upon kiln chaff:
there the Beast was given birth
the honey-paw was turned round—
in the moon, in the sun's cleft
upon the Great Bear's shoulders
where the air's lasses live, where
    nature's daughters are.
A lass stepped at the sky's rim
and a maid at heaven's pole
walked along a cloud's circle
and along heaven's border
in stockings that were bluish
    in bright well-heeled shoes
a box of wool in her hand
a sewing-basket under her arm.
She flung wool on the waters
dropped a thread upon the waves
    and the wind lulled it
the wanton air wafted it
    the sea breeze swung it
the billow drove it ashore
to the mead-sweet backwoods' shore
a honey-sweet headland's tip.

'Mielikki, forest mistress
Tapiola's careful wife
grabbed the bunch from the waters
and the fine wool from the waves
and then she laid it swiftly
swaddled it beautifully
in a basket of maple
    in a fair cradle;
she had the swaddle-cords raised
the chains of gold she conveyed
    to the lushest bough
to the widest leafy twig

and she lulled the one she knew
    rocked her beloved
beneath a shock-headed spruce
beneath a bushy pine tree:
there she brought forth the Beastie
brought up him of noble pelt
beside a mead-sweet thicket
inside honey-sweet backwoods.
The Beast grew beautifully
came up to be most graceful—
short his leg, buckled his knee
    a chubby smooth-snout
his head wide and his nose snub
his fur fair, luxuriant;
but as yet he had no teeth
nor had his claws been fashioned.

'Mielikki, forest mistress
    put this into words:
"I would fashion claws for him
    teeth too I would fetch
if he were to do no harm
and get up to no mischief."
So the Beast swore an oath at
the forest mistress's knees
before the God known to all
beneath the Almighty's face
that he would work no mischief
undertake no ugly deeds.
Mielikki, forest mistress
Tapiola's careful wife
went off in search of a tooth
    and to ask for claws
    from sturdy rowans
    from tough junipers
    from knotty tree roots
    from hard tarry stumps;

but from there she got no claw
neither did she find a tooth.

'A fir tree grew on the heath
a spruce on a mound came up
on the fir a silver bough
a golden bough on the spruce:
the girl took them with her hands
    from them fashioned claws
and fixed them in the jawbone
    in the gums set them.
Then she let her lazybones
    go, sent her pet out;
she put him to rove a swamp
to beat his way through thicket
to step along a glade side
to clamber upon the heath.
She told him to walk nicely
    to trot prettily
    to live merry times
to spend the days famously
on open swamps, amid lands
on the furthest playing-heaths
to walk shoeless in summer
    in autumn sockless;
through the worse seasons to dwell
to endure the winter chills
in a bird cherry cabin
skirted by a pine stronghold
at the foot of a fine spruce
under a juniper's arm
    beneath five woollen
    cloaks, beneath eight capes.
That's where I have got my catch
and brought this prey of mine from.'

    The young folk speak thus
    the old folk utter:

'What action pleased the forest—
pleased the forest, charmed the wilds
delighted the woods' master
and bent matchless Tapio
that he gave his peerless one
and dispatched his Honeyman:
was it a spear's finding, or
    an arrow's fetching?'

Steady old Väinämöinen
    put this into words:
'We greatly pleased the forest—
pleased the forest, charmed the wilds
delighted the woods' master
and bent matchless Tapio.
Mielikki, forest mistress
Tellervo, Tapio's maid
the forest maid fair of face
the forest wench so tiny
    went pointing the path
    and blazing the trail
marking the sides of the path
and teaching the way: she carved
notches all along the trees
blazed a trail upon the slopes
to the noble Beastie's doors
to the money-island's shores.
    Then, when I got there
    when I reached my goal
there was no spear's finding, no
aimed shot striking home: he rolled
off the collar-bow himself
    toppled off the log;
the brushwood broke his breastbone
the twigs shattered his belly.'

Then he put this into words
    he declared, spoke thus:

'My Beastie, my matchless one
my little bird, my sweet pet:
take off now, here, your head-dress
    splice up your snappers
    cast out your few teeth
    shut up your wide jaws
    and don't take badly
whatever occurs to us—
    bone-crunch, head-crack, loud
    clattering of teeth!
    I take the Beast's nose
    to help my own nose;
but I don't take to leave him
bereft, or me with but one.
    I take the Beast's ear
    to help my own ear;
but I don't take to leave him
bereft, or me with but one.
    I take the Beast's eye
    to help my own eye;
but I don't take to leave him
bereft, or me with but one.
    I take the Beast's brow
    to help my own brow;
but I don't take to leave him
bereft, or me with but one.
    I take the Beast's snout
    to help my own snout;
but I don't take to leave him
bereft, or me with but one.
    I take the Beast's tongue
    to help my own tongue;
but I don't take to leave him
bereft, or me with but one.
Now I would call him a man
I'd reckon him a fellow
who could count up the chompers
    get the row of teeth

out of the steel jaw
with his iron fists.'

But no other came at all
there was not such a fellow.
He counts the chompers himself
tells the row of teeth
below his kneebones
his fists of iron.
He took the teeth of the Beast;
he uttered a word, spoke thus:
'Forest Beastie, apple, fair
chunky one of the forest
now there's a journey for you
to make, and a trip to take
from this little den
this lowly abode
to a higher home
a vaster dwelling:
go now, darling, on your way
precious dear, treading
beside the pigs' paths
across piglets' tracks
up the scrubby hill
to the high mountain
to a bushy pine
a fir with a hundred sprigs!
'Tis good for you to be there
sweet for you to tarry there
within earshot of a bell
where cowbells tinkle.'

Steady old Väinämöinen
now came home from there.
The young folk speak thus
and the fair folk talked:
'Where have you carried your catch
which way have you brought your prey:

have you left him on the ice
    or drowned him in slush
or smothered him in a swamp
or buried him in the heath?'

Steady old Väinämöinen
uttered a word and spoke thus:
'I've not left him on the ice
    or drowned him in slush:
there the dogs would disturb him
the wicked birds would hide him;
nor smothered him in a swamp
or buried him in the heath:
there the maggots would spoil him
and the black ants would eat him.
Yonder I've carried my catch
I have brought my little prey—
to the golden knoll's peak, to
the copper ridge's shoulders;
I've put him on a clean tree
a fir with a hundred sprigs
    on the lushest bough
on the widest leafy twig
    to gladden mankind
and to honour those who pass.
I've put him with gums eastward
placed him with eyes north-westward.
    Nor right at the top:
had I placed him at the top
there the wind would spoil him, the
    gale would do him wrong;
nor yet put him on the ground:
had I put him on the ground
the pigs there would disturb him
the low-snouts would root for him.'

Then the old Väinämöinen
    burst into song, to

honour the famous evening
to gladden the closing day;
the old Väinämöinen said
    he declared, spoke thus:
    'Hold your flame now, splint
so that I may see to sing!
    The hour comes to sing
and my mouth longs to ring out.'
And there he both sang and played
made merry all evening long;
he declared at his song's end
    uttered finally:
    'Grant again, O God
next time, steadfast Creator
that this may be thus enjoyed
    may be done again—
this, the buxom boy's wedding
and the feast of the long-wool!
    Grant always, O God
and again, true Creator
    that trails may be blazed
    that trees may be notched
    among the fellows
    in a crowd of men;
    grant always, O God
and again, true Creator
that Tapio's trump may sound
that the forest's pipe may shrill
    in these little yards
    these narrow farmyards!
Days I'd give up to music
evenings to merrymaking
    on these lands, mainlands
    on Finland's great farms
among the youngsters rising
among the people growing.'

47. *Fire from Heaven*

Steady old Väinämöinen
    played the kantele
    long, both played and sang
rejoiced in other ways too.
The music rang in the moon's cabins
the joy at the sun's windows:
the moon comes from its cabin
stepped on to a birch's crook
and the sun emerged from its stronghold
squatted on top of a pine
to hear the kantele, to
marvel at the merriment.

Louhi, mistress of Northland
the gap-toothed hag of the North
then lays hold of the sun, caught
    the moon with her hands
the moon from the birch's crook
and the sun from the pine's top
    and she brought them straight
    home to dark Northland.
She hid the moon from gleaming
within a bright-breasted rock
she sang the sun from shining
into a mountain of steel
    and there she spoke thus:
'Don't get out of here alone
    don't rise, moon, to gleam
and don't get out, sun, to shine
unless I go and let you
out, come and raise you myself
    with nine stallions borne
    by a single mare!'

—

When she had conveyed the moon
    and had brought the sun
into Northland's rocky hill
into the cliff of iron
    she stole the flame, the
fire from Väinö-land's cabins
and the cabins lost their fire
    and the rooms their flame;
    and now it was night
perpetual, long, pitch dark night
    in Kalevala
those cabins of Väinö-land
and yonder in heaven, where
the Old Man of the sky sits.
It is hard to be fireless
and great woe to be flameless—
tiresome for mankind, tiresome
even for the Old Man too.

    That Old Man, chief god
he, the sky's great creator
began at that to feel strange;
    he thinks, considers
what wonder blocks out the moon
what fog is in the sun's way
that the moon gleams not at all
and the sun shines not at all.
He stepped along a cloud's rim
and along heaven's border
in stockings that were bluish
    in bright well-heeled shoes;
he went in search of the moon
and to catch the sun, but he
cannot find the moon at all
cannot catch the sun at all.

He struck fire, the sky's Old Man
    and he flashed forth flame

with a sword of fiery blade
    with a sparkling brand;
struck fire on his fingernail
made it crackle on his limb
    in heaven on high
level with the firmament.
Yes, he got fire by striking
and he hides the spark of fire
    in a golden purse
    in a silver case
and he had a maid lull it
a lass of the air wag it
    to form a new moon
    to start a new sun.
The maid on a long cloud's top
the lass upon the sky's brink
    she lulled that fire, she
    wagged that little flame
    in a gold cradle
    in a silver sling:
    the silver beams sagged
and the gold cradle jingled
the clouds squirmed, the heavens mewed
the lids of heaven tilted
    as the fire was lulled
as the little flame was wagged.
    The lass lulled the fire
    wagged the little flame
trimmed the fire with her fingers
cherished the flame with her hands;
but the silly girl dropped the
fire, the careless girl the flame
from her hands, the one who turned
from her fingers, she who trimmed.
Heaven was split into holes
the sky all into windows:
the spark of fire broke away
    the red tine whizzed off—

down through the heavens it spilled
and pierced the clouds flickering
  through the nine heavens
  clove the six bright lids.

The old Väinämöinen said:
'Brother, smith Ilmarinen
  let us go and look
  let's get there and learn
what that fire is which has come
that strange flame which has tumbled
out of the heavens above
  down to mother earth—
whether it is the moon's ring
  or else the sun's disc!'

And off the two fellows went;
  they stepped, considered
  how they might get there
  and which way might reach
the spots where the fire shifted
the lands where the flame poured down.
They came upon a river
like a sea to reckon with
and there old Väinämöinen
began to carve at a boat
to tap out one in the wilds;
next the smith Ilmarinen
  made paddles of spruce
  solid rods of pine.

The little boat was finished
with its rowlocks, with its oars;
  so they launched the boat.
They row along, speed along
  round Neva's river
and they skirt Neva's headland.
Air-daughter the lovely lass

eldest of nature's daughters
    she comes to meet them
    chattering, talking:
'What manner of men are you
    and what are you called?'

The old Väinämöinen said:
    'We are mariners;
I am old Väinämöinen
he's the smith Ilmarinen.
But say who your own kin are
    and what you are called!'

The wife put this into words:
'I am the eldest of wives
eldest of the air's lasses
    the first of matrons
who has five wives' finery
    the face of six brides.
Which way are you going, men
where are you off to, fellows?'

The old Väinämöinen said
    he uttered, spoke thus:
    'Our fire has gone out
    our flame has died down.
Long we have been without fire
    hidden in darkness:
now we have a mind to go
and find out about the fire
    which has come from heaven
    fallen off the clouds.'

The wife put this into words
    she declared, spoke thus:
'Fire's harsh to find out about
so is flame to ask about:
    the fire has done deeds

and the flame has wrought damage!
    The spark of fire flared
the red ball fell from the halls
the Creator created
and the sky's Old Man beat out—
    fell through level heaven
    cleaving that clear sky
piercing the mucky smoke-hole
    past the dry roof beam
    to Thor's new cabin
the Worshipful's boundless one.
    Then, when it got there
    to Thor's new cabin
it set about evil work
it started on dirty work—
broke the breasts of the daughters
fingered the maidens' nipples
    it spoilt the son's knees
singed the master's beard. There was
a mother suckling her child
in a woebegone cradle:
when it got to it the fire
    now did the worst job—
burnt the child in the cradle
and burnt the mother's bosom.
    The child went to Death
yes, the boy to Tuonela
who'd been born only to die
looked after but to be lost
in the pain of fire the red
in the hardship of white flame.*
The mother knew better, she
    did not go to Death:
she knew how to banish fire
    and how to tame flame
through a little needle-eye
    cleaving an axe-poll

piercing a hot ice-pick's slot
    along a field edge.'

Steady old Väinämöinen
    he hastened to ask:
'Where did the fires go from there
    where did the sparks dash
    after Thor's field edge—
to the forest or to sea?'

The woman answering says
    she uttered, spoke thus:
    'When from there the fire
    went and the flame whirled
at first it burnt many lands—
many lands and many swamps;
finally it plunged in the water
in the billows of Lake Alue:
    this nearly caught fire
    and as sparks glistened.
Three times in a summer night
nine times in an autumn night
it foamed high as the spruces
    roared up to the brims
in the hands of that harsh fire
in the force of that hot flame;
it foamed and stranded its fish
    on ledges its perch.
    At that the fish look
    the perch consider
how to be, which way to live
and the perch wept for its sheds
the fish for their little farms
the ruff for its rock stronghold.
    A crook-necked perch went
and reached for the tine of fire
but the perch did not get it.
So a bluish whitefish went:

it swallowed the tine of fire
    it gulped the flame down.
Now Lake Alue turned back
to water, came off its brim
to where it had been before
    in one summer night.

    'A little time passed:
pain came to the swallower
and hardship to the gulper
suffering to the big eater.
It swam about, swashed about;
it swam one day, it swam two
beside the whitefish islands
in between the salmon crags
past a thousand headlands' tips
below a hundred islands.
Every headland gave advice
every island brought the news:
"In the quiet water, in
anguished Alue there's none
to swallow the wretched fish
    to lose the mean one
    in these pains of fire
    in these woes of flame."

    'So a pale trout heard
swallowed that bluish whitefish.
    A little time passed:
pain came to the swallower
and hardship to the gulper
suffering to the big eater.
It swam about, swashed about;
it swam one day, it swam two
in between the salmon crags
    among the pike's farms
past a thousand headlands' tips
below a hundred islands.

Every headland gave advice
every island brought the news:
"In the quiet water, in
anguished Alue there's none
to gobble the wretched fish
 to lose the mean one
in the pains of burning fire
 in the woes of flame."

 'A grizzled pike came
 swallowed that pale trout.
 A little time passed:
pain came to the swallower
and hardship to the gulper
suffering to the big eater.
It swam about, swashed about;
it swam one day, it swam two
 betwixt the gull-crags
past the sea-mew's rocky reefs
past a thousand headlands' tips
below a hundred islands.
Every headland gave advice
every island brought the news:
"In the quiet water, in
anguished Alue there's none
to swallow the wretched fish
 to lose the mean one
in the pains of burning fire
 in the woes of flame."'

Steady old Väinämöinen
next the smith Ilmarinen
 weave a seine of bast
click up one of juniper
dyed it with willow waters
with goat willow bark made it.
Steady old Väinämöinen
put the women to the seine:

the women went to the seine
and the sisters to lug it.
    They row and they glide
by headland and by island
    betwixt salmon crags
and beside whitefish islands
    to a brown reed-bed
a bed of fair bulrushes:
    they try and they trap
    they pull and they ply
they cast the seine upside down
    they pull it in wrong
and they do not catch the fish
    which they vie to trap.
    The brothers launched out
the husbands go to the seine:
    they coax and they cast
    they pull and they pitch
    at bay mouths, crag tops
at Kaleva's rocky reefs;
but they do not catch that fish—
    the one they needed.
The grizzled pike would not come
from the bay's quiet waters
    nor from the great main:
fishes are small, meshes few.

Now at that the fish complained;
a pike says to the pike-folk
a whitefish asked an ide, a
salmon another salmon:
'Have they died, the famous men
have Kaleva's sons been lost—
knitters of the hempen seine
makers of the net of yarn
wielders of the great beater
workers of the long handle?'

The old Väinämöinen heard
and he put this into words:
'No, the fellows have not died
Kaleva's people fallen:
one has died, two have been born
who have better beaters, who
have handles a span longer
and seines twice more terrible.'

48. *Fishing for Fire*

Steady old Väinämöinen
the everlasting wise man
from that comes to the idea
    arrives at the thought
of weaving a seine of hemp
making up a hundred-mesh;
now he put this into words
    he declared, spoke thus:
'Is there a sower of hemp
    one who sows, who ploughs
for me to prepare a net
and to get a hundred-mesh
one to kill the wretched fish
    to lose the mean one?'

    A bit of land is
    found, a spot not scorched
on the largest open swamp
    between two tree stumps;
a stump root is dug out, there
    a hemp seed was found
in Tuoni's maggot's hideout
    in the earthworm's hoard.
There was a heap of cinders
and a pile of dry ashes
where a craft of wood had burnt
    a boat had smouldered;
    there the hemp was sown
and into the dust was ploughed
upon Alue lakeshore
    in a clayey field:
there and then a shoot arose
    flax sprouted immense

and enormous hemp came up
    in one summer night.
    By night the hemp was
sown, by moonlight it was ploughed
    it was cleaned, swingled
    was pulled up, rippled
    sharply it was wrenched
    smartly it was dressed;
    the hemp was retted
and soon the retting was done
and swiftly it was hung up
and hurriedly it was dried;
    it was brought straight home
    and soon it was hulled;
    briskly it was braked
    nimbly it was scutched
    keenly it was combed
    at dusk it was brushed
    straight away bunched up
more swiftly on a distaff
    in one summer night
    in between two days.
    The sisters spin it
the sisters-in-law thread it
the brothers weave it into a net
the fathers-in-law put it on ropes;
and then how the needle turned
    the drawknife returned
as the seine was got ready
and the toils of yarn prepared
    in one summer night—
    even half of that!

Well, the seine was got ready
and the toils of yarn prepared
its bag a hundred fathoms
and its wings seven hundred;

they gave it sinkers sweetly
    and floats fittingly.
The youngsters go to the seine
and the old at home wonder:
    will they really catch
    what they want to trap?
    They pull and they pitch
    they trap, they travail
they pull along the water
they coax across the water:
    they catch a few fish—
    some ruff, mere tiddlers
    some perch, bony ones
    some roach, bitter ones;
but they did not catch that fish
    the seine was made for.
The old Väinämöinen said:
    'Smith Ilmarinen
let us go yonder ourselves
    and launch with the nets!'

And off the two fellows went
    took their nets and launched;
    one seine-wing was slung
to an island on the main
and the other wing was slung
to a meadow jutting out
and the warp was made fast to
    old Väinö's moorings.
    They coax and they cast
    they pull and they pitch:
    they catch fish enough—
    some bass and some perch
    gillaroo, sewin
    some bream, some salmon
    all manner of fish;
but they do not catch that fish
    the seine was made for

and the toils of yarn prepared.
Then the old Väinämöinen
    added more nets; he
lengthened the wings at the side
    five hundred fathoms
and the rope seven hundred.
He uttered a word, spoke thus:
'Let's take the nets to the deep
    bring them further out
let's drag the water again—
yes, make yet another draught!'

They took the nets to the deep
    brought them further out;
they dragged the water again—
yes, made yet another draught.
There the old Väinämöinen
    put this into words:
'O Wave-wife, water mistress
water dame of reedy breast
    come and change your shirt
    and exchange your dress!
You have a shirt of reeds, a
    cloak of sea foam on—
the work of the wind's daughter
the gift of Billow-daughter:
I'll give you a shirt of hemp
put on you one all of lawn—
one woven by Moon-daughter
    spun by Sun-daughter.

'Ahto, billow-master, you
who govern a hundred troughs
take a shoot five fathoms tall
seize a seven-fathom pole
    to punt the main with
    stir up the sea bed

raise bony rubbish
drive a shoal of fish
towards this seine's warps and where
the hundred-float is let down
out of the fish-haunts
the salmon-crannies
from the main's great heart
from its gloomy depths
from where no sun shines
from where no sand scrapes!'

A tiny man rose out of the sea
a fellow came up from the billows;
he stands upon the high seas.
Then he put this into words:
'Is there need of one to beat
someone to wield a big stick?'*

Steady old Väinämöinen
put this into words:
'Yes, there's need of one to beat
someone to wield a big stick.'

The small man, puny fellow
yanked a fir tree from the shore
for a big stick a tall pine
fixed a boulder to beat with;
he asks and he speaks:
'Shall I beat with all my strength
properly with might and main
or beat as the tools allow?'

Old Väinämöinen shrewdly
uttered a word and spoke thus:
'You beat as the tools allow:
that will be beating enough.'

The small man, puny fellow
    at that now bashes
and beats as the tools allow;
and he drove a lot of fish
towards that seine's warps and where
the hundred-float was let down.
The smith holds fast with the oars;
steady old Väinämöinen
his job is to raise the seine
    jerk the toils of yarn
and old Väinämöinen said:
'Now there is a shoal of fish
within this seine's warps and where
the hundred-float is let down.'

    Then they raise the seine
they unload it, shake it out
into Väinämöinen's boat
and they catch the shoal of fish
    the seine was made for
and the toils of yarn prepared.
Steady old Väinämöinen
    sped the boat landward
and put in at a blue quay
at the end of a red stair;
he swept out the shoal of fish
he shed the bony rubbish
got from it the grizzled pike—
    the one long trapped for.
Then the old Väinämöinen
    thereupon he thinks:
    'Dare I handle it
without gauntlets of iron
    or mittens of stone
    or mitts of copper?'

    Now, the sun's son heard
and uttered a word, spoke thus:

'Were it me, I'd split the pike
I'd risk laying hands on it
had I my father's dirk, my
    honoured parent's knife.'

A knife spun out of the sky
from the clouds a dirk came down
its tip gold, its blade silver
to the belt of the sun's son;
so the worthy sun's son caught
    that knife with his hands
and with it he splits the pike
    slashes the wide-mouth:
in the grizzled pike's belly
    the pale trout is found;
in the pale trout's belly, there
    was the smooth whitefish.
And he split the smooth whitefish
    and got a blue ball
    from the whitefish's
    gut, from the third twist;
    unwound the blue ball
    and from the blue ball
    a red ball dropped out;
    undid that red ball
    and in the red ball
    found the tine of fire
    which had come from heaven
    through the clouds had dropped
    off the eight heavens
    down from the ninth sky.

While Väinämöinen wondered
    how it might be brought
into the fireless cabins
    into the dark rooms
the fire flared up and escaped
from the hand of the sun's son.

It singed Väinämöinen's beard;
    but worse for the smith
    the fire burnt his cheeks
    and it scorched his hands.
It went from there on its way
past Lake Alue's billows;
it leapt to some junipers—
the juniper heath caught fire;
it rushed into some spruces
and burnt the splendid spruces;
    it swept further still
    and burnt half the North
a strip of Savo's border
both halves of Karelia.

Steady old Väinämöinen
    stepped out himself, went
    up over the wilds
    after that harsh fire
    and he found the fire
    beneath two stump roots
    in an alder log
tucked under a rotten stump;
and there old Väinämöinen
    put this into words:
    'Dear fire, God's creature
the Creator's creature, flame:
you had no cause to go deep
and no business quite so far!
You'll do better when you go
    back to the stone hearth
commit yourself to your dust
peter out to your embers
    to be kept by day
in the cook-house birch-faggots
    and hidden by night
within the glowing fireplace.'

And he snatched the spark of fire
put it on burning tinder
    on hard birch fungus
    in a copper pan
carried the fire in the pan
on the birch bark conveyed it
to the misty headland's tip
to the foggy island's end
and the cabins got their fire
    back, the rooms their flame.

As for smith Ilmarinen
he plunged broadside in the sea
pulls himself up on a rock
on a shore boulder he lands
in pain from the burning fire
and in hardship from the flame:
    there he dimmed the fire
    and he doused the flame.
    He says with this word
    he spoke with this speech:
    'Dear fire, God's creature
    blaze, son of daylight:
    what put you to ill
    that you burnt my cheeks
    and heated my loins
    and angered my sides?
    How now shall I dim
    the fire, douse the flame
    make the fire harmless
    and the flame helpless
    lest it smart for long
    and nag for ages?
    Come, girl, from Turja
    maid, down from Lapland
slushy your stockings, icy
your shoes, frosty your skirt hems
a pan of slush in your hand

and a ladle of ice in the pan:
    toss some chill water
    some thin ice sprinkle
    on the burnt places
    on fire's bad fury!

'Should not enough come of that
    come, boy, from Northland
child, from the heart of Lapland
    tall man, from Darkland
large as spruces of the wild
    big as a swamp pine
mittens of slush on your hands
boots of slush upon your feet
a cap of slush on your scalp
belted with a belt of slush:
    bring slush from Northland
and ice from the cold village!
There's lots of slush in Northland
and ice in the cold village—
slushy streams and icy lakes
all the air a sheet of ice;
    slushy the hares hop
and icy the bears caper
on a snowy hillside, on
    a snowy slope's edge;
    icy the swans glide
and icy the ducks paddle
amid a snowy river
on an icy rapid's brink.
    Pull slush on a sled
lug ice along on a sledge
    from a harsh fell-top
    a mighty slope's edge
    and with the slush cool
and with the icy chill freeze
    the hurts dealt by fire
done to a turn by the blaze!

'Should not enough come of that
O Old Man, chief god
Old Man, keeper of the clouds
governor of the vapours:
rear a cloud out of the east
from the west send a cloud-mass
push them together edge-on
knock them against each other;
rain slush and rain ice
rain a good ointment
on the burnt places
overcome by hurt!'

Smith Ilmarinen
with that dimmed the fire
and calmed the flame down
and he got better
became his old self
after fire's harsh hurts.

49. *Moon and Sun*

Still the sun is not shining
nor the golden moon gleaming
on those Väinö-land cabins
on the Kalevala heaths:
the wealth grows chilly, the herds
get into a dreadful state
strange to the birds of the air
    tiresome to mankind
that the sun will never shine
    nor will the moon gleam.
The pike knew the sea-trough's depths
the eagle the birds' movements
the wind how far a day's sail;
but man's children do not know
when the morning will begin
    when the night will try
on the misty headland's tip
at the foggy island's end.
    The young hold counsel
and the aged consider
how they'll be without the moon
    live without the sun
    on those poor borders
the luckless lands of the North.
    The maids hold counsel
the charges deliberate;
they come to the smith's workshop
    and say with this word:
'Smith, rise from below the wall
craftsman, from behind the stove
    to forge a new moon
and a new sun-ring! It is

bad without the moon gleaming
strange without the sun shining.'

And the smith rose from below the wall
and the craftsman from behind the stove
to forge a new moon
and a new sun-ring;
and a moon he wrought in gold
out of silver made a sun.
The old Väinämöinen came
stations himself at the door
and uttered a word, spoke thus:
'Smith my dear brother!
Why in the workshop do you
clatter, hammer all the time?'

Smith Ilmarinen
uttered a word and spoke thus:
'I'm working a moon in gold
in silver a sun
for heaven's top up yonder
to go on the six bright lids.'

Then the old Väinämöinen
put this into words:
'Ho-ho, smith Ilmarinen!
You have been wasting your time:
no gold gleams as the moon, nor
as the sun does silver shine.'

The smith wrought a moon
and finished forging a sun;
raised them with a will
had them beautifully borne—
the moon to a spruce's top
and the sun up a tall pine.
Sweat rolled from the carrier's head
and dew from the bearer's brow

in the very hard labour
in the difficult lifting.
Well, he got the moon hoisted
    and the sun in place—
the moon at the spruce's peak
the sun up the pine, and no:
the moon will not gleam at all
nor will the sun shine at all.
Then the old Väinämöinen
    put this into words:
'Now is the time to cast lots
and to ask for a man's sign
where the sun has gone from us
where the moon is lost to us.'

He, the old Väinämöinen
the everlasting wise man
from an alder cut slivers
    laid the slivers out
set about turning the lots
his fingers arranging them;
    he says with this word
    he spoke with this speech:
'I ask the Creator's leave
and require, yes, an answer.
Tell truly, Creator's sign
    reveal, lots of God:
where has the sun gone from us
where is the moon lost to us
that they never in this world
    are seen in the sky?
    Tell, lots, as it is
not as a man would have it;
    bring here the true news
deliver what is destined!
    If the lots should lie
    their worth will lessen:

they'll be cast into the fire
the sign of men will be burnt.'

But the lots brought the true news
and the sign of men answers:
they said that the sun had gone
and the moon was lost yonder—
    in Northland's rocky
hill, inside the copper slope.
Steady old Väinämöinen
at that put this into words:
'If I go now to Northland
in the tracks of the North's sons
I shall get the moon to gleam
and the golden sun to shine.'

    He both went and sped
    off to dark Northland:
he stepped one day, he stepped two
    till by the third day
    the North's gate appears
    the rocky mounds glow.
At first he shouted out loud
at that river of Northland:
'Bring a boat here so that I
    can cross the river!'

    When the shout was not
    heard, nor a boat brought
he gathered a stack of wood
    dry spruce foliage;
he made a fire on the shore
    produced a thick smoke:
    the fire rose skyward
the smoke thickened in the air.

Louhi, mistress of Northland
    went to the window

looked out towards the strait-mouth
and uttered a word, spoke thus:
'What is the fire burning there—
there at the island's strait-mouth?
It is small as war-fires go
big as fishermen's flames go.'

The son of the Northlander
quickly pushed into the yard
    to look, to listen
    to inspect with care:
'There beyond the river is
    a hero walking.'

At that old Väinämöinen
shouted now a second time:
'Bring a boat, son of the North—
a boat for Väinämöinen!'

So the son of the North says
    he declared, answered:
    'No boats are free here:
come with your fingers as oars
with your palms as hand-paddles
for crossing Northland's river!'

At that old Väinämöinen
    thinks and considers:
'He is not a man at all
who turns back upon the road.'
He went as a pike into the sea
as a whitefish in the smooth river
quickly swims across the strait
    swiftly strode the gap;
he took one step, he took two
to the North's shore he hurried.
So the sons of the North say
    the evil swarm roar:

'Just walk into Northland's yard!'
He went into Northland's yard.
And the boys of the North say
    the evil swarm roar:
'Come into Northland's cabin!'
And he went into Northland's cabin;
he set foot in the doorway
laid his hand upon the latch;
    then he pushed indoors
made his way under the roof.

    There men are drinking
    honey, quaffing mead
the men all girded with swords
the fellows with war-weapons
out for Väinämöinen's head
to slay him of Calm Waters
and they asked the newcomer
    they said with this word:
'What is the wretched man's news
the swimming fellow's business?'

Steady old Väinämöinen
uttered a word and spoke thus:
'Of the moon there's wondrous news
of the sun mighty marvels.
Where has the sun gone from us
where is the moon lost to us?'

    The boys of the North
say, the evil swarm declared:
'There the sun has gone from you
the sun gone and the moon lost—
into a bright-breasted rock
into a cliff of iron.
They'll not get out unless they're let out
not be free unless they're freed.'

Then the old Väinämöinen
    put this into words:
'If the moon does not get out
from the rock, nor from the cliff
the sun, let's fight hand to hand
    let us take up swords!'

He drew his sword, wrenched the iron
snatched from the sheath the harsh one
upon whose point the moon shone
upon whose hilt the sun flashed
upon whose back a horse stands
where the peg went a cat mewed.
    They sized up their swords
they tested their cutlasses:
a tiny bit longer was
the old Väinämöinen's sword—
    by one barley grain
    a straw stem higher.
They went out into the yard
side by side on to the ground.
Then the old Väinämöinen
    smote with one flashing
    stroke—smote once, smote twice;
    sliced like turnip roots
    severed like hemp tops
heads of the boys of the North.
Then the old Väinämöinen
    went to look the moon
    to collect the sun
out of the bright-breasted rock
out of the mountain of steel
    and the iron cliff;
and he stepped a bit of road
    walked a little way
till he saw a green island—
on the isle a splendid birch
beneath the birch a boulder

beneath the boulder a cliff
    with nine doors in front
a hundred bolts on the doors.

He spied a mark on the rock
a false line upon the cliff.
He drew his sword from the sheath
cut a pattern on the rock
with the sword of fiery blade
    with the sparkling brand:
    the rock broke in two
into three the boulder burst.
Steady old Väinämöinen
looks through the crack in the rock:
there vipers are drinking beer*
    worms are swigging wort
    within the bright rock
the cleft of the liver-hued.
The old Väinämöinen said
    he declared, spoke thus:
'That is why poor mistresses
are getting less beer—because
vipers are drinking the beer
and worms are swigging the wort.'
He cut the head off a worm
he broke the neck of a snake;
    he says with this word
    he spoke with this speech:
    'Never in this world
    from this day forward
    shall vipers drink our
    beer, worms our malt drinks!'

Then the old Väinämöinen
the everlasting wise man
with his fists tried the doors, the
bolts with the force of the word;
but the doors will not open with hands

nor do the bolts care for words.
Then the old Väinämöinen
    put this into words:
'A man unarmed is a hag—
useless without axe or hoe.'
    And he goes straight home
his head down, in bad spirits
for he has not got the moon
    yet, nor found the sun.

Wanton Lemminkäinen said:
'Oh, old Väinämöinen, why
    didn't you take me
    with you as crooner?
The locks would have slid aside
the inner bolts would have snapped
and the moon got out to gleam
and the sun risen to shine.'

Steady old Väinämöinen
    put this into words:
    'Bolts won't snap with words
locks won't crumble with a spell
nor with the touch of a fist
    the turn of an arm.'

He went to his smith's workshop
and uttered a word, spoke thus:
    'Smith Ilmarinen
    forge a three-pronged hoe
and forge a dozen ice-picks
a whole bunch of keys, with which
I will let the moon out from
the rock, the sun from the cliff!'

He, the smith Ilmarinen
the everlasting craftsman
forged the things the man needed:

he forged a dozen ice-picks
    a whole bunch of keys
    a good bunch of spears
    neither big nor small—
forged them for once middle-sized.

Louhi, mistress of Northland
the gap-toothed hag of the North
gave life to wings with feathers
    and away she flew;
    she fluttered near home
then flung herself further off
across the sea of Northland
to smith Ilmari's workshop.
The smith opened his window
looked out: was the wind rising?
But the wind was not rising:
    it was a grey hawk.
He, the smith Ilmarinen
uttered a word and spoke thus:
'What is it you're after, fowl
perching under my window?'

    The bird sets about
    talking, the hawk speaks:
    'Smith Ilmarinen
    perpetual craftsman
how very clever you are—
yes, what a skilful craftsman!'

The smith Ilmarinen said
    he declared, spoke thus:
'It is no wonder at all
if I'm a careful craftsman
for I have forged the heavens
hammered the lid of the sky.'

    The bird sets about
    talking, the hawk speaks:

'What are you making there, smith
what are you building, blacksmith?'

The smith Ilmarinen says
    a word in answer:
'I am forging a collar
for that Northland hag, with which
she is to be chained fast to
    a mighty slope's edge.'

Louhi, mistress of Northland
the gap-toothed hag of the North
felt her ruin coming, her
day of trouble catching up:
    at once off she flew
    escaped to Northland
let the moon loose from the rock
let the sun out of the cliff.
She changed into something else
turned herself into a dove
    and she flaps along
to smith Ilmari's workshop
flew as a bird to the door
as a dove to the threshold.
    Smith Ilmarinen
uttered a word and spoke thus:
'Why did you fly this way, bird
and come to the threshold, dove?'

The fowl answered from the door
the dove spoke from the threshold:
    'I'm on the threshold
    to bring you this news:
the moon's risen from the rock
the sun is out from the cliff.'

    Smith Ilmarinen
    went himself to look.

He steps to the workshop door
looked carefully heavenward:
he beheld the moon gleaming
    saw the sun shining.
He went to Väinämöinen
he uttered a word, spoke thus:
    'Old Väinämöinen
O everlasting singer
    go, look at the moon
    and inspect the sun!
Now they are in the sky, right
    in their old places.'

Steady old Väinämöinen
    pushed into the yard
went and lifted up his head
glances heavenward: the moon
was risen, the sun was out
the daylight had reached the sky.
Then the old Väinämöinen
    began reciting;
    he says with this word
    he spoke with this speech:
    'Hail, moon, for gleaming
fair one for showing your face
    dear sun for dawning
and daylight for coming up!
Dear moon, you're out from the rock
    fair day from the cliff
you've risen as a golden
cuckoo, as a silver dove
up to where you used to live
    on your old travels.
Rise always in the mornings
    from this day forward;
    bring us wellbeing
shift the catch to the catching
the quarry to our thumb-tips

and good luck to our hook-ends!
Fare well now upon your way
upon your journey sweetly
end your curve beautifully
come at evening into joy!'

50. *The Newborn King*

Marjatta, nice youngest child
spent ages at home growing
at her high-born father's home
in her dear mother's cabins:
    she went through five chains
    six rings she wore out
    with her father's keys
    glinting at her hem;
half the threshold she wore out
    with her glittering hems
half the timber overhead
    with her silks so smooth
    half of the doorposts
    with her cuffs so fine
as much as a floorboard with
    her leather shoe heels.
Marjatta, nice youngest child
    she, the tiny wench
    long remained holy
    all the time bashful
    and she eats fine fish
    pine-bark bread that's soft
but she would not eat hen's eggs
where a cockerel had frisked
    nor meat from a ewe
    that had been with rams.

Mother bade her go milking
but she would not go milking
and she put this into words:
'No maiden who looks like me
will touch the teat of a cow
that has dallied with a bull

if there is no trickle from
heifers and no gush from calves.'

Father bade her board the stallion's sledge
but she'll not sit in the stallion's sledge.
    Brother brought a mare;
the maid put this into words:
'I'll not sit in a mare's sledge
that may have been with stallions
    if foals cannot pull
    nor month-olds convey.'

Marjatta, nice youngest child
    lived on as a wench
    as a modest maid
    as a shy braid-head
    became a herd-girl
    went out with the sheep;
    the sheep climbed a hill
and the lambs a mountain peak
and the maid stepped through a glade
    through alders she tripped
while a golden cuckoo called
while a silver one warbled.
Marjatta, nice youngest child
    looks, listens; she sat
down on a berry-hummock
sank on the side of a slope
and there put this into words
    she declared, spoke thus:
    'Call, golden cuckoo
    silver one, warble
    tin-breast, tinkle forth
German strawberry, tell me:
shall I go long as a maid
for ages as a herd-girl
    in these open glades
    on these wide grovelands—

one summer or two
five summers or six
maybe ten summers
or not all of that?'

Marjatta, nice youngest child
lingered long at her herding.
It is bad to be herding—
for a girl-child most of all:
the worm in the grass
lies, the lizards dart.
But there was no worm
lying, no lizard darting.
A berry shrieked from the hill
a cowberry from the heath:
'Come, maid, and pluck me
red-cheek, and pick me
tin-breast, and tear me
copper-belt, choose me
ere the slug eats me
the black worm scoffs me!
A hundred have come to look
a thousand to sit about—
a hundred maids, a thousand
women, children unnumbered—
but not one would touch
me, pick luckless me.'

Marjatta, nice youngest child
went a little way
went to look for the berry
and to pick the cowberry
with her good finger
tips, her fair hands. She
spied the berry on the hill
the cowberry on the heath:
'tis a berry by its look
a cowberry by its shape—

too high to eat off the ground
too low to climb a tree for.
She snatched a rod off the heath
with it brought the berry down;
the berry rose from the ground
towards her fair shoe-uppers
and from her fair shoe-uppers
    towards her pure knees
    and from her pure knees
    to her glittering hems
rose from there to her belt-ends
from her belt-ends to her breasts
from her breasts towards her chin
from her chin towards her lips
from there slipped into her mouth
    swung on to her tongue
from her tongue down her gullet
then into her belly dropped.
Marjatta, nice youngest child
was fulfilled, was filled by it
    she grew fat from it
    and she put on flesh;
she began to stay unlaced
to slouch about unbelted
to take a bath in secret
and to slip out after dark.

    Mother keeps thinking
her mamma keeps wondering:
'What's wrong with our Marjatta
and what's up with our home-bird
that she stays unlaced, always
slouches about unbelted
and takes a bath in secret
    slips out after dark?'

A child brings itself to say
a little child to declare:

'What's wrong with our Marjatta
what's up with the poor wretch, is
she has been herding too much
walking too much with the flock.'

She bore a hard womb
a difficult bellyful
for seven, eight months
for nine months in all
and by old wives' reckoning
half of a tenth month.
Now in the tenth month
the lass feels a pain:
her womb becomes hard
presses till it hurts.
She asked mother for a bath:
'O my mother, my darling
prepare a place of shelter
a little warm room
for a wench's sanctuary
for a woman's room of woe!'

Mother brings herself to say
her own parent to answer:
'Fie upon you, demon's bitch!
Who were you laid by?
Was it an unmarried man
or else a married fellow?'

Marjatta, nice youngest child
this one answers that:
'It was no unmarried man
nor yet a married fellow.
I climbed a hill for berries
and to pick a cowberry;
I took a berry I liked
a second time I tasted
and it went down my gullet

then into my belly dropped:
I was fulfilled, filled by it
and by it became with child.'

She asked father for a bath:
'O my father, my darling
give me a place of shelter
    a little warm room
where one sick may get relief
a wench endure her torment!'

Father brings himself to say
papa knew how to answer:
'Go, you whore, further than that
scarlet woman, further off
to the bruin's rocky dens
into the bear's craggy cells—
    there, you whore, to breed
there, scarlet woman, to teem!'

Marjatta, nice youngest child
    skilfully answered:
'I am not a whore at all
no kind of scarlet woman:
I am to have a great man
to bear one of noble birth
who will put down the mighty*
vanquish Väinämöinen too.'

The wench is in a tight spot:
where to go, which way to turn
and where to ask for a bath?
She uttered a word, spoke thus:
'Piltti, littlest wench of mine
best of my hirelings, go now
for a bath in the village
for a sauna at Sedgeditch
where one sick may get relief

a wench endure her torment:
    go quickly, press on
for the need is more pressing!'

    Piltti, tiny wench
uttered a word and spoke thus:
'Who shall I ask for a bath
who shall I beseech for help?'
Our little Marjatta said
    she uttered, spoke thus:
'Ask for Herod's bath, for the
sauna at Saraja's gates!'

    Piltti, tiny wench
who was meekly obedient
and prompt without being told
quick without being extolled
    as a mist goes out
as smoke she reaches the yard;
with her fists she grasped her hems
with her hands she rolled her clothes
    she both ran and sped
    towards Herod's home.
The hills thudded as she went
and the slopes sagged as she climbed
pine-cones jumped upon the heath
gravel scattered on the swamp;
she came to Herod's cabin
and got inside the building.

Ugly Herod in shirtsleeves
eats, drinks in the grand manner
at the head of the table
with only his lawn shirt on;
Herod declared from his meal
snapped, leaning over his cup:

'What do you say, mean one? Why
wretch, are you rushing about?'

    Piltti, tiny wench
uttered a word and spoke thus:
'I've come for a bath in the village
for a sauna at Sedgeditch
where one sick may get relief
one in anguish may find help.'

The ugly Herod's mistress
    walked with hands on hips
bustled at the floor seam, paced
in the middle of the floor;
    she hastened to ask
uttered a word and spoke thus:
'Who do you ask a bath for
who do you beseech help for?'
Piltti the little wench said:
'I ask for our Marjatta.'

The ugly Herod's mistress
    put this into words:
'The baths are not free for all
not the saunas at Saraja's gate.
There's a bath on the burnt hill
a stable among the pines
for a scarlet woman to have sons
a whore to bring forth her brats:
    when the horse breathes out
    bathe yourself in that!'

    Piltti, tiny wench
    hurriedly returned
    she both ran and sped
    said when she got back:
'There's no bath in the village
and no sauna at Sedgeditch.

The ugly Herod's mistress
uttered a word and spoke thus:
"The baths are not free for all
not the saunas at Saraja's gate.
There's a bath on the burnt hill
a stable among the pines
for a scarlet woman to have sons
a whore to bring forth her brats:
    when the horse breathes out
    let her bathe in that!"
That's it, that is how she spoke
that was her only answer.'

Marjatta the lowly maid
thereupon burst into tears
and she put this into words:
'The time comes for me to go
as of old for the gipsy
    or the hireling serf—
to go off to the burnt hill
to head for the lea of pines!'

With her hands she rolled her clothes
with her fists she grasped her hems
took a bath-whisk for cover
a sweet leaf for her shelter
    and she trips along
    in hard belly-pain
to the hut among the pines
the stall on Tapio Hill;
    she says with this word
    she spoke with this speech:
'Come, Creator, my refuge
and my help, merciful one
    in this hard labour
    in these most hard times:
free a wench from a tight spot

a woman from belly-throes
    lest she sink in woes
    perish in her pains!'

    When she arrived, she
    put this into words:
    'Breathe now, O good horse
    sigh now, O draught-foal
    and waft some bath steam
    send a warm sauna
that, sick, I may get relief,
in anguish, I may find help!'
    And the good horse breathed
    and the draught-foal sighed
over her heavy belly
    and what the horse breathes
is like steam being stirred up
like water tossed on hot stones.

Marjatta the lowly maid
the holy, the tiny wench
bathed her fill, bathed her belly
in all the steam she wanted:
there she had a little son
she brought forth her baby child
on the hay beside the horse
at the rough-hair's manger-end.
She washed her little offspring
swathed him in his swaddling-cloth
took the boy upon her knees
set the child upon her hem;
she concealed her baby boy
    she reared her fair one
her little golden apple
    her staff of silver
and in her arms she feeds him
and in her hands turns him round;

she laid the boy on her knees
    the child in her lap
and began to comb his head
    and to brush his hair.

The boy vanished from her knees*
the child from about her loins:
Marjatta the lowly maid
because of that feels great pain.
She dashed off in search of him:
she sought her little baby
her little golden apple
    her staff of silver
underneath the grinding quern
and the gliding sledge-runner
under the siftable sieve
under the portable tub
shaking trees, parting grasses
    scattering fine hay.
Long she sought her baby boy
her baby, her little one—
sought him on hills, among pines
on stumps and among heather
checking out each heather flower
through each patch of scrub sorting
digging up juniper roots
splaying out the boughs of trees.

    She steps deep in thought
and she trips lightly along
    till she meets a star;
    to the star she bows:
    'O star, God's creature
don't you know of my baby—
where my little offspring is
my little golden apple?'
The star knew how to answer:
'If I knew I would not say:

'tis he who created me
    for these days of ill
to glimmer amid the cold
and to twinkle in the dark.'

    She steps deep in thought
and she trips lightly along
    till she meets the moon;
    to the moon she bows:
    'O moon, God's creature
don't you know of my baby—
where my little offspring is
my little golden apple?'
The moon knew how to answer:
'If I knew I would not say:
'tis he who created me
    for these days of ill
to keep watch alone of nights
and to go to bed by day.'

    She steps deep in thought
and she trips lightly along
till she came upon the sun;
    to the sun she bows:
    'O sun, God's creature
don't you know of my baby—
where my little offspring is
my little golden apple?'
The sun skilfully answered:
'Yes, I know of your offspring:
'tis he who created me
    for these days of good
    to jingle with gold
    to clink with silver.
Sure I know of your offspring:
woe, luckless, for your baby!
There is your little offspring
your little golden apple—

in the swamp up to his waist
in the heath to his armpit.'

Marjatta the lowly maid
searched for her son on the swamp:
the boy was found on the swamp*
and from there he was brought home.
 Then our Marjatta
had a handsome son growing
but no name is known for him
what name to mention him by:
mother called him Little Flower
but strangers said Fly-by-night.
Now a christener was sought
and a baptist was looked for:
an old man came to christen
Virokannas* to baptize.
But he put this into words
 he declared, spoke thus:
'I'll not christen one bewitched
no mean one baptize at all
before there's an inquiry—
an inquiry, a judgement.'

Who will inquire into this—
 will inquire, will judge?
Steady old Väinämöinen
the everlasting wise man
he will inquire into this—
 will inquire, will judge!
Steady old Väinämöinen
thereupon passes judgement:
'The boy was got from a swamp
begot by an earth-berry?
Let him be put in the earth
beside the berry-hummock
or be taken to the swamp
hit on the head with a stick!'

But the half-month-old boy spoke
and the two-week-old piped up:
    'You wretched old man
you wretched, sleepy old man
for you have stupidly judged
    laid the law down wrong!
    For better causes
for still worse deeds you were not
taken to a swamp yourself
hit on the head with a stick
when you as a younger man
yielded up your mother's child*
    to save your own skin
    to redeem yourself;
    nor were you ever
nor yet taken to a swamp
when you as a younger man
used to dispatch the young maids
down below the deep billows
    upon the black mud!'

The old man quickly christened
and briskly baptized the child
    king of Karelia
guardian of all power. At that
Väinämöinen was angry—
he was angry and ashamed
    and he stepped away
towards the shore of the sea
and there he started singing
    sang for the last time—
    sang a copper boat
a coppery covered craft
and he sits down in the stern
he cast off on the clear main
and he uttered as he went
declared as he departed:
    'Just let the time pass

one day go, another come
and again I'll be needed
    looked for and longed for
to fix a new Sampo, to
    make a new music
    convey a new moon
    set free a new sun
when there's no moon, no daylight
    and no earthly joy.'

Then the old Väinämöinen
    goes full speed ahead
    in the copper boat
    the coppery punt
to where mother earth rises
    and heaven descends
and there he stopped with his craft
with his boat he paused; but he
left the kantele behind
the fine music for Finland
for the folk eternal joy
the great songs for his children.

* * *

    Now I should shut up
    and bind my tongue fast
make an end of tale-singing
and have done with striking up:
    even a horse pants
after going a long way
    even iron tires
after mowing summer hay
    even water halts
after rounding river-bends
    even fire flickers
after burning all night long;
so why should a bard not be
weary, gentle tales not halt

from an evening's long-drawn joys
and from singing at sunset?
I have heard it put this way
    argued differently:
no rapid however swift
    runs out of water
nor does a good singer sing
    everything he knows;
it makes better sense to stay
than break off in the middle.
So I'll give over, I'll stop
I'll have done, I'll leave off too:
I'll wind my tales in a ball
in a bundle I'll roll them
put them up in the shed loft
    inside locks of bone
from where they'll never get out
never in this world be free
unless the bones are shaken
    the jaws are opened
    the teeth are parted
    the tongue set wagging.

But what of it if I sing
if I chant ever so much
and sing in every valley
and in every spruce clump moan?
My mother is not alive
my own parent not awake
nor is my dear one listening
my own darling observing:
the spruces listen to me
    the pine boughs observe
the birch foliage fondles
    the rowans hold me.
Small I was left motherless
lowly without my mamma—
left like a lark on a rock

to be a thrush on a cairn
    as a lark to soar
    as a thrush to chirp
in a strange woman's keeping
    a stepmother's care.
    She turned poor me out
    drove the orphan child
to the cabin's windward side
    to the home's north side
to face the wind unsheltered
    and the gale unloved.
I, a lark, began roaming
and, a wretched bird, walking
a weak one, strolling abroad
a woeful one, wandering
    knowing every wind
    suffering the roar
    shaking in the cold
    howling in the frost.

    Many now I have
    and a lot there are
who talk with angry voices
who with harsh voices attack:
    one has cursed my tongue
another yelled at my voice
slandered me, said I mumble
declared that I sing too much
    that I chant badly
    twist a tale awry.
    Do not, good people
    don't take it amiss
if I, a child, sang too much
and, small, I chirruped badly!
I have not been schooled, not been
in the lands of mighty men
    have not got strange words

phrases from further away.
    Others were all schooled;
I could not be spared from home
helping my matchless mother
fussing round the lonely one:
I had to be schooled at home
underneath my own shed beam
at my own mother's distaffs
on my brother's wood shavings
and I was small too, tiny
a scamp in a ragged shirt.

    Be that as it may
I've skied a trail for singers
skied a trail, snapped a treetop
lopped off boughs and shown the way:
that is where the way goes now
    where a new track leads
for more versatile singers
    more abundant bards
among the youngsters rising
among the people growing.

NOTES

1:21 *Let's strike hand to hand*: the traditional gesture when two men sat down to sing. See the Introduction, which these Notes supplement. English words not in the *COD* are glossed.

1:36 *Kalevala*: primarily a place name meaning (according to Lönnrot) the abode of Kaleva, an obscure gigantic ancestor like Greek Titans. Lacking articles, Finnish makes no distinction between the place name and the title of the epic; the English article before the latter is conventional. The ending *-la* (or *-lä*, according to vowel harmony) is a 'locality formative'. Tapiola is the abode of Tapio, lord of the forests, Tuonela that of Tuoni, lord of the dead; Sibelius named his house Ainola after his wife Aino (named after the girl in canto 4); *kahvila* is a café, from *kahvi* 'coffee'. The present translation renders *-la*/*-lä* '-land' (e.g. *Väinölä* 'Väinö-land', 3:3), except for Kalevala itself, and Tapiola and Tuonela which, thanks to Sibelius, are already familiar.

1:66 *poems*: *runoja*. *Runo* is of old Germanic origin, and cognate with English 'rune', but they are not equivalent: a rune is a letter or inscription (not necessarily a poem), whereas a *runo* in the Kalevala tradition can only be oral, referring to both poem (as here) and bard (e.g. 12:456). Lönnrot also uses the word for the fifty sections of the epic, but the 'poems' do not correspond with the 'old poems' of his title, so the word is there rendered 'canto'. Scholars often translate *runo* as 'song', but the usual word for song (*laulu*) is also used in the epic (e.g. 1:82). The bards themselves called an epic-style narrative poem *virsi* (modern Finnish 'hymn'), which is rendered 'tale' (e.g. 1:5).

1:68 *sea*: the word clearly refers in the epic mainly to large lakes, 'lake' to smaller ones.

1:76 *kiln*: *riihi*, a building where grain is dried in mild heat and threshed.

1:77 *shed loft*: memory.

1:112 *nice nature-daughter*: *korea* (modern Finnish 'showy') usually means 'proudly handsome', but here and in canto 50 describing Marjatta it has sexual overtones. 'Nature-daughter' is *luonnotar*, formed of *luonto* 'nature, created world' plus the feminine suffix *-tar*/*-tär*; cf. *Kanteletar*, 'female spirit, muse, of the kantele', and *tarjoilija*, 'waiter', *tarjoilijatar*, 'waitress'.

1:285 *patterns*: *kirja* and related words refer to patterns both natural and man-made, often with a magical significance. (In modern Finnish *kirja* and *kirjoittaa* mean 'book' and 'to write', but the old meaning survives in *kirjava*, 'many-coloured, mottled, speckled, brindled'.) As the first element of compounds, *kirja-* or *kirjo-* has usually been rendered 'bright'.

1:304 *Great Bear*: the constellation *Ursa major*, alias the Plough, alias Charles's Wain. For the cult of the Great Bear see note to 46:13.

1:319 *stronghold*: used here metaphorically, *linna* (modern Finnish 'castle', colloquially 'jail') is equivalent to Anglo-Saxon *burh*, but 'borough' or 'burgh' is too elaborate for the epic, where the word usually refers to no more than a secure dwelling.

2:14 *Sampsa*: Sampsa Pellervoinen, an agriculture spirit whose first name is probably derived from Samson on account of his strength (see note to 11:311 below), his second from *pelto*, cognate with, and meaning, 'field'.

2:255–6 *clearing . . . fire*: slash-and-burn (or burn-beat) agriculture, in which the ashes are ploughed in as fertilizer.

2:372 *tin-breast*: used here metaphorically, *tinarinta* refers to an unmarried girl wearing trinkets of semi-precious metal.

3:45 *sang*: bewitched. The verb often connotes magic. When its object is a person it is sometimes rendered 'sing at' (e.g. 3:57); when the object is a thing, this is being called into existence, as in 302 ff. and 27:221 ff.

3:86 *wise man*: *tietäjä*, literally 'knower' of secret lore, i.e. magician, wizard, shaman. In the Finnish Bible the word is used for the 'wise men' from the east in the Christmas story.

3:179 *Häme*: province of south-west Finland.

3:181 *Vuoksi*: river in south-east Finland flowing from the Saimaa lakes to Lake Ladoga in Russia.

3:182 *Imatra*: here the once spectacular rapids where the Vuoksi runs off the granite table-land; now the site of a town, Finland's largest paper mill and a hydroelectric power station.

3:403–4 *with clear water . . . rumps*: they are glossy and well fed.

3:471 *He sits on the rock of joy*: this and the following line mean little more than 'he starts singing'. 'Joy' often means music in the epic, as here: the translation keeps the ambiguity, partly because there is another word for music—though this in turn usually refers to an instrument, the kantele; see especially canto 40.

3:536 *brother-in-law*: merely to parallel 'son-in-law' in the previous line. Such parallelisms are common—cf. 'fourth / . . . fifth' (4:307-8).

4:4 *bath-whisks*: the accepted but misleading English equivalent for leafy birch twigs used to stimulate sweat in the sauna.

4:25 *cogware*: 'a coarse cloth, resembling frieze, made of the poorest wool' (*OED*, latest use 1483), presumably related to 'cog', an early cargo boat. Rendering *haahen halja-koista*, literally 'about vessel-jackets', i.e. imported clothes.

4:38 *farm*: *kartano* (modern Finnish 'manor', cognate with English 'garden') is one of many more or less synonymous words for a dwelling, choice depending more on alliteration than on size or status.

4:94 *the Great One*: referring to Väinämöinen. The original invokes him here in terms of illustrious but obscure ancestors—*Osmoinen . . . Kalevainen* 'the descendant of Osmo . . . of Kaleva' (see note to 1:36).

4:334 *untimely died*: literally 'died an excessive *surma*', this being one of the two basic Finnish words for death.

Kuolema is what happens to the old and infirm; *surma* is what a coroner investigates. When *kuolema* and *surma* are parallel (e.g. 15:99–100) the latter has been rendered 'doom'.

5:112 *a lifelong mate on your knee*: 'lifelong' and 'on your knee' translate the same word, *polviseksi*, to maintain the parallelism. *Polvi* means both 'knee' and 'generation, lifetime'; the semantic link is childbirth—cf. Latin *genu*, *genus*.

5:178 *priceless*: the Finnish word has the same irony as the English.

6:43–6 *a horse stood . . . the rack was*: these four lines describe the decorations on the crossbow. Cf. Väinämöinen's spear (46:36–40).

6:200 *not in a month of Sundays*: literally 'not in a month (moon) gold-white', i.e. never.

8:86 *only a maid when wed*: regarded as grown up only when wed.

8:271 *dwelt on the stove*: the top of the traditional stone stove (*uuni*, cognate with English 'oven') used for heating and baking was a favourite haunt of old people and cats.

11:58 *splints*: thin narrow strips of resinous wood used as candles. Finnish *päre* in this sense has no ready English equivalent.

11:266 *Cowberry*: cows are often named after flowers. Lemminkäinen is too poor to own cows, so he names flowers, hoping his bride will misinterpret them as cow names. The cowberry (*Vaccinium vitis-idaea*), a kind of bilberry, plays a crucial role in canto 50.

11:311 *before the God known to all*: literally 'before the public God', i.e. in church, in front of the icons—a Christian element Lönnrot saw fit not to remove; cf. 'Sampsa' (2:14—see note), 'judases' for forest spirits (13:106), 'Jordan' (17:572).

12:137 *a Lapp will sing*: the Lapps have a traditional reputation among the Finns for magic, like the Celts among the English, for similar reasons.

12:199 *Turja's tongue*: '. . . can be explained thus, that . . . by tongue she meant not speech but magic skill peculiar to Northland' (Lönnrot's 1849 preface).

12:463 *Rutja*: modern Ruija, Finnmark, the Norwegian far north; left untranslated (to alliterate with 'rapid') because its otherworldly location (Tuonela) is paramount.

12:477 *Dripcap*: may be only an epithet—*märkähattu*, 'wet-hat(ted)'—but is more conveniently rendered as a name.

13:39 *left ski*: this pointed the way while the shorter right ski propelled—hunters could not be encumbered with ski-sticks. 'Snowshoes' (43) inadequately renders a synonym for skis.

14:248 *camel-colt*: to show this is no ordinary horse.

14:385 *whooping*: the Finnish swan is the whooper (*Cygnus cygnus*).

15:104 *king of beasts*: literally 'noble reindeer', now synonymous with 'lion'.

15:427 *Thor's new cabin*; presumably the outside world; cf. 47:185, 188, 219. Finnish *Tuuri* is the Norse god of thunder.

17:13 *Antero Vipunen*: a shaman whose barrow grave Väinämöinen visits to top up his repertoire of magic. Like Aino (4:363–70), Vipunen has become part of the landscape; a Western parallel is Arthur (see David Jones, *The Sleeping Lord and other fragments*, London, 1974). The considerable antiquity behind this canto has been obscured by the Judeo-Christian myth of Jonah: the shaman consulting his predecessor is swallowed, whereupon 'little' tradition supplies charms against indigestion.

17:22 *on a man's sword tips*: since this is to be another trip to the world of the dead, the risks are spelt out.

17:497 *God's trance-hour*: literally 'God's hour', referring to a shaman's trance, when he is possessed by (here) a healing spirit. The phrase occurs again at 32:115, where according to commentators it means 'God's wish'.

17:524 *buried*: literally 'into a chasm'. Inaccessible gaps in rocks were thought to contain magic; cf. the chasm at the Delphic oracle. A shaman going into a trance went 'into a chasm', perhaps a metaphor of a predecessor's grave. Here the chasm is Antero Vipunen's mouth, i.e. his grave.

18:59 *Finlandia*: rendering the unique *Suomela*.

18:116 *sedgy ditch*: *saraoja* (*sara* 'sedge', *oja* 'ditch') with its variants appears many times in the epic as a proper name. Most often, as Sariola, it is another name for Northland and is left untranslated; in canto 50 it appears as both *Saraoja* and Saraja.

18:137 *German straits*: presumably where ships of the Hanse plied their trade. In Finnish tradition 'German' and 'Germany' connoted quality, applied in the epic also to boots (18:352), planks (21:168), feminine beauty (25:289), shoes (25:594), soap (36:224), salt (46:311), and even strawberries (50:46).

18:368 *cummerbund*: *kussakkainen*, from Russian *kushak*, which is from Turkish *kuşak*; the exotic word suggests something rich and rare.

18:395 *cuckoos*: the bird connotes none of the mockery of Western tradition, besides which the reference here is to a cuckoo-shaped sleigh bell. The bluebird (396), by Maeterlinck out of Vera Lynn, is equally vague in the original; an explanatory 'bell' has been added.

18:403 *sea beast's*: *turskan*, literally 'cod's'; but since fish-skin is worthless, this must refer to a creature like *Tursas*, the 'Beast' of 2:67.

19:23 *viper-field*: Ilmarinen's first task is humdrum enough, for hibernating vipers are a common hazard in spring ploughing. When Gallen-Kallela illustrated this episode on the ceiling of the Finnish pavilion at the Paris World Exhibition of 1900, he fell foul of his Russian masters, who, after grudgingly allowing the Grand Duchy a pavilion of its own, were anxious about any expression of national feeling. They were pacified on being told that the fresco depicted 'a farmer's difficulties in the struggle against snakes'.

19:51 *And the bride gave help*: cf. Ariadne helping Theseus slay the Minotaur, one of many unexplained parallels between Finnish and Greek mythology.

19:369 *iron roof*: the eagle-bridegroom tries to enter three 'strongholds' (see note to 1:319 above). Prosperous farms often had men's and women's quarters for itinerant workers. The men with their iron helmets were not interested, nor were the women with their copper head-dresses; only the girls with their linen (hempen) kerchiefs welcomed the visitor.

20:6 *the godly*: because Northland is identified with Sariola (10), which has otherworldly connections—see note to 18:116 above.

20:20 *a calf and a half*: literally 'a right (proper, real, hell of a) calf'. This description of a great ox may have begun as a ritual poem to accompany a sacrifice; it was later used as a charm against burns, recited as fat was smeared on. The Church countered with a grotesque poem about a great pig (see FFPE 51, 52).

20:22 *Kemi River*: in Lapland.

20:54 *Virokannas*: god of oats, according to Agricola. Here Christian elements are concerned to discredit the pagan god. For his other, more impressive appearance in the epic, see note to 50:434 below.

20:612 *gipsy*: *kasakka*, an itinerant worker, popularly supposed to be of Cossack origin, as English gipsies were thought to hail from Egypt, whence their name. Not the same as the Finnish Romany, *mustalaiset* ('the swarthy ones'), who do not figure in the epic.

22:101 *trumps*: *torvi* is a herdsman's horn of birchbark, strips of which were wound into a cone; in modern Finnish it is also an orchestral horn. But in canto 33 it is parallel with *sarvi*, an animal's horn; whence 'trump'.

22:521 *cairns*: *raunio* (modern Finnish 'ruin') is a pile of stones left after ploughing, the original meaning of the English word (from Celtic).

23:203 *duster*: literally 'wing', perhaps a feather duster.

23:482 *parish*: *miero* (modern Finnish 'cold cruel world') is from Russian *mir* as in the expression *khodit' po miru* 'to go about the village', i.e. to live by begging. Because this old woman left her brutal husband, she and her children had no choice but to 'go on the parish'. For the rest of this canto Lönnrot drew extensively on the daughter-in-law lyrics of his *Kanteletar*.

23:505 *honey-berry*: a literal rendering of *mesimarja*, since both elements connote endearment. Otherwise *mesimarja* is Arctic bramble (*Rubus arcticus*), from which a liqueur is made.

25:620 *open*: reading *aukeilta*, an early emendation in the light of a formula (e.g. 1:126) of Lönnrot's *ankeilta*, 'anguished', perhaps a misreading of handwriting.

32:157 *going lost*: literally 'getting to Death'. When a cow stopped producing milk, it was thought to have been bewitched so that its milk went to the otherworld. Happily, no witch-hunt followed: the antidote was superior magic, as displayed for nearly the rest of the canto.

32:315 *Beastie, forest apple, bear*: literally '*Otsonen*, the forest's apple'. *Otso(nen)* is one of many words by which the animal is named, the word 'bear' itself being ritually taboo; 'apple' is a term of endearment (cf. English 'apple of one's eye'); an explanatory 'bear' has been added. See note to 46:13 below.

33:291 *That was how the young wife went*: with the help of formulas, Lönnrot makes creative use of an otherwise awkward join. How can the sweet bride of canto 22 have become the vindictive harridan of canto 32? Lönnrot offers no explanation—he could not anyway—but reflects sadly on how people can change.

35:203–4 *waif . . . stray*: *tuiretuinen . . . keiretyinen*—both rare. The first word is derived from Tore or Ture, a character in a Scandinavian ballad of incest and murder; but (thanks to this line) it has come to mean either 'stupid' or an endearing 'poor little', whence Tuire as a girl's name. The second word remains obscure.

35:352 *Savo*: province of central Finland adjoining Karelia.

35:372 *well-treatment*: an ironic variation on Kullervo's 'ill-treatment' (34:100).

40:48 *Rocky Horror, son of Dread*: *Kivi-Kimmo, Kammon poika*, literally 'Rock–*Kimmo*, Dread's son'—*Kimmo* (modern Finnish 'bounce') being here, according to commentators, only a variation of *Kammo*. The name of a rock musical came in handy.

40:224 *kantele*: over the centuries the original five-stringed zither was supplanted by the louder and more versatile fiddle (*viulu*) till the epic invoked the kantele as the 'national instrument'. Since then it has grown in both size and status: there are now kantele consorts whose largest instrument has thirty-six strings, and it can be studied to diploma level. Its chief exponents today are Martti Pokela and his family, who have made many recordings.

44:217 *toe-rags*: originally strips of cloth wrapped round the feet in the absence of socks. Elsewhere in the epic (and in modern Finnish) the same word means 'vapours', wisps of cloud, toe-rags of the sky-god. (In modern Finnish also 'candy-floss'.)

46:13 *bear*: cantos 46–9 embody three aetiological myths—the origin of the bear, the origin of fire, and the departure and return of the winter sun. The cult of the Great Bear (*Ursa major*) was widespread in the northern hemisphere from the Stone Age. The Arctic was named after Greek *arktos* 'bear'; Arthur was Arcturus after the star *Arktouros* 'Bear-guard' (cf. Welsh *arth* 'bear'); an Old Norse *berserkr* was a reckless warrior (cf. English 'berserk') apparently named after a protective 'bear-shirt'; Beowulf was 'Bee-wolf', i.e. Bear, observing the ritual taboo mentioned earlier. Bear ritual was prominent in early Finno-Ugrian cultures, surviving into modern times when Bartók noted down bear dances. The taboo survives too in some modern European languages, e.g. Russian *medved'*, literally 'honey-eater', whence Hungarian *medve* (cf. English 'mead'). Finnish *mesikämmen*, 'honey-paw', like *kontio*, 'bruin' (literally 'crawler'), is an affectionate alternative to *karhu*, 'bear'. In the Finnish rite as reflected in this canto, the hunter tells of hunting, catching, and killing the bear; he excuses himself, declaring that his victim is an honoured guest in the village; he recites its heavenly origin and apologizes for dismembering it, assuring its inedible parts a worthy resting-place.

47:206 *white flame*: translating *valkeaisen* twice. The Finnish word parallels 'red fire' (205).

48:156 *big stick*: *puu pitkä* means both this and 'tall tree'. The original plays on the ambiguity.

49:255 *vipers are drinking beer*: an uncharacteristic obscurity, like 32:157 ff. and related to it. Like the milk 'going lost' to the otherworld, here the beer, thanks to Louhi, is going the same way: 'The Hag of the North was now refreshing her snakes with Kalevala's beer' (Lönnrot).

50:199 *who will put down the mighty*: literally 'who will have power over power itself'. The echo of the Magnificat (Luke 1:52) was irresistible.

50:351 *The boy vanished from her knees*: the sudden switch is also in the source, a loosely connected sequence of Christian legends sung by Orthodox Finns. 'The Tale of the Creator' (*Luojan Virsi*, rendered 'The Messiah' in FFPE 59–62) consists of five legends—the Berry, the Search for a Sauna, Looking for the Lost Child, the Resurrection, the Shackling of Satan—of which Lönnrot uses the first three. This third is based on the story of the boy Jesus going missing from his family, and being found among the Temple doctors (Luke 2: 41–52).

50:423 *found on the swamp*: recalling the practice of leaving illegitimate babies to die if no one admitted paternity. This explains the problem of naming (427 f.), the 'inquiry' (439 ff.) and the baptism without a name (477–8). The source is now a poem about Väinämöinen's departure (FFPE 57, 58).

50:434 *Virokannas*: the old oat-god comes into his own as John the Baptist. Perhaps the faithful associated the unkempt figure on icons with the look of oats growing; this is one of many interpretations. In Orthodoxy his principal feast falls on 7 January, immediately after Christmas; the feast of his Nativity is universally celebrated at Midsummer, when wild oats are sown.

50:466 *yielded up your mother's child*: the boy is clearly confusing the old man with Joukahainen (canto 3); but such things happen in oral tradition.

APPENDIX
SIBELIUS AND THE KALEVALA

Kullervo, op. 7 (1892)

Symphonic poem for soprano, baritone, male chorus, and orchestra after the Kullervo cycle, cantos 31–6. Five movements: 'Introduction', 'The Youth of Kullervo', 'Kullervo and his Sister', 'Kullervo goes to War', 'The Death of Kullervo'. The third movement includes a setting of lines from canto 35, the fifth a setting of 36:297–346.

Piano Sonata, op. 12 (1893)

The principal theme of the second movement is adapted from an abandoned setting of the charm against rapids beginning at 40:23.

'Hail, moon', op. 18 no. 8 (1901)

A setting for male chorus *a cappella* of 49:403–22.

'The Voyage', op. 18 no. 9 (1893)

A setting for male chorus *a cappella* (also for mixed chorus) of 40:1–16. The five-beat rhythm imitates the epic singing-style of oral poetry.

Lemminkäinen Suite, op. 22 (1893–1939)

Orchestral work, also known as *Four Legends*, after the first Lemminkäinen cycle, cantos 11–15. Four pieces: 'Lemminkäinen and the Island Maids', 'The Swan of Tuonela', 'Lemminkäinen in Tuonela', 'Lemminkäinen's Return'. The second piece (the first to be written) was originally intended as the overture to an abandoned opera, *The Building of the Boat*, based on cantos 8 and 16. Tuonela is the abode of Tuoni, lord of the dead.

The Origin of Fire, op. 32 (1902–10)

Also known as *Ukko the Fire-maker*, a setting for baritone, male chorus, and orchestra of 47:41–110.

Kyllikki, op. 41 (1904)

Piano suite of three untitled pieces evoking the 'Island maid' whom Lemminkäinen abducts, marries, and leaves in cantos 11–15.

The Daughter of Northland, op. 49 (1906)
Symphonic fantasia evoking the first encounter between Väinämöinen and the Maid of the North in canto 8. The opening cello solo echoes epic singing-style. The composer wanted to call the work *L'Aventure d'un Héros*, but his German publisher preferred *Pohjola's Tochter*, adding for good measure at the head of the score his own unfortunate verses based on a prose 'synopsis' by the composer.

The Nature-daughter, op. 70 (1913)
Tone poem for soprano and orchestra setting lines from canto 1 about the creation of the world. The Finnish title *Luonnotar* means a female nature or creation spirit.

The Song of Väinö, op. 110 (1926)
A setting for mixed chorus and orchestra of 43:385–434. Väinö is Väinämöinen.

Tapiola, op. 112 (1926)
Orchestral tone poem evoking the abode of Tapio, lord of the forests, most prominent in the hunting charms of canto 14 and the bear ritual of canto 46. The epigraph is by the composer.

Tiera (unnumbered, 1898)
Short character-piece for brass ensemble and percussion recalling the abortive winter expedition in canto 30. Written, like *Finlandia*, op. 26, at the height of the Russian censorship, the work, with its hidden reference to spells against the Frost, could have been a gesture of defiance.

Outside the epic but within the tradition, six lyrics from the *Kanteletar* are set in *The Lover* (*Rakastava*), op. 14 (there is also a version for strings and percussion), and in the part-songs op. 18 nos. 3, 4, and 7. The six *Finnish Folk Tunes* for piano (unnumbered, 1903) are outside the tradition.

En Saga, op. 9, has no connection with the *Kalevala*, nor for that matter with Norse saga. The title is Swedish for 'A Fairy-tale'; the Finnish title *Satu* has this meaning. *The Bard*, op. 64, refers to an Ossianic figure in Finland-Swedish poetry, and the original title is in Swedish; Gray's ode 'The Bard' comes from the same world. *The Oceanides*, op. 73, refers to Classical myth; the Finnish title *Aallottaret* ('The Billow-daughters', one of whom is mentioned in canto 48) is a translation authorized by the composer to promote the work in Finland.

The list above includes some retranslations where existing English titles (supplied by the original German publisher) have been misleading: e.g. Pohjola is a place, not a person; Luonnotar is not an individual name.

See Robert Layton, *Sibelius* ('The Master Musicians', London, 1965, 1977) and Erik Tawaststjerna (trans. Layton), *Sibelius*, vol. i: 1865–1905 (London, 1976), vol. ii: 1904–1914 (London, 1986), vol. iii: 1914–1957 (London, 1997).